RISKING LIFE AND LIMB

Celebrating fifty years of the Ogwen Valley Mountain Rescue Organisation

Judy Whiteside

Foreword by
HRH The Duke of Cambridge

First published 2015.

Published by Ogwen Valley Mountain Rescue Organisation.
Bryn Poeth, Capel Curig, Conwy LL24 0EU.
web: www.ogwen-rescue.org.uk

A catalogue record for this book is available from the British Library.

ISBN: 978-0-9934949-0-1

Printed and bound in the UK.

This book is dedicated to all those whose lives have been touched by
the Ogwen Valley Mountain Rescue Organisation
— the team members, their families, friends and supporters
and, of course, all those who have needed our help.

Contents

Tryfan: Illustration © George Manley.

Preface

In 1964, 'Top of the Pops' first aired on BBC TV, Winston Churchill retired from the House of Commons, 'The Sun' newspaper went into circulation and, on the last day of the year, Donald Campbell achieved his seventh water speed record at 276.33 mph — the first person to set both land and water speed records in the same year.

In North Wales, a small team of volunteers at a local mountaineering school, led by Ron James, formed the Ogwen Valley Mountain Rescue Organisation. Now in its fiftieth year, this organisation remains true to its founding principle — providing a search and rescue service for people in difficulties in inhospitable terrain.

However, a number of things have changed over those fifty years. The team has grown to almost fifty members. There have been huge advances in technology which, in turn, have changed the way people request assistance and how that assistance is delivered. Casualty care has come on in leaps and bounds. The team has a supporters' group who help to raise money. The number of rescues continues to fluctuate and grow — peaking at over 140 in 2010 — and it's not uncommon for two, three or more incidents to occur over the same twenty-four hour period. All of which puts an ever-increasing strain on our volunteer team members.

Mountain rescue is no longer just about a small team of people going out on the hill. There are lots of activities behind the scenes, with working groups, committees and, of course, the all-important fundraising. The team has had to adapt and embrace change to be able to continue to meet its objectives.

This book tells the story of Ogwen Valley Mountain Rescue Organisation, from its inception to the present day. You will read how the mountain rescue service developed, how the team was formed and how it has changed. Through a number of real-life rescue stories you will see what team members do when a call-out comes.

Of course, we haven't worked alone. In 2015, the helicopter search and rescue service provided by 22 Squadron, at RAF Valley on Anglesey, has been replaced by Bristow, operating out of

Bryn Poeth in winter: Photo © OVMRO.

Caernarfon. The RAF, and now Bristow, are just two of the partners who have helped the team to deliver services. I would like to take this opportunity to thank all those who have helped and supported us. Unfortunately, there isn't room to mention you all in this book, but please be assured we are grateful for your assistance.

Throughout the fiftieth year the team held a number of celebratory events, including lighting up the ridgeline of Tryfan with head torches, a formal dinner on top of Tryfan and a picnic on Idwal Beach. We were fortunate to have Sir Chris Bonington as principal guest at our 50th Anniversary Grand Dinner, which was attended by team members past and present.

I hope you enjoy reading this history of the Ogwen Valley Mountain Rescue Organisation. We now look forward to the next fifty years. What will happen during this time we can only guess. In 1964, Ron James could hardly have imagined that, fifty years later, a pocket sized telephone would be able to pinpoint a casualty's location to within a matter of metres! One thing we hope, however, is that this volunteer service of which we are all proud to be members — remains firmly volunteer led.

Rhagair

Yn 1964, gwelwyd 'Top of the Pops' ar deledu BBC am y tro cyntaf, ymddeolodd Winston Churchill o Dŷ'r Cyffredin, dechreuwyd cyhoeddi papur newydd 'The Sun' ac, ar ddiwrnod olaf y flwyddyn, enillodd Donald Campbell ei seithfed record am gyflymder ar ddŵr, ar 276.33 milltir yr awr — y cyntaf i ennill recordiau cyflymder ar dir ac ar ddŵr yr un flwyddyn.

Yng Ngogledd Cymru, daeth tîm bach o wirfoddolwyr at ei gilydd mewn ysgol fynydda leol, dan arweiniad Ron James, i ffurfio Sefydliad Achub Mynydd Dyffryn Ogwen. Yn hanner cant oed erbyn hyn, ceidw'r sefydliad yn ffyddlon i'w egwyddor sylfaenol — darparu gwasanaeth chwilio ac achub ar gyfer pobl mewn anawsterau ar diroedd geirwon.

Er hynny, newidiodd nifer o bethau yn yr hanner can mlynedd hynny. Tyfodd y tîm i bron hanner cant o aelodau. Bu cynnydd enfawr mewn technoleg sydd, ac yn ei dro, wedi newid sut y mae pobl yn ceisio cymorth a sut y rhoddir y cymorth hwnnw. Gwellodd gofal anafusion o naid i naid. Mae gan y tîm grŵp o gefnogwyr sy'n helpu codi arian. Mae nifer y galwadau'n amrywio ond yn tyfu — y ffigwr uchaf oedd 140 yn 2010 — ac nid anghyffredin yw derbyn dau neu dri galwad neu ragor mewn cyfnod o bedair awr ar hugain. Mae hyn i gyd yn pwyso'n drymach drymach ar aelodau gwirfoddol ein tîm.

Nid dim ond mater o nifer fach o bobl yn mynd allan ar y mynydd yw achub mynydd mwyach. Ceir llawer o weithgareddau y tu hwnt i'r llen, gyda grwpiau gweithio, pwyllgorau ac, wrth gwrs, y codi arian hollbwysig. Bu'n rhaid i'r tîm addasu, a chroesawu newid, er mwyn gallu cyflawni ei amcanion.

Mae'r llyfr hwn yn adrodd hanes Sefydliad Achub Mynydd Dyffryn Ogwen, o'i ddechreuad hyd heddiw. Byddwch yn darllen sut y datblygodd y gwasanaeth achub mynydd, sut y ffurfiwyd y tîm a sut y newidiodd. Trwy nifer o hanesion achub go iawn, cewch weld yr hyn a wna aelodau'r tîm pan ddaw galwad.

Wrth gwrs, ni fuom yn gweithio ar ein pennau ein hunain. Yn 2015, daeth i ben y gwasanaeth chwilio ac achub â hofrenyddion a ddarperid gan Sgwadron 22 yr Awyrlu Brenhinol, yn y Fali ar Ynys Môn, gyda Bristow, sy'n gweithredu o Gaernarfon, yn cymryd ei le. Mae'r Awyrlu Brenhinol, ac erbyn hyn Bristow, yn ddau'n unig o'r partneriaid a helpodd y tîm i ddarparu gwasanaethau. Hoffwn gymryd y cyfle hwn i ddiolch i bawb sydd wedi'n helpu a'n cefnogi. Yn anffodus, nid oes lle i sôn amdanoch i gyd yn y llyfr hwn, ond cewch fod yn sicr ein bod ni'n ddiolchgar am eich cymorth.

Trwy gydol ein hanner canfed flwyddyn, bu'r tîm yn cynnal nifer o ddathliadau, gan gynnwys goleuo llinell crib Tryfan â thortshis pennau, cinio ffurfiol ar ben Tryfan a phicnic ar y traeth yng Nghwm Idwal. Buom yn ffodus i gael Chris Bonington fel ein prif westy yng nghinio Mawreddog ein Pen-blwydd yn hanner cant oed, lle daeth aelodau o'r tîm presennol a rhai o'r gorffennol at ei gilydd.

Gobeithio y byddwch yn mwynhau darllen hanes Sefydliad Achub Mynydd Dyffryn Ogwen. Bellach edrychwn ymlaen at yr hanner can mlynedd nesaf. Ni allwn ond ceisio dychmygu'r hyn a ddigwydd. Prin, yn 1964, y gallai Ron James fod wedi dychmygu y byddai ffôn maint poced, ym mhen hanner can mlynedd, yn medru lleoli claf o fewn ychydig fetrau. Un gobaith sydd gennym, beth bynnag, yw y bydd y gwasanaeth gwirfoddol hwn — yr ydym i gyd yn falch o fod yn aelodau ohono — yn parhau'n bendant dan arweiniad gwirfoddolwyr.

ANDY HARBACH
CHAIRMAN

OGWEN VALLEY
MOUNTAIN RESCUE
ORGANISATION

As Patron of Mountain Rescue England and Wales and as a former RAF Search and Rescue pilot, I have been privileged to witness first-hand the invaluable work of the Ogwen Valley mountain rescue volunteers - on the mountain and in the communities of Snowdonia.

Through the years, this dedicated group have been both pioneering and creative in their pursuit of better care for those they help, and there are many who owe a huge debt of gratitude to them.

This book celebrates the crucial part the team has played for fifty years, responding to those in need of support - be they injured climbers, the lost and afraid separated from their friends and families, or those in their community affected by civil emergencies such as flooding.

Enjoy this book; and join me in thanking a remarkable group of people for all that they do in the beautiful landscape of Snowdonia.

OGGI SNIPS

The Ogwen patch boasts eleven peaks all topping the magic 3000 foot mark — all true 'Munros' and all south of 'the Border'.

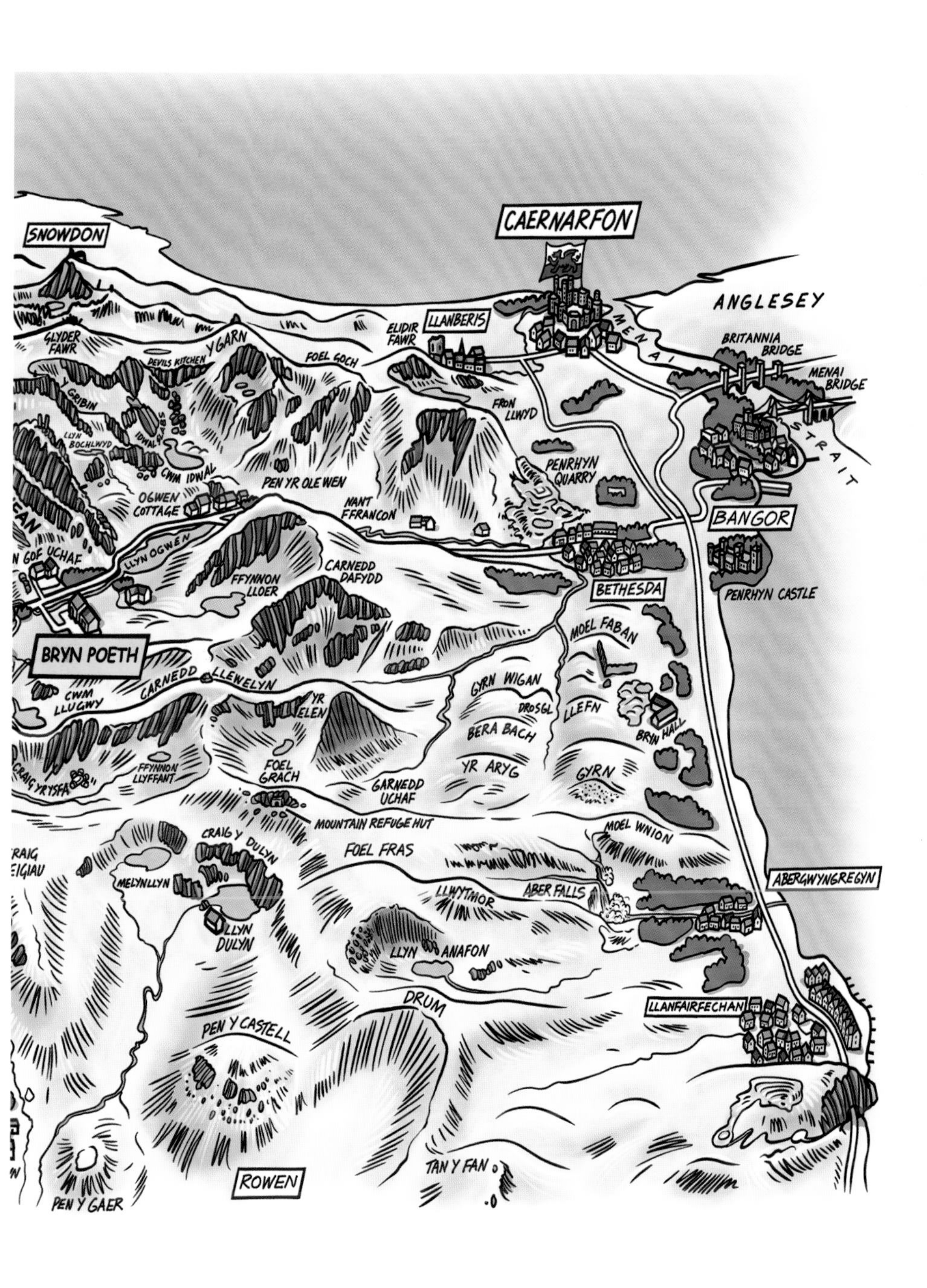
SNOWDON
CAERNARFON
ANGLESEY
GLYDER FAWR
Y GARN
DEVILS KITCHEN
ELIDIR FAWR
LLANBERIS
FOEL GOCH
MENAI
BRITANNIA BRIDGE
MENAI BRIDGE
GRIBIN
LLYN BOCHLWYD
IDWAL SLABS
FRON LLWYD
STRAIT
CWM IDWAL
PENRHYN QUARRY
PEN YR OLE WEN
OGWEN COTTAGE
NANT FFRANCON
BANGOR
LLYN OGWEN
CARNEDD DAFYDD
FFYNNON LLOER
BETHESDA
PENRHYN CASTLE
MOEL FABAN
BRYN POETH
CARNEDD LLEWELYN
GYRN WIGAN
CWM LLUGWY
YR ELEN
DROSGL
LLEFN
BERA BACH
BRYN HALL
FFYNNON LLYFFANT
FOEL GRACH
YR ARYG
GYRN
CRAIG YR YSFA
GARNEDD UCHAF
MOUNTAIN REFUGE HUT
MOEL WNION
CRAIG Y DULYN
FOEL FRAS
ABERGWYNGREGYN
MELYNLLYN
LLWYTMOR
ABER FALLS
LLYN DULYN
LLYN ANAFON
DRUM
LLANFAIRFECHAN
PEN Y CASTELL
TAN Y FAN
ROWEN
PEN Y GAER

OGGI SNIPS

The team's operational area covers approximately 125 square miles, from a line extending west to east along the Glyderau and from the Conwy Valley westwards to Bangor.

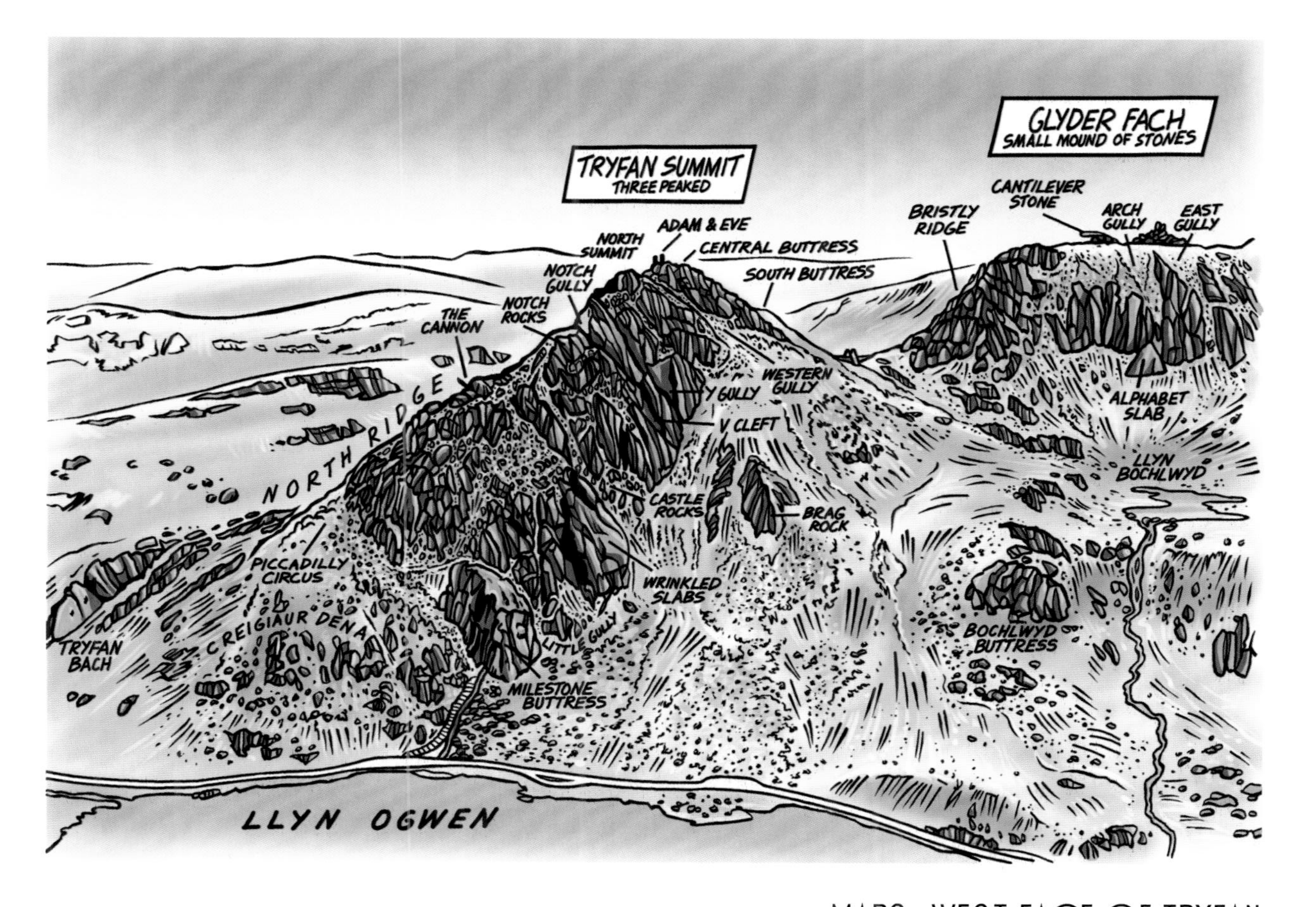
GLYDER FACH
SMALL MOUND OF STONES
TRYFAN SUMMIT
THREE PEAKED
CANTILEVER STONE
ARCH GULLY
EAST GULLY
BRISTLY RIDGE
ADAM & EVE
NORTH SUMMIT
CENTRAL BUTTRESS
SOUTH BUTTRESS
NOTCH GULLY
NOTCH ROCKS
THE CANNON
NORTH RIDGE
WESTERN GULLY
Y GULLY
V CLEFT
ALPHABET SLAB
LLYN BOCHLWYD
CASTLE ROCKS
BRAG ROCK
PICCADILLY CIRCUS
WRINKLED SLABS
CREIGIAUR DENA
LITTLE GULLY
BOCHLWYD BUTTRESS
TRYFAN BACH
MILESTONE BUTTRESS
LLYN OGWEN

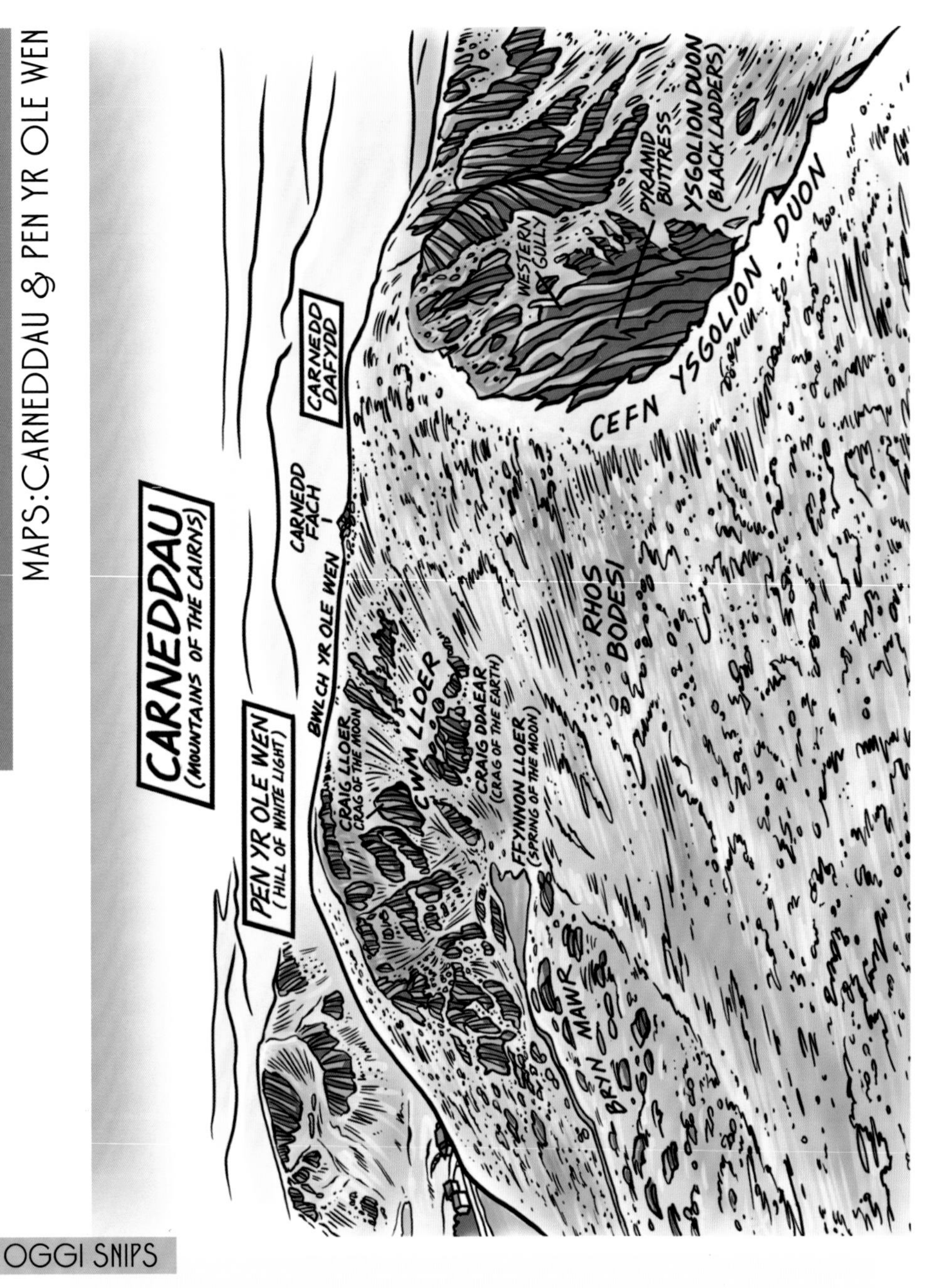

OGGI SNIPS

From the 'pink' incident report forms September 2002: His wife advised him to burn his boots and take up another hobby.

MAPS: CWM IDWAL & THE DEVIL'S KITCHEN

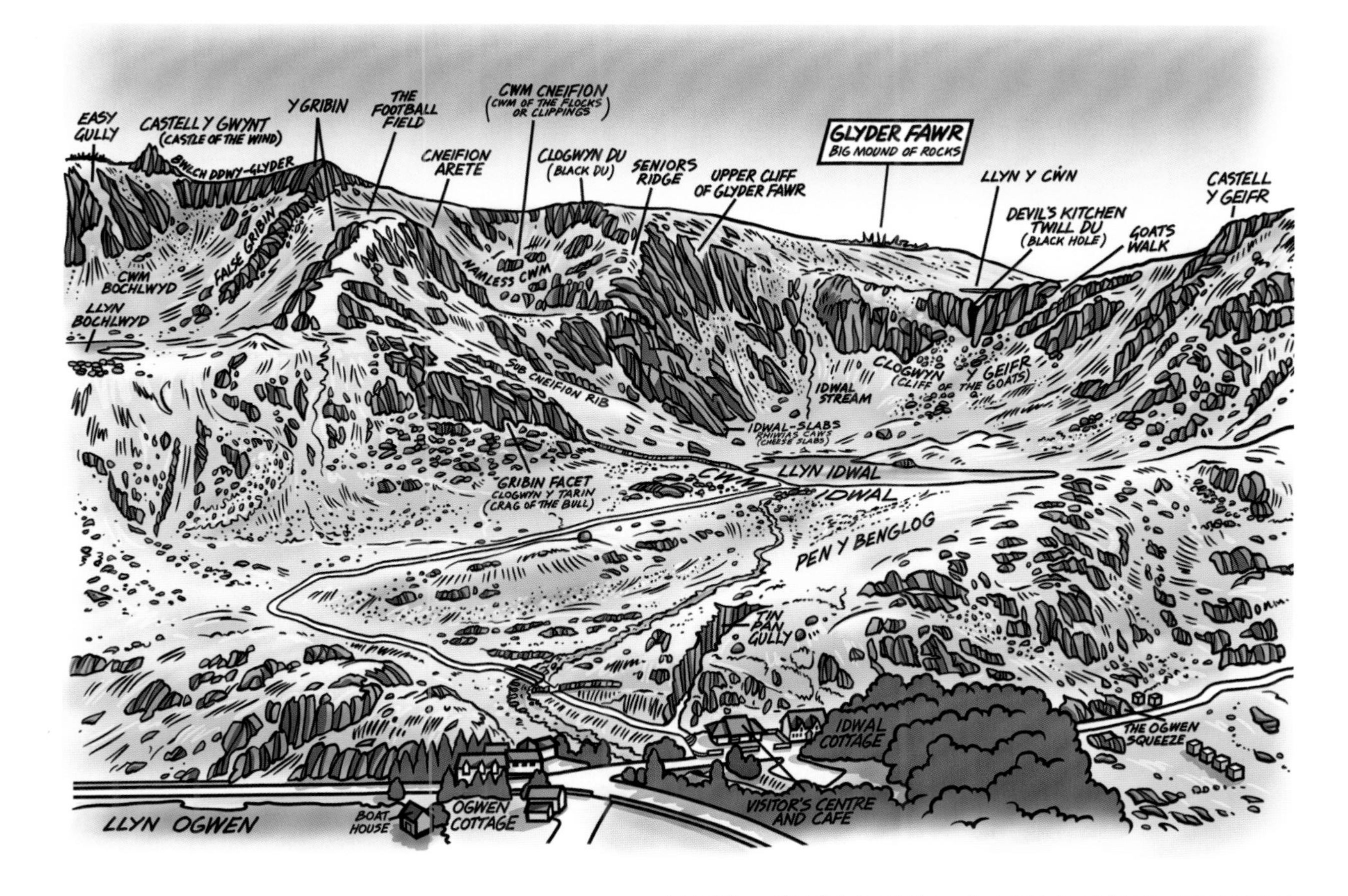

Left: Stretcher practice © OVMRO. **Map illustrations** © George Manley.

CHAPTER ONE

Cometh the moment, cometh the mountain men

People have been happily scrambling over the rocky outcrops and grassy slopes of Wales for centuries and, no doubt, extricating themselves from many a scrape and tumble, living to tell the tale over tea or tipples. There is evidence of activity on the summit and slopes of Snowdon, and the flanks of Tryfan, dating back as far as the Bronze Age. The first recorded 'recreational' ascent of Snowdon was by the botanist Thomas Johnson in 1639. During the late eighteenth-century, Thomas Pennant, the Welsh naturalist, writer and antiquarian, was busy bagging summits in North Wales and recording his experiences. In 'A short account of Caernarvon and Beddgelert', he noted that Edward I, after his conquest of Wales in 1284, held a 'triumphal fair' at the top, or at least very high 'upon this our chief of mountains' and 'adjourned it to the plains of Nevin to finish the joy of his victory with tilts and tournaments', indicating the likelihood of significantly earlier descents.

In 1862, English gentleman George Borrow, whose writing mainly focused on his travels around Europe, produced 'Wild Wales: Its People, Language and Scenery', an account of his tour around Wales alone and on foot after a family holiday in Llangollen in 1854. Alongside Pennant and Borrow, Cumbrian-born William Gilpin was recording his appreciation of the wild and rugged mountains in his travel journals and Cambridge student William Bingley explored the cliffs and ledges of Snowdonia in search of botanical specimens.

Their lyrical prose, detailed descriptions and sketches fired the public

Mariner at work: Ron James with the Mariner stretcher © OVMRO.

imagination and whetted the appetite for travel. It was inspiring stuff but, until the Victorian era, hill walking and climbing for pleasure remained very much the prerogative of the rich — the gentlemen and ladies who could afford to be adventurous with their time, money and life. Those less fortunate may have toiled in the mountains, working the farmsteads, herding cattle, building roads and walls or quarrying slate, but these things were born of necessity and the need to earn a living.

Anyone unfortunate enough to be injured in the mountains either died at the scene of their misfortune, or relied on their companions to rally local farmers, shepherds and quarrymen into makeshift rescue parties using makeshift equipment. Even then, they might die anyway, their injuries made worse by the bone-jangling journey across rough terrain, without the benefit of pain relief or protection from the elements.

The earliest record of an organised search and recovery in the area is in 1832, when a visitor called Philip Homer was reported to be missing on Moel Siabod. A search party was organised, led by local guide Robin Hughes of Capel Curig, but Homer's body was found on the mountain. He had died of exhaustion. In 'Notes and Recollections of an Angler: Rambles Among Mountains, Valleys and Solitudes of Wales' by John Henry Cliffe, originally published in 1860, the author writes that 'Homer's remains lie interred in the churchyard at Capel Curig. He appeared to have been exceedingly rash and venturesome and, regardless of advice and warning, wandered on Moel Siabod, got lost in the mist, and at last perished from exhaustion'.

Records of early mountain rescues are scant — or buried deep — but Hazel Robbins (née Pierce), a local historian and Fellow of the Royal Historical Society, has uncovered some gems amongst the archives. And it would seem that knowing where to look is the key to all manner of detail barely available to the twenty-first century journalist. One such is the story of John Price Hunt, who lost his life in the Carneddau, on 23 July 1856. While it would be many more years before a formalised mountain rescue service took shape, all the elements are there: the mustering of help, the rudimentary search tactics, the rapidly assembled 'stretcher' carried by all hands across the unforgiving terrain.

When John Price Hunt persuaded his friend of eighteen months, one Thomas Titmus, to accompany him to Wales — thinking it unwise to take his pregnant wife and child on a trip which involved a great deal of walking — he could hardly have imagined what would be his fate. Their intention had been to visit Beaumaris, the Britannia and Menai bridges and the Penrhyn quarries but, having completed a tour of the latter in mixed weather, they were struck by how beautiful and clear the day had become and changed their plans. Rather than viewing the bridges next, they would walk to the summit of Carnedd Llewelyn.

Once at the summit they rested for a short time, enjoying the spectacular views — although, unbeknown to them, they had actually ascended Carnedd Dafydd. Their problems began when they began their descent. Not only were they unfamiliar with the area, neither of them were experienced mountain walkers. John took the lead and proceeded along a narrow way 'where he stood knocking bits of stones with his stick'. Thomas, seeing that there did not appear to be any track and considering it to be a very dangerous way to go, advised John not to go that way.

'I'll go, if you will go with me', said John, but Thomas refused and turned back up. 'If you go up again we shall lose one another', shouted John. 'No, we shan't', countered Thomas, as he retraced

OGGI SNIPS

14 April 1990. Rucksack found at base of First Pinnacle Rib, East Face of Tryfan. Owner found incapable in hostelry in Betwys y Coed, claiming he lost it the previous December.

his steps before turning down to the left of the spot where John stood. It was 3.50pm and these were the last words the two friends exchanged.

When Thomas reached the bottom, there was no sign of John so he 'roamed about for some time and shouted for him', but it was no use. So he set off for Bethesda, which he reached at 5.45pm. By now tired and thirsty, he visited the Swan Tavern and told the landlady he had missed his friend. Soon after that, he began walking back to Bangor and came across a 'man on the mountain digging turf' and asked him if he had seen John. Then he called at the toll gate and asked the keeper if he had seen John go through and gave a description.

The keeper said he had and when Thomas told him he thought he must be mistaken, the keeper replied that he was certain John had gone by because he'd seen him pass through with Thomas earlier that day. Filled with hope of finding John, Thomas walked all the way back to Bangor, only to find that John wasn't there. Now he knew for certain that his friend was missing.

The following day, Thursday, it rained very heavily in the morning. Thomas left Bangor at 2.00pm for the two-hour walk back to Bethesda to see the local police officer, John Evans. He told Evans that his friend was lost on the mountain and Evans recommended he take Owen Thomas, a local man with a thorough knowledge of the mountains, to look for John. They both went up and walked about a good deal but found nothing. Later, they went again to the Swan Tavern where Owen Thomas gave an account of where they had been. Thomas also reported back to the police officer and they swapped addresses so they could keep each other informed of developments. Although John had been missing for a day, Evans thought he had probably descended on the other side of the mountain.

On the Friday, Thomas felt he should write home and inform friends and relatives what had happened, unsure what to do or where to go for help. He went up to the railway station and asked the guard for advice. The guard suggested Thomas see the local magistrate, Mr Williams, who appears to have been a local bank manager. Thomas called at the bank twice but Williams wasn't there, so the gentleman in attendance advised him to go and see Mr Francis, the quarry manager, and ask him if he would allow the quarrymen to go up and search the mountain.

This advice must have been a great relief to Thomas. At last, some decisive action could be taken. Because it had not been obvious where he could go for help, the whole of Friday had been wasted as he walked around Bangor trying to find someone to advise him. Consequently, it was not until Saturday, three days after John went missing, that a proper search took place. On that day, Thomas went with PC Evans and two others to see Mr Francis at the quarry to request the quarrymen's help. Francis agreed and, after 'dinner', about seventy quarrymen came out to search.

The search party made its way up the mountain, with Thomas amongst one of the groups that went to the summit while others searched lower down. Thomas's group had barely reached the summit before they heard Owen Thomas shout that John's body had been found. It was about 2.30pm. According to Thomas, John was not near the place where he had left him and he thought that, rather than turning right or left, John must have 'gone straight on a little way then fallen over.'

Thomas described the place as 'extremely precipitous' while Evans said it was 'a frightful place — not fit for any man to go to by himself'. The drop was estimated to be about 240 feet and the journalist reporting on the incident speculated that it was likely 'a man like the deceased probably quite inexperienced as to mountains would, on finding himself in a situation beset with so much danger, lose all presence of mind and become powerless to extricate himself or to avert his impending fate'.

In what could only be described as an early example of media sensationalism, the journalist expressed surprise that, despite continued warnings, strangers still persisted in 'meeting the dangers of mountain gorges without a guide', informing his readers that the skeleton of a man had been found some years earlier at Cefn Tir, to the north of Carnedd Llewelyn and not far from where John had been killed. Continuing in his stride he reported that at 'Ysgolion Duon, fox hounds and foxes have been seen to break their necks over the tremendous precipice referred to'. From this, it appears that John must have fallen to his death somewhere on the Black Ladders.

John was found lying on his left side, his face turned towards the rock with his right hand underneath his head. There were two or three injuries to the head including a deep wound at the back from which some blood had flowed, but not a great deal. There was some bleeding from the nose and scratches to the face but apart from that the face was uninjured. The ribs on the left side of John's body were flattened due to the force of the fall, his shoes were torn and both ankle bones had been dislocated. The conjecture was that he must have slipped over the rock for some distance during which his shoes were torn and he injured his head, before falling over the precipice. His cap had caught on a projecting piece of rock about thirty feet from the bottom.

Having found the body, the quarrymen prepared to bring it down from the mountain. This was done by making a litter out of ropes and sticks. By this means 'it was with great difficulty brought over the rocks' and carried for some three or four miles to the Douglas Arms Hotel in Bethesda, where the inquest was to take place two days later. And, when John's stepfather, John Reynolds, arrived in Bethesda, expecting to assist in the search for his son, he was met with the tragic news that his body had been found.

COBWEB CORNER

Efforts to document the team's history over the years have been many, with varying degrees of enthusiasm. The newsletters record several attempts to collate scrapbooks of press cuttings and photographs. In May 1980, team members were reminded of a request the previous month, largely unheeded. 'Clive has been underwhelmed by the response,' it admonished, with a liberal sprinkling of capitals and underscores. Attributing the 'wave of apathy that greeted the suggestion' to the 'inherent shyness of team members', it asked that they find it in themselves to overcome this personal problem and help document the history of your organisation...' Sadly, the struggle continued for some time to come.

OGGI SNIPS

Newsletter, 1981: Unusual call-out to assist in the search for missing documents stolen from the University of Bangor, later found strewn around the edges of Llyn Ogwen.

Secrets shared – the birth of the mountaineering club

As mountaineering grew as a sport, so too did the desire to share the experience and the mountaineering clubs took shape — first the Alpine Club, in 1857, followed by the Scottish Mountaineering Club in 1889 and the Climbers' Club, nine years later.

The intention of the Climbers' Club had initially been to 'encourage mountaineering, particularly in England, Wales and Ireland', but with the subsequent birth of other, more regionally focused clubs, it remained primarily a club for those who climbed in North Wales, having evolved in part from the Pen y Gwryd Hotel and the Society of Welsh Rabbits — a loose association of climbers founded by C E Matthews, the first president of the Climbers' Club.

Mountaineering club members spent their weekends in search of new routes in the Lake District and Wales. Then, in 1903, a tragic accident high on Scafell Pinnacle — the worst British climbing history had known — saw four climbers fall to their deaths as their leader slipped, still roped together. The first fatal climbing accident in twenty-one years of adventurous climbing in the Lake District, the 'Scafell Disaster' was a pivotal moment in mountain rescue history as a shocked climbing fraternity began to consider the increasing incidence of mountain accidents and the lack of rescue resources available.

Within a year, a supply of first aid and mountain rescue equipment, with instructions for its use, was in place at the Gorphwysfa Hotel (now Pen y Pass youth hostel), including a Furley stretcher, complete with extra carry slings, delivered on 24 December 1903. Similar arrangements would soon follow at the Pen y Gwryd and Ogwen Cottage as climbers increasingly turned their attention to the mountains of North Wales, with regular 'meets' at these three key locations.

Alan Hankinson describes in 'The Mountain Men' an air of reluctance, amongst those pushing up new routes and stretching the boundaries, to share their discoveries in print, perhaps fearing the cliffs of Snowdonia would become 'uncomfortably cluttered at holiday times'. Guide books might take away the sheer joy of 'savage solitude' and route discovery. There was a secrecy to it all, to be shared only amongst club members.

But publish they did, despite the 'caustic remarks' bandied by their peers about 'inaccuracies or misleading statements'. Geoffrey Winthrop Young began a scheme to combine English club journals and produce some local guides to 'stop these terrible accidents'. The first of these, 'The Climbs of Lliwedd' by J M Archer Thomson, a schoolmaster from Bangor, and A W Andrews, was published in 1909 and swiftly followed by Archer Thomson's 'Climbing in the Ogwen District', featuring all the known routes on the Glyderau, Tryfan and the Carneddau, which he had personally checked out. Archer Thompson was a Welshman, and one of the leading rock climbers in Britain at the time. With this guide, the Climbers' Club officers were said to consider that 'the epoch of exploration had then closed', which may have owed more to the desire to keep things 'in the club', than any real thought about how the appeal of climbing might widen beyond their hallowed circles.

It was Archer Thomson who climbed up to the scene to investigate the accidental death in 1901 of Percy Weightman, a fellow member of the Climbers' Club. The 'Tryfan Cross' commemorating

Weightman's death, carefully carved into the rock in a place rarely visited save by birds and wildlife, was rediscovered in 2014 by four Ogwen team members on a training exercise, as their path took them below Heather Terrace on a goat track. In torrential rain, high winds and sleet the four stood for a full five minutes looking in amazement at the large cross, with letters and numbers just visible above it. In such a desolate spot and quite off the beaten track, they were intrigued as to why and how it was there. Hazel Robbins uncovered a fascinating story.

Percy Weightman had arranged to spend the Easter weekend climbing in the company of four friends. Armed with ropes, ice axes and spiked boots, their intention was to climb Tryfan on the Sunday so, once the weather had cleared, they made their way to the North or Central Gully, which they reached at about 1.30pm.

John Milton, later reported that there 'was a great deal of snow for the time of year, and several pitches were entirely covered'. As they approached the top, it began to rain and became misty. Once at the summit, which they reached at about 3.30pm, they had a hasty lunch, not wanting to remain there any longer than necessary due to the weather. Their intention was to descend 'by the arête... but the mist by this time having hidden the main ridge, we inadvertently followed the slight deviation to our right which, after descending fifty or sixty feet, brought us onto the buttress running east, which skirts the North Gully.'

Despite a 'precipitous edge', Milton was adamant they were not in any danger, claiming it would have been easy for them to go back the way they had come to regain the main ridge. To spare them this additional climb, Percy — who was a few feet below the rest of the party — shouted that he'd look around. Taking his ice axe with him, he went down some thirty feet and disappeared to his right. It was about 3.40pm and the last time he was seen alive.

As Percy descended, not one of his companions suggested using the rope but, as Milton explained, he 'was a capital climber, strong, active and peculiarly sure-footed'. It never crossed their minds to use the rope. After a short time, having heard nothing from him, they began shouting. Receiving no reply, Milton descended in Percy's footsteps and saw, with horror where his friend 'had glissaded or slipped, and where the trough made by his boots ended abruptly over a protruding rock about two yards square', just before 'an almost sheer drop'.

Although what he had discovered was alarming, at this point Milton did not think that Weightman had fallen down the face, but had slipped in the direction of Nor Nor Gully. Returning to the rest of the party, he kept calm and, according to newspaper reports, did not tell them he had seen marks suggesting that Percy had slipped over the ledge, to avoid agitating them.

The party divided into two groups of two with each pair roped together to go down 'the open space', roughly at right angles to, and leading into, Nor Nor Gully. The lower they descended, the more hope they lost. And when they finally reached the bottom their worst fears were confirmed.

Percy was quite dead. One boot torn off, his body lay across the gully below the grassy traverse, five or six hundred feet from where his friends had last seen him alive. He had evidently fallen down the face of the mountain almost immediately he left their view. Milton unroped himself and went to where Percy lay, head downwards and jammed between some rocks. His skull was fractured and he appeared to have struck the rocks many times in the course of his appalling descent.

A party of climbers, no doubt men like Percy on holiday in the area, made a valiant attempt to

OGGI SNIPS

Cwm Idwal was the first National Nature Reserve (NNR) in Wales, officially recognised in 1954 by the Nature Conservancy.

reach the gully but were defeated by pouring rain, wind and 'the intense darkness of the night' and the search was abandoned until the morning. On Easter Monday, amid showers of hail and snow, Percy's body was extricated from the rocks, wrapped in canvas sheets then lashed to an improvised stretcher before being 'borne by a circuitous path slowly down the mountainside'.

There were newspaper reports that Percy had 'a great desire to do what had not been done before', prompting speculation that this might be a contributing factor to the accident but this was hotly denied by his friends.

'Mr Weightman,' said Milton, 'was an experienced climber, who climbed from sheer love of climbing, and never showed any desire to make or break records either in speed or in endeavouring to do what others had failed to accomplish. The immediate cause of the accident we may never know, but I am unwilling to leave uncontradicted a statement which is an aspersion on the name of one who will ever be held in high respect by his fellow climbers'.

It was some time later when Archer Thomson suggested that Percy had 'slipped on easy ground, and lost his balance through stepping on snow overlying a tilted plate of rock'. Whilst the accident was not due to any 'reprehensible negligence' on Percy's part, he reminded climbers of 'the advisability in such places of using the axe as a prop or a probe'.

In his account of the accident, Milton mentions a cross, cut into the rock to indicate where Percy's body was found. A small pile of stones also marks the spot where Percy's ice axe was found seven weeks after the accident. As this area is difficult to get to and not part of a popular walking or climbing route, it's safe to assume that the ice axe's discovery was the result of human activity at the scene related to the construction of the cross. It is not documented who commissioned the cross but it was most likely Percy's family — possibly his sister, Jane Alice, who was apparently very fond of her brother.

Archer Thomson too noted 'the cross carved in low relief on the right wall of the channel'. Yet this carefully constructed memorial to a beloved brother may have remained unseen and lost to time's memory if four individuals, descending in similar weather conditions, had not inadvertently come across it over a hundred years later.

'Perhaps it is fitting,' says Robbins, 'that, in the same way as Percy's body was retrieved and brought back to his family by fellow climbers in 1901, in 2014 another group of fellow climbers have ensured that his story is remembered once more and his cross, once lost, is now found.'

A perilous playground

As the hills have become more accessible, many more guide books have been written. A pattern was set: more climbers and mountaineers, more accidents. And gradually, the joys of standing atop a mountain have become less the preserve of the 'pure' climber. In North Wales, the Snowdon Mountain Railway played a part in this change, ferrying folk up the hill who might otherwise have stayed firmly at the bottom! This was the Victorian age, the age of the sightseeing tour, when those who could afford it might indulge in the European Grand Tour or, closer to home, tours of the Lake District or the mountains of Snowdonia — long, sinuous journeys by rail and road punctuated here

and there by opportunities to gaze at wondrous sights. And where better to gaze in wonder than the summit of Snowdon? Cloud permitting, of course.

The Swiss-engineered rack and pinion railway itself fell victim to a mountain accident on the very day it opened. On a fine Easter Monday in 1896, at 10.50am, with eighty passengers aboard, the first train of two carriages set off from Llanberis towards the summit, swiftly followed by a second train. They both reached the summit an hour later. By this time the cloud had descended. The second train to arrive, driven by William Pickles, set off on its return journey to Llanberis at 12.30pm. A few yards above Clogwyn station, the wheels jumped the rack and the locomotive careered down the slope into the bottom of Cwm Glas Bach.

Climbers coming up the mountain towards Clogwyn were reported to have thought they saw a large boulder falling towards them through the mist as the engine 'toppled and fell gracefully over the side of the mountain'.

In 'A Perilous Playground', Bob Maslen-Jones's study of two centuries of 'misadventures in the mountains of Snowdonia', he tells how William Pickles and the fireman jumped clear of the tumbling carriage. The guard in the rear coach applied the safety brake, shouting to the passengers as he did so, to stay in their seats. In the panic which must have ensued amongst the eager, unsuspecting sightseers, dressed in their 'Sunday best', two of them ignored this sanguine advice and jumped from the carriage. The surprise, perhaps is that they were the only two to do so!

One, a visitor from Shropshire, escaped injury but 'local man Ellis Roberts hit a rock on the side of the track and rolled back onto the line', where his leg was 'crushed between the footboard of the train and the rail'. Despite immediate first aid, it was some hours before a doctor arrived at the accident. He declared that Roberts had 'no blood in him.' He had been bleeding profusely from his crushed leg. The doctor did what he could and injected 'two quarts of warm saline into him.'

It was some time before the relief engine could get up sufficient steam to make the trip, a delay which may have cost Roberts his life. Strapped onto a makeshift stretcher, at some time on the way down he had died from loss of blood and was declared dead on arrival at the hospital. It was a long way still from the efficient casualty care and speedy helicopter evacuations available to today's casualties.

COBWEB CORNER

May 1967 newsletter: Eight members of the team were involved in the making of an ITV film about a rescue on Tremadoc. The 'patient', team member Dave Siviter, was attached to a 'few pegs' on the wall just right of the Vector and rescued by a horizontal lower on wire plus terylene ropes. The programme had originally been planned as a support to Joe Brown's 'Blond versus Buttress' film but, after seeing it, ITV decided to show it as a programme in its own right. Brown, who was watching, was reported to be 'very impressed'.

Team practice on Vector Buttress, Tremadoc, 1967: Left to right: Neil Adam, Barbara James, Roger Jones, Tony Jones with KC Gordon and Ron James guiding the stretcher. Team member Dave Siviter acts as casualty © OVMRO.

Of posts and gate posts

During the early 1920s, the climbing community was finding the lure of the Lake District somewhat stronger than Snowdonia but, noted Iwan Arfon Jones in his 'Climbers' Club Guide' to the area, things 'were soon to change' partly due to 'the purchase of Helyg which George Borrow had referred to as a wretched hovel'. The Rucksack Club too had a cottage in the valley, with Tal y Braich Uchaf. And in 1921, the Ogwen guidebook had been reissued with an appendix of new climbs (so much for their confidently heralded end to the epoch of exploration) by the intriguingly named H E L Porter. The generation of Everest luminaries and polar explorers led by the likes of Geoffrey Winthrop Young were said to dominate the Ogwen scene using 'fast cars to get them to the hills as quickly as possible' and generally lending an air of romance to the whole thing.

Yet, for all their fast cars and adventurous spirit, those who ventured into the hills and mountains for sport had to be able to look after themselves out of necessity. There has always been an inherent self-sufficiency about those who climb — perhaps less apparent in our twenty-first century world of GPS and internet-enabled mobile phones. And in those early pioneers, this brought with it a ready camaraderie and willingness to help others in distress in that same environment, characteristics undoubtedly manifest in those who volunteer as mountain rescuers today.

So, if a climber had an accident, it was other members of their party who were forced to deal with the consequences, with little more than their personal resources and dogged determination to see them through. There was no specialist equipment, limited knowledge of first aid and no formal training. Stretchers and splints were invariably improvised from whatever was available — gateposts, finger posts, five-barred gates and ladders were wrenched into service and knotted together with whatever rope or bits of clothing there was to spare. But the mood was changing and what was happening in North Wales was being reflected across the mountains of the UK.

An accident elsewhere, during a meet in the Peak District, and the extreme difficulties encountered by rescuers, proved pivotal. Edgar Pryor, an ex-president of the Rucksack Club, was knocked off his stance by a lady climber, who was not in the party, falling down the upper pitch. It was a rough hillside, covered with steep rocks, and Pryor fell about forty feet into an adjacent gully breaking his skull and thigh bone. A relay of runners brought up blankets and hot water bottles and Dr Findlay, a police surgeon and club member, devised a splint from a rucksack frame and organised evacuation of the casualty, using the finger post torn from the path as a stretcher.

Despite the ingenuity and care in the improvisation of stretcher and splint, it was an agonising business — a four-hour carry, using relays of stretcher bearers over rough going almost all the way, followed by a ninety-minute journey to the Manchester Royal Infirmary. Wilson Hey, the consulting surgeon, later observed that Pryor was so shocked he needed blood transfusion before he could be operated on. In fact, the transport and shock had so damaged the limb, Hey was forced to amputate some months later. 'The absence of morphia with the transport had done more damage to the limb than the mountain', he said. As a result of his experience, Hey began to agitate for the formation of an organised mountain rescue service, with the assistance of morphia [better known now as morphine], which he regarded as essential.

A keen and experienced climber himself, Hey had witnessed the inventiveness of mountain

OGGI SNIPS

Llyn Ogwen lies alongside the A5 between the Carneddau and the Glyderau. At 310 metres above sea level it covers an area of 78 acres, but is only a little over three metres deep.

rescue at first hand when climbing with two medical friends on the Glyderau in North Wales. Near the summit of Glyder Fach they came across a man with a broken leg in need of urgent medical attention. As one kept vigil with the casualty, the other two went to fetch help and a stretcher from the Pen y Gwryd. On the way down, they came across a gate which they 'borrowed'. Mindful that time was of the essence, they carried the gate up to the ridge and made the man as comfortable as was possible, before fixing him to the 'stretcher' and setting off down the mountain. The journey, needless to say, was traumatic for the casualty — the gate was uncomfortable, their makeshift splint was causing extreme pain to his injured leg, and there were no pain killing drugs available.

An accident in 1931, on Crib Goch, brought Alfred Sefton Pigott — one of Britain's most outstanding climbers between the wars — to the same conclusion. As a member of a carrying party which brought the injured man down, he experienced first hand the woefully inadequate equipment — an old stretcher and a few bandages — and the extreme difficulty in bringing the man off the mountain without doing him further harm.

Shortly after the accident, he began to discuss the possibility of forming some kind of rescue organisation with Hey, a fellow member of the Rucksack Club. The club set up a subcommittee to look into the growing concerns — at the same time as the Fell and Rock Climbing Club formed their own 'stretcher subcommittee' tasked with finding a satisfactory stretcher for mountain rescue purposes. In 1932, the two joined forces to become the Joint Stretcher Committee, charged to produce a suitable mountain stretcher and a list of first aid equipment.

It was the Thomas stretcher, designed by Eustace Thomas in Manchester, which was chosen as most suitable. This original design consisted of wooden runners made of ash, an aluminium frame and a stout canvas bed. Its telescopic handles locked automatically into their extended position, allowing the end carriers to see their feet and avoid stumbling. The wooden runners gave sufficient ground clearance to allow easy movement across rock, scree, grass or snow, although it was not strong enough to be dragged over very rough ground. The search for the 'perfect' mountain stretcher wouldn't end there — with hindsight it was heavy to carry and clumsy in use. Indeed, some years later, the Ogwen team set about producing their own eponymous stretcher. But it was a start. A significant step forward in casualty care.

Alongside this, the committee drew up a list of recommended first aid equipment to be left at designated posts for use by climbers and post supervisors along with local volunteers. This comprised a double Thomas splint, wooden arm splints, iodine, bandages, kettle, primus stove, eiderdown, feeding cup and urine bottle. The Thomas splint, incidentally, although sharing the same name as the stretcher was devised by Hugh Owen Thomas, a noted pioneer in British orthopaedic surgery, whose belief that rest and immobilisation were of more benefit to the patient than excision or amputation, had led him to invent a variety of splints and a wrench for the reduction of fractures.

Official 'rescue posts', were established in some of the more popular climbing areas around the UK, managed by the clubs with the help of donated funds and under the supervision of a designated individual. These 'Good Samaritans of the mountain valleys' were set to become the 'foundation of the whole service'.

In September 1936, the First Aid Committee of Mountaineering Clubs — made up of

MOUNTAIN RESCUE
RESCUE POST

representatives of the mountaineering clubs and bodies with allied interests such as the Ramblers Federation and the Youth Hostel Association — was set up to maintain the posts and administer donations. A central fund was organised from a 2% levy from the clubs and all accidents and use of equipment had to be reported to the committee.

The number of posts continue to grow as demand grew. By 1946, Wales had five official posts: Idwal Cottage Youth Hostel, the Climbers' Club hut at Helyg, the Pen y Gwryd, Glasfryn and the Outward Bound Sea School.

Public humiliation and a swift about turn: the dogged pursuit of morphia

Wilson Hey's determined efforts to relieve the suffering of those injured in the mountains laid the foundations for the level of casualty care experienced by today's casualty — not least his belief in the use of morphia to relieve pain.

Despite being refused permission by the Home Office in 1934, and convinced that 'morphia reduces suffering, and suffering produces shock, and prolonged shock causes death', Hey decided to issue morphia to the posts without a licence, at his own expense. He continued to do so for fifteen years — and made no secret of the fact. Its use was so widely advertised in pamphlets and journals that he freely admitted he almost took for granted that the government would be so impressed with the saving of lives and prevention of suffering, due to the use of morphia, that they might overlook the fact that formal permission had not been given.

In the beginning, the drug was administered via ordinary syringes and needles but, in 1938, La Roche Chemical Works provided tubonic ampoule syringes. Instructions for their use were provided in every rucksack and practical training given. Hey's belief was that these same syringes had been used in the field of battle, often by non-medically trained personnel, so why should they not now be administered by non-medically trained civilians in the similarly extenuating circumstances of mountain rescue. In August 1949, having learned that the drug was now allowed in mines and at airports for use by lay people, Hey reapplied to the Home Office.

Five days later, a Mr Dyke from the Home Office arrived to see him, unannounced and accompanied by a detective sergeant. Angry at the impolite manner of his interview, Hey refused to produce the requested Dangerous Drugs Book relating to his dealings with morphia.

Whilst his frequent letters to Whitehall met with a wall of silence, Hey found himself under extreme pressure from the press, fed by Home Office leaks. In fact, the leaks were so endemic, Hey heard of his imminent summons for 'wilful obstruction' ten days before it was served. Despite the evident loyalty of some of the better papers, Hey was afraid 'the rag press' would 'make a song' of the whole thing. 'Already they have damaged my reputation considerably. I am thought to be either a drug addict or that I am making money out of selling drugs to addicts.'

Rescue post plaque at Bryn Poeth: Photo © Judy Whiteside.

Reluctantly, he called a Grand Council, including Monkhouse, the assistant editor of the 'Manchester Guardian', and wrote to the Home Office. If they were prepared to withdraw the summons, he would withdraw all morphia from mountain rescue posts and would not issue any more in the future. As a consulting surgeon, he said, he neither required nor possessed a Dangerous Drugs Book but kept careful records. And anyway, the quantity of morphia missing during the fifteen years 'would not satisfy a morphia addict for a single day!'

Hey was prepared to become a martyr, declaring himself on the warpath. It grieved him that 'Britain is probably the only country in the civilised world where morphia is not provided in organised mountain rescue for those injured when walking and climbing'.

Court proceedings were twice postponed, the charge reduced to obstruction and refusal to produce a drugs book — the maximum penalty a £250 fine and twelve month's imprisonment. The whole affair ended in something of an anti-climax with Hey convicted of the lesser charge and fined a mere £10 with ten guineas costs, which was settled by the Mountain Rescue Committee 'for the sake of propaganda'.

Within days, having publicly humiliated a man of exemplary character who had only ever acted with integrity and concern for the casualty, the government performed an about turn. Hey was invited to submit 'another' plan for consideration. As this was the first time he'd actually been asked for any plan at all, he related the procedure to date — mountain morphia stocks were kept in a locked steel safe and rescue kit was in the charge of a supervisor, generally at a hotel, police station or farm. The only exception was a mountain hut on Ben Nevis where it could not be kept under lock and key as it must be ready for use in an emergency.

Tubonic ampoules made overdose impossible and replacement of stocks was not made unless a full report of the accident, with the name and address of the casualty on whom the morphia was used, had been supplied. All equipment was also subject to periodic inspections. During fifteen years, he noted, he had only lost 1.25 grams 'which must be far better than the average of any hospital ward or general practitioner.'

A date was set for a meeting in London on the eve of the Alpine Club dinner. Hey and Fred Piggott represented the Mountain Rescue Committee, along with members of the British Mountaineering Council, the Alpine Club and the Scottish Mountaineering Club. They were joined by Lord Chorley (thanks to whose efforts Hey reckoned mountain rescue would 'soon be a brilliant performance instead of a shoddy affair'), Sir Cecil Wakeley (President of the Royal College of Surgeons) and Dr Raymond Greene of Bartholomew's Hospital.

With the weight of public opinion against them, the Home Office relented and agreed to the supply of morphia to mountain rescue posts, provided an annual return recorded details of issue and use. The supply would be three quarter grain ampoules for each post, except for Ogwen and Glencoe which would have six ampoules each due to the frequency of accidents there. Since that day, mountain rescue has appointed a medical officer responsible for the issue of morphia. The first, of course, was the redoubtable Wilson Hey.

As the morphia furore reached its denouement, there were developments aplenty to exercise the hearts and minds of mountain rescue. The Ministry of Fuel and Power offered petrol coupons for mountain rescue use, the Ordnance Survey department agreed to mark the growing number of

OGGI SNIPS

Daily Post, 2012. 'There is a risk with outdoor activities in Snowdonia. There is no such thing as a safe mountain.' North Wales coroner, Dewi Pritchard.

rescue posts on their new maps, and the Ministry of Health implemented the National Health Service Act in regard to mountain rescue, agreeing to supply all drugs and equipment such as blankets and stretchers through the Manchester Royal Infirmary.

As Hey's professional home, this hospital was instrumental in the supply of morphia to the posts, providing an interface between mountain rescue and the Ministry of Health and the Welsh Office and, later, the Department of Health and Social Security. The procedure for issue remained in place for many years. Today, mountain rescue teams are issued with morphine by their local medical practitioners on the understanding that complete records are kept, detailing the quantity, batch number and 'use by' date.

Hotels, hostels and holidaymakers

Since the early twentieth century, due to their geographic locations, the Pen y Gwryd and Gorphwysfa hotels had been the natural 'centres' for the muster of mountain rescue. At Capel Curig, the Royal Hotel — owned by Eugene Brunning and affectionately called the 'Royal' — had also long been a popular venue for mountaineers and a ready source of willing hands.

In 1933, as the climbing clubs began to work more closely together, the landlord of the Pen y Gwryd, Arthur Lockwood, is said to have agreed to coordinate search and rescue operations in and around the northern part of Snowdonia. The hotel had been a honeypot for climbers since the 1800s so it made perfect sense to site an official mountain rescue post there.

When the Second World War brought something of a hiatus to both mountaineering and tourism, the hotel was temporarily occupied by a prep school from Bexhill-on-Sea. Only when the numbers of pupils dropped and the school was forced to move did Lockwood return, but the upheaval had taken its toll. No longer enthused by the task, he moved next door and a Mr and Mrs Owen Ridett took over.

Two years later, in 1947, Ridett too was forced to retire due to ill-health and sold the business to William Hampson who installed a manager, Christopher Baskin Briggs, a thirty-four-year-old Yorkshireman who was said to have 'always remained an unmistakable Yorkshireman despite the fact that he lived in North Wales for the last 45 years of his life'.

Under his stewardship, the hotel rapidly became a focal point for mountain rescue activity for the whole of Snowdonia. In the evenings, the Pen y Gwryd smoke room was a regular meeting place for climbers, both resident and non-resident, often long after hours. Briggs soon found himself rallying his guests and leading them out onto Snowdon to carry out a variety of searches and rescues.

Meanwhile, just as guests at the three hotels provided a constant supply of volunteers when required, so too did the youth hostels at Idwal Cottage and Ogwen Cottage. At Idwal, Constance Alexander and Olive Pritchard, both wardens, were very active rescuers — although the emphasis gradually moved to Ogwen Cottage, where the indomitable Mrs Williams was firmly in charge.

The foundations of a more organised mountain rescue service in the mountains of Snowdonia had finally been laid. And not before time. The end of war heralded a massive increase in outdoor

P·E·N·Y·G·W·R·Y·D

activity and, it seemed, an ever-growing toll of mountain accidents. The 'Manchester Guardian' bitterly complained in the summer of 1948 that 'our hills are swarming with town-bred youngsters who have no idea how quickly and inevitably their untrained muscles and ill-clad bodies would succumb to exhaustion and exposure if they were trapped for the night without shelter in a blizzard or a freezing mist. For the most part they do not venture on rock climbs but they will blithely run the greater risks of scrambling on steep dry grass in plain leather soles or glissading down a slope of soft snow into a sunless gully, where they find themselves out of control on a sheet of ice'.

In May that year, Geoffrey Halliwell reported in the 'Daily Graphic' that, for the benefit of the thousands of would-be climbers who would be 'comin' round the mountain' in summer, a party of experienced mountaineers had spent a 'strenuous Whitsun' on the cliffs of Tryfan, making a film on the 'many risks the recruits will have to take on — and the easiest way out of them'. Many of the 'actors' were active members of the Mountain Rescue Committee. The film was scheduled for screening as a twenty-minute short by September of that year. Veteran climbers hoped it would bring a substantial cut in the number of climbing accidents 'caused by inexperience and rashness... without glamorising the work of mountain rescue in any way'.

Whether the film had the desired effect on those 'a comin' round the mountain' later that summer is not documented but it would appear to have done little to prevent the toll of accidents in Snowdonia during the winter of 1950–51, culminating in the events of Easter 1951, a 'drama unparalleled in the history of mountain climbing in Britain'.

The winds of change blow ever stronger

From the autumn, in 1950, there had been deep snow covering the mountains. The air was bitterly cold, strong winds a regular feature. And the snow just got deeper and deeper. At one point, snow 'lay so thick on the summit of Snowdon that it was possible to walk from the end of the station platform on to the roof of the building'. Day after day of freeze and thaw, relentless snow and

Daily Graphic 1948: 'Technicians and actors take a chance, as they make the safety-first film'. On a narrow ledge, the 'casualty' awaits the rescue party before the stretcher is lowered down the rock face.

The Pen y Gwryd Hotel: Photo © Judy Whiteside.

freezing winds made the mountains 'as dangerous as the Alps'. So fierce was the wind that the knife-edge ridge of Crib Goch — now deemed by the BMC, a 'thrilling Grade 1 scramble' strictly the preserve of the confident mountaineer — was scoured of ice and snow, leaving only bare rock, rendering it the safest way up the mountain!

On New Year's Day, a climber was killed and four others injured in an avalanche on Y Garn, 'triggered by two parties, one of two climbers who were roped, and one of three unroped' in a story that almost beggars belief. Both groups were trying to tunnel through a huge cornice. The party of two had succeeded but the other party decided to dig another tunnel about thirty yards away, 'just for practice'. They had penetrated to a depth of six feet when the party of two started to dig a third tunnel in between. As the three tunnels met, perhaps inevitably, the whole length of the cornice collapsed, sweeping all five down the rocky gully. One of the party of two smashed his head on a rock, suffering fatal head injuries. The party of three later admitted they had no experience of tunnelling through a cornice.

Later in January, a party of thirty-seven walkers from Derby set off on an ill-advised trip to the summit of Snowdon, apparently ignorant of the severe weather warning and the potential hazards ahead of them. They were without ice axes and crampons and later admitted they had no experience of winter conditions. A small group of six made it to the top, despite gale force winds whipping the snow into spindrift, then began their descent of the Llanberis path. When one of their party, Donald Pounder, 'slipped and slid 450 feet down the icy slope' — fortunately for him, eventually managing to stop his slide — one of his companions attempted to climb down to him. He too slipped, stopping just before plummeting over the edge into Cwm Glas Bach. So deep was the snow, he couldn't return to his previous position, which left him with no option but to flog his way through the drifts to the lower end of the Llanberis Pass. Meanwhile, the remaining four friends had found Pounder, who had somehow staggered up to the railway track, and together they made it down to Llanberis where they raised the alarm. The other thirty-one had been some way behind but managed to reach the summit. There they took shelter in the summit building where they had to remain for some time, as the weather closed in again and the rescue operation had to be abandoned until the following morning.

But it wasn't always the inexperienced who got into difficulties. In February, a young woman and her boyfriend, both experienced climbers, had just begun their descent of Bwlch Glas using ropes and axes, when the girl slipped and shot away down the slope. In a flash, her unsuspecting boyfriend was dragged down with her and the pair of them hurtled on for about 500 feet before coming to a halt. Doreen Harrison lay bleeding and unconscious. Unharmed but no doubt in shock, all Anthony Bolger could do was make his injured girlfriend as comfortable as possible and wait.

Above them, two older climbers, Dr Anthony Woodroffe and Albert Turner had seen the fall. From where they stood, on the summit of Cwm Glas, they could see the girl and her boyfriend about 200 feet down the slope. There was no direct easy way down but, without further thought, and 'impelled by the highest sense of altruism in taking an obvious risk' — and anxious to reach the injured girl before dark — they began making their way towards the couple, cutting steps in the frozen snow. Meanwhile, one of three climbers also on the ridge set off to the Pen y Gwryd while his two pals set about following Woodroffe and Turner down the slope.

OGGI SNIPS

Volcanic eruptions around 440 million years ago form the foundation of the rocks you find in Snowdonia today.

As the afternoon ticked away and the skies began to darken, the slope began to ease. To speed the process, they decided instead to 'do a roped-glissade', taking it in turns to belay each other with their ice axes. It started well, but after only two glissades, disaster struck. 'Dr Woodroffe had gone down past me and stopped at a boulder,' said Turner. 'When I was level with him I found myself on a perch of hard snow on which I could not brake myself. I went down, gathering speed and eventually reached the bottom. I was dazed when I reached the bottom and surprised that the doctor had come down too.' By the time they came to a halt, close to the couple whose lives they had sought to save, Woodroffe was dead and Turner had received serious facial injuries.

Bolger had heard the men 'chipping their way down', then there was a yell and a clattering and he saw two people coming round the corner of a gulf of rock. 'They were sliding and the doctor landed about ten yards below us'.

It was after 11.00pm before the stretcher party reached the injured climbers, guided to their location by Bolger's whistle blasts through cloud and fresh-falling snow. The girl died as rescuers were lowering the stretcher down the slope of ice, 100 feet at a time. It was 5.30am before the two injured men and the girl's body reached the Pen y Gwryd then, with only two hours rest, Chris Briggs and his team set off up the mountain again, to bring in the body of Dr Woodroffe.

Writing in the 'Climbers' Club Journal', Briggs concluded that 'an ice axe belay, even though it is well in, will only stop a man sliding down a steep slope if the weight comes slowly to bear on it'.

The moment was clearly ripe for education, even amongst those who were already possessed of mountain skills, but it was the events of 'Black Easter', as it became known, that tipped the balance, leading the way to the foundation of more structured training in mountain skills and with that the pioneers of a more structured mountain rescue service in the area.

'500 people reach safety through the ice trap', ran a 'News Chronicle' headline on Monday, 26 March. By the end of the Easter weekend, three climbers had lost their lives and four were seriously injured, in a series of incidents which kept rescue teams, the RAF, police and 'climbers staying in the neighbourhood' at work for virtually twenty-four hours. A party of senior Scouts, who were camping at Llanberis 'to receive instruction in mountaincraft from the Rector of Llanberis' also shared the rescue work. By Easter Monday, under the headline 'Protest from rescue base', Chris Briggs remarked that his hotel was 'full of wet climbers from the rescue parties' and that there were 'gangs of inexperienced youths going about', ending with, 'We have had about enough of it'. Strong words.

The weekend had begun with an accident on Maundy Thursday, 22 March, 1951. A party of seven experienced climbers were descending South Gully on Tryfan. Despite carrying ropes, they chose to come down unroped, through the hard-packed snow and ice. Most of the party were using the edges of the gully, taking advantage of any rocky hand holds, but one of the group, forty-four-year-old Norah Batty, a schoolmistress from Liverpool, followed a line down the ice chute in the centre. She slipped and fell 400 feet to her death.

Good Friday passed without incident then, early on Saturday afternoon, a man and woman fell several hundred feet over a precipice into Cwm Du'r Arddu. They had been walking beside the mountain railway track near Clogwyn station when they both slipped on a patch of ice, lightly covered with freshly fallen snow. A Scout who saw them fall and heard their screams, gave the alarm at Llanberis police station and Police Constable Robert Roberts organised a rescue party which included a number of the Scouts. They were joined by members of the RAF team who were staying under canvas at Bethesda over the Easter weekend.

The first rescuers found twenty-year-old John Orrel dead. He had sustained severe head injuries. His fiancée, Marjorie Huxley was 'severely cut about the head' but still conscious. It was 5.00pm before they were returned to the foot of the mountain, carried by relays of stretcher bearers. Huxley was admitted to hospital in Bangor with a suspected fractured skull.

COBWEB CORNER

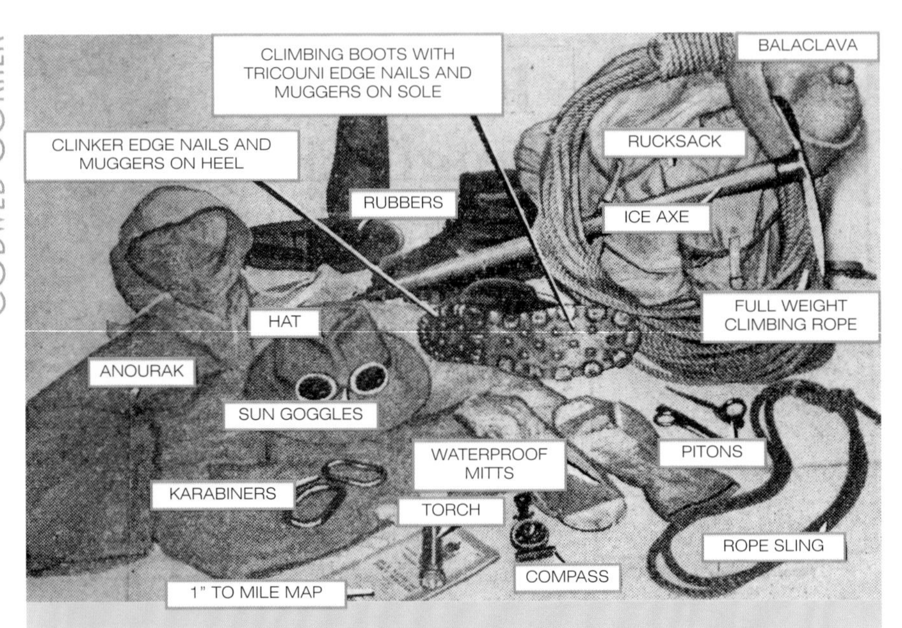

News Chronicle, March 1951: 'Equip yourself well and dodge danger — and don't forget the chocolate!' wrote Alfred Pigott. Although much of the advice remains sound, the recommended kit may well horrify the young climber of today. In the matter of boots (expected cost between three and ten guineas), he suggests walking in the rain 'to soak them to the shape of the foot', before fitting them with edge or tricouni nails. Two pairs of 'greasy wool' socks, with 'any old pair of trousers' tucked in, a gaberdine wind jacket or hooded 'anourak', topped off by his favoured 'old felt hat with a wide brim' complete the picture. Along with the essential rucksack, ice axe, maps, torch, compass and rope, he recommends the use of pitons (although 'our climbers' feel their use as bad 'as shooting a fox') and a supply of chocolate and sugary foods as a reserve. All for £10 to £15! How times change.

OGGI SNIPS

January 2014, 'Trail': 'Snowdon may be the superstar but Tryfan is the bristly underdog, with just the right mix of the accessible and the thrilling. A real mountaineer's peak'.

Chris Briggs and his party were making their way back to the Pen y Gwryd when they were intercepted at Pen y Pass and told of another accident, this time on Clogwyn y Garnedd. Peter Koch and his two companions, Gilbert Peaker and Arthur Clegg, were climbing near Trinity Gully above Glaslyn when one of the party slipped, dragging the other two from their stances. The three were experienced mountaineers and members of the Climbers' Club. They had made good progress, cutting steps in the hard snow as they climbed. However, at 600 feet, the hard snow turned into hard ice, and the wind started to gust strongly. The going was exhausting, their position precarious. They decided to retrace their steps down the mountain but quickly discovered that the steps they had cut on the way up were too far apart to be of use in descent. They were forced to cut more, this time beneath their feet, all the time teetering against the now gale-force wind. Quite suddenly, Peaker, who was leading, caught a gust mid-swing and fell, taking the other two with him to the bottom of the gully, variously described as five or six hundred feet below.

The accident was seen by Ivan Waller, who was skiing some distance away. When he reached the spot he found Koch was dead but his two friends were only slightly injured and able to walk down the mountainside unaided. Waller skied down towards the Pen y Gwryd to give the alarm and met the RAF rescue party only just returned from the previous expedition. 'It set out again without having a meal or a rest and, picking its way by the light of electric torches, brought down Koch's body direct to a stretcher fitted with sledge runners by about 8.00pm.'

But the nightmare wasn't over. Back at his hotel, Chris Briggs heard news of yet another accident. Climbing alone, George Hall had slipped and fallen at around 3.00pm, near the very same spot where John Orrel had fallen to his death, earlier that day. Once again, other climbers heard Hall shout as he fell. Anthony Hindle and G Addie made their way towards him. He was conscious when they reached him and they were able to carry him to a safer position about a hundred feet lower down the mountain, but later he lost consciousness and died some time before the rescue party arrived. It was 2.00am before rescuers reached Llanberis again with Hall's body.

And still it went on. Late in the afternoon, two parties of Scouts from Llanberis, twelve in all, were out on Snowdon when they met two Rover Scouts from another camp helping lone walker Arnold Dale to hobble down the mountain. Dale had slipped on ice while descending the last 800 feet of the Watkin path and fallen around fifty feet, badly cutting his knee. All three groups now pitched in

News Chronicle, Monday March 1951: Jim Greenhalgh and Ken Lord, who had 'kept an all-night watch over Arnold Dale' are given a hot drink by Mrs John Davies of York Terrace, Llanberis.

to help and all went well until they came across a patch of ice about 150 feet wide. Realising it would have been impossible to get Dale across the ice, they fashioned a rope stretcher from the ropes they had between them and carried the injured man back up to the summit building, joined in their task by some members of the Youth Hostels Association and another party of four climbers led by Jack Longland.

There they lit a fire, ate such food as they had — chocolates and sandwiches — and hunkered down for the night in the basement, unable to use the upper rooms of the building because they were filled with snow. They used snow to brew tea and found plenty of coal to keep the fire stoked. Longland abandoned any thoughts of taking the two youngest Scouts down. By now there were twenty people stranded on the blizzard-swept summit.

Soon after dawn, Longland took charge. Leaving a group of four men to look after Dale, he led the rest down the mountain, cutting steps and making good progress through the snow to Llanberis. At the police house, they met Briggs and his party, and the RAF team, ready to go up to the summit to bring down the five men. It was 9.30am. A blizzard was raging above the snow line and it would be a further seven hours before rescuers and rescued arrived back at Llanberis, having covered the last part of the descent by train.

The catalogue of incidents was heavily reported by the media, prompting calls for Easter to be fixed, by an Act of Parliament, to fall later in the year when the weather might be more clement — a campaign which rumbles on to this day without resolution. The 'News Chronicle' reported that the temperature had dropped to 27 degrees with 'five degrees of frost' and caught many of the climbers unprepared, with 'only light clothing and no proper climbing equipment'. A steady stream of climbers had arrived in the village throughout the night and day, 'their hands bleeding, clothing torn and boots slashed from stumbling over razor-sharp rocks'. Many suffered from exhaustion and exposure and the 'village women spent all might making tea and bathing the wounds of the injured while their menfolk formed rescue teams'.

In the 'Manchester Guardian', Jack Longland said that 'the accidents had emphasised the need for training young people in mountaincraft'. Others stressed the need for proper equipment 'if mountains are to be tackled in reasonable safety in wintry conditions'. Inevitably there were concerns that the publicity might lead to 'curtailment of the freedom of the hills', an anxiety swiftly countered by the assertion that 'education, not restraint, was the proper approach to the problem'.

The Ramblers Association lobbied that the 'quality of wildness' be retained but that scouts be appointed to send in reports on mountain conditions. Also, that the BBC should be encouraged to broadcast warnings based on this reports. Within a year, there would be National Park wardens in post in Snowdonia, tasked with that very thing.

It would be another eight years before three young men followed their passion for the mountains to start a mountaineering school at Ogwen Cottage, but the winds of change had blown.

Tragsitz practice: Tony Jones acting as casualty on the tragsitz, on a Plas y Brenin mountain rescue course (from a somewhat battered old photo) © OVMRO.

1904

RONALD WILLIAM HENRY TURNBULL HUDSON

Born 16 July 1876, died Devil's Kitchen 20 September 1904

by Hazel Robbins

Ronald Hudson began life at 1 Trumpington Street, Cambridge. His mother, Mary Watson Turnbull, who died when he was six, was the daughter of Robert Turnbull, a land steward and farmer of 290 acres in Hackness, Yorkshire. His father, William, was a distinguished scholar — Mathematical Lecturer at Cambridge University, Professor of Mathematics at King's College, London, 1882–1902 and Professor of Mathematics at Queen's College, London, 1883–1905 — but he was also a 'well-known advocate of higher education for women'. No surprise then, to hear that Ronald's two sisters were also successful scholars. Hilda entered Newnham College with a Gilchrist scholarship. She was appointed a fellow and was equal to Seventh Wrangler* at the Mathematical Tripos of 1903. Her sister was equal to eighth, her father third and her uncle second wrangler but, even amongst such gifted individuals, Ronald was exceptional.

Like his father he went to St John's College, Cambridge. Among his many achievements, he was Senior Wrangler in 1898, once regarded as 'the greatest intellectual achievement' in Britain. In 1902 he was appointed Lecturer in Mathematics at Liverpool University, 'one of the most brilliant mathematicians the university had'. By 1904 his publications formed 'a remarkable record for four short years of work', one book was in press, he had begun writing another on analytical geometry and had been asked to write one on elementary pure geometry. He was also an 'accomplished musician, and excelled as a solo pianist'.

An extremely likeable man, he was said to be 'remarkable for the vivacious energy which he threw into everything he did... in walking down the street, he danced along as if pedestrianism were the whole business of his life'. Even in the cut and thrust of academia it is hard to find anyone with a bad word to say. Indeed, the man ranked second wrangler to him in 1898 was John Forbes Cameron who alone was said to stand any chance of 'dislodging him from that glittering height.' It could be said that it was Hudson who had prevented Cameron from being ranked senior wrangler, yet they were firm friends and it was Cameron who accompanied Hudson on his ill-fated trip to North Wales in 1904.

The Mathematical Tripos was extremely difficult and demanding. The examinations were intended to be tests of endurance, taking place on consecutive mornings and afternoons for

OGGI SNIPS

Cwm Bochlwyd on Tryfan contains Llyn Bochlwyd, sometimes called 'Australia Lake' or 'Lake Australia' because its shape resembles the shape of the Antipodean country.

four and five days together. Students often 'found it necessary to build up their physical endurance'. Virtually every high wrangler participated in some form of regular physical exercise to preserve their strength and stamina including running, swimming and mountaineering. For Hudson, it was climbing. An enthusiastic climber, he had done most of his climbing in the Lake District, but in 1904 he decided to visit North Wales, where Tryfan and the Devil's Kitchen were becoming popular climbing venues.

The two friends arrived in Wales on Monday 19 September and stayed at the Pen y Gwryd. The following day, at about 9.30am, they set off to cross the Glyderau, eventually coming down to the Devil's Kitchen. According to the newspapers at the time, the Devil's Kitchen had already claimed three lives, 'one of the test pieces of mountain climbing in Wales'.

The two of them climbed the first part until, around 1.00pm, they came to a 'difficulty' that Cameron did not feel competent enough to climb. According to Cameron, they separated at this point on the understanding that Hudson would continue alone, but would attempt the entire climb. Hudson carried on and disappeared around the difficulty. A quarter of an hour later, he reappeared higher up on the left wall of the Kitchen and looking upwards. After that he disappeared for ever in life from his friend's sight.

Cameron waited another quarter of an hour in silence. Suddenly, he heard a noise which made him look around quickly and to see a huge mass of rock land with a loud crash beneath where he had last seen Hudson. Almost simultaneously he saw something else fall, something smaller which could have been a smaller rock or the body of his friend.

....the Devil's Kitchen had already claimed three lives, 'one of the test pieces of mountain climbing in Wales.'

Seriously worried, Cameron shouted his friend's name several times but without reply. Knowing his friend may be injured and in desperate need of assistance, he had to retrace his steps back down the first part of the Kitchen as quickly as he could, no mean feat for a non-climber who was alone and in a state of anxiety. He made his way to Llyn Idwal where the first person he found was a boatman who agreed to go back up with him.

The boatman and Cameron climbed as far as they could up the Kitchen but could see nothing from there. They climbed to the top by another route and looked down into the chasm where the boatman thought he could see a body, but Cameron could not. So they descended again with the purpose of trying to get a party together to help.

**A 'wrangler' is a student who gains first-class honours in the third year of Cambridge University's undergraduate degree in mathematics. The highest-scoring student is the 'senior wrangler', the second highest is the 'second wrangler', and so on.*

Fortunately, there were quite a few people around Llyn Idwal that day — some were tourists, others were working in the area and news of the accident spread fast. John Roberts, a 28-year-old fencer in the employ of Lord Penrhyn, played a key role in the search and recovery. He was alerted to the incident by a farmer's daughter who 'came racing up to him on her bicycle'. John, with several others, set off for the Kitchen and, with foresight, took a ladder with him which he carried for two miles 'for the purpose of carrying the body down if necessary'. Unbeknown to him, it would have a dual purpose.

Also at Llyn Idwal that day was Robert Thomas, a rate collector from Bangor who was cycling with a friend. Leaving their bicycles at Ogwen Cottage, they had proceeded up to Llyn Idwal and as they walked around the lake they noticed a lady and gentleman on the opposite side taking 'snapshot photographs'. They also noticed another gentlemen. Then suddenly, 'there seemed to be some commotion amongst the little party, and we saw the lady and gentleman hurry off in the direction of Ogwen'. Whilst Thomas and his friend wondered what had caused their abrupt departure, a young man came rushing up to them. The young man, they later learned, was John Cameron. He was in a great state of agitation — hardly able to speak. Pointing in the direction of the Devil's Kitchen he said, 'I am afraid my friend is either killed or hurt!'. Trying to calm him down as best they could, they proceeded up to the Kitchen 'impelled by the hope that we might still find Mr Hudson alive, although we feared that the worst had happened.' Along the way they were joined by several other people. Although they went as quickly as they could, 'the way was terribly difficult' and it seemed a long time before they came to the scene of the accident.

...People somehow seem to take more liberties with Welsh mountains than with others, but the laws of gravitation in Wales are the same as in the Alps.

Eventually John Roberts and his group, carrying the ladder, and Robert Thomas and his group, which included Cameron, arrived at the scene. Roberts climbed up first and reached an enormous boulder, the same impassable difficulty which Cameron had faced. To overcome it, he used the ladder. Laying it slantwise across the chasm and underneath the boulder, he crawled across and under the boulder before continuing 'up the further slippery face' of the Kitchen until he reached a ledge at the foot of a huge slab of rock which ran at an angle upwards from the ledge on which he

OGGI SNIPS

Believe it or not, the Ogwen valley is home to several carnivorous plants including Round-leaved Sundew, Butterwort and Bladderwort.

stood to the foot of another inward and upward running slope. Far above this, he could see the top of the chimney.

Roberts peered about in the gloom. Finally, he saw Hudson's body at the bottom of the huge slab of rock, resting on his knees with his face buried in a pool of water. His left temple was 'crushed like an eggshell', his right arm fractured at the elbow, he had a compound fracture at the wrist and his left leg was broken. There were two long tears down the back of his jacket, maybe caused by him sliding down the face of rough rock. Roberts felt Hudson's hands and ears, but they were quite cold. When he tried to lift his friend's body by the waist, he noticed it was still slightly warm — but it was clear Hudson had received fatal injuries. It was five o clock, some three and a half hours after he had fallen.

Roberts now had the problem of removing Hudson's body from the ledge, something he knew he could not do alone. Robert Thomas, standing with the rescue party twelve feet below the ledge, scrambled up with the aid of the ladder. He noticed there was a lot of blood and believed Hudson had bled from a severed artery in the fractured wrist. On lifting him, Thomas thought it seemed as if every bone in his body had broken.

Looking up, Thomas saw a ledge about thirty feet above and later said he believed Hudson had fallen after, or in trying to, reach this ledge 'because a stone which projected about halfway up between the two ledges was deeply splashed with blood, as if Mr Hudson's head had struck against there in the descent.' Down below, Cameron now knew that his friend was dead and all hope was lost. Thomas described him as being 'terribly upset', the one idea in his mind that if he had been able to reach his friend sooner he might have been able to save him. Even when he was assured that death must have been instantaneous, he scarcely seemed satisfied.

Roberts and Thomas began the difficult and dangerous process of removing Hudson's body from the ledge, assisted by Sam Jones, a quarryman who, Thomas noted 'showed great skill in doing so'. Roberts and Thomas placed a rope under Hudson's armpits and fastened another to his feet, then lowered the body down to the rescue party below. It was then carried down to the lake on the ladder, no doubt with some difficulty, over which it was ferried and from there down to Ogwen. From here it was conveyed to Glanogwen Church in Bethesda, exactly how is not stated. However, the local police officer, David Roberts, had gone up to the scene, meeting the rescue party just emerging from the Kitchen so he may have accompanied the body to Bethesda.

Both Roberts and Thomas marvelled at Hudson's skill in climbing to the point he had. Roberts, well-acquainted with the mountain himself, said he could not have reached the ledge without the use of the ladder. Thomas could 'only marvel at his daring in climbing so far up the rock. Looking at the smooth slippery surface, offering scarcely a foothold, I could hardly believe anyone would venture to risk such a climb'. He would never have gone up so far himself 'except that our party had but one idea, that Mr Hudson might still be alive and must receive assistance at all cost. A man never knows what he can do till he tries... descending from that ledge was a much more risky undertaking for us than going up.'

The inquest took place at Bethesda, two days after the accident. Cameron explained that Hudson was very fond of climbing and had done a good deal before, mostly in the Lake District, and was very sure with his hands and feet. He further explained that he had not continued because he himself was not a climber. Hudson knew this and knew that Cameron would not go any further. Whilst Cameron did not know how far Hudson had climbed, he knew he was not intending to complete the entire ascent of the Kitchen when they separated. He thought Hudson fell as a result of the rock giving way under his feet, not from any error of judgement on his part or loss of strength. Apart from locally, the press erroneously reported that Hudson had slipped and fallen in trying to pluck a rare fern. Many headlines read 'Life lost for fern' but Cameron was clear this was not true. 'It was a climb, pure and simple, attempted for its own sake and for the love of climbing.'

The coroner, Mr J Pentir Williams, described Hudson's death as 'a very sad accident'. The Kitchen was 'evidently a most dangerous place to attempt to climb' and 'people somehow seem to take more liberties with Welsh mountains than with others, but the laws of gravitation in Wales are the same as in the Alps.' He paid tribute to 'a brilliant young man' who had accomplished something 'to be proud of for a lifetime' and noted the exemplary conduct of Roberts and Thomas who 'had taken their lives in their hands to recover the body'.

The jury foreman, Mr Hughes 'Ty-amser', returned their verdict of 'Accidental Death' then a Mr Griffith Roberts, speaking in Welsh, said he hoped the press would publicise the dangerous nature of the place of the fatality and marvelled that people tended to choose the most dangerous places to visit, and without guides, 'of whom there were plenty'.

Hudson's death had a profound effect on the people of Bethesda, still suffering the after-effects of 'Y Streic Fawr' (the Great Strike) at the Penrhyn Quarries which had ended the year before. This three-year strike had a cataclysmic effect on the community, with friends becoming sworn enemies, families facing unimaginable hardship and husbands forced to leave their wives and children for coal mines further afield. At the end of the inquest the jury asked Hudson's father if they could testify their sympathy by forming a funeral procession to escort his son's body from Glanogwen Church to the railway station in Bethesda. William Hudson, 'much moved', agreed to the request.

The next morning a 'short but impressive funeral service' was conducted by the Rev R T Jones,

OGGI SNIPS

Tryfan is the fifteenth highest mountain in Wales. It was re-surveyed in June 2010, using accurate GPS measurements, and 'grew' a whole 2.4 metres, from 915 to 917.5 metres!

attended by members of the jury and the principle tradesmen of the town. The coffin was carried by members of the congregation with an escort headed by the vicar and a Dr Pritchard, most likely the local doctor. The sad procession made its way through Bethesda for three-quarters of a mile. As a mark of respect, all blinds in the houses were drawn and shops closed as the coffin passed by. From Bethesda, the body was taken to Bangor and thence to London. On Saturday 24 September, Hudson was buried in Wandsworth cemetery next to his mother. A few weeks later, a memorial service at St John's College, Cambridge was attended by the vice chancellor, Sir Robert Ball, Sir Richard Jebb MP, the Master of Trinity and other distinguished individuals.

The death of this exceptionally gifted and likeable young man had a significant effect on those who knew him. His father, the author of several publications on mathematics, never published anything after 1904. John Cameron never published any original work in mathematics but did go on to have a distinguished career. During the First World War he served in the Ministry of Munitions, in 1925 he was elected Master of his college, Gonville and Caius, and in 1933 became vice chancellor of Cambridge University. Married in 1905, he had two sons and a daughter, his elder son dying a prisoner-of-war after being captured at Dunkirk. He named his youngest, born four years after Hudson's death, John Ronald Cameron. When he died in 1952, aged 78, his obituary in 'The Times' revealed that his love of mountains continued. Perhaps it was there that he most remembered his friend.

Hudson's book 'Kummer's Quartic Surface' was posthumously published by Cambridge University Press in 1905. In his prefatory note, mathematician Henry Frederick Baker wrote that, for those who had known Hudson, the book 'will be a reminder of the enthusiasm and brilliance which compelled their admiration'. Liverpool University established one of the highest awards a student could attain in his memory. The Ronald Hudson Memorial Prize for Pure and Analytical Geometry is still awarded. At St Paul's School, London, which Hudson attended from 1888–1895, a memorial bronze was erected.

Ronald Hudson's death left his family and friends bereft and the world deprived of a brilliant and gifted man. Just twenty-eight years old when he died, he achieved more in his brief life than many do in a life long lived. But this should hardly be a surprise for such a man as Hudson who, in the words of someone who knew him, had a 'tremendous keenness to do his best, and grasp every moment of the fleeting hour'.

1938

QUARRYMAN SAVES 'VARSITY TUTOR ON PEAK

15 August 1938

At 10.30am on Monday 15 August 1938, Robert Leslie Beaumont, a Fellow of Corpus Christi College, Oxford, set out from the climbers' hostel near Ogwen, to climb the Black Ladders, a 'rather forbidding ascent', with two friends, Anthony Cox and Herbert Kneigschemer. Experienced mountaineers, they had reached the foot of the climb at around 1.15pm, stopping there to rope themselves together — Beaumont first, then Kneigschemer, then Cox.

The climb was such that half way up the gully, it was necessary to move out to the right to avoid an unclimbable obstacle. Beaumont negotiated the move, returning left to rejoin the gully before calling to Kneigschemer, out of sight below him, to come up. Kneigschemer had moved up some ten feet when he heard the sound of his friend falling. Beaumont had fallen the full length of the rope, some 80 or 90 feet, stopping only when the rope became tight. It was 2.45pm.

Doubtless stunned by the sudden turn of events, fired with shock and adrenalin, his two friends reacted with consummate speed. Cox clambered up to tie Kneigschemer onto a spike of rock before tending to Beaumont, hanging some feet below a narrow ledge, onto which he pulled him. Kniegschemer remained on the ledge — wrapping his own coat around his injured friend and undoubtedly putting his own self at risk of hypothermia — while Cox ran down the mountain and along the sheep track to Bethesda, to raise the alarm.

Haydn Jones, a teacher at Talysarn School, had been picnicking with his friends Nansi Williams and Lillian Jones on the way to Black Ladders when they saw a dishevelled figure rushing down the mountainside towards them. Jones — described, incidentally, by the 'North Wales Chronicle' as 'a Welsh dramatist' — quickly made his way towards the ledge, where he could see a figure in a white shirt, and called up to him. Cox, meanwhile, continued to the Water Works, where he phoned for a doctor and the police, then on to Helyg for a stretcher.

When later asked by the deputy coroner why it was necessary to travel all the way to Helyg for a stretcher, he replied that, had a suitable stretcher been available at Bethesda, it would have saved an hour. Police Inspector Jones confirmed that the stretcher at the police station was 'cumbersome and antiquated and not suitable for mountain work'.

News spread quickly and several parties of quarrymen and shepherds set out for the gully. A message was sent to Bangor for some experienced climbers and they too soon arrived. In

OGGI SNIPS

At the summit of Tryfan is a photogenic pair of rocks some six feet high and four feet apart, dubbed Adam and Eve.

fact, the response was described as 'astonishing'. Two police constables, Phillips and Williams, and doctors Pierce Williams and Mostyn Williams, who were in practice together in Bethesda, went along with the rescuers to deliver first aid, and a third doctor — Doctor Edwards, a brain specialist from Liverpool — had also joined the rescue party. Sergeant Edison Jones busied himself marshalling the rescue parties and arranging for an ambulance from Bangor. It was around 7.00pm before Cox made it back to the gully, and many of the rescuers were there already.

It proved a superhuman task to get the stretcher onto the ledge in the gathering darkness and pelting rain, but lowering the man 200 feet, once strapped to the stretcher, was by far the most difficult problem.

The rescue was fraught with difficulties, even for experienced climbers — although the press were later accused of over-dramatising events. Darkness had fallen, it was raining heavily and the wind was hurricane force. The climb was not a popular one, and accessible by a number of routes. One of these was through Gerlan, past the Bangor Water Works and along a sheep track which, in the main, ran parallel with a stream. Part of the path was unsafe — a landslide had almost obliterated it — and it was very boggy in places.

It proved a 'superhuman task' to get the stretcher onto the ledge in the gathering darkness and pelting rain, but lowering the man 200 feet, once strapped to the stretcher, was by far the most difficult problem. With six men on the ledge holding the ropes, the stretcher was gradually lowered to another ledge, with one of the rescue party guiding the way over protruding boulders, a process which lasted several hours. And by this time, 9.20pm, it was pitch dark. From the safety of the valley, figures could be seen carrying hurricane lamps and torches along the sheep track from Bethesda, a most eerie scene. A slip in the dark, it was reported, and they would have gone 'headlong into the river'. In fact, one man had a narrow escape when a large boulder fell close enough to rip some of his clothing away. But, despite the difficulties, there was no lack of willing helpers, anxious to assist.

At Ty Slatters Farm, a crowd had gathered, armed with lamps and torches — and a bugle, to add even further drama to the evening — made their way along the path towards the rescue party, lighting their way down. And the street lights of Gerlan were kept alight longer than usual to assist the extra traffic caused by the incident. The stretcher reached the foot of the climb around 11.15pm, and from there it as conveyed to Bethesda where it arrived at 2.30am.

There Beaumont was placed in an ambulance for the Caernarvonshire and Anglesey Infirmary at Bangor. Unfortunately, Beaumont's condition deteriorated on the Tuesday evening and he died, despite the best efforts of his rescuers and the intervention of specialists from Liverpool and elsewhere. On admission, he had been found to be suffering concussion and abrasions and remained unconscious. Later X-ray examination indicated a fractured vertebra and his brain showed signs of compression.

Newspaper accounts of the incident were prolific, discussing the 'rudeness' of climbers when questioned by the press, and haughtily reminding them that 'neither quarrymen nor pressmen desire to turn out at all hours and in all weather conditions in a neighbourhood which is in itself inhospitable, without having human inhospitality to accentuate it'! The Daily Express and the North Wales Chronicle focused on Glynne Jones, described as a '50s-a-week Bethesda quarryman' (and also, variously, described as being thirty-one and fifty-two-year-old!). They sought to remind the 'leisured classes' who climb in the region that the people who are first to offer help — 'nearly always

Newspaper accounts of the incident were prolific, discussing the 'rudeness' of climbers when questioned by the press, and haughtily reminding them that 'neither quarrymen nor pressmen desire to turn out at all hours and in all weather conditions in a neighbourhood which is in itself inhospitable, without having human inhospitality to accentuate it'.

at imminent peril to life and limb, because the climber who has fallen is usually to be rescued from an almost inaccessible spot — are not leisured people but men to whom the loss of even a day's pay is a serious matter.'

Jones had been on his way home from Penrhyn quarries, when he heard that a climber was lying on his back on a narrow ledge on Black Ladders. He was said to have climbed past the rescue parties, stopping only to gather a first aid kit, which he strapped to his waist before proceeding through the mist on the 'most difficult climb of his life'. He had neither ropes not climbing boots.

OGGI SNIPS

Legend has it that anyone who jumps the terrifying gap between Adam and Eve, known as the Leap of Faith, will then be given the Freedom of Tryfan. Cue cameras...

Such was his concern for the patient, Jones travelled with the ambulance to Bangor, until finally, exhausted, hungry and soaked to the skin, he returned to his worried wife at 4.00am, only to set out to work again two hours later. He later admitted it was the worst climb he had ever had. 'When I reached that ledge, I wondered how I'd got there. My only worry was that my jacket, which I left at the bottom of the mountain, was gone when I got back. It had eight shillings in it, all the money I had'.

A leader column in 'The Chronicle' discussing the incident four days later, was sternly disputed in a letter to the editor the following week, headed 'We shun pressmen'. 'The dangers of the rescue have been grossly exaggerated,' wrote R Glynn Williams. 'The track leading to the cliff is both easy and obvious, as most Bethesda people should know. To plunge headlong into the stream from it would be rather a difficult, manoeuvre, since gravity acts downwards and not horizontally.

'To a mountaineer, be he quarryman or climber, the problem of reaching the ledge and quitting it safely, together with the raising and lowering of the stretcher was more technical than hazardous. Darkness made the return a little harder, but a rope and safe conduct from the lower ledges were available for all who needed them. The danger of falling stones was chiefly due to so many being in the direct line of fire, at a time when they could have sheltered on the side ledges in safety.'

Constance Alexander, warden of Idwal Cottage youth hostel remarked that 'one is always reluctant to give information [to the press] because for some reason or other mountaineering accidents are always treated in a more sensational way than any other and a mountain accident is, to most climbers, a tragedy and not sensationalism.'

And Donald Duff — a Denbighshire doctor and climber who would become a pioneer in mountain rescue, creating the 'Duff stretcher' and establishing an organised mountain rescue service in Scotland, separate from his peers south of the Border — noted the 'public prejudice against climbers'. His remarks may still ring true. 'Their standard of good fellowship and helpfulness to others in trouble is one of which the rest of the community is still far short'. Which certainly echoes the closing comments of the deputy coroner that 'on occasion like this it is marvellous what feeling of human kindness and zeal is shown in the effort to save human life.'

CHAPTER TWO

Ogwen Cottage: from mountain school to mountain rescue

Ogwen Cottage began life as a stage coach inn. Set beside Llyn Ogwen in the shadow of Tryfan, it was once a key staging post on 'Telford's Holyhead Road' — the A5, as we now know it. Designed to allow stagecoaches and the mail coach to carry post between London and Holyhead — and thence by boat to Ireland — the road was completed with the opening of the Menai Suspension Bridge in 1826. Meandering amiably through the mountains of Snowdonia, via Llangollen, Corwen and Capel Curig, and on through the centre of Bangor it proved the perfect access road for mountaineers to, delivering eager young climbers to their adventures since the early nineteenth century.

By the 1890s, many of those climbers would stay at the Pen y Gwryd or Ogwen Cottage, where early accounts noted that the warden Mrs Jones 'always most good naturedly received and fed us if we turned up, no matter at what hour'.

The 1894 'Climbers' Club Journal' advertised for Ogwen Cottage as 'the chief centre for climbers visiting Snowdonia' and Ogwen Cottage features in many early climbing accounts. The 'Climbers' Club Guides to Wales' note one particular incident, on 3 March 1895, when Archer Thompson and H Hughes recorded the first winter ascent of the Devil's Kitchen after 'an epic battle'. In his own account of the climb, Archer Thomson wrote that 'according to tradition our ancestor Thor was

The early days: Roger Jones and Ron James during an early rescue © Ken Wilson.

OGWEN COTTAGE AND TRYFAN, NANT FFRANCON
W 6089

"IDWAL COTTAGE", NANT FFRANCON PASS. MERSEYSIDE YOUTH HOSTELS,

armed with a hammer for his battle with the Frost Giants, and with such a weapon we, too, were luckily provided in the form of a hatchet, surreptitiously removed from the worthy Mrs Jones's coal cellar at Ogwen. This implement proved of the utmost utility until the head took leave of the haft and, glissading the snow slopes, vanished from sight.

'The head was recovered and the hatchet, ingeniously repaired with string, continued to render us valuable service'.

They finally reached the top after seven o'clock, in the gathering dark and bitter cold, their clothes in tatters and one of Archer Thomson's hands so badly frostbitten, he was unable to use it for several weeks. There is no mention of whether the hatchet and Mrs Jones's coal cellar were ever reunited.

The main rescue centre for the Ogwen area had initially been Idwal Cottage, under the care of Constance Alexander and Olive Pritchard. A former quarry manager's cottage on the old main road at the head of the Nant Ffrancon Pass, and close to Idwal Slabs, Idwal Cottage is the oldest youth hostel in the UK although it was actually the second to open — the first, at Pennant Hall near Llanrwst, had opened in December 1930, but closed the following year due to problems with the water supply. The same year, Idwal opened its doors to customers. The price of an overnight stay was one shilling. Annual membership was five shillings for 'seniors' and two and sixpence for 'juniors' and life membership was available for three guineas. Accommodation was in single sex dormitories and self-catering facilities were provided.

The emphasis for mountain rescue moved to Ogwen Cottage when the Climbing Club moved the rescue kit there and Mr Hughes, son-in-law of Mrs Williams of Ogwen Cottage, began to help by using his taxi as rescue transport. Mrs Williams's parting words of advice, in case of a rescue call-out, were unequivocal. 'Fire a red flare from the car park — get the climbers together and put the one with the cleanest boots in charge!'

The association between the two cottages remained strong. For many years, until the team established its base at Bryn Poeth, team members travelling into the valley from elsewhere in the UK would camp at Idwal Cottage, often drying out post-rescue in front of the Aga before retiring to the pub. Cliff and Mal Randles served for many years there as warden, until they left to pursue other ventures, at which point Wally and Ellen Owen took over. Randles remained a good friend of the team through his life. He died on 25 September 2014, aged 90, fondly remembered by many who have been involved with Ogwen over the years.

By the end of the 1950s, more people were venturing into Snowdonia, whether by rail, road or through blagging a ride. Despite a boom in private car ownership, it was still more the reserve of the wealthy or those on their business travels. A favoured method of accessing the hills amongst those who wished to climb them was to stand by the roadside, rucksack at the ready, arm extended, thumb in the air.

With the rise in popularity of mountain recreation — no doubt fuelled by the media's recurring preoccupation with mountain accidents — education authorities began to look for suitable buildings to convert into outdoor centres. Plas y Brenin, the National Mountain Centre, had begun life as the

Postcards from the past: Top: Ogwen Cottage with the A5 road close by. Bottom: Idwal Cottage with Y Garn rising in the background. Postcards originally produced by Valentine's.

Capel Curig Inn, built by Lord Penryhn in 1801. Over the years, it was a popular stop for mountaineers and many distinguished guests, including Queen Victoria, Sir Walter Scott and Lord Byron — so much so that, some time between 1869 and 1871, the name was changed to the Royal Hotel. In 1954, Eugene Brunning, the owner, decided to sell the hotel, on the proviso that he would be the last landlord in the hotel's 153-year history and that the purchaser must 'use the building for some purpose other than an inn'. It happened that John Disley, a Welsh steeplechaser who had competed in the 1952 Olympics, was in the bar as Brunning discussed his plan. He contacted Justin Evans at the Central Council for Physical Recreation, which he knew was looking for a suitable spot for a mountain training centre in North Wales.

A sale was agreed and, on 1 April 1955, the Royal passed into the hands of the CCPR. It was renamed Plas y Brenin, meaning 'King's house', in memory of George VI whose trust fund had bought the building, but it would be known as the Snowdonia National Recreation Centre. The accommodation was limited to forty students and the first courses were held that summer with John Disley as chief instructor and Roger Orgill as chief canoe instructor. Over time they would build up a core of staff instructors with a pool of mountaineers and canoeists as volunteer staff.

The steady flow of students proved a further resource for mountain rescue purposes and Plas y Brenin worked very closely with Chris Briggs from the outset. Young, fit and enthusiastic, students made useful stretcher bearers. Within five years, mountain rescue courses had been included in the teaching programme — although involvement in call-outs was purely voluntary, even for the permanent staff — and the centre was designated an official post.

Meanwhile, three young mountaineers, from very diverse backgrounds and experience, were hatching a plan to set up their own mountaineering school. The idea of a private school began while Anthony Mason-Hornby, Ron James and Trevor Jones were climbing in Snowdonia. They were convinced that many climbing accidents could be avoided if climbers were properly taught and advised — so convinced that, by spring 1959, they had each resigned their 'comfortable' £750-£1000 a year jobs and invested £8000 in the project, to realise their vision.

Twenty-eight-year-old Tony Mason-Hornby, a former Etonian of Sandhurst, Berkshire, was a land agent in Bangor and lived at Bethesda, near Llyn Ogwen, with his family. A 1949-graduate of the Lake District climbing schools he believed tuition in mountaineering to be 'essential to the education of a young boy', teaching him self-reliance, self-confidence and the importance of teamwork and initiative.' It should also, he added, 'drill into him the importance of not leaving litter on the mountainside!'

On his death in 1994, the 'Caernarfon and Denbigh Herald' reported that Mason-Hornby had 'bought Ogwen Cottage on behalf of local men Ron James and Trevor Jones, to set up a mountaineering school for children from cities after a brewery had wanted it for a pub and outbid local efforts'.

Twenty-six-year-old Ron James, a science and athletics master from Birmingham, first 'clapped happy eyes' on the mountains as a child, when he was brought from Birmingham to Wales during the Blitz. 'We came by train and were delayed in a siding by bombing at Ruabon. We arrived at a dairy farm in Llan Ffestiniog at 2.00am. In the morning, I opened the curtains and there was this incredible view. I saw clouds with a mountain above them: Moelwyn Bach. I had never seen a

OGGI SNIPS

Newsletter 1987: Instructions for the team leader: 'If in danger, if in doubt, run in circles, scream and shout!'

mountain. The only grass I had ever seen was in parks and at Aston Villa's ground.' Thus began a lifelong passion — although, in 2009, he was reported to have hung up his climbing boots for the more challenging routes. By the age of twelve, he had climbed Snowdon, going on to be regarded as one of England's top mountaineers.

'The nice thing about climbing is that it's so intense, nothing else in your life comes to mind. When you reach a summit, there's a feeling of great satisfaction.'

Twenty-eight-year-old Trevor Jones, of Streetly in the West Midlands had resigned from his £1000-a-year career as a research chemist, believing the rewards of doing a worthwhile job would far outweigh the loss of salary. He would remain with the school for a year.

'Og Cott', as it would become known, opened during Whitsuntide 1959*. The centre could accommodate thirty students and four permanent resident instructors. Mason-Hornby would be the warden, living on the premises with his family. The high staff to pupil ratio remained unprecedented for some time.

The early months were not without their troubles. According to the Post Office, there would be no telephone lines for the first three months and the North Wales Electricity Board said 'No electricity for five years', the latter being resolved by an agreement to share water and generated supply with the nearby Idwal Cottage youth hostel.

The building was in a dilapidated state. Dry rot riddled the dining room and provision had to be made for a drying room and lecture room, staff rooms and accommodation. The back of the building had to be completely restored and all sorts of things were apparently hidden under the floor, including a coffin plaque.

But those early troubles did little to dent their enthusiasm, so determined were they in their efforts. And it seems the press were behind them all the way. 'A stone's throw from the cottage', noted the 'Liverpool Daily Post', 'stands Tryfan, one of the most majestic of all the Welsh mountains. It stands like a vast pyramid of rock — great, terrible and alone. These young people respect the smallest hill in Snowdonia just as much as this giant. Perhaps this is the quality which above everything else, will make this venture a success'.

'There has been a feeling among mountaineers that the tradition created by that great Welsh climber Owen Glynne Jones, sixty years ago, needs to be revived. The Ogwen tradition, we feel, is too fine a thing to be allowed to perish,' added Trevor Jones.

Over time, more than £12,000 would be invested in the project and, from their original intention to provide courses in rock climbing and mountaineering, the timetable grew to include a range of mountain-related pursuits: snow and ice work, botany, geology, forestry, photography and more.

The three men were helped in their initial task by Pat James, Barbara Bennett, a teacher, from Collyhurst in Manchester and George Thomas, one of Snowdon's best-known climbers.

Pat had resigned her teaching post to become the cook. 'I once cooked a three-course meal over a primus stove on a mountainside,' she was reported to say, promising guests plenty of good wholesome food and the occasional 'airy fairy' dish! Barbara, meanwhile, would continue to teach

**Whitsunday is the name used in the UK and Ireland for the Christian festival of Pentecost, the seventh Sunday after Easter. In 1959 this fell on 17 May. Whitsuntide referred to the week following Whitsunday*

not 'the three Rs' but the rudiments of hillcraft which she'd learned herself on her climbing expeditions in the Alps and the UK.

By August, Og Cott had been given official recognition as a mountain rescue post by the Mountain Rescue Committee, the first privately-owned school to be granted this recognition and the first fully-manned post in Wales. Notices were posted in hostels, hotels and police stations in Snowdonia, informing people what to do in an emergency: a two-starred red flare, fired by Pat James would break high above the Nant Francon Pass to signify that someone was in trouble on one of the surrounding mountains and 'call' the three 'leaders' back to base.

The newly formed rescue team had barely drawn breath before their first call-out came when a man fell fifteen feet at Cwm Lloer, breaking his leg.

Sometimes, reality bites

The idea of Og Cott was to provide training and advice to new and experienced climbers, along with affordable accommodation and good food. Long term, they hoped to persuade education authorities to send parties of children to literally learn the ropes. To achieve this, they decided not to charge for the accommodation of any teacher accompanying a party. They also planned to run classes in advanced rock climbing for those already capable of leading on a climb. Due to their links with Birmingham, for a fortnight at a time, they would teach the basic to groups of children and teenagers from the city.

But not least in the school's activities would be its role as a mountain rescue party, a requirement which quickly threatened to become a burden. As the centre was open throughout the year, there was always a core of competent mountaineers available but much of the problem lay in the ethos that instructors automatically became members of the Ogwen Cottage rescue team, available for call out at any time. It was often the case that the instructors would come back to Og Cott after a long day teaching, only to turn tail and go back out again to help an injured or lost climber — often

COBWEB CORNER

Newsletter June 1967: Incidents often seem to occur — completely coincidentally — when team members are in the vicinity, either practising their skills as a team or simply enjoying a spot of personal climbing. The June 1967 newsletter reports a couple of such rescues, one a Holly Tree Wall lower during the Whitsun team practice where the stretcher arrived 'within seconds of the climbers fall' and another a rescue on Glyder Fawr during the team's 'climbing weekend'. The team also dealt with a double rescue on Tryfan and Craig yr Ysfa involving a 1000-foot lower down Great Gully and two helicopters. And the month finished with the removal of a jammed knee from Slab Intermediate on the Gribin, 'with a climber still attached to it'. Tape étriers, prussiks and lard were put to good use on that one!

OGGI SNIPS

Newsletter December 1989: Reportedly overheard: 'Rules are made for the obedience of fools, the guidance of wise men... and for covering the backs of the progressive.'

in dark, deteriorating weather conditions. Exhausting stuff, however passionate an instructor might feel about their cause.

In April 1962, Mason-Hornby speculated in the 'Western Mail' that 'when we formed our team we had little idea of how busy we should be. We soon learned to dread weekends and Bank Holidays and as we return from the hard day's work on the hills on such days, vivid pictures of past rescues spring to mind: the crumpled figure lying smashed on boulder-covered scree, the companion numbed with cold and shock, helplessly standing guard.

'Three years ago, we must confess, there was a novelty in this work, although we never relished it. It has recurred so frequently that we now consider it merely as a task to be done quietly, quickly and efficiently. We ask ourselves yet again, Why has this to happen?

'People, especially young people, must climb, but need they fall? Why must they get hurt or even killed in this wonderful pastime with its ever-present background of danger?'

They set about looking at the causes. Since the opening of the mountain school, they had participated in 83 rescues involving 108 people, nine of whom were women.

'Seventy were stretcher cases, fifteen of which required lowering down a crag, a highly skilled and sometimes dangerous operation. Students, the services, school and scout parties accounted for over half of these. Three rescues were of those in charge of parties, two of soldiers and one of scouts, whilst 22 cases involved those apparently under tuition of some sort from a mountaineer, possibly proficient but in each case acting only in a temporary capacity and unused to instructing. This high proportion — 30 per cent — involving training parties inadequately led strengthens the demand made by professional mountaineers for some type of qualifications for those who wish occasionally to train parties in the hills.

'Whilst some rescues have involved people only stranded in difficult positions by their own folly, eighteen have been dead, the majority due to head injuries and 47 have been injured or suffered from exposure. Half the rescues have been carried out in fine weather. This would appear to give the lie to the theory that more accidents occur in bad weather. It is certainly true that walking or climbing expedition are more serious in adverse conditions, but there are many more people to be found on the mountains in good weather.

'Seventy-five per cent of those who have availed themselves of our voluntary services have been under thirty years of age, of whom 50 per cent have been in the 19-22 age group. Thirty-seven accidents involved rock climbers, excluding six who have been led to safety with a timely rope. Twenty-seven of these were falling leaders, four who were climbing second, and two of these fell when their belay gave way as they checked a falling leader, and six were unwisely climbing unroped. Not many years ago, to fall off while leading was both dangerous and a disgrace, but today there are many who think it is all right so long as they are not going to get hurt. This is a dangerous philosophy.

'We were called to the assistance of walkers who had been injured on 45 occasions. Twelve were due primarily to bad route-finding, eight to bad leadership, eight to inexperience, seven to various combinations of the above and eleven might be called unavoidable, or rather, they were the fault of none.

'Of 57 people who fell any appreciable distance, 34 fell between five and thirty feet, eight between

30 and 100 feet and fifteen fell more than 100 feet. Nearly all the latter group were walkers, unroped of course, who fell from high ridges down steep slopes, whereas nearly all of those who fell while rock climbing fell between five and thirty feet. This could be attributed to the technique of using running belays whereby a leader safeguards his progress, thus limiting the extent of a possible fall.

'Reports in our daily newspapers often tell of notorious black spots but it is impossible to state that certain areas are more dangerous than others. To the foolish, all mountainous areas are dangerous but to him with good judgement, the danger is lessened by choosing sensible expeditions.

'Of the 83 rescues, eighteen have been outside our area — in Llanberis Pass or on the Snowdon crags. This area is the responsibility of Mr Briggs, at the Pen y Gwryd Hotel. Apart from ourselves, the nearest rescue team is at RAF Valley, thirty miles away.

'Of the remaining 85 operations, 27 occurred on Tryfan where there are many routes suitable for beginners. From this and from the fact that so many have been in the 19-22 age group, one can argue, not particularly accurately, that young men who have successfully followed a number of rock climbs, eager to lead, make their way to Tryfan and perhaps, feeling a little over-confident, embark on a route too hard for them and come to grief.

'Very few accidents occur on rock climbs above 'severe' standard because such routes are frequented by those who have already acquired a measure of competence. It is hard to draw conclusions from our findings, but there are facts that cannot be argued. Firstly, fewer women are killed or injured because there are fewer women in the mountains. Secondly, more accidents happen on Tryfan because there are more people on Tryfan than on any other mountain except, perhaps, Snowdon when the trains are running.

'Thirdly, more casualties have been young men as most active mountaineers are in their late teens or early twenties. And fourthly, more accidents happen on easy routes because more people climb them.

'There can be no doubt that the majority of accidents could have been avoided by taking that extra bit of care, that extra torch, whistle of map, that extra bit of food, and by remembering that the extra mile at the end of a wet day, when the party's energy is spent, is an extra step towards the loss of limb or life. If people would only give a bit of thought to planning their route, checking their equipment and the strength of their party the day ahead would be more enjoyable and the outcome less tragic.

'To those who set forth poorly led, badly equipped, unfit and untrained we could say, 'You may have friends, you may have relations. They may be fond of you so think before you act rashly. And remember that all rescue teams are voluntary and they have more enjoyable use for their time than carrying heavy people on stretchers in pouring rain, in pitch darkness, falling into bogs and stumbling on boulders.'

Words which continue to echo round the mountains even today.

Anthony Mason-Hornby: One of the founder members, pictured outside Ogwen Cottage, 1969. Photo with thanks to Cicely Mason-Hornby.

1937

CONNIE ALEXANDER, IDWAL YOUTH HOSTEL

by Hazel Robbins

Connie Alexander was the first Warden of Idwal Youth Hostel, taking up the post in 1931 at thirty-four years old. Those who chose to live in such remoteness were often regarded as curiosities. In June 1937, the 'Dundee Evening Telegraph' ran an article, detailing the lifestyles of those 'hermits' who 'prefer the company of birds', including Connie. A rather romantic figure, she was said to live 'in her lonely surroundings', walking 'the wild mountain paths with no other companions than her dog, the birds and the noises of the wind'. Indeed, one of her walks made it onto the front page of several regional newspapers, from Gloucestershire to Dundee!

On Sunday 21 March, Connie left Idwal Youth Hostel with her dog. Her intention was to meet three friends who had gone out earlier that day. When her friends returned without her there was no immediate concern 'as it was recognised that she was an expert climber and thoroughly acquainted with the district'. But, at 7.00pm when hail and rain obscured the mountain tops, those at Idwal did become anxious and a search party was organised, comprising climbers from Oxford staying at Helyg, local farmers, quarrymen from Bethesda and even people from Bangor including the coroner, J Pentir Williams's son, Emyr.

Equipped with hurricane lanterns, ice axes and 'special lightweight first-aid apparatus' the search was initially conducted in bright moonlight but, at midnight, snow began to fall which developed into a blizzard. Most of the searchers were forced off the hill except one party comprising men with a thorough knowledge of the area. At 6.00am the next morning, the search was resumed, this time concentrating on 'the notorious Idwal Slabs and Devil's Kitchen.' It wasn't until 11.00am that word reached Idwal that Connie was safe in the Victoria Hotel in Llanberis, and no way of informing the searchers who were still out on the mountain, and who came back hours later. One of the last off the hill, Mr George Henry Garster, fell and lacerated his nose during the descent and had to receive hospital treatment.

However, Connie's ordeal had been no less arduous than the searchers. Following the recognised route over the mountains in the direction of the Pen y Gwryd, she found the going 'heavy' and when she had gone beyond half way, realised she was too tired to retrace her steps back to Ogwen and decided to follow the path down into the Llanberis Pass. Unfortunately, the weather changed and she suddenly found herself enveloped in a

OGGI SNIPS

From the 'pink' incident report forms, August 1976: Location: start of N Ridge Tryfan. Injury: lower leg. Footwear: clogs!

snowstorm which completely covered known landmarks making any further progress dangerous. So she found shelter from some rocks and remained there until dawn. With her dog beside her, she made her way down to the main road and near the Pen y Gwryd, at the junction of the Llanberis and Aberglaslyn passes, saw a furniture van coming towards her and hailed it, requesting a lift to Ogwen. The van was carrying furniture to Llanberis and was too unwieldy to turn round! So Connie had no choice but to take a lift into Llanberis.

During the journey the driver, George Simpson from London, 'shared his flask of tea and luncheon basket with Miss Alexander, and fed her faithful companion, the dog, which appeared none the worse for its adventure in the hills'. Connie, who was wet through, apparently 'made light of her experience' being 'more tired than exhausted'. Unavoidably, the search for her continued hours after she had reached safety and the 'Caernarvon and Denbigh Herald' sensibly reported that she had 'been a prominent advocate of the installation of a telephone at Ogwen', which could have averted a good deal of anxiety.

The 'North Wales Chronicle' and the 'Caernarvon and Denbigh Herald', reported the incident correctly on their inside pages. Elsewhere, sensational headlines such as 'Woman safe in hotel while party scours mountains', told how Connie had been safe and unhurt as the snow-covered mountains were being searched for her. The 'Dundee Evening Telegraph', took further dramatic licence by adding that a storm came on while she was walking on the main road and that she was taken in a passing van to Llanberis where she stayed the night. The suggestion was that while she was safe and warm in a hotel, people were risking their lives searching for her in a snowstorm!

However, seven months later Connie had the satisfaction of giving her version of events. On 11 October a new radio series on the Northern wavelength was launched called 'It might happen to you'. The first in this new series, entitled 'Night on the bare mountain' involved Connie relating her experience and 'her emotions during those long hours in bitter cold, awaiting the dawn'. Also taking part in the programme was Dr A W Wakefield, the Everest climber. He commented on Connie's actions, pointing out what she had done right and what she had done wrong. He also discussed matters such as clothing, discipline, carrying a compass, what to do if a climber falls behind schedule. The fact that she survived the night in such extreme conditions reveals that Connie was a sensible and resourceful woman and must also have been well-equipped. It was, Dr Wakefield said, 'easy to criticise by the fireside after the event' going on to praise Connie's 'pluck'. A review of the programme the next day described it as not only 'of full-blooded interest but a valuable piece of education'.

Friends across the water

A number of people helped shape the first five years of Og Cott and one of these was Flight Sergeant Johnnie Lees, leader of the RAF Valley MRT. The relationship between the RAF and the civilian mountain rescue teams has been long and fruitful, particularly in the Ogwen Valley, situated as it is just thirty miles and a few moments flying time from the RAF Valley base on Anglesey. But it owes its very beginnings to men like Lees and Flight Lieutenant George Graham.

Often acclaimed as the 'architect and saviour' of mountain rescue, Lees's involvement in the service began in North Wales. The RAF Valley team had been established by George Graham at RAF Llandwrog in 1943 and moved to Valley in 1951 — the same year that nine people lost their lives on Snowdon over that fateful Easter weekend and another five would before the year was out. Members of the RAF teams were volunteers too, taking on the task aside from any role they might play in their day job, and they played a key part in the rescues in Snowdonia, recovering bodies and casualties, struggling with the appalling weather conditions and kit that was unfit for purpose.

The previous week, an Avro Lancaster bomber had crashed near the summit of Beinn Eighe, in Scotland. It was five days before the wreckage was sighted. Over several days, the attempts to locate the wreckage and the bodies of the aircrew threw the inadequacies of the RAF mountain rescue service into sharp focus. Few of the rescuers had ice axes, one or two were wearing Wellington boots, and few were properly trained for the harsh conditions of the mountains in winter. Despite repeated efforts, the last body was not recovered until the end of August.

In the face of huge public concern, Whitehall stepped in. The Air Ministry demanded radical changes for the RAF mountain rescue service, including a structured training schedule, the introduction of an annual mountaineering course in North Wales, an instruction manual for mountain rescue and the posting of experienced mountaineers to the service. Johnnie Lees, an experienced mountaineer and pioneering climber, was asked to instruct on the first course, in October 1951. Three months later, at the age of just twenty-four years old, he was appointed as team leader of the RAF Valley MRT, a post he held for eight years.

Former RAF MRT members John Greenwood and Vic Bray knew Lees well. 'Vic was the man who held Johnnie's top rope during the rescue for which Johnnie was awarded his George Medal,' explains Greenwood. 'As far as I know, Johnnie was the only person ever to be awarded the George Medal for mountain rescue.'

Vic Bray wrote about Johnnie on behalf of the ex-members of his Valley team during the fifties. 'During this period he was largely responsible for remoulding the RAF mountain rescue service in this country, from poorly-equipped though willing amateurs, into rescue teams second to none at that time. He fought for and got better equipment, whilst at the same time organising summer and winter climbing courses for members of both home and overseas teams. He also introduced advanced rescue techniques using the Austrian Tragsitz rescue harness, which he demonstrated to both RAF and civilian teams'.

Bray describes the rescue which resulted in the George Medal, as recorded by Lees himself in the log book of the day.

OGGI SNIPS

February 1986 newsletter: The only thing to put in this issue is that the ropes have been colour-coded, the only one I can remember is that red ends are for practice only!

'The team was called out on the evening of 3 January 1958. Major Hugh Robertson of the Army Mountaineering Association, had fallen whilst leading Amphitheatre Buttress on Craig yr Ysfa — a high and remote crag in the Carneddau. Weather conditions were moonlight, a light covering of snow and very cold.

'No army personnel had been able to reach Robertson and his climbing partner, Lieutenant Roger Eagle. When the RAF rescue team arrived on the ridge above the buttress, it was decided that five team members would descend and assess the situation, using fixed ropes as handrails when needed.

'They descended for nearly 600 feet, sometimes over difficult ground, followed by a final abseil to land Lees, Andrews and Bray on the narrow ledge where Robertson and Eagle were situated, whilst Douglas and Pilot Officer North stayed above ready to pass down extra ropes as required.

'As the pair had been on the ledge for over five hours and Robertson was delirious and had head injuries, an immediate evacuation was decided upon. Robertson was strapped to Johnnie's back using a split 120-foot coiled rope, worn rucksack fashion, through which the casualty's legs were pushed. A pair of 120-foot knotted ropes were then attached to both Lees and Robertson along with various support slings attached to the active ropes by prussiks. The pair were then slid over the edge to where the vertical wall of the Buttress fell into the Amphitheatre and lowered some 140 feet.

'The remainder of the team plus army personnel recovered the casualty by Thomas stretcher from the Amphitheatre, and carried him about two miles down Cwm Eigiau, to the waiting RAF ambulance. In spite of his strenuous descent Lees took more than his fair share of the carrying, then it was on by road to Llandudno Hospital, where Robertson eventually recovered from a double fracture of the skull.'

A confident, often outspoken man, Lees didn't suffer fools gladly, but when the 'crunch' came he was always there, ready to do the business. One of his instructions to new team members was apparently 'when on an aircraft call-out, you will walk until the blood wells from the lace holes of your boots, stop, wash your feet in the nearest stream, put on a plaster and dry socks, and walk on'.

'Luckily,' says Ron James, 'Johnnie Lees was a friend and helped us to form a team from the Ogwen staff and friends'. And Lees continued to influence mountain rescue until his retirement from the RAF in 1961. The following year, he was awarded the British Empire Medal 'for services to mountain rescue'. After his retirement, he worked for a time with Ron James as a mountain guide at Og Cott. Alongside their mountain rescue work, the pair submitted proposals to the British Mountaineering Council for basic mountain training for leaders of school and youth groups — ideas which led to the formation of the Mountain Training Board and the Mountain Leadership certificate in 1964.

KC Gordon was there at the start and remained an operational team member until the age of seventy-five, in 2015. He recounts joining the RAF as an apprentice. 'After three years of technical training you had to give options where you'd like to be posted. I wanted to be near the mountains so I put down Kinloss, Leuchars and Valley. I got Valley. But I remember how disappointed I was that January day in 1959, coming along the coast, looking out as the mountains came and went and the train crossed over the Menai Straits, and gradually realising that my home for the next two

FROM THE ARCHIVE

Boy soldiers 'in danger' in Snowdonia, Sunday Telegraph 1970: Over the years, many groups and individuals from the armed forces, have come to the area to train or test their personal mettle by taking part in challenging events. The majority live to tell the tale, but every so often an accident occurs which underlines the sheer danger of the Ogwen terrain.

In 1970, there were concerns that young army recruits were being sent on exercise to Snowdonia, ill-equipped and insufficiently trained. A report in the 'Sunday Telegraph' speculated that the Army had the 'worst record of anyone in the mountains', with junior soldiers being sent up 3000-foot mountains in dangerous weather.

Earlier in the year, a junior soldier had been fetched from the Milestone Buttress on Tryfan, so far gone he could not move. In freezing rain, the boy was clothed in standard army combat jacket and denims. His clothes were not waterproof and the rain had soaked through to his skin. The group had been led by regular soldiers, but they were so inexperienced in the mountain environment, they'd failed to notice that the boy was suffering from exposure.

In another incident, a group of junior bandsmen, led by a sixteen-year-old sergeant, had been ordered to cross the mountains in bad weather, then bivouac on the other side before returning the following day — but they had no tents. They were found by the rescue team in low cloud, with no idea of their true position. The officer in charge of the party was not on the exercise and, when sent for, simply ordered the boys back to the mountain.

KC Gordon was so disturbed by this news that he called the Army depot at Menai Bridge to report that the boys were soaking wet and some had no change of clothing. There was a risk of extreme hypothermia had they returned to the mountain as instructed. Finally, a major arrived and the boys were allowed to spend the night in the mountain guides' hut at Ogwen.

The event only served to confirm Ron James's belief that no officer or NCO should lead a party on the mountains until he had passed a mountain leadership course. The Ministry of Defence clearly shared his concerns. By May 1971, following meetings between the Ministry, the British and Scottish mountaineering councils, the Outward Bound Trust and Lord Hunt, all leaders of army parties would have to hold a mountain leadership certificate or be full members of the Army Mountaineering Association.

and a half years was on the other side of Anglesey — a long walk from the mountains!'

Undeterred, the young KC joined the RAF mountain rescue team. 'We were always on exercise somewhere in Snowdonia. We'd often get stopped on the road to or from an exercise — or the pub! Except on Sundays, of course, because in those days that was a dry day in Wales. The local police would stop the trucks and say there'd been a call and we'd all go back up.

'The RAF team had a good relationship with the Ogwen Cottage school. Ron James was a guide and our team leader [Lees] was too. Sometimes one or two of us would help out in the centre, instructing. Ron said to me, if I ever got out of the service, there was a job for me there.'

OGGI SNIPS

October 1986 newsletter: 'There is a drill, stand and bits in the store. Please look after these as if they were your own. NB. That doesn't mean taking them home with you.'

After his two and a half year stint at Valley, KC knew he was due for an overseas post. He'd hoped to go to Nicosia, where there were mountains to be had, but once again fate had other ideas. Disappointed, he found himself on Malta — smaller than Anglesey and not a good hill in sight. He was, he says, heartbroken when he got there.

Things looked up a little when he discovered a kindred spirit in a civilian engineer on the base who also enjoyed climbing and the pair of them regularly went off to climb on the sea cliffs. Meanwhile, he 'made a nuisance' of himself and secured a transfer to Nicosia, which enabled him to climb in Turkey and Greece, all the while remembering what Ron James had said to him. Towards the end of his posting, he wrote to James to see if the offer was still on. It was. Now all he had to do was save £220 to buy himself out — on his seven guineas a week wage that was quite a task. But save he did and, in 1963 he was off to join Og Cott.

'I remember getting discharged from Lyneham and getting the night train to Bangor. The dawn was rising as I arrived. From there I had to hitch to Bethesda. I was in my demob suit, rucksack on my back with all my possessions in it. I walked the last five miles to Ogwen through snow and arrived at breakfast time. Everyone was still in bed because there was no course in, so I went round and woke everyone up with a cup of tea.'

Early epics

'Three epic rescues stick in my mind from this period,' says Ron. One involved lots of schoolchildren on the Carneddau, who he describes as victims of the 'newly discovered' hypothermia, and led indirectly to the development of the Mountain Leadership scheme. Another, on Lliwedd with RAF Valley, involved two jockeys and a 500-foot lower from the foot of Red Wall on a dark wet night. 'Johnnie Lees and the stretcher had 500-foot No 4 ropes, I had two 300-foot No 2 ropes joined with a knot. Halfway down my knot jammed. Foxy Cartledge carried on feeding out, I climbed up a bit and jumped off to free it, dropped 50 feet, passed the stretcher and re-caught it on the bounce. How Lees laughed!'

The third involved a broken femur on a wet Whit Sunday night on Cloggy on the wall just to the left of Pigott's Climb. 'Salient points included holing the van radiator on the drive up Snowdon, a Tyrolean traverse [rope rescue cableway] from the Eastern Terrace to the top of the routes and Terry Darby in nails sending up sparks as he slid across. The lowerers belayed to some poor-ish pegs and, as an afterthought before letting Dave Yates lower me, I used an odd end of rope to attach him to Pete Vaughan, the third lowerer.

'Dave lowered me over the edge, I paused on a ledge, stepped off, Dave's pegs failed and he appeared over the lip — luckily keeping hold and still attached to Pete. As the ledge with the patient on was small, the stretcher was supported horizontally by two pegs. I stood on it to lower him then had the magic moment of removing first the head end peg and finally, the foot end peg. A final memory of Dave Yates abseiling into our light in a flurry of snow. Snow at Whit? No, it was the feathers from a new but split duvet!'

Although, as an aside, snow in late May hasn't proved quite the impossible notion Ron then suggested. Famously, in 1975, an inch of snow stopped play at a county cricket match between Derbyshire and Lancashire in Buxton. And in June 2011, the summit of Snowdon was pictured by the BBC under a white blanket of snow. 'It started hailing around lunchtime, then it snowed for about an hour,' said Jonathan Tyler, the manager of Snowdon Mountain Railway's visitor centre. 'It wasn't cold, but people were arriving at the summit looking quite bemused. It was summer at the bottom of the mountain and winter at the top'. An all-too familiar occurrence in the mountains!

School gets new masters

When KC Gordon had arrived at Ogwen Cottage, freshly demobbed and raring to go, the school was still private but, says Gordon, 'it wasn't making any great profit'. Eventually, financial pressure forced their hand.

'It was a time of expansion for the education authorities', adds Gordon, 'inspired by Jack Longland's pioneering efforts in Derbyshire*'.Ron James still had a lot of contacts with his native Birmingham and many of the students already came from there, so it was an obvious first place to go for help. 'They bought the centre and saved it'.

So, on 6 April 1964, the school gained new masters with the sale to Birmingham Education Authority for £11,500. The authority planned to spend a further £10,500 on improvements. And, instead of remaining a free house, it would now be primarily for Birmingham students. A dinner in Llanberis marked the changeover, set to take place at midnight on 5 April.

Tony Mason-Hornby and Ron James would remain in charge, with Ron as warden and chief instructor, and Tony as senior instructor. Alice Jones, the 52-year-old cook who had been 'mother' to the climbers at the cottage, would also stay on. The agreement was that the rescue team would continue and from then on, the number of team members would grow significantly.

Up to that point, 4000 pupils had been instructed in rock climbing and mountaineering with 33,000 more attending one-day courses and the school had also gained a reputation for exploration in the field in North Wales, with an impressive list of new routes achieved. The school was also proud of its safety record — with no serious incidents over their five-year tenure — which they attributed to the ratio of one instructor to only two or three pupils. And they had earned a good name for themselves in mountain rescue.

When the Ogwen Cottage Mountain School opened, it heralded the start of a new era. In five years, those three visionary men and their staff had given the climbing fraternity a new household name, but it was very much a business gamble. Now was the start of a new phase.

With Birmingham's ownership came many changes. 'Everyone was relieved,' said Barbara James, 'when a big generator, a more powerful source of electricity, arrived. No longer did the last person to go to bed have to run across the car park to switch off our old Lister!'

**In 1950, Longland had established the outdoor centre at Whitehall, near Buxton, one of the first of its kind in the UK.*

OGGI SNIPS

October 1986 newsletter: 'The base tape recorder has been fixed and is now operational again. Bet most of you didn't know it was missing, did you?'

Barbara first met Ron James at Capel Pinnacles some time before the sale to Birmingham. When she became an instructor at Og Cott, she entered a world of 'work and play that was mainly the prerogative of men'. She was, however, perhaps well-prepared for the task having struggled against the odds herself to gain fitness — particularly the debilitating challenge of dealing with eczema in the unforgiving outdoor environment. She recalls coming to the mountains of Snowdonia as a teenager from the Wirral, ill-prepared for the strenuous task of mountain climbing. Regular trips soon fixed that and, shy by nature, she quickly found, when she 'had enough breath to talk', that it was easier to initiate conversations on the mountain, her reserve disappearing 'as if by magic'.

She had returned to North Wales throughout her college days, but eventually met and began climbing with Ron. In September 1964, she took a job as assistant warden at the Towers Outdoor Pursuit Centre. By Easter 1965, Birmingham Education Authority was advertising for an instructor at the Ogwen Cottage Mountain School. The job was hers 'on condition that I stopped work immediately if I became pregnant!' Such were the strictures placed on women in those days.

'Og Cott was situated in a veritable wind funnel where the A5 road was at its highest point, about 1000 feet, and the valley at its narrowest. Our front door gripped tightly onto one side of the road and Llyn Ogwen lapped against the other. When conditions allowed, the downward pointing wing of passing, steeply-banked, low-flying jets seemed about to slice through the surface of the lake. Unsuspecting visitors nearly jumped out of their skins. For city youngsters, it must have been another world.

'Our only neighbour was the busy Idwal Youth Hostel and the nearest pubs were about five miles drive in either direction to very different villages. Capel Curig had attractive cottages dotted along its length and a dramatic open vista to the perfect postcard view of the Snowdon massif. Convenient campsites were within easy access of the three hotels' bars, while the youth hostel, climbing shop and cafes catered for the needs of tourists, climbers and walkers. In contrast, throughout the length of Bethesda's main street, shops were wedged in between terraced housing, and chapels and churches were on the opposite side of the road to the pubs but relatively few visitors were tempted to stop.'

Barbara recalls that the school ran alternate courses for thirty boys or thirty girls at a time, with every pupil from a different school, so no child knew any other and they were 'all in the same boat'. Most had never ventured away from home before, let alone seen a mountain. The syllabus included hill walking, skiing on the artificial ski slope at Plas y Brenin, a one-night camp and a mountain rescue day.

She has a number of memories of Mrs Jones, the cook, who she describes as being 'small in stature but large in adaptability'. From Mynydd Llandegai, Mrs Jones had spoken little English before starting work at Og Cott. Mason-Hornby would drive her to work in his Rolls Royce every day. When he decided to leave the school, despite being close to retirement, this remarkable lady decided to learn to drive. 'We were thrilled when she passed her test, in English, the second time round, and from then on drove to Og Cott in her Mini as though in a Rolls Royce!'

Landed with any matters to do with 'housekeeping' — no doubt due, she speculates, to being the only female instructor — James was allowed one day off per course to check stock, order food and undertake cleaning chores. Whilst this meant occasionally missing 'the torture of a night out

camping' it also often meant returning from a wet day on the hill to be greeted by Mrs Jones with a 'Mrs James, the fish has not arrived'! Needless to say, nobody else had thought to call the shop — and from then on tins of salmon were always available for emergencies!

Despite being expected to carry out the gender-typical roles about the place, one suspects Barbara James was perfectly capable of holding her own — as any woman in a man's world had to do in those times. 'The competitive, all-bachelor atmosphere created a frequently hard hitting, never vindictive and rarely unkind sense of humour. After work, at weekends and in the summer evenings, the instructors went climbing, competing with each other to make first ascents of routes of extreme difficulty and their day ended with a pint and female company.' Ogwen Cottage Mountain School, she adds, 'influenced and changed the lives of most who had worked there and those on the courses'.

The 'John Glews incident'

Now that the school was in the hands of Birmingham Education Authority, the instructors were able to enjoy the same school holidays as other education providers. The long six-week break provided the glorious opportunity to explore mountains further afield. During that first summer, when most of the instructors had, as KC Gordon says 'hightailed it to the Alps' and the RAF Valley team were training elsewhere, an accident happened which had a significant effect on how mountain rescue would be delivered in the valley.

John Glews was left to 'house-sit' at Ogwen Cottage for the summer, with instructions to call Plas y Brenin if necessary. While he was attempting a new route on Clogwyn Ddu, a crag at the top of Nameless Cwm above Idwal Slabs, a peg came out and he fell. He was, says Ron James 'badly smashed up'. Someone ran for help but whilst he was waiting, it occurred to Glews that the intermittent rescue service provided, dependent as it was on the availability of Ogwen Cottage staff and the RAF, was insufficient. What Ogwen needed was continuous mountain rescue cover, delivered by an independent group of rescuers who could be available throughout the year.

When the hastily gathered rescue party arrived, Glews was unimpressed by their lack of skill and attempted to tell them what to do even as he lay on the stretcher. Apparently, he was so badly injured that when colleagues visited him in the orthopaedic hospital at Gobowen in Shropshire, he was still in intensive care. They resolved there and then that the need for a permanent rescue team was a priority.

By autumn 1964, a new team had been conceived, guided by Ron James and Mason-Hornby. It would consist of a number of team leaders, mainly the instructors from Ogwen Cottage, with a pool of skilled rescuers at their disposal, on call round the clock. It would be an entirely voluntary enterprise. The Mountaineering Club of North Wales was also very much involved.

The inaugural meeting of the Ogwen Valley Mountain Rescue Organisation was held in March 1965. Mason-Hornby was in the chair, Ron James was senior team leader and Barbara James was

Top: John Glews. **Bottom:** The salubrious 'mountain rescue' caravan, purchased for a fiver in May 1965. Is it any wonder they took it away? © OVMRO.

secretary. 'When it was first set up,' says Ron, 'it was an amalgamation of the newly created team and the two rescue posts at Ogwen and Idwal but it was heavily biased towards the team because we provided the numbers. The committee included reps from the posts, so we called it an organisation. Mountain rescue work was starting to be recognised as a skill in need of practice and training'.

During the next five years — indeed, ever since — the team continued to experiment with kit and ways of doing things. There would be experiments with a split Thomas stretcher, developments with radios and collaboration with Plas y Brenin and Glenmore Lodge to refine team member skills. A significant change came with the arrival of Dr Ieuan Jones at the Caernarfon and Anglesey Hospital in Bangor, where he worked as the senior accident officer. Like Wilson Hey before him, he realised that the skills of mountain rescuers, and the treatments they could offer, were inadequate for the bigger emergencies they might face and set about improving them, often by exposing team members to the shocking reality of trauma.

They were interesting times, to which hindsight lends a wry humour, as Chris Lloyd explains. 'In May 1965, OVMRO purchased a small caravan for £5 which was sited at the rear of the Cottage. But it wasn't long before eagle-eyed authorities thought its presence might encourage travellers and the council ordered the caravan to be removed in September of that year — an exercise which cost more than it had to purchase it!

'In February 1966, Birmingham Education Authority kindly dedicated a room (the old generator room/garage) to mountain rescue. However, there were strict rules about use of this room. This included no overnight stays and certainly NO girlfriends or women were permitted in there at whatever time of day or night!' We can only speculate whether any girlfriend or woman ever actually harboured a burning desire to spend any time in said generator room.

Like KC Gordon, long-standing members Roger Jones and Neil Adam were involved during the Ogwen Cottage rescue team days — Adam while still a student and Roger through the Scout movement. 'My father was the local commissioner and I got involved with the Scout hut at Hafod when it was opened in 1959 and that was my introduction to mountaineering,' says Jones. Trained as a mechanical engineer, he was employed at Bangor University where several members of staff were members of the team. 'A lot of students come to Bangor because it's near the mountains and the university was quite happy that if students got into difficulty, there would be staff around to bring them home! We were never penalised if we were out on the mountain'. Spending so much time at the hut, he was often called upon by the instructors at Og Cott to help out on rescues so it was a logical step to be part of the newly-formed team.

He recalls the early days, when Mason-Hornby's Roll's Royce would be pressed into service, often taking team members away from their pints the Douglas Arms in Bethesda to go rescue someone. As an 'ambulance' it certainly seemed better from a casualty's point of view than being slung in the back of a coal truck! 'The boot folded flat,' says Neil Adam. 'The stretcher stuck out a bit but we could slide it in and two people would sit in the back holding onto it'.

OGGI SNIPS

November 1977 newsletter: 'Scran night', Idwal Cottage. There will be approximately 3.5 pints of beer each, so those of you who fancy more, please bring it with you.'

Suited, booted and ready for action

The experiences of the school's first five years may have given Mason-Hornby pause for thought but they also set a template for the innovative, forward-thinking team that Ogwen continues to be. At the time of the team's Silver Jubilee in 1990, Ron James recalled that the team 'got hold of a film of rescue in the Alps by Mariner and practised, for the first time in Britain, many of the improvised techniques now very much part of guide and instructor training'. There was also a Tragsitz from Austria, a Perche Barnarde from Frendo in Grenoble and later the Mariner stretcher and wire lowering gear. And James himself was the 'master of improvisation'.

On one occasion, he was driving back from Birmingham when, as he approached Milestone Buttress, he was flagged down by police, who recognised his car. He was wearing a suit and leather-soled shoes but fortunately had a pair of trainers with him. It seemed a climber was in difficulty in Ivy Chimney. The man had slipped and his leg had shot into a crack where the knee had become completely jammed. He had been there for at least three hours and both the police and the RAF MRT had tried everything they knew without success.

Dr Ieuan Jones had also been called to the scene and was considering whether he might have to amputate the man's leg. Someone came up with a car jack, hoping to prise the sides of the chimney apart, but James wasn't happy with the risks implied by this solution. Who knew how the rocks might behave?

So, without further ado, he climbed up to the casualty in his immaculate suit. The man was manoeuvred into a sit-sling to take the weight off his knee, which enabled James to straighten the leg. Then with a pair of scissors, he cut away the trousers, in front and behind, and removed the boot from the stuck leg. That done, he asked if anyone had any sandwiches. Fortunately, they had.

Quickly dispensing with any fillings, James rubbed what butter he could find around the trapped limb then, clipping his waist belt tightly to the back of the sit-sling, he placed his feet firmly against the rock before suddenly straightening both his legs. The man popped out of the crack like a cork. Subsequently, James undertook two more, similar rescues. He recalls one when the team used washing up liquid — there were bubbles coming off the rocks for weeks afterwards — and another using engine oil 'as no one had any sandwiches left!'

The methods of calling out were varied. There were no telephones to speak of, and certainly no such thing as a 'mobile phone'. The local 'bobby' would go round knocking on doors, gathering known volunteers. KC Gordon describes how news of an injured or missing climber frequently disrupted his Saturday evening plans. 'Just as we were heading off to Bangor to chase after the college girls (there were two women's colleges in Bangor at the time), someone would come rushing in and say there was someone stuck. If it was just 'someone stuck', we'd toss up for which two would go out and the rest would carry on to Bangor. If it was a proper accident, we'd all go'.

Barbara James recalls that the resident instructors accepted that living-in at a rescue post brought responsibilities. All too often after dark, the 'unmistakably urgent knock at the door' signalled a call-out. And sometimes they happened right in front of you. Gordon remembers seeing a girl going the whole distance of Idwal Slabs and sadly not surviving. 'It was like picking up a bag

of sticks'. Then as now, even if you were roped up, if you fell, you could go quite a distance — and there were no helmets in those days.

In 'Itching to Climb', Barbara James describes her first encounters with the 'grim results of mountaineers' misjudgements', shortly after she began working as an instructor at Ogwen Cottage.

One November weekend, the weather warnings had been severe. As she and Ron drove back up the Nant Francon valley after a lunchtime pint, the freezing rain had turned to sleet. On arriving back at Og Cott, they learned that three members of a group had not returned to their base, a hut a few miles away.

'They'd set off to climb a long route on a crag high above the A5. Apparently one of them was not feeling well before he started out. Conditions deteriorated rapidly and soon gale force winds were blowing the snow into drifts, blocking the road.

'After the road was opened the next morning, we heard the full story. They had reached the climb and we were told that they had battled up several pitches before deciding to retreat downhill. This they did but into a valley far from their base! Seemingly determined to return to the Ogwen Valley they'd retraced their steps uphill, but couldn't descend the steep path they'd walked up. They had to walk uphill in order to descend an easy ridge, in the teeth of a gale. Only when the

FROM THE ARCHIVE

City couple in ledge ordeal at 2000 feet, September 1968: Two lift attendants, doubtless accustomed to guiding the odd nervous passenger between floors at Lewis's department store in Liverpool, found the tables turned, when they became stuck 2000 foot up Tryfan for seventeen hours — on a narrow ledge, with no more than 'an inch to spare'.

Neville Wright and his girlfriend, Michelle Edwards, both in their thirties, had set off around 1.30pm on the Saturday morning, intending to 'walk over the mountains', but quickly became caught by a swirling mist. They clambered down a big gully, thinking it was a route back to the valley, but arrived at the very narrow ledge and could go no further.

As darkness fell, there was nothing else to do but huddle under Wright's plastic mac with the wind howling round them. They dared not go to sleep in case they fell from the ledge, keeping each other awake by trying to sing songs. At one stage, a big rock dislodged, sending their duffle bag crashing down with their flasks, sandwiches and camera inside. The apples and oranges tucked into their pockets, in anticipation of later enjoyment, now the only nourishment they had.

Early next day, a party of Army cadets from Sutton Coldfield who had spotted the couple high above them on the ledge, valiantly tried, and failed, to climb the gully. So, they hurried back to Ogwen Cottage Mountain School to fetch help. Ron and Barbara James went to the ledge and lowered the couple down using a rope seat. Neville Wright and Michelle Edwards, cold, tired and hungry, finally travelled home by train, twelve hours later than they'd planned.

Safe at last: Roger Jones carries Michelle Edwards to safety © OVMRO.

sick man and his colleague, who had been supporting him, could go no further did they stop on the tarmac road, between a huge mountain wall and the leat (a drainage ditch that crossed the hillside). The third man continued downhill to alert their companions but the blizzard conditions were so severe they could not find their missing colleagues.

'The men were found next day about ten to fifteen minutes walk from the A5 road, still 'sitting' on their ropes but hidden from view, and quite dead. Shortly afterwards, Ron and I were testing our new, wooden skis for the first time on an easy slope near the road, when I was shocked to see two pairs of legs protruding from the back of the Land Rover taking the bodies to Bangor.'

One rescue recalled by Ron James demonstrates the sheer satisfaction rescue work gives, and he reckons it was one of the most technical rescues the team had done. He later noted that 'the relationship between the team, the Llandudno Rescue Team and Plas y Brenin had become very close due to a number of well-coordinated searches'. So, when a call came in to a double incident on Soap Gut, on the Milestone buttress, Plas y Brenin came too. It was October 1968, and twenty-four-year-old Valerie Wright, said to 'know next to nothing about mountaineering', was roundly praised for her part in saving the lives of two other climbers in the incident.

Wright had been roped together with her fiancé, Neville Sanderson, and Leslie Gadman — both also in their twenties — when disaster struck. Gadman had been climbing about twenty feet above the couple, when he dislodged a large rock and plummeted past the ledge his friends were standing on. The rock hit Sanderson, knocking him unconscious before hurtling on down to hit Gadman as he dangled on the end of the rope, crushing his foot against the rock face.

Without a thought for herself, Wright grabbed her fiancé to stop him falling over the edge and somehow managed to hold on to Gadman's rope, lowering him gently to a ledge below. Then began a lonely five-hour vigil until the rescuers arrived with floodlights and two stretchers just before midnight.

'I only started climbing two weeks ago', she said, once safely back on terra firma, 'and I suppose I reacted instinctively just as anyone else would have done. Neville just went all limp and he was being choked by the ropes which had slipped up from his waist. He kept swaying about on this narrow ledge which was all muddy after the rain. He still had Leslie's rope in his hands and I grabbed this and eased it out until Leslie got onto another ledge.

'When the rescuers arrived, they strapped me to a tree a short distance away, because I could do nothing but stand there with blood-stained clothing in my hands.'

Ron James later praised the young woman to the press, saying she'd done an excellent job keeping her head in a tricky situation 'for the ledge she was on was very slippery and only the width of a biscuit tin', adding that all the 'lads' were full of praise for the way she acted in saving the lives of two men. The rock had virtually severed Sanderson's foot and causing serious arterial bleeding.

Neil Adam, still a student in Bangor and fresh from the rigours of Ieuan Jones's advanced first aid course, was thrust in at the deep end as the delegated first aider. He bandaged the man's foot then the two men were lowered 150 feet, on two separate stretchers side by side, with Ron James guiding one and Adam the other.

The rescue lives on in the memory for the enduring reputation it bestowed on one particular

OGGI SNIPS

September 1978 newsletter: 'A chance to see the coastguard in action on the Little Orme. Very little to say apart from the fact that mountain rescue is definitely not a spectator sport.'

team member. Having just been given three new Pye Bantam radios — in return for support for a film with climber Joe Brown — the team had decided to try out its new toys that very day. As team members arrived at the roadside, the girl shouted down that the leader had fallen and the second was injured and James headed off up the hill, radio at the ready. Or so they thought on the ground. After a good deal of frustrated fiddling, and getting no response from James, Roger Jones stuck his head out of the window and the words 'Ron! Stick your *** radio on!' echoed loud around the crag. Radio now 'stuck' on, matters could proceed. And Roger Jones would forever be the 'Voice of Ogwen'.

That same month, circumstances prompted a rescue of a different sort when fifty-six-year-old William Brandwood collapsed with a heart attack. Constable Eric Roberts had collected the ten tiny pills required for treatment from the chemist in Bethesda, before dashing the two miles to Ogwen Cottage in a police van. Instructor John Hesketh then set off with the tablets to join Ogwen team members who were already searching in the darkness for the sick man.

Brandwood was found with two friends, sheltering from the gale-force winds behind rocks on the aptly named Castell y Gwynt (translated as Castle of the Wind), an exposed prominence atop the 3200-foot Glyder Fach. Four other members of the original climbing party had retreated down to Ogwen Cottage to get help.

Pills duly delivered, a tedious three-mile walk down the mountain began. It was bitterly cold and the wind threatened to wrench the stretcher from the handlers' grasp. At times the men were on their knees. Shortly before midnight, a rescue team from RAF Valley set off from Pen y Gwryd to relieve the Ogwen team — but the two teams passed each other in the darkness! However, watchers in the valley below could see the meandering glowworm shapes above and managed to bring the two teams together with the help of radio contact. Medical advice was also relayed by radio from Pen y Gwryd to the rescuers on the hill and, four hours later, Brandwood was delivered to the ambulance and on to hospital.

The farewells begin

Inevitably, before too long people began to move on, lives and careers calling them to fresh pastures.

In 1966, Tony Mason-Hornby left North Wales to take over the family estate in Cumbria. During his time in the area, he had done many fine climbs, some first ascents, and qualified as a mountain guide. Here too he met his wife Cicely Barbara Carter. They were married for thirty-five years before he succumbed to Motor Neurone Disease, in 1994. Away from Ogwen, he had nevertheless left his mark. His memorial service was attended by several members of the local climbing community. 'Tony had a super sense of humour', recalls Barbara James, 'and a wonderful way of dealing with the authorities. Even to the last with the evil illness he suffered from, he did not lose his strength and faith'.

Cedric Milner assumed the chair but only a year later, he emigrated to Canada and Tony Jones took over. Three years later, in April 1969, Ron James too left the area, to become principal lecturer

in outdoor education at IM Marsh College of Physical Education in Liverpool, a position he held for sixteen years until he retired and returned to North Wales in 1985.

'By 1968', explains Ron, 'the repetitive nature of the Ogwen work meant that I was applying for other jobs. I'd been involved in over 300 rescues and felt that my enthusiasm for rescue might not be shared by future wardens and so the use of the caravan and outbuildings were all steps towards independence'.

Rescues linger on in the memory for many reasons — gory, amusing, humbling, exhausting — and they have a way of popping up whenever prompted. Ron's last rescue before heading to his new life in Liverpool in 1969 was one such, and another double rescue at that. It was a perfect day. He was alone in the office, everyone else out on the hill, when the call came in that a fourteen-year-old boy had collapsed with a heart attack near the summit of Tryfan.

'A helicopter in the area picked me up, we lifted the lad and saw him to Bangor, just in time for a second call, this time to a broken leg below the cave in Great Gully on Craig yr Ysfa. So it was back to Ogwen for a 1000-foot wire and winch, then up to the gully top where KC had luckily arrived with his walking group.

'He lowered and I collected the casualty and used the second as an assistant jockey. The winchman helped us with the short carry and away they sped to Bangor. Everything was fine except for me. Alone in Cwm Eigiau in a suit plus boots, a first aid kit, a stretcher and both blokes' kit!' A situation which he reckons Gordon found highly amusing from the safety of the ridge!

'In the first five years,' concludes Ron, 'it was pretty much half a dozen professional people running a mountaineering school and combining that with rescue work. It was very quick, very efficient and hopefully straight back down to the pub afterwards. The staff at Ogwen Cottage were very close knit. We did what we did as a pleasure. It was a service by climbers for climbers. That's what we must never forget. I did enjoy living in Ogwen Cottage. It was a great place to live, where you had the ability to get into the mountains quickly'.

Barbara James, as Ron's then-wife, left at the same time, a prospect she looked forward to with dread. City life did not appeal despite the idiosyncratic nature of living at Ogwen Cottage. One of the greatest problems, she recalls, was the lack of mains electricity. 'The supply line was on the other side of the road but despite frequent letters, the electricity board maintained there was insufficient power available for us.' Coincidentally, just as they were about to leave, 'the generator crankshaft exited through the housing'. Not long after, mains electricity was magically connected — and a full-time housekeeper was appointed.

Within seven years, Barbara and Ron too had parted company. Undeterred and in urgent need of employment (and ever the survivor), she continued to seek challenges, in what was still very much 'male territory'. She became the first and only female civilian to be employed by the MOD to train Infantry Junior Leaders. After eleven years, she took early retirement and travelled to the Falkland Islands soon after the conflict, unaccompanied, for a walking holiday. And she achieved her private pilot's licence — a fiftieth birthday present to herself — before flying a Cessna solo for forty hours round Florida. Now back in North Wales, her fondest memories are of being 'at the

The way things were, 1968: Top: The old kit store, 1968. Bottom: Rescue party for a heart attack victim on the Pyg Track. Photos © OVMRO.

cutting edge of a new initiative. There were no qualifications for that kind of work, so it was an exciting time. What we were doing was revolutionary. It was very tiring, it was extra hard work, it was enjoyable and interesting and it certainly was an adrenaline rush!'

Dr Ieuan Jones also left the area, to work for the Coal Board. But he would return to continue working with the team until the 1990s.

Alice Jones, who had served as cook for so many years, retired in 1975. This remarkable lady, who local press reports called the 'mother of the mountains' had, they said, become 'mother' to thousands of children over the years, often struggling through snow storms just to get to Og Cott to feed the children and staff. By way of thank you she was treated to a 'slap-up retirement dinner and a gold watch'.

'I can well remember the first day at Ogwen', she said. 'There were four serious accidents on that first day and some people were killed. I did not think I would be able to carry on… but I did'. She also recalled many happy moments with the youngsters coming off the windswept hills to enjoy a bit of home cooking.

FROM THE ARCHIVE

Learner climber saves falling companion, Liverpool Daily Post May 1969: Stories of novice climbers saving their climbing companions are not unusual. A Liverpool University student was reported to have been saved from certain death by the actions of a 'girl learner-climber' although, in fact, the young man had suffered little more than an injured elbow.

Cheryl Jones had managed to take the strain on the rope as Ernie Ward hurtled past her on Idwal Slabs. With the runners pulled from the rock face, there was nothing else preventing Ward from falling further. Neil Adam led the eight-strong team to rescue Ward from his ledge, assisted by members of a rescue team from RAF Kinloss, in Scotland, who were on exercise in the area. They lowered Ward 100 feet, with Roger Jones guiding them down the cliff. Had it not been for Cheryl wearing gloves, her hands would have been badly burnt by the rope and the outcome would not have been good.

Later that month, another incident, also on Idwal Slabs, saw twenty-one-year-old John Pratt held by his climbing companion when he fell. And once again, his friend was able to lower him gently to a ledge, fifty feet below.

Rescue practice at Gogarth, 1968: Photo © Dai Rowlands.

1967

THE 'HENRY SADLER' INCIDENT ON CARNEDD LLEWELYN

10 September 1967

Stories of incidents during the earlier years of the team are often hard to verify. Press reports, if they even exist, vary in their detail, memories change and fade over so many decades, paper records are lost or were never written in the first place. But sometimes, years after the event, new information comes to light, a relative of a fatality or a surviving casualty comes forward with detail only known to the family. Such was the case with the tale of 'Henry' Sadler, who died on Carnedd Llewelyn in September 1967.

Phil Williams-Jones was a SARDA dog handler and Ogwen team member at the time. He wrote a report on the incident some time afterwards. 'It was some time around noon when the call came in: a missing person, last seen somewhere on Carnedd Llewelyn. Could I go to Trasbwll, near Llyn Eigiau, with my search dog as soon as possible, to meet the inspector and police constable from Ty'n y Groes and members of the Llandudno Rescue Team.

'Once there, I heard that two teachers and three sixth formers from a school in Worthing, had been attempting the fourteen 3000-foot peaks, from Yr Wyddfa to Foel Fras. One of the teachers and two boys had been going strong and, after Yr Elen, had gone on ahead while the other teacher, 48-year-old Henry Sadler, followed slowly with a third boy, John Friars.

'Earlier that morning, Friars had been found on his way down to Dolgarrog via Cwm Eigiau, looking for help. He was interviewed by the local constable, 'Big Tom' Thomas. It seemed the teacher had become exhausted and unable to continue.

'We later learned that the other teacher and two boys had arrived on Drum, in the early hours, where a colleague was waiting in a Land Rover. Dawn broke and, although visibility was good at the time, there was no sign of either Sadler or Friars. Eventually, the group made their way to Bangor police station, to report two of their party as overdue. OVMRO was alerted and commenced a search of the route from Ogwen, by which time the weather had deteriorated.

'I was fortunate in being able to get a first-hand account of Constable Thomas's interview with John Friars. From the description of the terrain at the point where he had left his teacher, I was certain they'd come up from Yr Elen and were on the upper slope of Carnedd Llewelyn when they parted. Friars had then gone over Llewelyn and down into Cwm Eigiau. It was still dark when Friars had left Sadler.

'In those days we had no radio communications, so we didn't know that the team was

OGGI SNIPS

June 1974: Team member bends his nose by tripping (in broad daylight!) over a tussock — allegedly induced by his nocturnal habit of studying moths and their nocturnal habits.

already on the hill. Bangor police had received the initial report and called out Ogwen. Conwy police, who were dealing with the information given them by Friars, had called out Llandudno team. Consequently, there were two searches going on independently, completely uncoordinated.

'There were no suitable vehicles at Trasbwll to travel up the track to Llyn Melynllyn, so three of us — Constable Thomas, Malcolm Burrows from Llandudno and me with my dog, Tina — set off to walk up past Melynllyn to Foel Grach and onward to Carnedd Llewelyn. The weather by this time had deteriorated still further. As we crossed Foel Grach, a particularly strong gust of wind picked up Big Tom (six foot five and sixteen stone plus) and carried him quite some distance, then dropped him on his back amongst the rocks. I was fearful he was hurt — how could two of us carry him down? Thankfully he was unhurt, so we took a few moments at the old refuge for coffee and biscuits, before setting off again.

'It was around 7.00pm when we found Sadler. He was in a crawling position but had fallen forward in the lee of a low rock ridge, heading towards the summit of Llewelyn, about 300 yards away. His torch was still in his hand but there were no vital signs in evidence. His dog, a Springer spaniel was sitting patiently by his master's head. Sadler was dressed in an ex-army lightweight anorak, shirt and lightweight trousers, thin socks and lightweight boots, with no hat or gloves, although he had both in his pockets. It was a classic case of hypothermia. Still moving towards his goal, if only he had turned right downhill, he could have escaped to warmer and safer ground.

'In view of the bad weather, with darkness approaching and no way of communicating with our base, we decided to make our way down and return to recover the body the next day. Big Tom took the spaniel into protective custody. We built a cairn of white stones on the rock ridge and left.

'The following morning, the weather had improved. A party from the Llandudno team, including Ron Williams, Constable Thomas and me, walked back up and evacuated Sadler's body down Melynllyn to a Land Rover, for transport on to Llandudno mortuary.

'The photo [overleaf] shows the recovery party, just above Melynllyn, taken by Johnny Reay of Llandudno. Ron Williams is on the extreme left of the picture, at the rear, Big Tom is next with the motorcyclist's helmet, the next two nearest the camera were PCs from Conwy. I am the one in the hat and breeches and the remainder are Llandudno team members.

'It was later that we learned of Ogwen's participation in the search. As a result of this incident, better cooperation was introduced between police divisions in mountain rescue matters. It also helped the push — already well in hand — for better radio communications between base and hill parties. Another direct result of the incident was that Ron Williams and I joined the Ogwen team.'

On 6 September, the 'Liverpool Post' reported that 'after a ten-hour search in rain, sleet and gale

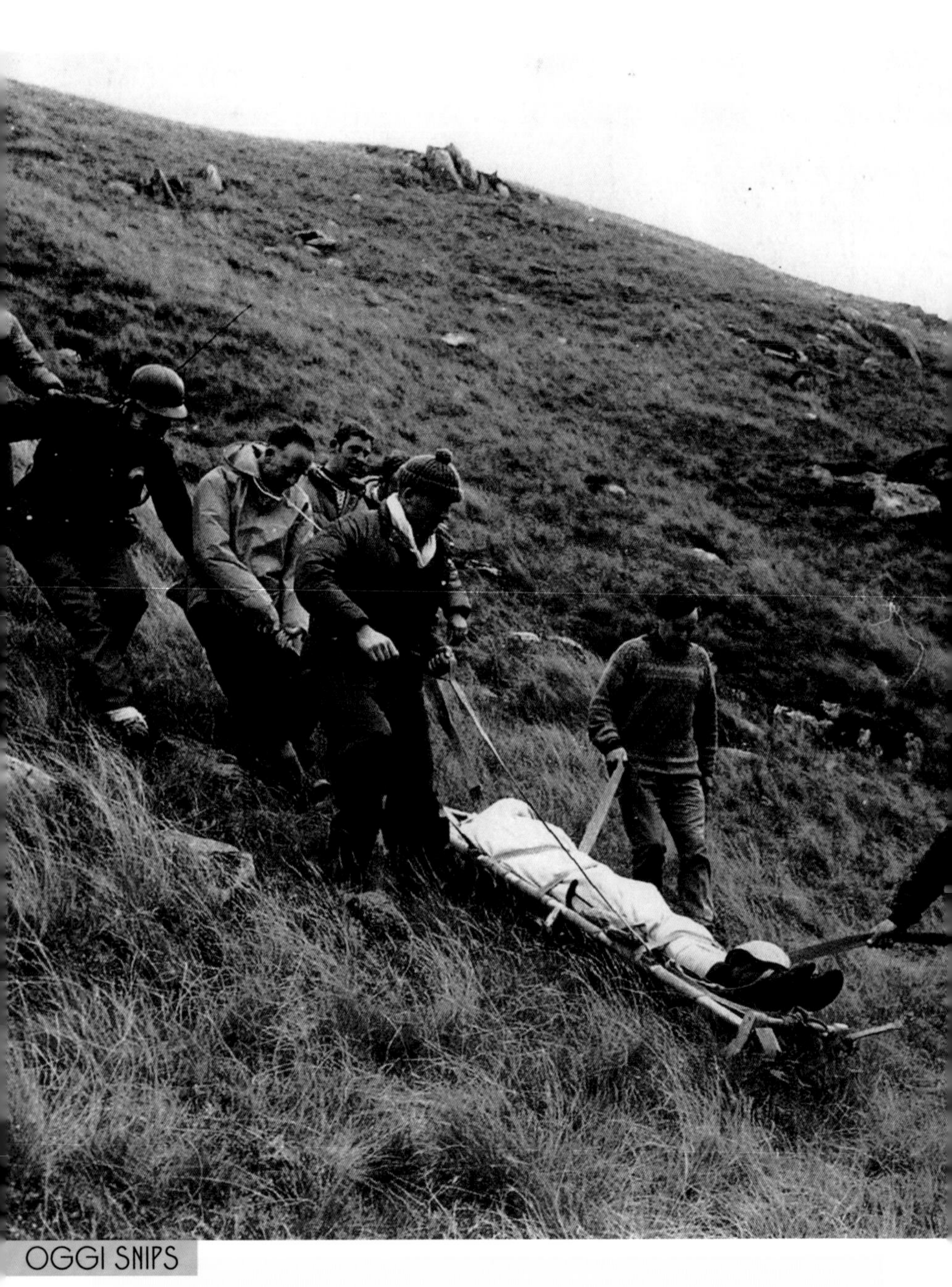

OGGI SNIPS

September 1999. 333 members are a whiz with the knitting needles, producing a variety of clowns, sailors, dolls, teddy bears and cats in fantastic detail. More wool now required…

force winds', the team had found the body of a 'middle aged schoolmaster. Standing guard over the body of Henry Sadler from Worthing, Sussex, was his brown and white spaniel which refused to move from his master's side and in the finish had to be led away on an improvised lead by one of the rescue team. John Friars had struggled nearly eight miles to safety, crossing mountain streams in full flood and arrived in Dolgarrog in the Conwy valley as rescuers were starting out on a dawn search'.

The facts of the incident, however, were not entirely correct. In 2001, a letter received by Chris Lloyd from Sadler's niece, Christine Higgs (née Sadler) threw new light on the story.

'Several of the details were actually incorrect,' she wrote. 'My uncle's name was John Harley Sadler [not Henry] and he was generally known as Harley. He was 49 years old at the time of his death. He was not a teacher but an agricultural contractor and he was the leader of a Boys' Covenanter group at his church which was a little chapel in Storrington, Sussex. He often led the lads in expeditions and they had not only climbed the fourteen 3000-foot peaks in Wales in 24 hours, but had also climbed the three highest peaks in the UK, also in 24 hours with a bit of mad driving in between! He knew the mountains well, therefore, and had also taken me up Snowdon by the Crib Goch ridge when I was in my teens.

'He was probably not as fit as he might have been having suffered earlier in the year from flu and having had a very hectic time before he drove to Wales with the group. His dog was a Welsh Springer spaniel called Theophilus (Theo for short!). He was a lovely animal, very well trained and after Harley's death he was adopted by a neighbour who was able to take him on the walks over the South Downs which he had been used to. The name of the lad who went for help was John Fairs [not Friars as reported].

'I heard that Harley was missing on the 6.00pm news in the evening, but did not realise it was him because of the inaccuracy of the report,' she adds.

The recovery party: Left to right: Ron Williams, Big Tom, two PCs from Conwy, Phil Williams-Jones in the hat and breeches. The remainder are Llandudno team members © Johnny Reay.

CHAPTER THREE

Building a home: lotteries, Land Rovers and lamb

Og Cott had served them well, but the team was fast outgrowing the space available. Times had changed too in their relationship with Birmingham Education Authority. The writing had been on the wall for some time. In late 1973, the authority had revealed plans for an extension which meant the loss of storage for OVMRO in the garage. It was proposed that the team begin fundraising for its own 'Oggi base' and later that year the education authority gave notice that the mountain rescue room would be required for their own purposes.

'There was a suggestion,' adds Chris Lloyd, 'that the shed could be relocated and used by Ogwen but — as the caravan before it — this fell foul of 'planning'!'

Whilst they had already begun looking at Bryn Poeth as a potential home, in the short term, the team's only choice was to move into the generator shed behind the old school at the back of Idwal Cottage, courtesy of the Youth Hostels Association. It was a space which afforded even less room than before. There was barely room to stand upright. It served only as a dump — in more ways than one — but it would be 'base' for two years. Some repair work was required but, by August 1975, it was weatherproof and team kit was relocated from Ogwen Cottage to Idwal Cottage and the garages of team members Tony Jones and Roger Jones.

Comfort for meetings was achieved by holding them in Tony's flat on the Bangor University campus and any social activity would invariably gravitate to Cobden's

Bryn Poeth: Pre-garage days © OVMRO.

Hotel, allegedly the 'unofficial HQ' for OVMRO, according to a newspaper report in May 1976.

Bryn Poeth, once employed as the Water Bailiff's cottage, belonged to the National Trust. During the 1950s, a man called Dudley Stevens — often heard to introduce himself to people as 'The ghost of Bryn Poeth' — had run a one-man outdoor education from there but now it stood empty.

'He certainly gave his students the feel of the Great Outdoors,' says Chris Lloyd, 'with facilities such as earth floors, outside loo and water collected from the stream'.

Without doubt, it was a very primitive building but the location was ideal, just 200 yards from the main road with space to land a helicopter behind but planning permission would be required for change of use if Bryn Poeth was to become the new base.

The Trust was happy for the team to move in but there was strong opposition from some quarters of the local community — the Snowdonia National Park Society, led by Esmé Kirby, amongst them. Esmé was a passionate conservationist and campaigner whose life had been immortalised in an international best-selling book by her first husband Thomas Firbank, in 1940. 'I Bought a Mountain' told the story of how Esmé had taken on a Snowdonia sheep farm in Capel Curig without any experience of keeping the hefted flock which had lived there for centuries.

With similar determination she initially thwarted the team's efforts to move house. Chris Briggs too, perhaps protective of his status as a figurehead in mountain rescue in Snowdonia, believed there to be no need to base a mountain rescue team in the Ogwen valley. They objected to the National Trust applying for planning permission to turn the building into a mountain rescue base.

As a result, in 1974, Gwynedd County Council refused planning permission for the change of use, arguing that the cottage might be needed for a farm worker's family. They also claimed that the beauty of the valley would be spoiled by the large numbers of vehicles which would surround the cottage at the time of a rescue.

The National Trust was reluctant to appeal the decision themselves, not wanting to incur further costs on the property. So, determined to succeed, the team approached the Welsh Office, assisted by Coventry solicitor Richard Brindley — at a cost the charity could really ill-afford. After an initial adjournment, the appeal went ahead on 13 July 1976, in the Memorial Hall at Betws y Coed. In the report of the public enquiry, the inspector said that the work of the team should be considered against the possible effect of a rescue base on the beauty of the area.

The inquiry was told that the team had to store equipment in a shed at the back of Idwal Cottage and when briefings had to be given during a search or rescue they had to be given in a car park in all weathers. Added to this, RAF rescue helicopters were obliged to land on the A5 to refuel, blocking the road. Welsh Secretary John Morris upheld the appeal against the council's decision. The team was reported to be 'delighted to have won, and won completely'.

Finally, in 1975, planning permission was granted. The National Trust employed the services of the Manpower Services Commission [Jobseekers] to refurbish Bryn Poeth. On Sunday 2 October 1977, Ogwen Valley MRO moved in to Bryn Poeth 'shortly after Prince Charles had popped in to see the work of the National Trust,' says Chris Lloyd. The original proposal had been for full occupancy but the agreed lease only allowed for use of a small operations room at the front of the building and a small, newly-constructed lean-to shed at the back, for use as a store. There was no facility for the team to use any other parts of the building except in an emergency. In fact, the

OGGI SNIPS

Everything comes to those who wait... In 1990, the landlords confirmed that they would erect a stock-proof boundary to Oggi Base. In 1998, it finally appeared.

remainder was available to the National Trust conservation parties.

The operations room was less than half the width of the room currently used for this. The back wall of the whole building was on the line of the back wall of the existing kitchen, the steps in the corridor and back wall of the bunk room. The lean-to stores were where the store room is now. The electrics were hit and miss, there was neither heating nor hot water — just a cold water tap out the back. A kitchen sink and two toilets were located in the current kitchen but accessed from an external back door. There was a potato patch some two metres below the existing car park and room for two 4x4 vehicles in front of the building. Nothing else could get up the track. Parking was limited to the grass verges of the A5. It was primitive. But it was home.

And, as with any home, there were rules. One, except during mountain rescue operations, no more than one vehicle could be parked in the vicinity of the base. Two, no dogs were allowed in the grounds, unless they were search dogs, which would be leashed the whole time, unless they were working. Three, no one was permitted to sleep in the ops room or the store room (except during ops!). And four, no litter was to be left at or in the vicinity of Bryn Poeth. A special note added the caveat that 'mountain rescue operations' included 'official exercises'.

Feeling the chill

As the years passed, it became increasingly evident that their new home was unfit for purpose. The structure was old and clearly suffering the ravages of its harsh environment, exposed to the elements, 1000 feet above sea level. And, it was cold. Very cold.

Oft repeated and variously remembered by those around at the time, is the 'hypothermia story'. The team was particularly stretched that night, with a number of calls one after the other. 'We'd three fatalities in the end,' recalls Roger Jones. 'The call had come in for someone missing on Y Garn, there were people missing on the big crags… and while all this was going on, the climbing partner of one of the casualties was 'sheltering' in the unoccupied area of Bryn Poeth while the rescue of his friend was carried out. As time went on, this chap became more and more gaga and it became apparent he was hypothermic, the base was so cold. That was the tipping point for refurbishment. We said it must never happen again.'

Jerry Gallienne, who with Jones was responsible for the renovation of Bryn Poeth, recalled that the gentleman in question had suggested 'there was more chance of getting hypothermia in Bryn Poeth than there was on the Carneddau'. Whether the hypothermia was actual or hypothetical, we'll never know, but without a doubt, it was the final straw. And a well-loved story!

Besides the need for warmer surroundings, the operational needs of the team had changed too. Search operations were frequently long, drawn-out affairs and Bryn Poeth was often headquarters for a considerable number of people. It was also vital as a training base.

It was thought only proper that the National Trust undertook some repairs but when approached, late in 1985, the Trust declined, suggesting that Ogwen do the work — and pay for it. Working with the National Trust's design team, a scheme was drawn up. The estimated cost was £55,000. The team's accounts held just £3,000. And thus began three years of fundraising.

BEDFORD
UGY 829F

Enthusiastic though the committee were, it wasn't an easy task. Initially, their requests for support seemed to receive very little consideration. Progress was slow. Then, in a change of strategy, they began targeting specific companies and organisations and this immediately brought rewards. There was much discussion about whether work should begin before the necessary cash was in the bank and generous offers to either lend the money or act as guarantor. But wisdom prevailed. Far better to reach a stage where the team could pay for any work undertaken, rather than commit members to fundraising just to pay back any loans.

By 1988, there had been just £9000 in the pot but the Sports Council for Wales had pledged £10,000, the Worshipful Company of Drapers of London £5000. Slowly but surely, persistence paid off. In the end there was £64,000 in the bank.

By February 1989, planning consent had been granted, full working plans had been drawn up and the team was in a position to start work. But not, it transpired, without a few more hitches.

'We'd been granted planning permission by Arfon Borough Council', wrote Gallienne, in the Silver Jubilee newsletter, 'but unfortunately the building we were renovating was situated in Aberconwy, despite the fact that Aberconwy denied any knowledge of its existence or location!' A change in the authority granting the planning permission became necessary to comply with the appropriate regulations. A draft lease had been with the landlords for some time, with little progress and some time and energy was required to push things forward.

'Because of the legal complexities of our working on a building which didn't belong to us and which, at this stage, wasn't leased to us, we needed two legal agreements — one the actual lease, the other a licence to carry out the work and ensure that once work was completed the aforementioned lease would be granted to us as a condition of us having satisfactorily carried out the work!'

Finally, immediately after Easter, builders were instructed to enter the premises and start work. The reconstruction of Bryn Poeth had begun. Or so they thought. Two days later the team was informed by the landlord that there was a 'minor problem' with the plans. They should be submitted to the landlord's own architectural panel for rubber stamping. This was said to be a 'mere formality' and work could therefore continue as planned. However, fourteen days later, says Gallienne, the landlord's architectural panel had indeed rubber-stamped the plans — 'by means of rejection'!

'The rejection was on the basis that the rear of the building, which consisted of our old store room and a lavatory block were of significant historical interest, having stood for all of approximately thirteen years and should, therefore, be preserved. We had to inform them that, unfortunately, the parts of the building in question now formed a substantial part of the car park having been demolished as one of the first operations and all of the rubble spread out to the front of the property. We were now confronted with a landlord who indicated that the builders should be told to stop work immediately whilst they reconsidered the plans.

'To protect the interests of the organisation, we were forced to inform the landlord that, should they find it necessary to instruct the builders as such without obtaining our prior consent, then we would find it necessary to discontinue the renovation of the building and seek alternative accommodation.'

Bryn Poeth and Blue Alex: Photos © OVMRO.

Happily, the problem was resolved and work continued in accordance with the plans — which had by then been in the possession of the landlord for ten long months. During the building work, the team was once again temporarily homeless but, thanks to North Wales Police and their loan of a Bedford Signals wagon, they had a base while building progressed.

Just before Christmas, the keys to their new base were handed back to OVMRO. Totally gutted, Bryn Poeth had doubled in size, rearranged to suit the needs of the team: the ops room was 25% wider, there was a crew room with quarry-tiled floor and two small bunk rooms, capable of sleeping twelve people. A new kitchen came equipped with commercial stainless steel units, there were two showers, wash basins and two toilets. The old lean-to stores were now an integral part of the building. There was a new electricity supply and an LPG boiler to heat the water and radiators. And the potato patch became the current car park. At last, a building fit for use and one to be proud of! By early 1989, they had moved back in.

On 12 May 1990, the new rescue base was formally opened, the ribbon cut by Bob Borradaile, the Master of the Worshipful Company of Drapers of London, in the company of 130 guests — including VIP guest, Tony Mason-Hornby. The Chronicle even reported the presence of the 'centre's rescue helicopter' — alas, funds hadn't quite stretched as far as the purchase of a helicopter. However, five team members did perform a 'hover jump' as part of a rescue demonstration, having been winched from a crag behind base.

FROM THE ARCHIVE

© Peanuts.

Have we all gone soft? Newsletter 2001: Remember those pre-Goretex days when on the hill you'd get through an Ogwen wetting then return to a damp little tent pitched opposite Idwal YH? Now we all go home to a brick tent, hot shower and central heating but, in the early days, many team members came from afar at weekends to camp in the trees.

There was an art to pitching your tent. The site may look level and green, but it's actually an old spoil tip from the Tin Can Gully quarry. The art was in remembering exactly where you'd pitched the previous week — and which bent and twisted peg fitted at each corner. And, strangely, the tent always went up better if we'd called at Cobdens first!

Many have memories of 'camping at Og', some not always so happy. One team member dislocated her kneecap when her dog bounded past, knocking her to the ground. She refused the offer from team members wanting to practise their first aid and reduce the dislocation. One happy camper witnessed his tent, complete with contents, fly past en route to Capel, one very windy day. And another was rudely awoken when team members forced a sheep into the tent — to give his dog some company!

OGGI SNIPS

September 1998: 'Oggi base remains helpless in the face of sheep who nibble the grass to a number one shave and cattle who push topsoil down the hillside better than a JCB.'

The Drapers had been long-time supporters of the team. In 1982, they had donated £500 towards binoculars. Six years later, they sent £5000 towards the Bryn Poeth fund, so it was only fitting they cut the ribbon. The minutes for September 1973 record an invitation for the Master Draper to become a member and a proposal that the Drapers 'receive metal badge number one'.

The new metal badge had been designed by Ron Williams early in 1972, inspired by a coiled rope and twin ice axes on the wall at Plas y Brenin — which, in turn, inspired the same arrangement on the chimney breast above the wood burner in Oggi base. At the April meeting, it was noted that the cost of the die was £30 with a subsequent cost of 87p per metal badge. The February newsletter reported that the new badge would be £1.50 to team members and that, as a general guideline, a person should have been a full team members for two years and have participated in twenty 'significant rescues' before earning the right to wear it (a cloth version was still available). Team members who wished to sport the metal badge were required to apply for one and the committee also reserved the right to ask for it back, at which point they would receive a refund of one pound.

The system is still in place. 'Attending base to make the tea or holding someone's hand to walk them around Llyn Idwal does not count,' says Chris Lloyd. 'After written application to the committee, the qualifications are checked and the award made or not. Team members still have to pay a deposit for the badge — an incentive not to lose it as it remains team property. In theory, it should be surrendered upon resignation and the deposit refunded but usually it is gifted to the retiring member. The first batch were numbered and number one was indeed presented to the Master Draper. After the three-day search for four missing boys in Easter 1973, the Drapers donated a good sum to OVMRO.' Lloyd himself holds badge number 58.

Prior to this, there wasn't an 'official' team badge as such. During 1972, name tags had been introduced. 'The original concept,' says Lloyd, 'was to have a number of people available for call-outs in the valley at weekends. Team members would arrive for a day or a weekend's climbing. They'd sign in on a board in the 'garage' giving their name, route and number in the party then try to complete their day by early afternoon, ready for the witching hour of 4.00pm. Team members — especially Tony Jones — would sit on the wall next to the old Brew Shack on the A5 above Ogwen Falls, drinking tea (Tony engrossed in a cowboy book) and await the call-out or the pub opening. One member, Vic Simpson, made a new board which is still upstairs in Oggi base, though it was never used. Vic's wife', he adds, 'was known as Plus One, because he always signed her in on the board as '+1'. Nobody knew her first name!'

The idea was that team members would remove their engraved Bakelite dog tag from their necks and place it on the board. After the rescue, they'd pick it up again. That way they knew everyone was off the hill.

'In those days,' says Lloyd, 'there were only about three hill set radios and no mobile phones. So a member could easily be mislaid. The system died out after we had to leave Og Cott for the small generator shed at the back of Idwal YHA. I suppose as there wasn't a proper base with a wall where you could hang such things, the concept died out and it was never reintroduced when we moved to Bryn Poeth. It's a good job we don't do this now, as some members are renowned for leaving things behind — rucksacks, wallets, boots… cars!'

Sharing, growing and making space

The team had made huge strides forward, but there were still a few hurdles to leap. The National Trust, impressed by the vastly improved facilities now available at Bryn Poeth, decided it would be ideal as accommodation for their Acorn holidays. It was a further two years before an agreement for shared use was finally made, in late 1992, but it wasn't easy having a building that served two purposes.

'For the next fifteen years or so,' says Lloyd, 'these hard-working footpath builders and conservation workers risked being woken up in the night by team members on a call-out!'

The Trust eventually backed out because the property no longer suited their use and the lease was renegotiated when Ogwen became a charitable incorporated organisation in June 2015.

Despite initially being forced to share their space, Ogwen continued to invest heavily in Bryn Poeth. In the late 1990s, transport options were limited. Team members were forced to make do with Tony Jones's own vehicle during rescues. That, or share the backs of Land Rovers with bales of hay, whilst the local farmers transported them up the mountain. With the new base now up and running, they decided it was time to invest in their own vehicle and, in January 1995, the team took delivery of their first Land Rover Defender 110, at the cost of £18,000. Now they had a new problem to solve: they needed a secure, weatherproof home to house it in!

To fund building a garage, the team applied for Lottery funding through Sportlot. Established in 1999, the Sportlot Community Chest was set up to support locally-based sport and physical activity projects throughout Wales. But, disappointingly, their initial response was that Ogwen's garage was outside their remit, despite — some might say — a clear connection with physical activity of the highest order.

Not to be beaten, Ogwen set about challenging the Sportlot response. A good number of telephone conversations and a huge amount of determination on the part of team member Paul Henshall, and some 350 letters later, Sportlot agreed it may be in their interests after all and offered £17,500, including VAT, towards the £40,000 project to not just build a garage, but refurbish and convert the loft space.

'During the work,' explains Chris Lloyd, 'we realised that if we called it an annexe rather than a

FROM THE ARCHIVE

Casualty escapes with only a 'hurt shoulder' in 200 foot fall, September 1970: Two young men had more adventure than they'd bargained for when they nipped to a disused slate quarry near Bethesda to tinker with a derelict car. The car went over the edge of the quarry, swiftly followed by one of the men, Ronald Watson, when he lost his balance. Two fire officers, an ambulance driver, a PC and a doctor went down the quarry pit on a rope to find Watson had escaped with only a hurt shoulder. There followed a tug-of-war-like rescue as Ogwen team members hauled casualty and stretcher up the sheer quarry face.

OGGI SNIPS

October 2015: Overheard. Over beer. On the nature of call-outs. 'We're entering a new era of incompetence. We've had the brilliant mountaineers... now we're back to the idiots.'

garage, it would be zero-rated for VAT. We duly informed Sportlot, only to be told we'd now be receiving just £14,000 towards the garage!

'Then, shortly afterwards, Sportlot advised us we had been overpaid by a thousand due to the grant being given as a percentage of the overall project and that by saving the VAT, the percentage was effectively reduced and we owed them a thousand pounds!'

This seemed somewhat unfair and a meeting was called.

'It was a memorable meeting,' recalls Lloyd. 'Feelings were running high. So much effort by so many and now this. At one point, one team member reached across the table towards the Sportlot representative, clearly intent on making the man see sense, before being swiftly reminded we might need them again! But he had a good point — we'd saved three thousand pounds on the project and now they wanted a thousand back!'

The application form itself had been no mean feat, with 72 pages to complete, and the team had to change their constitution to allow disabled people to carry out rescues. Henshall was a keen negotiator, not given to early surrender. Dave Worrall clearly recalls Paul's mantra, when in discussions with the Lottery: 'No is not an acceptable answer'.

Work on the new garage began in September 1996. William Hague, then Secretary of State for Wales, visited in January 1997, just before completion of the building works in February. On another sunny May day, Anne Ellis (newly appointed as an honorary team member) officially opened the new garage and loft conversion. Anne had been a generous benefactor over many years. Alongside her, the team had appointed another two honorary members in Dennis and Louise Johnston who had recently retired from the Llyn Ogwen café. Other guests included the Chief Constable of North Wales Police, Michael Argent, who had agreed to act as patron.

The day also saw the launch of Ogwen's new support organisation, Treble Three, to help with vital tasks like fundraising and giving talks to local bodies.

The lamb factor

Paul Henshall would later be responsible for fundraising when the first Land Rover needed replacing, by way of a sponsorship deal with the Welsh Lamb Association and Safeway supermarkets, HM Bennett and Lynpak.

HM Bennett Limited (now part of Randall Parker Foods) was a privately owned processor of beef and lamb based in Andover, Hampshire. A lamb specialist, they serve a range of markets from retail to wholesale, at home and abroad and all the Welsh hill farmers were loosely contracted to them. In 2000, they were providing Welsh lamb to 260 Safeway stores. That's a lot of meat and a wide marketplace — and a fantastic opportunity to promote mountain rescue.

Negotiations took some time, culminating in a fantastic deal, quite unique in mountain rescue: for one month, Ogwen would receive 5% from sales of all the Welsh lamb in all 260 Safeway stores and the packaging would feature the team logo.

The promotion launched on 24 July at the Royal Welsh Show in Builth Wells, with the team Land Rover on proud display for the day, nestled into its very own rustic flowerbed. So successful was

RESCUE
X958 RJC
Safeway

MEWN BUSNES FARMERS IN BUSINESS
WFS
Group
WELSH
LAMB & BEEF
PROMOTIONS
PHOENIX
MOUNTAIN RESCUE
AMBULANCE
WELSH
LAMB
SUPPORTED BY
Safeway
DONATIONS MADE TO WELSH MOUNTAIN RESCUE WHEN YOU BUY THIS PRODUCT
OGWEN VALLEY MOUNTAIN RESCUE ORGANISATION
RESCUE TEAM

the promotion that the Welsh Lamb Association and Safeway agreed to continue for a further month, enabling the team to buy outright a new £25,000 Land Rover.

When the Land Rover was delivered, in 2001, the team put on a party at Bryn Poeth, welcoming members of the Welsh Lamb Association, local farmers and dignitaries, as well as fellow rescue organisations. They'd hoped it would be good PR for all concerned but sadly the TV news carried nothing on the story. Foot and Mouth had broken out that day.

With refurbishment, Oggi base became a comfortable, social place to be, a focal point for the team, but in many ways Bryn Poeth has remained a work-in-progress. In 2003, an assortment of rotten windows were replaced with Danish custom-made windows — some if which are rotten again, in 2015 — and the driveway from the A5 was surfaced with heavily reinforced concrete, making base a great deal more accessible to non-4x4 vehicles. A second garage was built over the winter months of 2004. It was officially opened by Richard Brunstrom, the then Chief Constable of North Wales Police, in August 2005.

In 2012, with the National Trust finding Bryn Poeth no longer suitable for their use, the operations room was extended into the first bunkroom and the remainder of that bunkroom knocked into the second bunkroom, with overall accommodation reduced from twelve to eight. This gave a more practical ops room and a comfortable second bunk room which could be used as a private area for relatives and friends of casualties — hopefully a little warmer these days.

'Oggi base has come a long way from its caravan in 1965,' says Chris Lloyd. 'Whilst Bryn Poeth might not be as practical as the modern 'custom built' mountain rescue team bases, it's in the heart of our operational area. And it boasts many facilities, including an en suite landing zone for the helicopters and one of the best views in Wales!'

Business as usual

In amongst all the fundraising, of course, there was much to occupy team members. An increasing number of incidents involved young people, but not just in Snowdonia. Across the UK, a series of fatal accidents involving school parties led to long debate in Parliament, about the 'safety in outdoors pursuits' for youngsters heading to the hills in search of adventure. But it was an incident in the Lake District which prompted concerns about the safety of team members.

In June 1969, on Low Crag in Buttermere, members of the Cockermouth team gathered with their team leader Jock Thomson and his friend, Kathryn Walton who had just achieved her mountain instructor's certificate at Plas y Brenin. The exercise was the opportunity for Walton to demonstrate a new technique of stretcher lowering with the stretcher horizontal, guided by two barrowboys. The first run went smoothly, with the 'casualty' (cunningly concocted from a sleeping bag and rucksack) delivered safely to the foot of the crag. On the second lower, with a real person strapped in the stretcher, an extra rope attached, and Thomson and Jim Coyle as barrowboys, disaster struck. The huge belaying rock gave way, sending everyone involved tumbling down the crag in a shower

Land Rovers and lamb: Top & inset: New vehicle launch, just as of Foot and Mouth breaks out. Bottom: Team vehicle on display at the Royal Welsh Show in Builth Wells © OVMRO.

of debris. The heavy stretcher, casualty still inside, landed on Walton. Trapped by her legs, her pelvis and one arm were broken. Thomson lay quite still, with fatal head injuries, despite wearing a helmet. One of the belayers had been catapulted onto the scree about four yards away. He later died in hospital. And Coyle remained hanging from his safety line, about four feet from the ground, his arm broken.

News of the accident travelled quickly through the mountain rescue community. In August that year, the Ogwen minutes record a donation of £10 to be sent to the Cockermouth team appeal fund — half of a £20 fee the team had received from the BBC filming of a rescue practice at Tremadoc — heartfelt support for their rescue colleagues in the Lakes.

Neil Adam recalls that after the incident, team members went back to Tin Can Gully, a regular training spot, and drilled bolts into the rock. Up until that moment, mountain rescue teams by and large comprised groups of young mountaineers, giving something back to an activity they loved, pooling their skills and experience to help fellow climbers in trouble. Clearly there were concerns about safety, but now they were having to think beyond the safety aspect. Now there were serious concerns about insurance.

In September 1959, an insurance scheme for rescuers had been set up through Lloyds, which gave £1000 cover at death at a premium of £100 per annum. It had seemed perfectly adequate at the time, according to Noel Kirkman, then chairman of the Mountain Rescue Committee. In his potted history of mountain rescue, he explained that the insurance had been arranged after 'considerable effort', largely due to the difficulty of defining 'genuine rescuers'. This was solved by the phrase 'using official MRC kit'. No claim was made until the Cockermouth accident. The insurance company paid out but the terms of renewal were unacceptable and in any case the cover had become too small due to the effects of inflation.

With help from other quarters, including Lord Hunt and the Prime Minister, Jim Callaghan, the Mountain Rescue committee persuaded the Association of Chief Police Officers to support an insurance scheme arranged through the police. 'So far as the law is concerned,' wrote Kirkman, 'mountain rescue teams act on behalf of the police in rescuing the injured and removing the dead and over the years the police have in fact become much more involved in mountain rescue organisation'. The result was that, in 1972, the Home Office agreed that chief constables might, 'if

COBWEB CORNER

Newsletter June 2001: A group of Scottish climbers learned the hard way not to get stuck, the day after being overheard slating mountain rescue teams in the pub. 'One Saturday night,' recalls Chris Lloyd, 'we were called out to a group stuck on the Devil's Kitchen. We approached from the top and called down. 'Are you alright?' 'Aye,' came the response, 'throw us a rope'. 'Are you the members of the young Scottish Climbers' Club who've been reported missing?' 'Aye, we are', came the response. 'Now throw us the bloody rope!' 'Are you safe and uninjured?' 'Aye, we're safe and okay.' 'Well... if you're safe and not injured, we'll be back in the morning to rescue you!'

OGGI SNIPS

'That prince of Welsh peaks which from all angles is grand and unmistakeable'. Hamish Brown, English writer and mountaineer, speaking about Tryfan.

they considered it necessary in their police area, pay an insurance premium for mountain rescue teams, sufficient to give cover of £32,000 at death [the 1977 figure].

In November 1971, the Ogwen team received confirmation that North Wales Police would be supplying personal accident insurance cover and, by March 1973, the police had agreed to insure members for up to four practices a year. The names of those involved would be required up front. It was later found that this was insufficient to cover any self-employed member so the team offered to pay a top-up premium to enhance the police scheme. The regional body now pays this for all the teams in the region.

Slips and trips

'Missing youngsters' and 'death plunges'regularly topped the press reports of the early 1970s. Frequently, the stories involved a missing person, a plunge and a shocked girlfriend or family member left to cope with the aftermath, all wrapped up into one 'good' news story!

In early March 1971, a young climber saw his father slip and fall to his death while scrambling along Bristly Ridge between Tryfan and Glyder Fach, 3000 feet up. Fifty-year-old Bernard Richardson sustained severe head injuries after slipping on soft snow. His twenty-one-year-old son was unhurt save for a slight injury to his leg as he came down the mountain to get help.

Later that month, a girl student watched in horror as her companion 'plunged head first to his death' off a cliff. Roped together with his girlfriend, John Francis had begun climbing the first pitch of the 400-foot Spiral Stairs on Dinas Cromlech when he slipped. He'd barely climbed twenty or thirty feet when he fell on his head, the piece of tree he'd grabbed still in his hand. From the ground, his girlfriend could only watch in horror, unable to prevent his fall. Ten miles away, in the Ogwen valley, a rescue helicopter rushed another man to hospital after he fell off Idwal Slabs.

In January 1972, a young Army officer 'plunged' 500 feet into a gully on Crib y Ddysgl, grabbing the headline 'Snowdon plunge kills officer', despite another incident unfolding across the mountain. Earlier that day, nine students had been found huddled together in Cwm Tryfan after another big rescue operation. Not wanting to risk the lives of the young soldiers in his charge, twenty-five-year-old Lieutenant Andrew Marshall had gone on ahead in very poor conditions to explore a possible route. An officer with the King's Own Scottish Borderers — and an instructor at the Army's Outward Bound Centre in North Wales — he had travelled to Snowdonia with other officers and a group from the Junior Infantry Battalion. Having instructed his group to remain where they were, he struck out to find the route. Two hours later, when Marshall failed to reappear, they were led off the mountain along another route by a sergeant.

Police officers, rescue teams from Ogwen, Llanberis, RAF Valley and RAF Stafford, and search dogs and handlers took part in the operation — some passing within feet of the lieutenant's body in the darkness. It was 8.45am the next morning before dog handlers found his body in Parsley Fern gully, lightly covered in snow. He had died of shock, following multiple injuries.

Meanwhile, the six men and three girls who'd been rescued earlier were reported to be 'lucky to be alive', in something of a journalistic afterthought.

On Wednesday, 9 November 1988, fifteen-year-old Anna Humphries walked out of school and disappeared. Hours later, farm labourer David Evans, who lived close to Anna in the village of Penley, had also vanished. Anna would routinely walk home from school, to be met halfway by her parents but, as their daughter was being attacked, Rosemary and Trevor Humphries were trapped in a traffic jam.

Anna was a keen 'Neighbours' fan. That very evening, her two favourite soap stars would finally tie the knot. But, as Charlene and Scott exchanged vows in Ramsay Street, Anna was nowhere to be seen. 'We tried not to worry,' said her mother, 'but we knew something was wrong. She would have called. That was the kind of girl she was.'

A hundred and fifty people joined the search, from a number of mountain rescue teams — a search which would last nineteen days. On the Friday, Evans was named as a suspect, as forensic experts examined his car, a green Austin Allegro. By Saturday, it became clear that his passport, £200 in cash and clothing had also disappeared. On the Sunday, searchers found one of Anna's black pointed shoes and, by Tuesday, her school friends had re-enacted Anna's last known movements. A week later, the police discovered that a passenger named Evans had taken a hovercraft to Boulogne on the day they had both vanished.

Anna's distraught father offered a reward on the head of the 31-year-old bachelor and the search wore on. Then, finally, Evans was arrested while hitchhiking on a deserted country road near Lyons. Interviewed for ninety minutes by Detective Chief Inspector Colin Edwards and Sergeant Philip Thompson, the information he gave was a breakthrough. The hunt switched to the Severn and West Mercia police searched a fifteen-mile stretch of the river throughout the weekend. Anna's body was less than a hundred yards from the base established by the Cheshire Police Underwater Unit at Hampton Loade. She was fully clothed and wedged under a tree overhanging the riverbank.

More details emerged. Evans was a violent man and convicted rapist, and this was a sex attack that had gone badly wrong. As he struggled with Anna, the car windscreen shattered. With her body still in the boot, he went to a garage to get a new windscreen fitted, drove forty miles to dump her body, then travelled to France. His mother, it was said, aware of her son's previous violent behaviour, informed the police, who published his face widely. A lorry driver in France recognised him several days later.

Evans confessed. It was later reported that he had approached Anna for directions. As she leaned into his car, he bundled her in. Forensic tests also proved his guilt. Blood in his car was the same group as Anna's. Fibres and a button from her clothes were also found and there were fragments of glass in the car and on his clothes. He was sentenced to life imprisonment, with a recommendation that he serve at least thirty years.

Tragsitz rescue practice: Jerry Gallienne carries Clive Hughes during a practice in Tin Can Gully. Note the lack of 'safety' rope and karabiners © OVMRO.

1973

THE DAY SEEMED SO GOOD: THE BATTLE TO FIND FOUR LOST BOYS

Easter weekend 1973

Four teenaged schoolboys from Hertfordshire kept themselves occupied with sing-alongs and snacks from their rapidly dwindling rations, when they found themselves marooned in the mountains for three days and nights in April 1973, on what should have been a very different weekend. It was the final stage in their Duke of Edinburgh Gold Award, a four-day trek, over fifty miles of challenging terrain and the culmination of many months of training — an exercise for which they were well-prepared.

All of them had some experience with map-reading and compass work and with them they carried a tent, food, two primus stoves and emergency rations. Each boy had a polythene survival bag, sleeping bag, anorak, waterproof over-clothing, a change of dry clothing, first aid kit, map and compass, torch and whistle. But Stephen Attwood, Terry Hankin and Graham Brown, aged sixteen, and fifteen-year-old Christopher Dell survived because they remembered their first lesson on walking in the mountains: when in difficulty, just 'sit tight'.

At 9.00am, on Good Friday morning, 20 April, they were all set to leave Capel Curig. The weather was 'quite fine', confirming an earlier forecast from the BBC. But what the boys didn't know was that the Manchester Met Office had painted a very different picture — with temperatures in the mountains dropping towards freezing, cold rain and hill fog throughout the day. With characteristic bluntness, Tony Jones was later to remark that the boys should never have been allowed out in such conditions. 'It was cold, wet and horrible and when you are only fifteen or sixteen, you do not have much in the way of reserves, either mentally or physically, if things go wrong.' Thankfully, these four boys proved themselves to have plenty in the way of reserves.

The boys were in the charge of 29-year-old Roger Baldwin, Youth Officer for South East Herts, with other instructors on hand as assessors. Confident that reasonable weather was assured, Baldwin saw the boys off from Capel Curig, along the old drovers' route to the track junction and down towards Llyn Crafnant and Trefriw in the Conwy valley. Five miles and three hours later, they were seen by one of their assessors, all in good spirits.

From Trefriw, they were to climb steadily to Llyn Eigiau, then more steeply up to Foel Grach, a lonely mountain refuge, where they were due to meet two of their assessors at 5.00pm, and

OGGI SNIPS

North Wales is home to a community of relict plants known collectively as arctic-alpine plants more common at the end of the last Ice Age in the mountains of Snowdonia.

bed down for the night. At 3.50pm, they were reported to have been spotted by other mountaineers, some way off-course by the side of a stream and 'less than half way' along their planned 16-mile route for that day. And the weather could no longer be described as 'quite fine', as the boys faced driving wind and rain and plummeting temperatures.

Cold and tired, they struggled on through fog-shrouded rocks and deepening gullies, as the rain turned to sleet, then snow, their way forward barely visible. Finally, an hour after they should have checked in at Foel Grach, and with one of the youngsters, Christopher Dell, showing signs of hypothermia, they reached an agreement: to pitch their tent and 'sit tight'.

They settled down in their tent to eat the last of the day's food supply — sausages, peas and potatoes. All they had now were their 'iron rations' — Kendal mint cake, chocolate, glucose, soup and condensed milk — the same kind Edmund Hillary and Sherpa Tenzing had taken to the summit of Everest. But surely they would not be there long?

When they woke the next morning, six inches of snow lay on the ground. It was foggy and freezing. Realising they were safer where they were, again they reached agreement: to ration their remaining food and continue to 'sit tight'.

In his later statement to the police, Graham Brown noted that at noon, he and Terry left the tent to attempt to find the mountain refuge hut but were unable to because of the dense mist. They retraced their footprints back to the tent, arriving there about 12.30pm. At around 6.00pm, he said, they heard voices outside. 'Thinking it was our instructors we called out and I went to the front of the tent, opened the flap and saw it was a man and a woman. The man said 'We are lost'. I laughingly said, 'So are we.' He got out his map and I too got a map. We compared where we estimated we were and agreed.

'I cannot remember the exact conversation, but the man and his wife told me they were making for Bangor and hoped to continue over the summit. I think I mentioned that Christopher wasn't feeling so well but I can't be sure. I certainly did tell them we were working for our Gold award. About this time, visibility improved slightly and we could see quite a distance downwards, although it was still misty above. The man went down the slope looking for a landmark. Stephen and I walked down to where he was, about 200 yards below, and saw a track in the valley, about half a mile from where we were standing.

'He told us he didn't think the weather would improve and was considering going down and leaving by way of the track. We walked back to the tent, leaving the man and woman outside and didn't see them again. At no time did we tell the couple we were worried about our position — we were not worried and quite confident we'd be able to move off the following morning.'

OGGI SNIPS

Cwm Idwal was designated as a National Nature Reserve in 1954. It was the first such site in Wales.

Meanwhile, when the boys failed to arrive, Baldwin and the other staff members grew concerned for their safety and carried out their own 'minor search operation' along the route the boys should have taken, but to no avail.

As Saturday night came and went, the weather began to ease. Keen to continue on their way, the boys began to retrace their own steps, back to lower ground but, two miles on, the weather closed in again and it started to snow resulting in 'white out' conditions. Good sense prevailed and once again they resolved to stay put, pitching their tent on the Sunday afternoon on the Gledrffordd plateau. There was nothing more to do but sleep, listen to the small transistor radio which Graham Brown had taken with him, and sing their favourite hymns — including, somewhat appropriately, 'Guide me, Oh Thou Great Redeemer'!

Throughout Saturday and Sunday, Baldwin and his group of assessors continued to search as best they could but who could rule out the possibility that one of the boys had fallen ill? Or simply fallen? So, at 3.45pm on Easter Sunday afternoon, they were forced to admit that 'it was bigger than they could cope with' and reported the situation to Ogwen Cottage.

There was little could be done in the failing light, bar a low level search by Ogwen and RAF Valley team members and local police officers, with a large-scale search planned for first light. Tony Jones and Ron James would be the search coordinators. By then, seven mountain rescue teams had been drafted into the task, alongside SARDA, the RAF, helicopters from C Flight and the North Wales Police. On the second day, an informal 'search panel' was set up, including the search coordinators and representatives of all the organisations taking part, to plan the most effective use of all the resources available. It was a pivotal point in the way mountain rescue is organised in North Wales. The experience gained in this extensive operation proved invaluable in the setting up of a more formal search panel by the North Wales Mountain Rescue Association, in November 1973.

On Easter Monday, fifty people searched the Carneddau in very poor weather, joined later in the day by search dogs and the helicopter. Alistair Haveron, one of

Rescuers assembled: Image courtesy of Stephen Attwood, one of the four 'lost boys'.

the RAF Valley party leaders reported over the radio at 10.30am that conditions were 'just about a white out' and too bad for a line search of the easterly slopes leading up to Foel Grach. News very quickly spread. The press and BBC were quick to pick up on the story, keen to discuss the implications and, almost immediately, more volunteers began to arrive at Ogwen Cottage, climbers and hill walkers from across North Wales.

Multi-agency, multi-team operations have become more commonplace in recent years, but not in the 1970s. The sheer numbers involved in this search (which gave rise to it being dubbed 'The Easter Riots') required significant organisational skill: briefing and debriefing, establishing search areas, liaising with the police and the RAF, dealing with willing 'outsiders' wanting to throw their weight into the search effort. Not to mention engaging with the families and those who had been instructing and assessing the boys.

The incident highlights too, the changes in communication technology which have radically altered the way missing persons are reported, searched for and communicated with. With the advent of the mobile phone, 'lost' and injured persons can not only report themselves as such and continue to communicate with the rescue team but, thanks to smartphones — with their integral GPS capability — and the SARLOC app, a lost person can be located to a precise grid reference, enabling rescuers to go direct to that location. [More about SARLOC on page 227.]

Bob Maslen-Jones, in 'A Perilous Playground', describes the process in some detail in his account of the incident. 'As they arrived, each group or individual was asked to report to a command centre manned by the police where details of their experience, age, fitness, home address and so on were recorded, and each group of twelve people was briefed by Tony Jones to carry out a detailed search of a given area. The search area was gradually being expanded to cover the possibility that the boys had travelled further than had been thought.

'After a day's searching, the search parties returned to base perplexed that they had found no trace of the boys. Every news bulletin from then on carried up-to-date information about the progress of the search operation and, at 6.00am on Tuesday morning, Stephen Attwood's father, who knew that the boys had a small transistor radio with them, broadcast a message telling the lads there was an extensive search going on and they must carry out their survival procedures and wait for help to arrive.

'The message was heard inside the tiny tent. It gave Stephen quite a jolt to hear his father's voice, but it cheered them up to know that a lot of people were out looking for them. Any thoughts of making another attempt to rescue themselves were forgotten and knowing that it could not be long before they were found, they just sat and waited.'

OGGI SNIPS

Since 1999, Cwm Idwal National Nature Reserve has been 'rewilded', leading to a reduction in grazing and a change in the vegetation around the reserve.

At 7.00am on the Tuesday morning, 483 searchers, five search dogs and their handlers gathered at Ogwen Cottage for their briefing and, by 8.00am, the first parties were on their way to their allotted search areas.

With the cloud base still low, the RAF helicopter was initially restricted to searching lower down the mountainside but, as the cloud lifted, they were finally able to fly higher up. And as the clock ticked through to mid-morning, still huddled together in their tent, the boys heard the distant rumble of the Whirlwind helicopter. Knowing their tiny shelter would barely be visible,

...changes in communication technology which have radically altered the way missing persons are reported, searched for and communicated with... Thanks to smartphones — with their integral GPS capability — and the SARLOC app, a lost person can be located to a precise grid reference, enabling rescuers to go direct to that location.

shrouded in the mist, Stephen clambered out of the tent and headed towards the noise. It was almost a mile before he emerged from the mist, waving his arms above his head.

The boys were found at Gledrffordd Ridge, half a mile up the Carneddau range, in what was described as 'a courageous piece of airmanship' by the pilot, Flight Lieutenant Gordon Mitchell, navigator Flight Lieutenant Stan Burt and Master Aircraftsman Stan Ormiston.

They had taken the aircraft along a corridor only twenty foot high, between the snow-covered ground and the low mist — with visibility less than 100 yards. 'I suppose it was a bit tricky', said Mitchell, modestly. 'We went to have another look today at areas we could not reach yesterday because of the low cloud. I suddenly spotted an orange object on the ground. We landed near it and it turned out to be the cover of some sort of equipment. We thought we would search the area more thoroughly. Almost immediately, my winchman saw one of the boys running down the hill waving something over his head'. The boys were duly picked up and flown to Ogwen Cottage and the curative properties of hot soup.

The team's newsletter, later that year, recorded the grateful thanks from the boys and their parents. Mr and Mrs Attwood expressed 'very great feeling of relief', thanking the team for the

OGGI SNIPS

During the annual stretcher race, 'casualties' often jumped off to run alongside when out of sight. These cheating ways were overcome by replacing the casualty with a telegraph pole.

tremendous amount of work and personal hardship they endured to rescue their son and his three friends, a sentiment echoed by the other parents. The boys themselves said they would 'be eternally grateful for the marvellous work', apologising for the 'large amount of trouble' they had caused. Other thanks came from Lord Snowdon, the Private Secretary to the Duke of Edinburgh, the Hertfordshire Education offices and the BBC.

Debate continued for some time afterwards. Ron James speculated that the boys may have survived 'perhaps another four or five days', adding that they had done just as they had been instructed to do. However, he was critical of the hike itself.

'Fifty miles is an awful long way for teenage boys to go in these mountains at this time of year. This is the most appalling part of the episode — that the 50-mile walk is laid down in the rules for the gold medal. Perhaps,' he suggested, 'the rules should be looked at again. Fifty miles on Dartmoor in June is one thing. Fifty miles in Snowdonia in wintry conditions, is quite another matter.'

There were concerns about the delay in reporting the boys missing and Baldwin's reliance on a seven-hour-old weather forecast. Had he taken heed of the updated forecast, the boys might never have set off or, at the very least, been able to halt their hike at Trefriw. But there was no doubt that the boys' decision to sit tight had saved their lives. There was speculation whether the boys would be required to re-take the expedition section of the award scheme, possibly in Derbyshire. An official of the Hertfordshire education authority said it was possible that they be granted the award anyway, because of the initiative and courage they had shown and the fact that they had obviously absorbed their training. One of the rescuers was reported to say he thought it unlikely they would gain the award, because they did not report back by 7 o'clock on Sunday night and did not finish the fifty miles,' adding that 'they should have the medal for their sheer guts'.

In fact, the boys were offered the Gold Award but, with great strength of character, chose to repeat the expedition the following Easter 1974, again in North Wales, along a different route — as Stephen Attwood confirms.

Eye in the sky: RAF Whirlwind helicopter searches the area.
Image courtesy of Stephen Attwood.

OGGI SNIPS

En route to a call near Harlech, four Land Rovers drove over the timber toll bridge at Penrhynduedraeth, each claiming the 'one behind' would pay. Who did remains a mystery...

'Our 'retake' corresponded with the BBC's 'Tuesday's Documentary' feature 'The Day Seemed So Good', filmed in the October half-term of 1973 in North Wales, and timed for the first anniversary of our little adventure.'

The programme aired on 9 April 1974, at 9.25pm. A further note in the team's newsletter, in May 1974, reads that 'comment from lay people suggested that it was well received.' However, 'the two tone sirens were by courtesy of the BBC — no one else knows anything about them!' Perhaps a degree of artistic licence had prevailed, yet Stephen Attwood confirms that the reconstruction of the actual expedition and their life in the tent held pretty true to events. And, finally, the boys had achieved their Gold awards. They remain in touch to this day and, certainly for Stephen, the episode had done little to curb his enthusiasm for the mountains.

'After successfully completing the Gold expedition, I and several others went on to complete the Mountain Leader Course Summer training and were associated with further John Warner School expeditions in North Wales as instructors for many years. Summer 1988 saw a group of these expedition helpers have their own two-week walking holiday in the Austrian Alps. I went on to follow groups around the North Wales countryside until 1989, when work took me to the US for several years.'

Now back in the UK, both Stephen's children have achieved the Gold Award and he celebrated his 50th birthday by walking with his son from Rhyd Ddu through the old mine workings — very familiar ground — to meet his daughter. She had just finished a week in Wales for her Silver Expedition at the Herts Snowdonia Centre at Nant Gwynant, where he used to stay 35 years before.

'I still love walking,' adds Stephen, 'and completed the 40-mile Lyke Wake Walk (a sixteen-hour trek) a couple of years ago with a group of work friends, more than 25 years after completing it the first time'.

On their way down: With the RAF crew (left to right) Stephen Attwood, Graham Brown, Terry Hankin and Christopher Dell. Ogwen's Tony Jones in the foreground. Image courtesy of Stephen Attwood.

Inset: A year later, the boys return to Wales to complete their Gold Award in the company of a BBC film crew for 'The Day Seemed So Good'.

CHAPTER FOUR

Taking care of the casualty

Whatever happens in the name of mountain rescue, whatever research, whatever developments, the one guiding point of focus is the casualty. Always. Long before the Ogwen team took shape, mountaineers who also happened to be eminent doctors, accustomed to receiving into their emergency care the broken bodies of those who fell, were putting their minds to improving the lot of the injured hill-goer. Wilson Hey had set the tone in the early twentieth century, risking his good name and freedom pursuing the use of morphia, so convinced was he in the benefits of pain relief for mountain casualties.

Legal recognition, after years of resistance from the Home Office, wasn't just a huge leap forward, it was a line in the sand. Never again would mountain rescue step back behind that line. Care of the casualty could only move forward. Nowadays, not only do teams expect to train and be proficient in the delivery of first aid — the casualty expects to receive it. Whatever the casualty's injuries, that bunch of people who turn up to help them must surely know what they're doing? But how did we get from strapping people to finger posts with nothing more than a prayer to relieve their pain, to the professional, often highly-advanced casualty carers of today?

Ideas have come and gone over the years, protocols changed, techniques and equipment grown more sophisticated, but still the 'casualty is king'. The constant

Casualty care: Practice on the hill © OVMRO.

striving to better what went before, to learn from experience and the evidence gleaned, has always been strong in Ogwen, but one man is regularly credited with taking casualty care to another level entirely. As a climber himself, Dr Ieaun Jones understood that team members were doing the best they could with what knowledge they had, but their medical skills weren't enough for the bigger emergencies.

Having qualified in 1959 from Guy's Hospital, specialising in trauma and orthopaedics, Jones moved to what was then the Caernarfon and Anglesey General Hospital (C&A) in Bangor the following year. Concerned by the flow of patients coming in from mountain accidents, he tells how he went along to Chris Briggs to offer his services, but Briggs turned him down. Not so Ron James, however, and thus Ogwen Cottage became the first rescue team in Britain to have full formal medical training.

He describes how he 'bargained' with the team. 'They had practically no idea of first aid, so I suggested that if they taught me to climb, I would teach them first aid.

'They were given equipment and bandages, but if they saw somebody lying down, they only had a rough idea what to do with them. They'd focus on getting the person down as quickly as possible, practically running back down the hill with the stretcher, which was great — but not necessarily great for the patient!'

Despite morphine having been made available at the posts, it was rarely used. When a casualty was in pain, the attitude tended to be 'You're a big strong lad, you don't need morphine.' So Jones set about teaching team members about the properties and effects of using the drug on a patient. This teaching was extended when Tony Bennett, leader of the RAF Valley MRT, asked him to sign the certificates that allowed the RAF team members to carry morphine. 'I found they knew nothing about the properties and effects of morphine and gave them instruction in the subject such that they could answer questions when I tested them.'

First aid courses were uncommon, apart from the St John's Ambulance, but even then the course material didn't address the kind of problems rescuers might encounter. Jones contacted the St John's Ambulance Brigade in Bangor, and arranged to run a course under their auspices. The idea was that they would then issue a certificate to those who passed an assessment at the end of the course.

Based in the hospital's physiotherapy department, the classes used a combination of practical demonstrations and colour slides — many of which left little to the imagination. And they were definitely not for the faint-hearted, as Tony Jones recalls. 'His live lectures, often delivered while smoking a cigar, would last some two hours, the audience enlivened by comments such as 'the next rather gory slide shows...' It wasn't unknown for the occasional candidate to faint when a particularly gory slide appeared on the screen.'

Barbara James too remembers the seemingly 'coded' cigar puffing which punctuated the slide shows. 'We always knew a three-puff would be one heck of a gory slide!'

Ieuan Jones invited St John's members, ambulance men and mountaineers to attend his classes but, he recalls, it soon became clear that it was easier to teach first aid to mountaineers than to teach anything about mountain conditions to first aiders!

In 1964, he had reached a crossroads in his career and wanted to specialise, so left the area for

OGGI SNIPS

From the 'pink' forms, October 1982: Two passing leprechauns stopped this party's aimless circling and showed them the way down.

the East Midlands, to work for the National Coal Board as their medical officer. As part of his duties, he ran courses of lectures on first aid as Assistant County Medical Officer for St John's. Perhaps not surprising to those who have undergone Dr Jones's rigorous testing, that year the brigade annual report showed a big increase in the number of those who had failed their tests!

'I realised,' he said, 'that I was responsible for half the national failures. This explained to me why the Bangor division had looked rather shocked the previous year when most of them too had failed my test!'

Two years later, he returned to Bangor as head of the accident unit. Current team doctor, Glynne Andrew spent six weeks as a medical student at this unit. 'Ieuan was in an unusual position being in charge of the accident unit at the C&A, as the unit was properly integrated with the trauma ward and the trauma theatre. Thus he was working in a well set-up emergency department before the specialty of emergency medicine existed in the UK. During my six weeks there, I was very impressed with how well organised it was compared with the units in Sheffield, where I was a student — and Ieuan was largely responsible for that.'

There had been a rumour Jones was coming back, so the team was all set for him to run a course on his return. 'I turned up at Ogwen Cottage to find the new team had been created in my absence! I was invited to sit on the committee and promptly got stuck into delivering courses in first aid for mountain rescue'.

Ieuan Jones's lectures ran on one evening a week at the University College of North Wales. His 'First Aid in Mountaineering' course won the support of the St John's Ambulance Brigade headquarters in Wales, thanks to their senior officer, Don Williams, and they issued a special certificate for the course. Jones slowly increased his collection of faint-inducing slides but, he says, 'it took me many years to complete the collection with a slide of fern-shaped lightning burns'!

Barbara James was one of the first to attend the lectures. They brought memories of an early encounter with trauma. 'The group of schoolgirls were testing their newly acquired boots on the lowest reversible holds on Ordinary Route, Idwal Slabs. The day was warm. Observers, passing comments, were sprawled on rocks that offered the best viewpoints from a horizontal position. Ron James was soloing about fifty feet up Hope, when there was an unforgettable thud.

'Instinctively, I pushed the girls around the corner, as one thud followed another. Ron froze and held on tight. She landed where I had been standing, having missed her grab at the rope of a leader on Faith. A pretty eighteen-year-old lay unconscious, clothes in disarray. It was in the days before airways and she bit Ron's finger in her death spasm as we carried her down.

'I thought of her as I watched Ieaun pace the stage at the university lecture theatre, and in the pregnant pause as he puffed on his cigar. I thought of her as I struggled to select the best of two seemingly equally correct answers. And I especially thought of her as I scrambled up a dirt bank in the forest near Betws y Coed to reach a 'victim' draped with ropes and suspended from a tree. For this was 1967 and the first of Ieuan's courses. The 'victim', by the way, was none too happy when I extricated the lump from under his tongue with a very dirty finger — as had most of the other candidates!'

The practical training sessions and the individual practical examinations were run by Jones's wife, Joan, who by all accounts was a highly competent, and very strict, nurse. After the lectures, everyone would migrate to the pub — a great opportunity to discuss the topics raised.

'Ieuan,' adds James, 'was a very brave doctor and those unlucky enough to be injured owed him an enormous debt. For over twenty years, his hand guided rescuers throughout the whole of Britain, yet most of the casualties never even knew his name'.

Dr Ieuan Jones's course became well established as a standard for first aid in the mountains — far beyond the mountains of Snowdonia — and it would be the cornerstone of the team's training until the late-1990s. As demand grew, he continued to develop the courses, introducing first an advanced, then an instructor course. The first instructor course ran in November 1968, based on his famous collection of taped lectures and slides. It was clear that the standard of first aid training in Wales was far above any being delivered elsewhere.

'Between 1978 and 1983,' says Tony Jones, 'some 2359 candidates had attended the basic course with a pass rate of 69% but many found the contents and standards required anything but basic. His slides not only illustrated the range of injuries, but also laid the foundation for what could be encountered on the hills. Unintentionally, this proved to be an early example of 'psychological

FROM THE ARCHIVE

Hot dog, 14 June 2010: Three team members took it in turns to carry a tired and injured Labrador down hill, during a hot summer's day in June. Exhausted ten-year-old Nero was on an expedition with his owner Alex when they got into trouble and had to call mountain rescue. The two of them had walked through Cwm Idwal and the Devil's Kitchen onto Y Garn, when Nero began to feel the effects of the warm day and the hard surface beneath his feet, suffering 'raw paws and failing back legs'.

Alex had been assisted by several passers-by who noticed the dog was in distress and, having aborted their planned route over Glyder Fach, they progressed down Y Gribin. The descent starts with a steep and time-consuming scramble and Alex quickly realised she needed help. She dialled 999 around 2.00pm.

A party of four team members went to her location, carrying with them a pack frame and large zipped bag. Initially, Nero was placed in the bag and strapped to the pack frame then carried down as if on a small stretcher. But there was some concern that he might be overheating in the bag so it was decided that faster progress would be made by carrying him over team members' shoulders. So three of them took it in turns while the fourth escorted Alex off the mountain. Needless to say, dog and owner were delighted to be reunited at Bryn Poeth some fifteen minutes later.

OGGI SNIPS

Bryn Poeth means 'hot hill' or scorched earth owing to the top soil there being so thin on the bedrock.

inoculation' to reduce stress.' The rigorous final examination tested his students' skills and clinical knowledge to the extreme but Dr Jones grew increasingly concerned that non-mountaineers could pass the exam without ever having been on a mountain. His worry was that such a person might be drawn into a difficult rescue situation and prove to be a danger to themselves and others. So he introduced an intermediate theory test which included questions about basic mountaineering skills such as navigation and compass work. It was an effective filter for the non-mountaineers.

I didn't want anyone to have a certificate who wasn't able to get to the casualty in the first place,' explains Jones. I was testing people who were very much better at it than me, but I needed to know they had competence on the mountains.'

Stuart Dethick, who was instrumental in developing the Ogwen stretcher, recalls how Jones would invite selected team members to the hospital to see how things worked at the sharp end — with all the sights, smells and sounds that accompany traumatic injury. 'He was a bit of a maverick in his own way, but his training was very good. You'd go into the operating theatre and accompany him on his rounds. In the casualty department, you'd see people coming in and he'd put you on the spot, getting you to suggest diagnoses without access to the X-rays, using what clinical knowledge you had. He'd ask tough questions — very scary but if you were there, you knew you had his trust.'

Team members would see how a casualty might respond to pain and treatment and, under supervision, learn at first hand the art of handling broken limbs and damaged people, and it was an element of Jones's teaching style from the very beginning.

Barbara and Ron James were students in Jones's first advanced course. She recalls that once the theory and practical exams were complete, they were required to attend the accident unit at the hospital. The day remains etched on her memory. On the previous evening, two girls had been in a road traffic collision in their Mini. 'One unbroken limb remained between them. One girl was unconscious and unable to be taken into theatre because of chest complications. Examination revealed that she had a missing bony prominence in her left elbow and other injuries. While I was at her bedside, she became critical and internal cardiac massage had to be tried there in the ward. Sadly, she died.

'Next we were taken to the foot of a bed with a huge dome — similar, Ieuan said, to the treatment used for hypothermia. Unwisely, I relaxed. As the sheet was pulled back I was unprepared for the sight of an old lady with third degree burns from head to foot, who was conscious and able to talk. The smell finished me and I had to find fresh air and a tap to quench a desperate thirst — a classic symptom of shock!

'Ron survived to carry on and hold the bowl while a knee was aspirated. He received certificate number one. I returned the following day and survived, achieving the number two certificate.'

Jones would go out on a rescue if he was available but, he says, he didn't see himself as a full team member, more an instructor who might go out if needed. 'The belief was still that a doctor's place was on the ground not on the mountain but I always believed that whatever skills I had in dealing with trauma, I was prepared to offer to the casualty. You have to remember there were no paramedics in those days — we'd go out to these awful accidents and do what they do now.'

His teaching, he says, 'broke the barrier that first aid only went up to a certain point beyond which it should be in the hands of a doctor. I was teaching the techniques that were needed, how not to make things worse. The first aid books until that point were written in chapters, each specialist writing their own bit, but some of the things in one chapter might interfere with stuff in others. It wasn't joined up.'

In 1973, the team published a booklet on the topic of mountain rescue, linking the thoughts and skills of Tony Jones, then team chairman, with those of Dr Ieuan Jones. The somewhat long-winded title was perhaps characteristic of the academic discipline whence each author came. 'Some thoughts on the organisation of mountain search and rescue operations' by Tony Jones, with 'Notes on mountain rescue first aid' by Dr Ieuan Jones was, wrote Tony Jones, a 'short essay' aimed at their own team members but he hoped 'others in the mountain rescue service might find something of interest' there. Ieuan Jones's notes were very specific to the difficulties of dealing with frostbite, hypothermia, lightning strikes and stretcher handling in the mountain environment.

'People underestimate,' says Tony Jones, 'what Ieuan did. He really was very significant.'

Proud, and yet quietly modest, about his achievements, Ieuan Jones is frank too about the things which didn't work out as hoped. A bit of a 'radio ham', he persuaded Dr David Last, a lecturer in the electronics department at the university, to cooperate on a device which might aid in the diagnosis and treatment of a casualty. Described as an 'audio modulator facility', the device would send back data from the incident site to the hospital such as pulse rate, blood pressure, respiration rate and ECG readings. It had its drawbacks. As a piece of additional equipment to carry up the hill, it was fairly bulky and initial trials showed there to be a lot of interference for a constant signal. Perhaps most significantly, if Ieuan wasn't available at the hospital to receive and interpret the information, it proved an impractical tool. The idea was shelved and it was back to the radios.

Efficient radio communications between hospital and rescuer could be vital in saving a life. On one occasion, a walker had suffered a heart attack high on the Glyderau. Ron James radioed Jones

FROM THE ARCHIVE

18 November 2003. Three 'young lads' lost on the Glyderau: The message that came through said simply that 'a seventeen-year-old was distressed after a hard day' but the reality was a little different. Three 'young' men were lost somewhere above the Plas y Brenin to Pen y Gwryd road and in need of assistance. The day had started out well enough. The three were staying at a hotel in Capel Curig, and had left their car in the village car park before taking the bus to Ogwen, then walking up via the Devil's Kitchen. Their intention was to climb the ridge to Capel but, on the plateau south of Caseg-fraith, they realised they were running out of time and daylight. With no torch between them, a boulder field ahead of them, tired and aching limbs and immense common sense, they dialled 999.

They were gratefully escorted off the hill in high winds and driving rain, highly amused that the original call-out had described them not just as one individual but, more importantly, as 'a young lad', comprising as they did two sixty-eight year olds and one mere youngster of sixty-five.

OGGI SNIPS

The Guardian, 5 June: Police received 70 calls after jubilee revellers set of flares and fireworks in the mountains above the Ogwen Valley fearing they were distress flares.

to ask for advice. He explained the symptoms and was told not to rush the man down but to put him in a tent, keep him warm and quiet and wait 'and I will get some pills up to you'. The pills duly arrived by runner and, soon after, the man was carried back to the Pen y Gwryd and a waiting ambulance. He made a full recovery but it could have been a very different story.

Another project involved a cocoon-style stretcher, which might prevent a casualty becoming hypothermic during evacuation. Peter Ellis, a design student at Birmingham Polytechnic, asked Ieuan for some ideas for a project he was doing on the design of a new type of stretcher. The result was a human-shaped fibreglass cocoon in two parts: the body and a lid. A see-through panel in the lid reassured the casualty that he hadn't been entombed. Hot air from a portable heater would be fed through ducts into the shell, the temperature adjusted as necessary. The design was developed and the prototype built but it proved 'too heavy and cumbersome,' wrote Bob Maslen-Jones. 'It ended up as a huge yellow sledge which was once seen floating across Llyn Idwal and was later used as a carriage for Santa Claus!'

Beyond the valley

Throughout the late-1970s, there were the first stirrings of change at national level — doubtless influenced by Ieuan Jones's ground-breaking work in North Wales. Others too were working hard not just to raise standards in first aid but to ensure those same standards were adhered to by all the teams. Dr Peter Andrew, a GP in New Mills, was already credited with moving the cause of mountain rescue in the Peak District forward. In 1977, he was elected to the Mountain Rescue Committee and immediately appointed as secretary to the medical subcommittee, serving jointly with Oliver Cowpe as the honorary officers for morphine provision

He was keen to see a certificate accredited by the MRC for first aid training for mountain rescuers. In 1980, arrangements were made with the British Red Cross Society for a certificate to be over-stamped 'Mountain Rescue Approved Syllabus.' And in 1989, the Department of Health agreed to fund first aid equipment provision to mountain rescue teams. This was a significant achievement, enabling the then Northern Regional Health Authority to supply equipment to teams throughout England and Wales, with an initial budget of £30,000.

Work was also going on to improve the understanding of hypothermia. In July 1979, Neville Marsden, a GP and member of the Rossendale Fell Rescue Team produced 'Diagnosis Before First Aid: A Manual for Emergency Care Workers'. He too was running courses locally but, in the main, teams were dependent on St John's and the Red Cross.

In 1982, the MRC decided to establish its own syllabus, course, examinations and certification. As with Ieuan Jones's courses, the emphasis was very much on the practical and it was around this time that the term 'casualty care' became more generally used, perhaps a more accurate reflection of the various aspects of mountain rescue.

It was some years before publication of any standard written teaching material, however. 'Casualty Care in Mountain Rescue' was launched in September 2000 and continues to be a base line training manual across the UK but this is just a foundation on which the Ogwen team has continued to build.

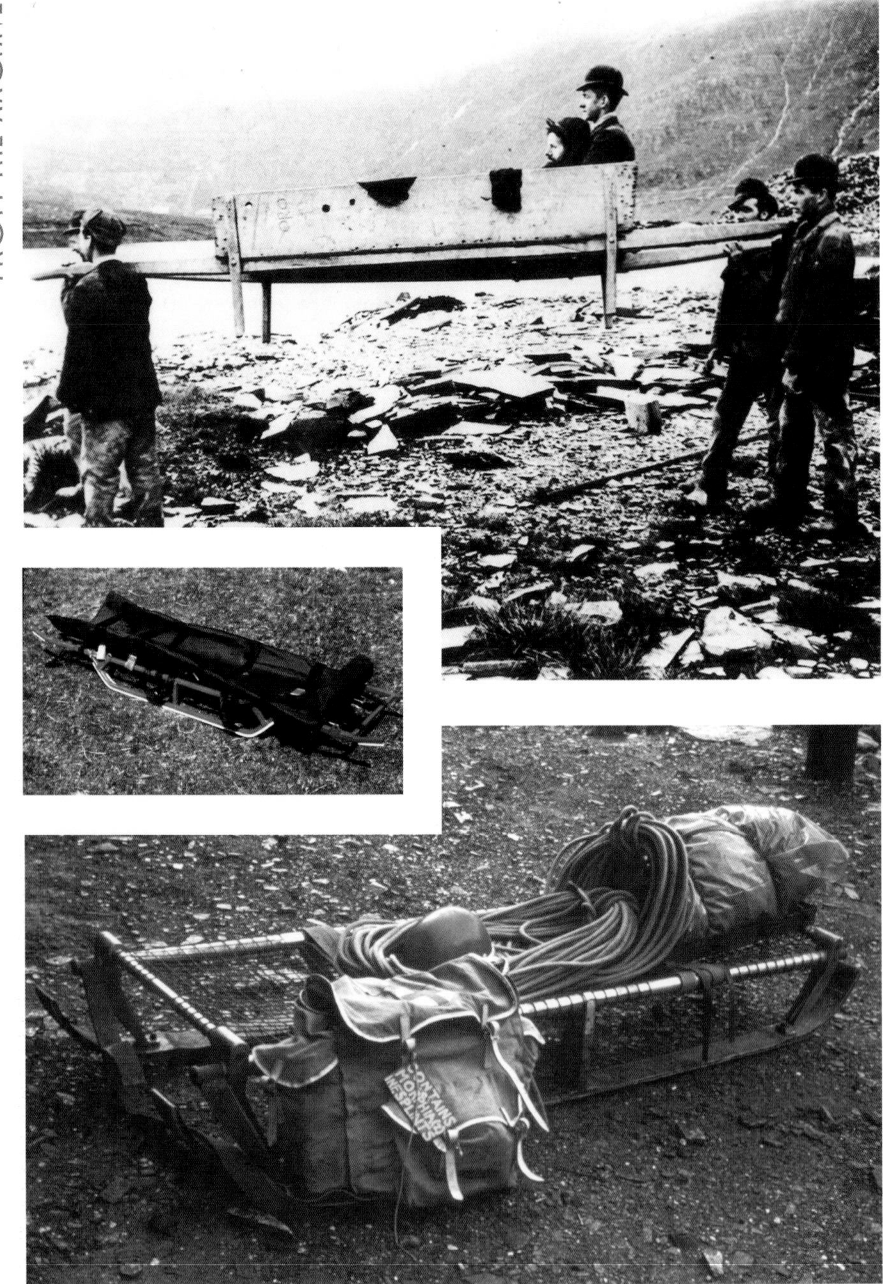
CONTAINS

Boy, you're gonna carry that weight...

One of the driving factors in any developments has been the frequently extreme nature of incidents and the difficulties of transporting equipment up to an incident site on team members' backs! The search for a more efficient means of extracting and carrying a casualty has been a constant — as was the desire to lighten the load.

In 1968, Ron James published in the 'Alpine Journal' a comparison of mountain rescue stretchers used in Britain at the time. Many of them have figured in Ogwen's history. Some of the older relics still hang around at base, and some fell by the wayside.

The Thomas stretcher, then standard equipment at the posts, was originally designed to collapse sideways, to make it easier to carry by two people along narrow paths and tracks but this feature had been dropped at an early stage to reduce production costs. Consequently, the Thomas became a rigid one-piece stretcher. It was, said James, 'awkward to carry and particularly difficult in scrambling territory such as the north ridge of Tryfan'.

Peter Bell, well known across mountain rescue for his eponymous Bell stretcher, had already begun the manufacture of a hood-style head cage in 1967, designed to match the Thomas. The following year, George Fisher, team leader of Keswick MRT, sought his guidance on the possibility of dividing the Thomas across the centre to enable a two-person backpack carry. Bell had actually already devised a way of achieving this, also incorporating a revolutionary wire mesh bed. In came the orders and he had carried out about twenty such conversions when the further supply of new Thomas stretchers for conversion was abruptly refused by the manufacturer. Some four months later, they offered their own 'transverse split' version of the Thomas, complete with a wire mesh bed.

The new Split Thomas was 'cheaper, simpler and lighter', noted James. The two pieces could be carried over the shoulders of two teams members whilst following 'a face route of Grade 3'. The mesh head guard protected the casualty — and the 'jockey' on vertical lowers — and could be reversed as a back support for sitting injuries. The canvas bed had been replaced by plastic-covered wire net. This, he said was now used for almost every rescue for two of the Welsh posts and it withstood rough usage 'exceptionally well'.

The folding stretcher designed by Hamish MacInnes, for use in the difficult terrain and long distances found in the Scottish Highlands, wasn't as comfortable to carry up hill and it was shorter than the Thomas, prompting James to speculate that 'overall, one gets the picture (which Scottish rescuers tend to encourage) that all patients come from south of the border and are under five foot six inches, and all rescuers are Scotsman over six foot!'

Two years before his article, James had introduced the Mariner stretcher to the team. It was widely reported to be the first new stretcher to be introduced to British mountaineering for thirty years, although MacInnes had produced his Mark 1 folding stretcher in the early 1960s. It cost £150 and should have attracted an import duty of 25% but an appeal by the team resulted in this being waived.

Sebastian 'Wastl' Mariner was an Austrian alpinist and a pioneer of mountain rescue, dubbed

Carrying the load: Top: Thankfully, the wooden, coffin shaped stretcher no longer in use! Slate quarrymen transport a casualty © Gwynedd Archive. Inset: The 'Oggie' stretcher. Bottom: Thomas stretcher. Photos © OVMRO.

the 'father of mountain rescue' in Europe. Affectionately christened the 'Sosban' by team members, this 'one wheel litter' could be lowered down the highest crag in Wales. It could be handled by just four men, rather than the usual eight and required 'only' three reels of wire to be carried onto the hill, rather than a thousand feet of rope. It meant, it was said, that areas that once were inaccessible with a conventional stretcher could be reached quicker — and the casualty brought down much sooner. 'Sosban', incidentally, is Welsh for 'saucepan'.

Made of thin tubular steel and glass fibre, it was collapsible and also had a clip-on wheel. The casualty could be secured in the stretcher by means of four pairs of straps. 'No longer,' ran the press reports, 'will ten men have to struggle with six or seven ropes 300 foot long to rescue a climber in trouble', enabling a rescue to be 'done in half the time taken by an ordinary British stretcher.'

These were high hopes. Unfortunately, they were set to be dashed as the wire and winch were so heavy. Neil Adam remembers an occasion on the Black Ladders, when there were two casualties on a cliff. 'The idea was to lower them to the bottom. We had five members at base, two stretchers, cas bags and 2000 foot of wire, the winch and all the gubbins and somehow we had to get it up the hill! The five of us stood there scratching our heads. In the end, we got the RAF to haul it up!'

The Mariner never really took off. 'It seemed ideal for sea cliffs,' says Roger Jones, 'but it didn't work. The wire was spiralling and bunching. In the end, it was consigned to the bin'.

The Tragsitz harness was another Austrian invention, essentially a carrying seat for use with casualties who could be transported safely in a sitting position. It was very portable and easy to use on crags when lowered by means of a friction device. However, on scree and poor paths even when using a long pole for support, James concluded that it was difficult to carry a patient by this means for very long.

The Perche Barnarde was a French stretcher which was very portable, breaking up into five loads, each about six pounds in weight. When assembled, it resembled a pole with a patient in a hammock below it. It couldn't be slid on rock, snow or the ground but on searches for exposure cases it was, he said, 'quite useful to take into high hills'.

Thanks to James, a number of bits of kit found their way to the team from Europe. Neil and Maggie Adam recall travelling to Austria on a climbing holiday, taking with them a wish list for the

COBWEB CORNER

Newsletter June 2001. The wonders of the mobile telephone: These days, mobile phones are often the first bit of kit to be used but things aren't always quite as straightforward as simply picking up the phone. When one man witnessed an accident on the Glyderau and immediately phoned for help, little did he know that Dublin was the nearest available receiver. After many minutes of confusion, the operator realised the problem and phoned a friend in Merseyside Police. They, in turn, phoned North Wales Police, who made a call to Ogwen. Who then telephoned the informant... who was only one mile away.

OGGI SNIPS

Weekly News, May 2012: Too many people reach for the mobile before thinking to get themselves out of trouble. And when we get there, they're sitting next to the path!

team and a couple of banker's orders, with strict instructions on how much they could spend. Mission accomplished, their next task was getting past Customs officers who didn't take too kindly to the 'bullet connectors' in their baggage. 'We had a letter from the Customs and Excise HQ,' says Maggie, 'but the guys still wanted us to leave the kit behind. Eventually, they let us through but not before we'd demonstrated how it all worked. The bullet-shaped connectors joined two bits of wire so it didn't snag on the rocks.'

Meanwhile, Peter Bell had been pipped by the manufacturers with their own a split stretcher design. With orders to fulfil, he set about designing and manufacturing his own stretcher. With the full patent through in 1972, the robust Bell stretcher was set to become a standard workhorse across mountain rescue. This too is heavy but, ironically, it would be the development of a lighter stretcher which finally prompted the team to buy the Bell!

Lighter, leaner, faster

Stuart Dethick first got involved with the team in 1981. An outdoor instructor, young and new to mountain rescue, he became frustrated by the 'old' way of doing things. 'The philosophy was old-fashioned. Team members were going at the pace of the slowest person, with huge items of equipment like the Thomas stretcher on their backs. The rucksacks weighed a ton, chock full of stuff. The med kit was a nightmare — everything for every eventuality and 95 per cent of it for no reason at all! There were still guys around wearing Tricouni boots and tweed plus-fours.'

Like Ron James before him, he was inspired by what he'd seen in the Alps. 'Going light was quicker. It was the way forward. I wanted to change the philosophy.'

The first thing he tackled was the medical kit. 'Tony Jones loaned me maybe fifteen, twenty years worth of incident forms. I tabulated every single injury we'd dealt with to see where the real work was. Leg injuries were top of the list, head injuries, then fatalities, followed by flailing limbs, fractures and wounds. Some of the stuff we carried just wasn't necessary. If we were going to someone with a broken ankle, why did we need to carry collars?'

There were younger team members, says Dethick, who wanted to be able to run up the hill — often in trainers, not boots — so he set about designing a modular sack, one that would be easy to carry. 'Then we needed to look at other things. The Thomas stretcher was okay, the Bell was strong. They reckoned you could lift a Mini on one, so we gave it a go and bent the thing! But when do you evacuate a Mini? We needed something light, easy to put together, and quick to deploy.'

The result was the 'Oggi stretcher'. Dethick cracked the design in time-honoured fashion, on the back of a beer mat! The team agreed a £400 grant for its development and by 1989 they were being marketed. A second one was commissioned in 1991 and five years later they were structurally tested for winching into the Wessex helicopter.

'There was a practicality to it. Everyone else was making stretchers with a join in the middle, so I designed a solid centre with separate ends to slot in. The bed lets light through so the casualty can be X-rayed while still in the stretcher — useful in the case of suspected spinal injuries.'

'Team members loved this stretcher,' says Chris Lloyd, 'because the five pieces could be divided amongst team members and no one or two people were left carrying what felt like a hang-glider on their backs, but this too had its disadvantages. One of these was that, to other teams, it looked rather like a Meccano set without the assembly instructions — and, of course, all five people had to arrive on scene in order for the stretcher to be assembled!'

It was at this point the team addressed that problem by purchasing a Bell stretcher, so that stretcher carries in northern Snowdonia were not exclusive to those who had mastered the Oggi stretcher!

'The next thing,' says Dethick, 'was prompted by Ieuan's concerns about stretcher bed sag and how that might affect the management of spinal cases. The upshot was we moved to a plastic bed, a bit like the Sked [a stretcher designed specifically for use in confined spaces. Made from a heavy sheet of plastic, it becomes rigid when folded around the patient]. I took a prototype down to show people and it went out the same day. We were a bit nervous, but it worked.'

One of the characteristics of Ogwen's work is the steep terrain and, occasionally, the team has to lower a stretcher a very long way. 'The old fashioned method was with someone at the top and a barrowboy. The trouble with that was you went down like a yo-yo and somehow always managed to go past the ledge. The RAF were starting to look at abseiling with the stretcher. The principle was good so I went to Denny Moorhouse and said I wanted to build something.

'Denny was the founder of DMM, the first guy to make aluminium karabiners. He put me in touch with a chap called Fred Hall and I spent weeks building an auto-locking descender. The idea was you pulled a handle and you could control your abseil with the stretcher and static ropes. The stretcher moved down the rope. That device established the whole idea of standing on the stretcher.

It meant the good climbers in the team could run on ahead as the advance party to set things up. The rest of us could leg it in with the bum bags and do our stuff, then hand over to everyone else. The whole aim was to move from the siege mentality to being a little bit smarter.'

Resourcefulness was still the name of the game. He recalls one time on Tryfan when the 'ledge bag' hadn't arrived, so between them they cobbled together about 200 karabiners just from the contents of people's rucksacks. 'You realised you could do things without all the heavy stuff,' he explains. 'In the early days you were carrying mega-ropes. But why not do as they do in the Alps and keep it light. Keep things moving through. The biggest challenge was that the RAF guys were 'just round the corner' with their helicopters so it became a race to beat them to it. 'You had to run to do that, so you had to be streamlined.'

John Hulse was experimenting too, stuffing a fishing vest with medical kit so he could get up the hill fast without the weight of a rucksack. All of which is fine for the 'hasty parties' but, of course, team members still need to carry the stretcher and the heavy ropes and technical equipment required to lower it safely, so it's not all lightweight kit and bum-bags.

Dethick left the team after twenty years when he moved away from the area, but the pursuit of that holy grail of speed, efficiency and lightness of weight continues. Now there are lightweight oxygen and Entonox cylinders and lightweight blood pressure monitors. There are AEDs in the team vehicles and finger pulse oximeters carried by the front line cas carers. There are neoprene splints, lightweight cas bags and vacuum mattresses. The medical kit contains lightweight thermal jackets or bags to keep the casualties warm. And, of course, science and technology have helped hugely with all of this through the development of ever lighter, more efficient materials.

In terms of stretchers, one Oggi stretcher is still available for use — 'great in windy conditions,' says Chris Lloyd, 'because it's demountable. We have two up-to-date Bells. In 2014, we bought the Ferno Titan stretcher as used by the RAF and we've recently had the Tyromont bag on trial but see little use in holding one'.

A recent investment in equipment has been a medical training manikin, the most expensive piece of kit purchased after transport. This inflatable doll can breathe, has a pulse, a chest that moves and even makes throwing-up sounds. The complete casualty experience! 'It has already proved its worth during diamorphine training,' says Andy Harbach, 'to demonstrate how to treat someone recovering from an overdose'.

Continuing professional development

All the kit in the world is worthless without training and the team has been fortunate from the start in having dedicated and resourceful doctors, trained nurses and, more recently, paramedics to guide and train them in the necessary skills. By the late-1980s, the reduced availability of Dr Ieuan Jones's advanced level course meant the team had to look elsewhere for high-level training.

At one stage, Louise Dethick helped organise training for a number of members at Sheffield

High level travel: Tony Jones takes a hi-line in the Perche Barnarde © OVMRO.

University hospital in advanced level trauma care. She was also one of the tutors. 'It was a truly hospital-based course,' wrote Clive Hughes, in a summary of casualty care in 2006. 'There were very few pre-hospital components and we even looked at the theory of invasive techniques such as peritoneal lavage and management of cardiac tamponade'. Over the top possibly, but there were many elements they could adapt and use in a rescue environment.

In fact, Clive Hughes and Marion Waters did much to advance the skills of team members over a thirty-year period, Hughes as a passionate and dedicated first aider, Waters in her professional capacity as an emergency care consultant. It was during 1997, whilst team members were assisting with a Children's Day at the Countess of Chester Hospital, and chatting with A&E doctors about their need for more advanced training, that Marion Waters first met 'mountain rescue'. It was a serendipitous meeting.

'We agreed to look into the provision of an advanced level course but then realised it would be difficult to do that without knowing what lay in between that and the basic one-day course. Consequently, we also ended up writing and running what became known as the Emergency Care for Mountain Rescue (ECMR) intermediate and advanced level courses. The drawback was that my previous experience in pre-hospital care didn't equip me for working in a mountain environment.'

In an echo of Ieuan Jones's bartered exchange of skills many years before, Waters struck a deal that the team would teach her about their environment if she helped them with the training. 'This,' she says, 'was at some personal cost, as I had to overcome my fear of heights!'

The principle of advanced trauma life support had arrived in the UK from the United States in 1989 and revolutionised the way things were done. The approach was to look for and treat life-threatening injuries first while upholding the principle of 'do no further harm'. This was new to mountain rescue too but the result was a continuity of care all the way through the process — from the hill to the paramedic or winchman, to the A&E department and onwards to the ward.

'Running that first course was an education for all concerned', says Waters. 'We found an open, friendly, enthusiastic, outrageously cheeky tribal community with the different tribes sitting very apart in different areas of the room. But by working in small groups, with scenario-based teaching, they had no choice but to work together and learn from each other.

'Take analgesia. Candidates had to practise giving intramuscular injections of saline (not morphine) to each other. It was a great confidence booster — and it meant more casualties could receive pain relief out on the hill.

'The primary and secondary survey approach to casualty assessment meant some long cherished concepts had to go too. First was the belief that the casualty should be carried on the injured side. Anyone who has ever broken a rib would probably agree this wasn't a great idea! If they didn't have a pneumothorax before they started, they might well by the time they arrived at the bottom of the hill.

'Second was the idea that the hypothermic casualty should be warmed up on the hill. Considering the amount of heat and time it takes to defrost a one pound pack of frozen peas in a saucepan, it seemed a little ambitious to consider achieving warming a whole person who is severely hypothermic — although this is not to disregard the hugely beneficial effect of shelter, warm drinks and food, even warm inspired air on the less severely hypothermic casualty.'

OGGI SNIPS

The mountains of Snowdonia were created during the Caledonian Orogeny some 380 million years ago.

Waters recalls the introduction of the laryngeal mask airway — for use by the advanced care providers — after two long and difficult carry-offs for casualties with a compromised airway. Now that the majority of calls for help come by means of mobile phone, team members tend to reach the casualty far quicker than twenty, certainly fifty years ago. Where once they might have to face a dead body, now they are more likely find a casualty alive but critically ill or injured. So live training was provided in a hospital setting on the use of LMAs and this, like every other aspect of training, has to be maintained.

'Training standards continue to evolve,' says Glynne Andrew, 'but, essentially, all pre-hospital care now functions to the same standards whether at road accidents, mountain accidents or whatever. After the introduction of Advanced Trauma Life Support (ATLS) methods from the USA, this has been nationally and globally the agreed standard methodology for initial management of trauma patients in hospital. Because of the success of this system, there is now a pre-hospital version (Pre-Hospital Trauma Life Support) PHTLS, which sets the standard expected for pre-hospital care. This is mainly directed at paramedics and other ambulance crew. Some elements of this are not realistic in some environments — such as mountain rescue or sea rescue — but most of the principles are applicable and this is what we strive to do.'

Regarding the mountain rescue casualty courses thus far, these have mostly not had external validation from professional bodies and this has been an issue. 'We are seeking to move to courses which have been externally validated,' adds Andrew.

In at the deep end

Every now and then, a day comes when team members' skills are stretched to the limit. When, whatever training they've gone through, however many slide presentations they've sat through or books they've read, they face something new and unexpected. One Saturday in October 2013, was just such a day.

Elved Roberts and Dave Canning were tackling a route on Pen yr Ole Wen. Roberts was leading when the rock beneath his feet came away sending him crashing onto the steep scree below. The tumbling boulder followed suit, striking him on the lower shin, before hurtling on towards his petrified friend. Imagining that 'this was it', his time had come, Dave Canning clung to the rock face, praying, cursing, urgently for his life. And someone, somewhere must have heard. On the rock hurtled, splintering and shattering as it went, before finally coming to rest on the A5 — fortunately free of traffic. It was a life-changing accident.

Experienced climbers, they had done everything right. They'd followed the guidebook to the letter. It was a route that doubtless many had trod before them, over rocks that have remained in place through centuries of footfall and erosion. Until that day. The rock had amputated Roberts's lower leg but, with amazing presence of mind, he set about stemming the flow of blood while Canning, in deep shock himself, sought to apply some basic first aid while battling against an intermittent mobile signal to alert the emergency services — not entirely convinced, when finally he made contact, that they believed his assertion that his friend's leg 'had gone'.

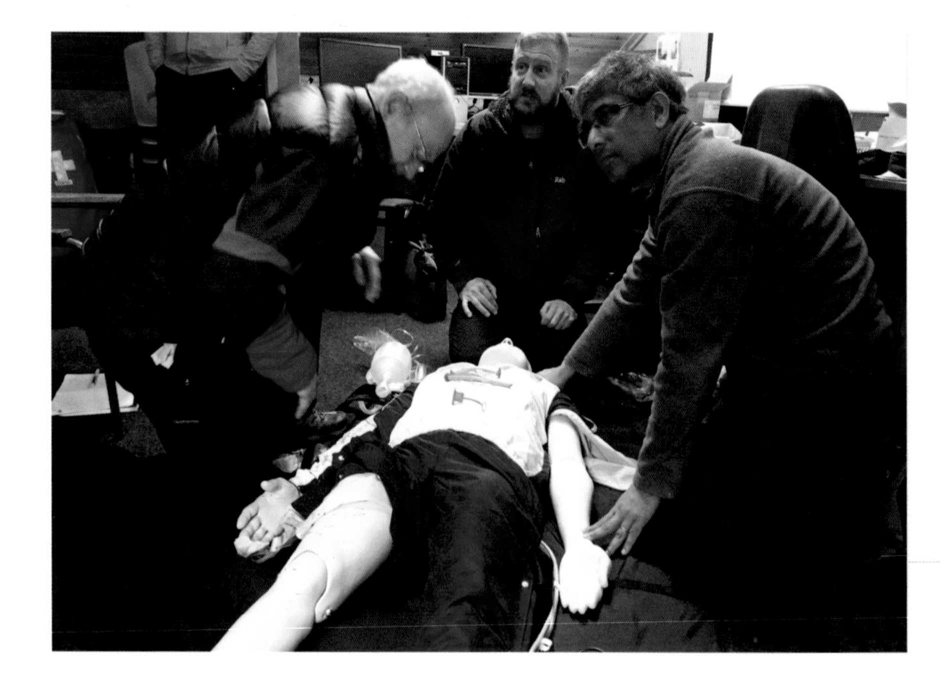

Canning describes the moment he saw his friend fall. 'He fell to the left as the block rolled away from the rock face and, to my utter horror, aimed itself directly at my head. I had no escape. I was tied to the anchors by a few centimetres of rope by a clove hitch, a knot designed to tighten under load. Elved was also attached to me and the anchors, via the belay device. Adrenaline and blood rushed and in that split second I managed to do the only things I could. I firmly locked off the belay and threw myself flat against the rock face, with only my helmet for protection, wanting to melt into its surface and waited for the impact.

'I truly believed I was about to be decapitated, but my life didn't flash before me. I didn't think of loved ones. Just a cold explosion of fear and an angry resistance against the inevitable. The rock thumped above me then flipped over my head crashing into the slope below, closely followed by one of Elved's rock shoes.

'I heard him rolling down the rock face to my left. Then, not wanting to believe my eyes, I saw his right foot had been sliced off. At the end of his right leg, a ragged, bloody stump was leaking blood over the ground. What had just flown over my head wasn't just his rock shoe.'

Perhaps fortunately for Roberts, the first team members on scene were highly qualified to deal with his injuries, including Glynne Andrew, himself an orthopaedic surgeon. They were soon joined by a stretcher party of Ogwen and RAF team members.

The initial call had gone out to attend 'male with leg injury on Pen yr Ole Wen'. Paul Smith and Pauline Hallett, both very experienced cas carers, would be driving past the site en route to base from home, so they agreed with the team leader that they would go to the scene of the accident. 'It sounded very serious,' says Smith. 'We needed to ensure that it was as serious as it sounded and that the team's response was appropriate.' He recalls that the incident had 'all the same ingredients as any other rescue but it's not often you have to send a foot to hospital!'

Team members suspected there was little chance of saving and reattaching the foot, but it was clear that Roberts was quite attached psychologically to the possibility. 'He wanted it to go to hospital with him,' says Smith, 'and we didn't want to disabuse him of that. That said, all the way through, Elved's heart rate never got about 60-ish. He was very calm. He knew his foot was gone. It made it easier for us to talk to him about it.'

Smith dealt with the stump while another team member dealt with Roberts's breathing. Only two or three could work on him at any one time with two others on their knees, the stretcher resting across them to keep it flat on the steep, loose slope. Others were further away, quietly going about their tasks — assembling the stretcher, communicating with Oggi base and the helicopter and organising the means for Roberts's foot to travel with him.

Initially, a 20-litre insulated plastic box, designed to keep liquids cool, went up to the scene, along with as much frozen bread and cheese as they could find (the classic 'recommendation' of frozen peas not being to hand). But there were concerns about the handle being good enough to sustain winching. Finally, the foot was packed into a stuff bag with what might otherwise have made a tasty lunch, and placed on the stretcher with Roberts.

Life-changing though his accident was, from the first dawning that this was as serious as it gets,

Top: Casualty care on the edge: Rescue on Crib Lem, 2 May 2010 © Dave Worrall.
Bottom: State-of-the-art cas care training with a breathing doll © Andy Harbach.

his recovery has been remarkable. After sixteen days in hospital, he was fitted for his first prosthetic limb in early December, 2013. By Christmas, he was popping into work a couple of short days a week and, by the new year, he had returned to two days a week. By Easter, he was back at work full time. A return to the rock face followed as soon as he was able, his 'disability' seemingly driving him to achieve more than he might have done otherwise.

'Whilst being an amputee is certainly frustrating at times it has also brought about a renewed appreciation of the moments and wonders of being alive. Without modern medicine and machinery it is almost certain that the injuries I had sustained could have proved fatal. But, due to the extremely long list of people who have helped me, my life has been able to continue in a manner very similar to before. This experience has opened my eyes to what people can do for others.

'I seconded HVS on my first weekend out. I've attended the LimbPower games and been coached in running. I've competed at Para-climb Scotland, organised by Jamie Andrew and the Mountaineering Council of Scotland, and came second in my category. I've done a bit of easy winter walking and a two-week tour of Orkney.'

It hasn't all been plain sailing — a fall on his stump in hospital was far more painful than the accident itself and there was a split in the scar and numerous blisters and sores to contend with — but it's a remarkable story, nevertheless. Read it in full on page 138.

The questions of fatality

In October 1999, an accident on Snowdon, [technically outside the team's area] began a gradual chain of events which led to another 'first' for mountain rescue — one that would impact significantly on Ogwen. Ten-year-old Jonathan Attwell was the youngest of a party of scouts from Bristol, descending the east ridge of Snowdon when he fell 500 feet to his death. A member of the 19th Kingswood (1st Warmley) group for just a month, Jonathan had been looking forward to his first

FROM THE ARCHIVE

Casualty saved by his torch, January 2000: A lone climber could have died had it not been for his quick thinking and a torch. The 56-year-old was walking on Tryfan when he fell nearly ten feet and injured his shoulder. Police were alerted at 6.45pm by someone who recognised SOS signals being flashed from the west side of Tryfan and the team was called fifteen minutes later. The man had fallen on a very steep and unstable ground at about 2000 feet. 'We set off at 7.00pm,' said Roger Jones, 'and didn't arrive until 10.30pm which gives you an idea of the difficult terrain of Tryfan. He'd strayed on to one of the steep places of the mountain. He was suffering from hypothermia but if he hadn't used his torch, it could have been a lot worse.' The unnamed casualty was praised for using good mountain sense. 'He had the sense to stay where he was and use his torch as a distress signal.'

OGGI SNIPS

From the Guestbook 2011: Just writing to say a massive thanks to all of you for rescuing me off Glyder Fawr. Pleased to say I've since done the route again. Got it right this time.

adventure away from home. They were a group of boys like any other of that age — boisterous, noisy, hungry for new experiences — yet they soon settled down to the matter of climbing a mountain.

Forty-nine-year-old Peter Finlay led the group to the summit, via the rocky ridge of Crib Goch. As Ed Douglas noted in 'The Observer', this is 'one of the most demanding options he could have chosen for a young boy's first experience of the great outdoors'. They posed for a photograph, taken by Finlay, a smiling group of happy youngsters. Jonathan, wrote Douglas, had just told one of his friends that it was his 'second-best achievement after going to Disneyland'.

Finlay's chosen route to the summit may have been questionable, but the descent was perhaps more so — littered with rubble and false paths. As they moved back downhill, Finlay had assumed the five younger boys behind him on the descent would see and follow his path down the ridge. But he later admitted there had seemed 'a hell of a distance' between himself and Jonathan when the youngster fell to his death yet, at the same time, it didn't feel as though it 'could have been that far'. He could remember going around a big rock where he walked to the top. At that point, he could see the boys following him, so continued down, assuming they could see where he was had gone. 'I had no reason to think they would not follow me down and four of them did and one didn't.'

When another boy asked what had happened to Jonathan, Finlay realised he was missing and tracked back up the slope but it was too late. Sam Roberts, a National Park warden, happened to be on the summit as Finlay searched anxiously for Jonathan and he radioed for help.

A Sea King helicopter diverted to the scene and found Jonathan's body on rocks below the East Ridge. Douglas paints a vivid picture. 'Winchman Philip Hill felt for a pulse, but the length of fall made death almost inevitable. Jonathan's new boots had been torn off, his wallet was halfway up a rock face, his rucksack and sweater some way below his body.'

An inquest into his death, two years later, heard that members of the troop had been 'full of life' when they reached the summit and none had appeared to be struggling with the descent down tricky ground. 'There were lots of people,' said Finlay, 'walking down, walking up. People with their dogs. The person with a dog was walking up. I met someone with a child walking down there'. Apparently unnoticed, Jonathan lost his footing and simply vanished from view.

At the inquest, the following February, the coroner ruled that while negligence had played a part in the young scout's death, Finlay was not guilty of the gross negligence required for a verdict of unlawful killing. Soon after the inquest, the Crown Prosecution Service began an investigation and Finlay was charged with manslaughter. The jury took three hours to acquit him, two years to the day after Jonathan's death.

Throughout those two years, there had been confusion around the circumstances of Jonathan's death, not helped by Finlay himself. Douglas describes how, at their only meeting with the scout leader — accompanied by Roger Starr, then Scout County Commissioner for Avon, and Field Commissioner Janet Hall — they'd looked for answers, but 'details were hazy'. He 'gave the family the impression that Jonathan had strayed from the path and effectively stepped off a cliff. He pointed through the window at a house eighty metres across the close and said Jonathan had been as far away as that. Interviewed in the autumn of 2000, just before being charged with manslaughter, Finlay said that it had been 'feet'.

'The Attwells asked the other boys who it was who had been at the back of the group with Jonathan to guide them down. The answer was that they had been left to descend alone. Despite Starr's assurances to other parents, the regulations of the association had been ignored and fundamental rules of mountain leadership flouted.'

It was reported that the Scout Association certificate which permitted Finlay to lead such trips had expired two years before Jonathan's death and he had not completed a 'nationally respected qualification' in leading mountain expeditions, despite attending a training course. Only after listening to expert witnesses at his trial, did Finlay appear to admit that the ground had been 'difficult, deceptive and dangerous terrain' and 'not suitable for ten to twelve-year-olds'. But perhaps more significant for mountain rescue, was that during the court case the judge asked whether the police had taken witness statements. So many questions seemed to remain unanswered.

Understandably, the press took a keen interest in the story. Suddenly, there seemed to be a rash of 'scout deaths'.

The previous year, eleven-year-old Scott Fanning had been on a camping trip in Rochdale with ten other boys and six scout leaders when Scott, who was at the front of group, fell 100 feet to his death. After Scott's death the coroner returned a verdict of accidental death, but he also made a number of safety recommendations about scouting trips. Mrs Fanning had forwarded these to the Scout Association in a seven-page letter. Had they been implemented on Jonathan Attwell's trip, she openly speculated, perhaps he might not have died.

A week after Jonathan's death, a 35-year-old scout leader died after falling on Cader Idris. He'd been scrambling up with one of the fourteen-year-olds in his charge, leaving a large, well-organised group to an easier path. The younger scout was said to be only feet from his leader when he fell.

A year later, tragedy struck again, this time closer to home. Fifteen-year-old year Jamie Chambers died of head injuries at Bangor hospital after being struck twice by rock falls in a 'million-to-one tragedy'. One of a party of nine boys aged twelve to fifteen years and five adult instructors from the Birkenhead area, he had been taking part in a supervised climbing and abseiling exercise on Tryfan Bach. Barely 500 metres across the road from Oggi base.

Other members of his party and other climbers immediately went to his aid, but they too fell prey to a second rock fall which struck the boy again and also injured a scout leader and another man, who were attending the boy. They both suffered leg injuries. It just so happened that team members were already at base for a session of first aid training, so they were at the scene in minutes. As they approached, still more rock fell.

The pathologist Dr Donald Wayte found Jamie Chambers had died from 'multiple lacerations to the heart due to blunt trauma to the chest consistent with a mountaineering accident'. The coroner admitted he been critical of scouts in the past but not this time. Everything had seemed to be in place — two ropes, eight feet apart, were hung on the rock face from which scouts could abseil or be lowered. One was slung around a pinnacle jutting away from the rock face. Jamie had climbed up and was about to abseil down but 'he was a big strong lad. The force of him pushing off — the rock went with him'.

Fatal incident investigations in action: Main photo © OVMRO. Inset © Dave Worrall.

Scout leader Matthew Harvey said a rock half the size of the coroner's desk hit Jamie in the midriff then tumbled away. The lad suffered a sore back, wrist and bloody nose but was conscious. Moments later, 'a six foot slab came from just behind where the pinnacle was. It started to slide. It hit the ledge and flipped over. It knocked Paul Beard and another climber down and landed on Jamie then continued down. It took Jamie slightly over the ledge.' Scout leader Graham Lysaght said the second rock sounded like 'a roaring noise from a train.'

Stuart Dethick was one of those Ogwen team members quickly on scene. He told the hearing he had been shocked. Ten minutes before, they'd heard of a person with head and back injuries. What they found was someone unconscious and unresponsive. 'He stopped breathing at least five or six times. I don't recall, in twenty years of climbing, there being an incident involving a rock fall.'

'This was quite an unusual incident,' said Chris Lloyd, 'especially for the boy to be struck twice by rock falls.' Just as thirteen years later, Elved Roberts would conjecture his own bad luck at being the final incremental footfall, wresting a seemingly solid rock from its anchors, Lloyd too talked of a rock, held in position for many years and bedded down by top soil, that may have become top heavy. Once it moved away, the one above it became loose and followed suit. It was simple bad luck, on a popular training ground for thousands of climbers.

The judge's comments following the trial of Peter Finlay hit home. This time there were multiple casualties — including one fatality — and the police wanted witness statements. A number of team members involved with the incident were taken on one side by police officers and 'grilled aggressively'.

Then, on 10 April 2002, came a tipping point. The team was called to help Llanberis team members search for a missing man in the Llanberis Pass. 'Half the team went up one side, half the other,' says Roger Jones. 'Found a body in Bryant's Gully. The team went up but we couldn't do anything. It was a scene of crime now because no one had seen him fall. It ground on and on, just waiting. Why were we being kept on the hill as volunteers, while the police found a 'scenes of crime officer' capable of getting into a difficult location? We waited for quite some time for the police officer — on a weekday morning when we needed to go to work.

'The outcome was an agreement that North Wales Police would allow team members to investigate fatalities. Now it's understood that if we're called to an incident more than 100 feet off the path, we can act on behalf of the police. The coroner is very happy with the reports we submit.'

When a fatality occurs in the mountains, the police are obliged to investigate, on behalf of the coroner. And the coroner is legally obliged to hold an inquest to determine the cause of death, based on the information gathered by the police from witnesses. Understandably, those left behind to grieve look to the coroner and police for answers, the why and the how of their loved one's death.

Perhaps the most important element of any investigation is the information gathered at the earliest opportunity from an accident location — a 'crime scene' until proved otherwise. This might include eye-witness testimony, photographs, video recording and the examination and recovery of equipment. The very nature of the mountains means any crime scene investigation can be incredibly difficult — well nigh inaccessible to the majority. It made sense for those people already trained in mountaineering to learn the necessary skills for this too.

Agreement reached, the Fatal Incident Protocol was finally launched in 2003, jointly negotiated

OGGI SNIPS

Britain's smallest tree, Least Willow, can be seen growing high in the mountains of the Glyderau and Carneddau at about 3cm tall.

Middle-aged casualty suffers heat exhaustion, 9 August 2003: One of the hottest days of a glorious summer and the team was called to assist a middle-aged casualty with heat exhaustion, some 2000 feet above the Ogwen valley on Pen yr Ole Wen. The casualty had endured a two-hour car journey from Manchester that morning before being let loose on the steep and direct assault on the south face of Pen yr Ole Wen.

As she carried no water, she was disappointed to find that this side of the mountain has no streams or pools. When she collapsed, her two colleagues soon exhausted their own water supply trying to revive her and one of them returned to the valley floor to collect more water. After a further three hours of nursing the casualty, without much success, the team was called.

The advanced party soon found the casualty lying conscious in the shade of some boulders near the summit. They radioed base requesting a stretcher party. 'At base,' says Chris Lloyd, 'we looked at the assortment of stretchers, from the straight Thomas of the 1930s design, the Mariner of the 1950s, the Neil Robinson (even older!), the Oggi stretcher and the Bell. That's the one. But don't let's bother with that great stretcher, let's just take the pack frames! Travelling so light, we were soon at the casualty site where we found Feathers, a seven-year-old Airedale terrier. She was carefully loaded onto the assembled pack frame stretcher and carried off the mountain. Peter Bell may not have thought of this type of casualty when designing his stretcher system, but it fitted the job perfectly. And, as for Feathers, she made a full recovery!'

between North Wales Police and the North Wales Mountain Rescue Association (NWMRA). It was the first of its kind in the UK and now a benchmark for mountain rescue teams across England and Wales. Essentially, it outlined best practice when dealing with fatalities, managing the incident, handling evidence and dealing with the families. 'We've built up a huge amount of information which helps inform how we do things,' says team member Tim Bird. And it massively supports the next of kin in situations like this.'

The team also now has an information sharing protocol — also developed through North Wales Police and NWMRA and trains team members to act as 'family contact officer', so there is always someone on hand to help friends and family if needed.

2013

BLOOD AND PATIENCE: A CASUALTY'S STORY

by Elved Roberts

There was a strong gusty wind from the NE with cloud at about 600 metres and the threat of drizzle. The normal Ogwen haunts were going to be fully exposed to the wind. Pinnacle Ridge on Pen yr Ole Wen was low on the mountain and south facing so out of the wind. Somewhere between V Diff and a scramble, it looked a reasonable choice to move fairly quickly on a marginal day. We fixed the belay below the route and took the precaution of placing a quickdraw in one of the anchor points, clipping in a lead rope. In case of a fall, the belay device would be orientated correctly.

I climbed up a metre or two onto a fairly large ledge. In the corner a large block, maybe 1.5 cubic metres, leant into a corner. The guidebook suggested climbing onto it before going up the corner. I thought about placing protection but looked at how the ropes would flow. There was the possibility of something out to the left but this would create rope drag. As the climbing was fairly easy and the ledge adequately large, that slip would land you back on it so I decided to forego protection until standing on the block. Rarely in climbing does not placing protection keep you from more harm than placing it.

The block leant at a very steep angle, but it was socketed into a crack system, the very thing that had kept it in place since the Ice Age. I dismissed my doubts, but, if there are two lessons to take from this story, it's to 'trust your instincts' and 'just because it was safe yesterday, doesn't mean it is today'.

With my hands on top of the block, things began to move. I was falling. The block rolled sideways like a cartwheel, dirt flying over my head. I tumbled down the slope, rolling in a ball. The ropes went tight. The quickdraw had done its job. I ended up somewhere between sitting and lying facing outwards, feet downhill, three or four metres below the belay. Things hurt but nothing was screaming. Then something caught my eye. Something red.

There was a pool of blood beneath me. Bright red and thick, like emulsion paint. My foot and about half my lower right leg were gone. Like a sausage with its contents squeezed out, the skin hung loose with bulges underneath it which were undoubtedly fragments of bone. The muscles in my calf twitched and knotted. Blood ran from my leg like a tap. Amazingly, it didn't hurt that much!

Direct pressure on the wound wasn't possible. It would hurt too much. Fragments of bone could come through the skin or do more damage. Plus the wound was right across the limb.

OGGI SNIPS

June 2010: Danielle [the owl] is now back with her chick and mate. He didn't recognise her at first but after she'd given him a damned good thrashing, he knew who she was!

It had to be either pressure on the femoral artery in the groin or a tourniquet. The artery would be tricky to find. If I passed out, would Dave be able to find it and keep the pressure on? Loss of blood pressure through shock and blood loss would make it increasingly difficult to find the pulse. And you're taught never to tourniquet. Though not yet knowing much about amputees, I knew having a knee was better than not. I knew that, once applied for an extended time, it was common for an amputation to be required from the site of the tourniquet down. The narrowing below the knee was where it was going to have to go.

I fumbled with a 120cm sling, got it covered in blood, discarded it for a 60cm sling. Applied that in a full turn below the knee and tightened it with a wire gate, then lay on my back as Dave reached me. He was reassuring but his voice indicated he was distressed. He phoned for help but the phone kept cutting in and out. Maybe six or seven calls. Then he was through. 'My friend's leg's been amputated, we need a helicopter.' By now, he was holding my leg and lying back on my rucksack. 'Dave, if I pass out, whatever happens, keep the tourniquet on and my leg in the air.'

I blew six blasts on the whistle from my chest pocket. Dave could see people on the road near Ogwen Cottage, waving. They could hear the whistle. People I would meet months later phoned mountain rescue. Sonny and Alex both independently put calls through.

The loosened boulder had crashed all the way to the A5, fragmenting as it went. We'd been 'lucky'. Dave had to duck for his life as the rock flew over his head and I'd only lost a leg. He's married with three children, two still at school. And, to cap it all, he'd only survived a rare cancer a few years previously. Thankfully, no one was on the A5 as the remains of the block slammed into it. Even a car would have been insufficient protection.

Now through on the phone, Dave told them about the tourniquet. They said to remove it but how else would they have dealt with it? The blood flow was down to a drip every four or five seconds. Not wanting to lose more of my leg than necessary, it was worth seeing if a viable clot had started to form. We slowly unwound the turns and watched the drips — no visible increase so we left the tourniquet loosely in place. If it started to bleed heavily, we'd retightened irrespective of advice. I tried to calm my mind to reduce blood pressure and heart rate and we waited.

Someone came up the hill, one of the people who waved from Ogwen Cottage. It was Jason. He and his friend Sonny had been planning to do the same climb. Sonny phoned mountain rescue, using the pay phone outside Ogwen Cottage, and they asked him to wait by the phone. Jason started up the hill to see if he could help. He came over the rib of ground and saw us. If he was squeamish, he hid it well. He sat close up, the back of my thigh against his back, the best way of supporting it but it meant Jason got the five-second drip. Fifteen, twenty minutes passed. By now, I knew I'd be okay. This was a bad day, but I was going live. It was a liberating feeling.

A rescue team 4x4 pulled up in the lay-by. Two people got out and one of them started to run up the hill. It was Paul. Before saying anything to us, he spoke into his radio. 'We need a helicopter'. If there had been any doubts about the seriousness of the injuries they were dispelled. We shuffled sideways onto a patch of clean dirt and he began placing dressings on the wound, inspecting me for other injuries and generally monitoring my situation. A second dressing went on top of the first. Blood seeped through and I could feel the crepitus. Meanwhile, Pauline held my hand and talked to me constantly, her knees either side of my head.

Before long the entire hillside was busy. Maybe twenty-five people. The RAF MRT had been training on the other side of Pen yr Ole Wen so they too came to help. Someone presented me with an Entonox mouthpiece. It didn't stop the pain but it did distort time. I'd breathe the gas in for a few minutes and things would get uncomfortably strange, stop for a few minutes, then restart.

Paul took my pulse at regular intervals, writing on a chart and passing it to the team doctor. The three of them chatted in quite an animated way outside my hearing. 'Do you know what's happened?' asked Pauline. 'Yes, my leg's been cut off.' More surreptitious discussion. 'How's my heart doing?' I ventured. 'You tell me,' countered Paul. 'Normally it'd do 50, but I reckon it's going faster than that now!' 'It's doing 60, cool as a cucumber.' With this, the excitement subsided.

I knew I'd need an operation. There was crushed bone and obviously non-viable skin, covered in grit, dirt and fragments of heather. I asked if they'd found my foot. They had. It was in a bag on ice. There might be a 5% chance it would go back on. Slim, but I didn't want my foot left on the hill.

I looked over to Y Garn, the Glyderau and Tryfan and wondered if I'd ever see a mountain again other than from a car. I felt very tearful but wanted to keep positive for my rescuers. Far harder for them if I fell apart mentally. I thought about my partner Claire. She also climbs. We could have done that route together. It could have been her.

Over an hour had passed. It was hard to see what was going on but I knew people were carrying out different tasks. They'd set up a belay in the groove to the right, to lower me down on a stretcher if the chopper didn't come. Then, suddenly, 'Below!!' and we all tensed as rocks clattered down the gully next to us. 'This whole mountain's rotten,' someone ventured.

By now, the spasm in my leg had spread to my pelvis and the top of my left leg. Partly the nervous system going haywire, partly through cold.

A radio crackled. 'The helicopter's five minutes away,' said Pauline. I was going straight to the University Hospital of North Staffordshire (UHNS), the main trauma centre for the north west. The flight would take about an hour. Had I been more distressed or my vital signs weaker, I'd have been taken to Bangor to be stabilised, then transferred to UHNS — but by then the foot would almost certainly be lost. This was good news. The 5% still had a chance of coming in.

OGGI SNIPS

March 2013: Shocked walkers found the body of a young man hanging from a tree during their walk. Team members recovered the body and took him to the mortuary.

Paul explained that Dickie, the winchman, would come down and supervise me being strapped into the cradle. The whole thing would take fifteen minutes or so. Looking straight up at the Sea King, the roar and wind was incredible. Strapped and blanketed in the cradle, I checked again that my foot was on board. It was somewhere down by my other foot, tucked away. I asked for Dave, now standing further back. We shook hands and promised to see each other soon.

It would be a long winch, nearly the full length of the cable — nearly a minute. Due to the steepness of the cliff they were as close and low as possible. The winch began. One of our climbing ropes had been used to secure the cradle to the hillside to stop it sliding down. As we rose, I could see it lifting up between the mountain and ourselves. We were tied to the mountain! The dynamic rope stretched taking the strain. I noticed Dickie had a rescue knife on his leg but even if he could get to it, the rope was tied to the foot end. It looked impossible for him to reach it. Then someone stepped forward. Luckily, it was a slip knot. Reaching up and leaning forward using the angle of hillside to good effect, he released the knot. We were free. A few seconds later, the spinning started, like a fairground ride possessed of demons. I was possibly the most scared I'd been all day.

Dickie stuck a leg out and leant into the spin. It stopped. Then moments later, it restarted as fast as before and we span all the way to the chopper. How were we going to get on board spinning like this? But, as we drew near, somehow Dickie caught the chopper and we were in. Dickie and 'Seaweed' (the radar operator) dragged the cradle into position and we headed off, door open with a view of the Welsh mountains I was still able to appreciate.

Months later, with Dave, Jason, Sonny and Claire, I visited 22 Squadron at RAF Valley. We met some of the ground team who'd attended the incident as well as the co-pilot, Rob Paul. Rob had been flying during the winch as he had a better view of the mountainside than the pilot due to the hovering position. He explained how serious the winch had been, details I'd been unaware of at the time. A Sea King can fly at 100% engine capacity for as long as it's got fuel but can dip 'into the red' when it needs a bit more power. It can do 109% for twenty minutes or 120% for five seconds. Beyond this, the gearbox could fail. Because we were climbing in the lee of the strong north-east wind, the air flowing over Pen yr Ole Wen was causing a serious downdraught on the blades causing the engine to need a lot of power to hover. At the start of the winch, the engine was running at something like 115%. When the climbing rope attaching the cradle to the hillside went taught, it did 120% for seven seconds. It could have been a far worse day.

An hour or so passed in a time distortion. Five minutes for the blades to stop rotating, then I was wheeled into A&E. UHNS is a major trauma centre yet it appeared empty. Where was everyone? Then round the corner, ten or twelve people. A couple of nurses took my hands and began talking reassuringly. A bank of machines to my left lay dormant. A doctor standing on what

OGGI SNIPS

The iconic and protected Snowdon lily is known to flower in the Glyderau on dark, north-facing cliffs, well away from grazing sheep and the collecting sticks of plant hunters of old.

could have been a pedestal called orders. My clothes where lifted and things stuck onto and into me. The machines sprang into life. Heart rate, blood pressure, breathing rate, oxygen saturation and more I didn't recognise.

An anaesthetist spoke to me. He was a climber. Good start. 'Your surgeon is Mr Dwyer. The best.' Ten minutes on, Mr Dwyer appeared. He was a climber too and had done that very route. We chatted about climbing, then his manner changed. 'I've been looking at your foot. The talus bone is badly damaged. If I put your foot back on it'll be fixed and painful. You won't be able to do sport again. In two years you'll be begging me to cut it off. I recommend we prepare the leg for a prosthetic.'

I'd pretty much worked out this would be the case. The 5% chance wasn't going to come in. A sister arrived. Who's your next of kin? We need to ring someone. That meant telling Claire. I tried to delay it, until there was a bit more certainty. I didn't want Claire told by a stranger that her boyfriend had lost his leg. But the sister wouldn't let it go. This was it. The phone rang, as the sister stood over me. Leaving a message wasn't an option. Claire picked up. 'I'm alright but I've been in an accident. I'm in a hospital in Staffordshire. I've injured my foot and need an operation.' I'd wanted to spare her the detail until she was with me but half an hour later, she knew anyway. Because the incident was going to be in the media, Dave and the rescue team had called to tell her.

My whole body was X-rayed — skull, spine, pelvis and about eight of the leg from different angles — then we were straight into the anaesthetic room. 'Look into my eyes and count to ten.' Without a dream or even seeming to sleep I was awake again and my new life had begun. So many people helped me along the way but some deserve special appreciation: Dave, Jason and Sonny, the team, 22 Squadron, the RAF MRT, all the staff at UHNS, Addenbrookes and Colchester prosthetics departments, my employer, LimbPower, the Mountaineering Council of Scotland, all my friends and family. And, most of all, Claire.

CHAPTER FIVE

Learning and leadership

As Dr Ieuan Jones observed, training people in first aid and casualty care, whilst hugely important to the wellbeing and future survival of casualties, is only part of the picture. All the first aid training in the world counts for nothing if your team members don't possess the skills to access the casualty in the first place — and then operate in a calm, confident, efficient manner in the harshest of environments.

Many have brought their own experience and skills to the team, usually accompanied by a deep thirst for learning and a desire to make things ever better.

Developing as it had done from a mountaineering school, in the early years of the team there was the core of instructors, professional mountaineers and willing volunteers who lived in the valley, all led by Ron James. KC Gordon, for example, was one of the original instructors from Ogwen Cottage. He has remained with the team throughout the fifty years, only standing down from operational duties in summer 2015. One of the older generation of British Mountain Guides, he had a reputation for running an incident 'with the fewest possible resources'. Dave Siviter was another instructor involved in the early days. John Banks was an RAF MR team leader, stationed at Valley. John Ellis Roberts was a mountain guide and national park warden. Neil Adam was a student when he joined. Still operational, he is now a hill farmer with his wife Maggie, who was a teacher when they met and she first became involved with the team.

Maggie Adam recalls some of her early 'training'. Like so many, she first became involved through Ieuan Jones's first aid courses. The following year she found

Technical rope rescue training: Photo © OVMRO.

herself pressed into service as a radio operator during a call-out — a task she had no previous experience in, let alone instruction. 'Sit in that, speak when you're spoken to! That was it! I sat in the old Land Rover. It was very cold and wet and I did as I was told!' Unlike today, when training is structured and leaders have to earn their stripes, she 'went from nothing to party leader in one go' when she was tasked to organise a group of volunteers during a search.

The 'weekend' members — those who came from across England and Wales — would appear through the evening on Fridays to camp under the trees at Ogwen, ready to climb and be on hand if needed. 'We'd arrive in the dark,' recalls Twiggy Price, then go up on the hill in the morning to walk or climb. Then in the afternoons we'd perhaps practise different things — rope skills or stretcher work, usually up Tin Can Gully. And we were generally together as a group. Then it was back to Cobdens Hotel in the evening.' In many ways, it was as much a gathering of friends as a rescue team. And, invariably there would be a bar involved!

Training largely consisted of team members sharing their skills with other team members but that didn't mean potential trainees had an easy time of it. Roger Pyves joined in 1980. 'You had a mentor in your first year — they showed you everything. You were pushed quite hard physically and mentally by the team to see where your breaking point was. You need to know the limits of those around you. It was part and parcel of the training.' It's a principle which still applies.

Ron James appointed Roger Jones and Tony Jones as deputies. Then, when James left, Tony Jones stepped up. During the 1990s, a system of having a number of team leaders was set up but, for many years, says John Hulse, Tony was 'always the de facto team leader'.

Tony Jones had joined the team soon after its formation. Having secured a degree in geology and chemistry from the University of Cape Town, he came to Aberystwyth University to study for his PhD. He was new to the area, several thousand miles from his native South Africa, but mountaineering and mountain rescue were already in his DNA, his first rescue on Table Mountain aged just sixteen. When Ron James ran a week's mountain rescue course at Plas y Brenin, in 1965, Jones attended. He learned a lot there. 'Ron was a superb mountaineer, a good rope technician.' In his 'Some thoughts' essay, Jones credits Ron James for sharpening most of his earlier thoughts on mountain rescue'. He believes James's skills added to his own technical abilities admitting that he was 'never a good rock climber' himself, adding that his childhood polio 'slowed me down a bit.'

FROM THE ARCHIVE

Man crushed by felled tree, 8 January 2010: When a 29-year-old man suffered serious crush injuries after a tree fell on top of him, team were called to help paramedics battle their way through snow to the scene of accident. The gentleman was believed to have been cutting down a tree in a field at Ty Nant near Corwen. Fire crews used specialist off-road vehicle to take lifting gear to the site while the paramedics were transported in mountain rescue vehicles. 'The man was quite badly injured, said Chris Lloyd. 'We were assisted by farmers who helped bring equipment to the scene and other teams were also on standby ready to help as well. It was a real team effort.

OGGI SNIPS

The Snowdon lily can be found far from 'home', around the northern hemisphere from the Alps to the Rocky mountains and from Greenland to Mongolia.

What he might have lacked in rock climbing ability, Jones more than made up for with inventiveness. John Hulse recalls an incident in October 1988, when three canoeists were in danger of losing their lives when they missed their last get-out point on the River Conwy, just above Betws y Coed. Gareth Cryer, Simon Hale and James Savage were washed downstream from Penmachno Bridge towards the fifty foot drop of Conwy Falls. They grabbed a rock in midstream to stop themselves going over the falls but, after several days of heavy rainfall, the river was so strong they couldn't swim to the bank. And, such was the force of the water, if a team member had gone in attached to only a rope, they would have been dragged under and drowned.

Tony Jones, says Hulse, 'devised a novel way of extracting the casualties' with an aerial ropeway from the bridge to the opposite bank fifty feet across the river. A fifteen-strong Ogwen team worked by floodlight to fix the ropes, attached to a Land Rover on one side and trees on the other. Then, with the rest of the team working from the bridge, team member Doug Jones 'volunteered' to be lowered down to the rock, eighty feet below. 'Doug was foolish enough to turn up in a wetsuit', says Tony Jones, with a wry smile, 'so he got the job!' The idea was that the system of pulleys could alter the tension of the rope and, once the casualty was in the harness, the tension could be increased. Both 'jockey' and casualty would be pulled up together.

Roger Jones describes the whole rescue as 'absolutely fantastic and very dramatic with the river roaring below' but, having been called out at 8.00pm, he 'was in the pub by 10.30, which speaks for itself!' The canoeists were 'none the worse for their experience', says Tony Jones. 'They asked us to rescue their canoes too but we told them we weren't a salvage company!'

Simon Hale later described to a 'Daily Post' reporter how he had escaped death as the three of them 'crashed out of control through white water. 'We were just coming to the end of the trip and were looking to get out of the river because we knew we were getting close to the falls. Four of the group managed to get ashore but we were carried along by the force of the water. One of us capsized and was swept down about eighty feet before he clung to the rock. We paddled on but got the canoes trapped between a bridge wall and a rock. The wall was too steep to climb, so we jumped over the rock to the middle of the river.'

The incident proved a seminal moment for the team as it dawned that the rescue techniques being used in the mountains were transferable to the water environment. It also featured in the BBC 'This Is Your Life' programme about Tony Jones, in 1993.

Over time, the tradition of training at weekends developed into the first Sunday of every month being dedicated to training. With such a wealth of mountaineering and teaching experience amongst team members, training should have been a doddle. 'The trouble was,' says Hulse, 'training was happening but it wasn't highly valued. It wasn't efficient in many ways. From the mid-1980s onwards, there were newer people coming in, trying to establish their own ways of doing things. Tony Jones was the driving force behind much of this — but he also gave people permission to think, and that's what they did! So we started to see things like the Ogwen stretcher development. Better ways of doing things.'

He remembers his first meeting with Jones. 'By reputation, he was fierce. The Ogwen warlord! And he definitely hadn't passed his diplomacy exams.' Jones himself defends his legendary lack of tact, describing one occasion at Oggi base when someone turned to him and said he was upsetting the informant. 'I was more concerned about my team members on the hill,' he says. He credits Pauline Hallett in particular with a tremendous ability to handle people. 'She helped me many times, taking panicking informants off my hands while I dealt with the rescue. If a casualty was dead, I'd say so. I see no sense in generating false hope.'

Not all the tales are harsh, however. Anecdotal memories of Tony Jones frequently revolve around his Land Rover — breaking down, crashing, going faster than maybe he should, or careering through walls. Jones himself recalls this particular incident, answering a call to a heart attack on Snowdon. 'It was a Series 1, long wheel-based Land Rover and a wet, greasy road.' Taking a bend too fast, vehicle met wall. Without further ado, he pulled into the side, jumped into the vehicle behind — driven by Roger Jones — and continued on to the call-out. Another tale has him parked up next to a farm vehicle outside Cobdens, very late at night. Jones allegedly 'borrowed' a bale of hay, placing it under the vehicle bonnet to 'feed it like an animal'.

'His personal vehicle was all kitted out like a big Tonka toy,' says Hulse. 'Driving to an incident was interesting!' But, eccentricities aside, he was a very dynamic, thoughtful planner on the hill, 'always thinking ten moves ahead whereas others would be reacting one move ahead. It was always a very paramilitary operation — surnames only — but he gave the focus and determination to get people to perform well in very challenging conditions.'

'Tony always made a lasting impression,' says Bill Dean, for whom Jones acted as best man at his wedding. 'He was a great practical joker.' He recalls someone's stag night when Jones plastered the groom's arm in Plaster of Paris, so the hapless groom woke the next morning believing he'd broken it. However, the evening before his graduation ceremony proved the perfect

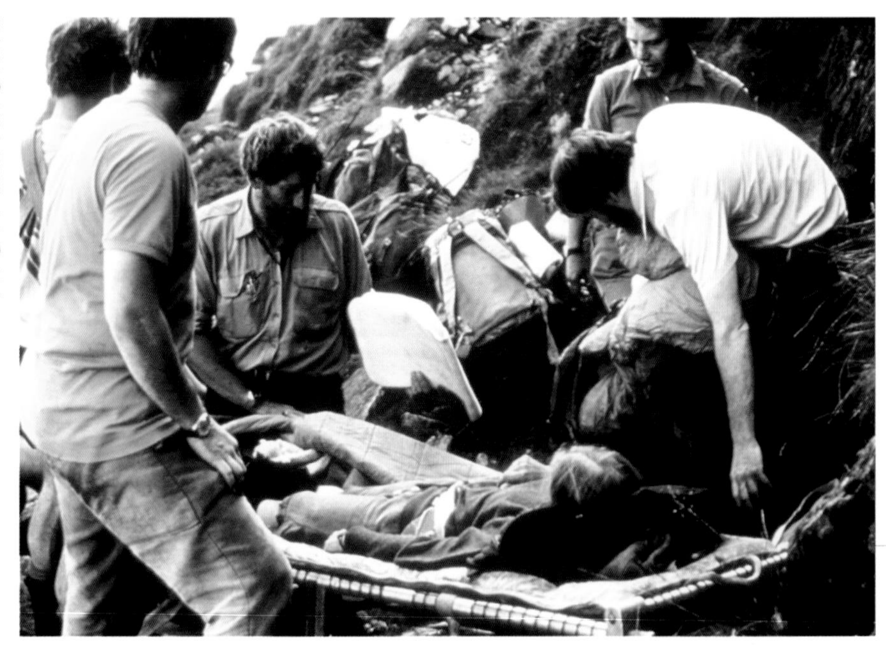

opportunity for some small measure of revenge. 'He'd imbibed rather a lot of his favourite Scottish tipple. We carried him home, all the while imagining what we could do to him, but all we could think was to paint his ears bright green. So next morning, as he doffed his mortar board to the assembled dignitaries, he still had bright green ears.'

There are many who talk about Jones with great affection. 'I have to emphasise from the start,' says Twiggy Price, 'Tony is like a big brother to me and he's godfather to my children'. They remain great friends, although neither is now actively involved with the team.

Al Read describes Tony as 'more of a father' to him. 'He has a very generous heart', he told Michael Aspel, during Jones's 'This is Your Life' television appearance. Read's first involvement with the team was something of a baptism of fire, with an all-night rescue on the east face of Tryfan. A student at Bangor University, where Tony Jones was one of his lecturers, Read would hitch up the Ogwen valley every weekend to climb. One weekend, in February 1981, he asked Jones for a lift. The response was characteristically swift and to the point. Yes — so long as he made himself available for mountain rescue. 'It seemed a fair bargain!'

The weekend had gone well — climbing done and no calls for assistance in the hills. But, as is the way with these things, it pays not to count your chickens.

At 5.00pm on the Sunday evening, the pair were in Jones's Land Rover, heading back to Bangor when they were stopped at the Brew Shack on Idwal car park. A twenty-one year old girl was stuck on the east face of Tryfan, whilst climbing with her university group. She was cold, hypothermic and scared. It was foggy and dark and there was snow on the ground. After a long search, the girl was located at the junction between the top of Little Gully and North Gully. It was a 250-metre stretcher evacuation down to Heather Terrace, then off to Cwm Tryfan.

'It was a long, cold and memorable night but I enjoyed it, perversely!' admits Read, who finally made it back to Bangor in time for his first lecture, at 9.00am on the Monday morning.

Despite his early experience with the team, as a student he wasn't encouraged to join. But, over his three remaining years at university he continued to stay at Helyg and to go on call-outs. By the time he joined the Royal Navy in 1984, mountain rescue had given him a good grounding for the Officer Corps. Through seventeen years service, his heart and mind remained firmly in the Welsh hills.

Letters from America

While his autocratic nature undoubtedly jarred with many around him, Tony Jones was a consummate networker, well connected in all sorts of areas, and it served both him and the team well, forging relationships far beyond the Ogwen valley in the cause of mountain rescue. When the US Air Force PJs (Para Jumpers) came to Snowdonia to train in the mountains, they needed somewhere to stay. Helyg became their base. Jones was hut custodian at the time and the relationship developed from there, with strong social and rescue links. Team members would travel

Tony Jones centre, oversees the rescue of an injured walker © OVMRO.

SNACK BAR
OPEN!
TEA COFFEE
MINERALS
HAMBURGERS
POSTCARDS
Wall's
ICE CREAM

out to the Alps to help train their guys, travelling down to RAF Woodbridge and flying out from there to Lyons. John Hulse recalls one occasion when 'ten Americans and three Oggi members went out to Chamonix for two weeks, flying from USAF Woodbridge to Lyon Airport in the back of a battle-scared C130 Hercules. Lots of ideas came out of that trip.'

Jones recounts travelling to Kirtland Air Force base in Albuquerque to join an advanced cascare course in 1978. It broadened his perspective and, incidentally, earned him an honorary membership. And, we hear, 'two green feet tattooed on his backside'. In turn, 'the PJs helped out on first aid courses in North Wales, adding to the work of Ieuan Jones.'

Such were the links between Ogwen and the PJs that one team member, John Evans, went to Albuquerque in the early-1980s, to join the US Air Force and train as a combat medic. He travelled the world with them over the next twelve years or so, experiencing life in the bigger mountains. When he left the PJs, he became a mountain guide in the Alaskan mountains which, in turn, led him to the Denali National Park Service and the high altitude mountain rescues on Denali and the surrounding ranges. He later returned home to Capel Curig — and the Ogwen team — where he would spend six months of the year. The other six months, he would return to Alaska, much of it at the Denali high altitude camp at 14,000 feet. 'John was never at home for long,' says Russ Hore. 'He instructed in mountain rescue technical rope work, wilderness first aid and search management which not only took him around Wales, England, Scotland and Ireland, but as far afield as South Africa and Hong Kong.'

Tragically, in April 2009, after thirty-six years in mountain rescue, John Evans died in a 200-foot fall at Clogwyn y Grochan, in Llanberis. He suffered severe head injuries whilst climbing with his partner, Lin, on a team climbing evening. Lin had turned to see him tumbling down the slope. 'There were twenty or so team members on hand,' says Hore, 'but we couldn't save him'. Recalling his friend soon after, Hore spoke of 'a real stalwart — the man to have with you when the going got tough on the mountains.' Three hundred people gathered to say farewell, a good number of them, in time-honoured fashion, retiring to Evans's favourite local, Cobdens, 'for a few beers and a few more beers after the service'. The PJs joined in the fun and 'older members sang songs in the corner'. Ultimately, the PJs resurrected the age-old OVMRO tradition of stripping off in the back bar, running across the A5 road with Newcastle Brown in hand, jumping in the river and downing the beer. 'John', says Hore, 'would have been proud!'

American influence has been strong across the years, in no small way due to Tony Jones, whose mathematical brain was perfectly suited to the developing science of search. He was, says John Hulse, the 'go-to guy for search activities', largely due to his extensive contacts within the police and his links with search and rescue experts in the US.

Jones had forged links with Rick Levalla and Skip Stoffel, when he attended his first search management course in Washington State in 1980. The US National Park Service had developed the course, following a couple of search disasters, and Levalla and Stoffel had pulled together a block of research into a text book, 'Search is an Emergency'. It was 1988 before anything of this nature ran in the UK when Peter Howells, from Central Beacons Mountain Rescue Team in South

Top: Early training at the edge. **Left:** Hi-line practice with doll. **Right:** The original Brew Shack © OVMRO.

Wales, contracted the Americans as the core instructors for a search course. Jones was also invited to be one of the instructors. The five-day course ran Monday to Friday at Crickhowell, followed, over the Saturday and Sunday, by a two-day tracking course run by Don Cooper, a search and rescue consultant from Ohio. Cooper and fellow American Ab Taylor had pulled together much of the early work on tracking from their own experiences and research in the field.

Jerry Gallienne, Roger Pyves and Bob Lewis went along to represent Ogwen. Gallienne wrote at the time that he had been 'somewhat sceptical', but now stood convinced that the principles could be used by the team.

Until 1992, the courses ran annually in different locations, until they settled on Bangor University. It was the ideal location, close to the mountains, with good teaching facilities and Tony was ideally placed, working at Bangor University and living on campus, to organise the bookings and the programme. Now sponsored by Mountain Rescue England and Wales, the search course became known as 'search planning and management' while tracking became 'field skills'. Whilst this wasn't an Ogwen initiative as such, Jones's involvement was 'enormous', says Peter Howells.

Billed by the 'Daily Post' in 2003, as 'a guessing game that can save lives', central to the theory was the study of missing or lost person behaviour. Search managers go through the records of past searches and categorise the missing person in a variety of ways such as age, or whether they're experienced or inexperienced walkers.

'One of the fundamental things is the straight line distance from the point last seen to where they were found,' explained Jones. 'Then we do an analysis of those distances so, in time, we can say from our database that 80% of people of a particular category were found, say 40km from where they were last seen. It gives you a planning tool. It's not psychological profiling in the way you might see it portrayed on TV, or the way it's used by police forces. Few in mountain rescue are either psychologists or psychiatrists but we do try to read ourselves into the mind of the missing person because we try to estimate what they're likely to have done.

'There are two sides to a search: the planning and management side and then the fieldwork. Both need to be right. If the planning is badly done, then the fieldworkers will be wasting their time. If the fieldworkers are not looking properly, then the planning is weakened.

'While the search is on, from the time the person is reported missing until the paperwork is done, we attempt to find out as much as possible about them: the equipment they carry, the experience they have, their characteristics, are they fit or unfit, what they're wearing, are they missing from home. The bigger your database, the more reliable are the inferences you can draw from it.

'I've used these methods in North Wales, the US, Iceland, South Africa and elsewhere. The principles apply everywhere but you should never forget that it is statistical and not absolute fact, nor infallible. But I don't think we have many open files. One way or another, he have found them in the end. We're not always successful but more often than not.'

Clive Swombow, chairman of Treble Three (the team's support group) since its inception, attended Stoffel and Lavella's courses through his work as a police officer and he too was an instructor on that first course at Crickhowell. A sergeant in 1972, he had been appointed search and rescue liaison officer for North Wales. As a climber, he was ideal for the role, working with all the teams and RAF 22 Squadron. Since the 1980s, he has instructed in search management

OGGI SNIPS

From the 'pink' forms, August 2003: Team members helped extract the police and ambulance vehicles that had been locked behind a gate by an irate farmer.

training, field skills, man tracking and disaster management throughout the UK and also in the US, Croatia, Iceland, Ireland and Sweden. In the latter case, he was engaged to teach the fundamentals of search and tracking through deep forests, from the back of a quadbike — not as counter-intuitive as it might sound. 'The secret is, if the missing person is on the track, you'll find them anyway. I was teaching them how to spot signs to the sides, away from the track.'

This relationship led to a contingent from Sweden visiting Ogwen in November 2014, to see how the team operated and learn how to develop a fundraising group similar to 333.

Swombow was also instrumental in setting up Tony Jones with a visit from Michael Aspel and his 'big red book'. The programme aired in January 1993. Asked if he knew anyone suitable for 'This Is Your Life', Jones was an obvious choice. 'Within three weeks, we'd fixed the whole things up, including Tony's sister flying across from South Africa. Tony thought he was coming out to meet the new police helicopter but then we turned up in the yellow Wessex'.

'By the way, I might be taking my life into my hands here,' announced Aspel to camera, before jumping from the helicopter, red book behind his back. 'The man we're hoping to drop in on doesn't own a television set, so he probably doesn't know who, or what, I am.' Yet, to his credit, Jones was happy — if a little bemused — to be swept along with the process. The whole thing happened on the same day, as friends and family, team members and past casualties paid tribute to a remarkable man at the filming in TV Studios at Manchester.

Growing an international arm

Cross-fertilisation of ideas and expertise has always been strong in Ogwen. In spring 2006, team members Al Read, Ron Williams and Davy Jones travelled to Makarska in Croatia, 5000 feet above sea level, to teach life-saving skills to local search teams. They were there to show their Balkan counterparts how to hunt for missing climbers, using search dogs in particular — an exercise which involved burying meat and then challenging the handlers and their dogs to find it. They also taught them how to splint broken limbs and work with helicopters. 'The safety aspect was a huge part of it,' says Read. 'These aircraft are dangerous on a good day! When it's dark or the weather is bad, they're even more so. We try to minimise the risk so they are aware of the hazards of approaching the helicopter. For example, if you work under a hovering helicopter in snow, the rotor blades can whip up 100 mph winds and an instant blizzard — you quickly lose your perception of what's around you. It's the same effect on a dry day with dust.'

Sadly, the four-day trip wasn't without incident. 'We were doing some demonstration work with the media,' explains Davy Jones, 'when the call came through that a man had fallen in the mountains, about 200km from where we were. The report was that one man had broken his leg. A small team went up there while we stayed to carry on the work we were doing, but it soon became clear it was a much bigger incident. Three men lost their lives. Al went out to help in the recovery of the bodies and I was there when they brought them back, so it was quite upsetting.'

Despite the tragedy, the training was a great success. While he was there, Davy Jones was awarded a framed Croation silver cross in recognition of his work, training Balkan rescuers to use

search dogs and he was also reunited with the three dogs he'd helped train for their new lives in Croatia, collies Meg and Manston and a spaniel called Diana.

In May that year, the Croatian rescuers travelled to North Wales for the second leg of their exchange. Ten workers and two government officials made the journey for seven days to learn more about how the emergency services work together. While they were here, they visited the coastguard, RAF, RNLI and the air ambulance, as each of the jobs carried out by these services are carried out by the mountain rescue service in Croatia. They also took part in practical sessions with Ogwen team members and learned more about working with search dogs. The relationship continues. Since 2006, a number of team members have been out to Croatia to undertake winter training, bringing benefits to the whole team.

Overseas trips are a regular feature of life in Ogwen. Any number of expeditions undertaken in the name of pushing personal boundaries, crossing icecaps, climbing the 'greater ranges', snowshoeing, skiing, ice-climbing, experiencing life at its most extreme. It keeps the skills honed, the mind sharp to risk. Then there are the 'exchange' trips to learn from other rescue environments — Croatia, Sweden, Iceland, the Crimean Peninsula and the US.

In another 'arm' of the 'international division', in February 2009, the team received a call from Dublin and Wicklow team in the east of Ireland. They needed assistance with a rescue on Lugnaquilla, the highest mountain in the province of Leinster, where two snowboarders in their thirties had been missing overnight in arctic conditions.

'We were asked because of our experience in winter conditions,' explains Tim Radford. 'Nine or ten of us assembled quickly and moved to RAF Valley where we were picked up by an Irish Coastguard helicopter and taken over the sea to Ireland — neatly bypassing passport control! He dropped us near the mountain then just flew off. We had no idea where we were — no maps and nobody there to meet us. Eventually, someone did turn up but those first few minutes were interesting, to say the least.

'Al Read and I got lifted in another helicopter. We were tasked with taking the ropes up. There was a huge trail of people going up the mountain. The two chaps were found on the summit and stretchered off but the most memorable thing for me was the sheer number of people involved: over two hundred. Every team in Ireland was there. We were treated very well by our Irish colleagues who put us up in a Dublin hotel before a morning ferry back to Holyhead. Even the RAF MR troops had to get the ferry, rather than fly back — and no sooner had they got back to Holyhead, they were called out to an air crash in South Wales.'

The two missing men, Keith McDonnell and Pat Doyle, had remained in touch with a paramedic from the rescue team throughout the rescue effort. They were advised to 'dig in' to the snow to protect themselves from the biting wind — the same wind which had whipped their map from their hands at around 4.00pm. In thick fog and temperatures several degrees below freezing, the race was on to find them.

Alongside the mountain rescue volunteers, police and coastguard were fifty members of the Irish Army Ranger Wing, qualified in Arctic survival skills, and five helicopters. Finally, at midnight,

Top: Preparing a casualty for lowering © Sally Armond. **Left:** Winter training in Scotland © George Manley. **Right:** Hi-line training Tin Can Gully © OVMRO.

came a breakthrough, when a group of rangers found the missing men, aided by a ping of their mobile signal and a lot of whistle blowing. It was another four hours before the cloud had lifted sufficiently to airlift them out — but not before their rescuers had carried them through thigh-deep snow for nearly four kilometres. It had been a twenty-four hour endurance for them, and pretty tough for their saviours too.

Keith McDonnell was diagnosed with frostbite on his toes and fingers, his condition made worse by the fact that he had been taking a blood-thinning drug since suffering a clot the previous year. His friend suffered some frostbite. McDonnell told the 'Irish Independent' that there was no point they felt they wouldn't be rescued, conceding that if they'd had to endure a second night on the mountain, 'they would have been in serious trouble'. He insisted they'd not been foolish and were carrying appropriate gear for the conditions and looked forward to 'a long hot bath and a glass of wine after his ordeal'.

The 'Irish Daily Mail' reported that hugging his girlfriend was a precious moment McDonnell feared he'd never see. 'When I was up there, I was thinking about my parents and my girlfriend and how they must be worried sick. That's what got me through'.

They had survived, he said, thanks to a spare mobile phone, a plastic bag and a chocolate bar. 'We wanted to build a snow hole but the ground was quite hard and we couldn't break through so we built a wind shelter using our ice axes and a waterproof plastic bag I had in my rucksack. We sat on our rucksacks. Luckily we had extra clothing — gloves, hats and extra equipment to keep warm — but our only food was a frozen Moro bar. My water bottle froze over. I had to shovel snow into my mouth for moisture. It was minus ten wind-chill and the gusts were strong.

'We knew we had hypothermia and shouldn't sleep but we'd drift off for thirty seconds at a time. We held each other for the whole night. At one point I started to hallucinate as the hypothermia set in.'

The making of a team leader

Besides cultivating international relationships, Tony Jones was involved both regionally and nationally, as well as representing the interests of mountain rescue at the government-led UK Search and Rescue (UKSAR). His interests and skills were diverse, his experience arguably unequalled (during his time with the team, he was involved in 904 search and rescue operations), yet he remains modest about his achievements. And he is generous in giving credit where credit is due. 'The vital word', he says, 'is in the title. Individuals are only part of the story. Without the team, my efforts wouldn't have come to anything'.

In a Mountain Rescue Committee newsletter in December 1980, he outlined a suggested syllabus for progressive training, suggesting that for a team to be properly effective, it was essential its leaders be 'proficient in all aspects of any work the team is asked to undertake. The foundation of a mountain rescue team is the commitment of the members to mountaineering'. He also recognised that the free-spirited nature of mountaineers tended not to coincide with a love of paperwork. 'Very few volunteers like administration. But a certain amount must be done'. Another

The most famous and influential of all the fables about Snowdonia are the medieval tales known as the 'Mabinogion', about the encounters between the mortal and underworlds.

observation which still rings true!

The issue of training became a frustration for John Hulse. He was concerned that the existing training structure lacked effectiveness. 'We had an archivist but no training officer!' Having expressed this very thought, he was duly designated team training officer in 1990 and, with this new-found 'authority', set about writing the team's training documents, including a logbook, 'brutally cloned from the RAF MRT logbook!'

He also led the introduction of the team leader evaluation process. 'The idea was to get some form of objective periodic review of team leaders so that the leadership cadre keep the respect of the team — and can be voted out if necessary. It ensures they keep their skills fresh, rather than resting on their laurels. It was a big change for the team but it needed to be done as part of the change from the autocratic form we had then, towards a more democratic and accountable model. The process is far from perfect but it was an important step forward.'

The Ogwen team is unique in having eight team leaders, rather than a single lead with deputies beneath them. Why so many? 'Because we can become quite busy,' explains Hulse, in something of an understatement. 'We realised having a single team leader didn't suit us. As a group, we're interdependent with complementary capabilities. It's very robust, consensual. We rarely disagree'.

It's a system that works well for them. When a call for help comes in, the team leader receives a text message and decides whether to call out the team. Team members then get a text to go to an RV point. Tim Bird is one of the most recent 'graduates', becoming a team leader in the spring of 2015.

'It isn't about hierarchy — more a sideways hierarchy. We have two team leaders on duty at the weekend and bank holidays. Whoever picks the call up, deals with it, then you've got to be using the computer to deal with the incident. Meanwhile, the second team leader can drive to base.'

He cites an incident in March 2015, when two men, aged 54 and 65, became lost on Y Garn in freezing temperatures. It was his first as a team leader. The men had made a brave effort to rescue themselves, wandering around the 3,107-foot mountain all night trying to find a path, but they were forced to call the emergency services at 6.30am when it became evident that the older man was developing hypothermia.

John Hulse was one of the duty team leaders that day. 'I took the initial call,' explains Hulse, 'and worked with the informant for at least an hour, including getting the 999 call sent to me to try to decipher where they were. It was a challenging incident as it was clear that both men were in trouble and getting close to succumbing to the cold having been out overnight in near-winter conditions. The way I handled the operation was to run the SARCALL log and the talking with informants from home, together with sorting the air assets and RAF MRT. The benefit of doing this at home where it is quiet is that I can do the work, share it electronically and have a lot of the preliminary stuff done by the time base truly comes online. Once at base, it's often far too noisy and busy! Meanwhile, Tim went up to base to start managing the hill response'.

'Other senior team leaders begin to arrive,' says Bird, but they don't interfere, just become team members. The strength is that you can then seek out the most appropriate person for advice — a skills audit, if you like. We all have different styles.

'The information was sporadic on the log — made worse by the initial message being taken by a non-mountaineering person with no knowledge of the area — and we couldn't use SARLOC [software capable of pinpointing a person through the GPS on their smartphone]. I requested the phone log from the police for clarification. The men were in a very exposed position. At one point, the information was that they were at the top of Devil's Kitchen, then the next was 'crossing a mountain fence'. It was a really interesting job — scaling it up as information came in.

'It was strange to be at the base organising the response rather than out on the hill leading a party but you have a progression in your team history. You see a job needs doing and you step forward. In terms of that rescue, I probably saved his life — so you can make a difference. The guy was in hospital for two days.'

'It's good that Tim had a challenging incident for his first team leadership role from base,' adds Hulse. 'You always remember the first incident as TL!'

The initial team leader evaluation scheme was adopted in March 1997. Leaders have the opportunity to stand down when they need to, and revert to ordinary team membership but, in any case, each team leader steps down from their post at the end of a three-year term. They can then apply for reselection, ratified by a secret vote at the AGM. Essentially, the system remains the same today as then, with only a bit of fine-tuning since. The committee and the other team leaders score each candidate, from nought to three with two the required standard, but candidates are also encouraged to score themselves, so there's a 'huge amount of self-evaluation', says Bird.

'You have to be honest with yourself. Going through the process is quite nerve-wracking. You never quite know how the team will support you — and they all have to vote for you. It took me eighteen months but it's a real opportunity, an honour and a privilege — you couldn't be parachuted in as you might be in other services. You need to come up from the ground and have the skills.'

FROM THE ARCHIVE

Head over heels in love, 30 July 2007: Sharon Parry felt on top of the world when her boyfriend proposed on a mountain but quickly fell to earth with a bump moments later when she slipped on scree, fell six feet and badly gashed her head above her right eye. She had been delighted to accept when partner Andy Laurence popped the question on bended knee on Moel Siabod and the magical moment was captured on camera by her seven-year-old daughter Olivia, who was in on the secret. The family, and their black Labrador, Devon, had to be picked up by the team and taken to hospital for the wound to be stitched.

'We got out our sandwiches,' said Sharon, 'and Andy got on his knee and popped the question. I was thinking it would have been so much nicer if we'd gone for a nice meal and I was in a dress instead of my walking gear! Then we were a quarter of the way back down when I just flipped. I was panicking, Olivia was screaming 'Help my Mummy!'

Andy bandaged her head and cleaned out Sharon's right eye which was covered in blood from the cut. But then feeling they were getting lost, he summoned help. A team member led them down to safety and the couple were taken by ambulance to hospital.

OGGI SNIPS

From the Guestbook, 2010: Many, many thanks again. All I can say is that we are damn lucky to have people like you in the world.

Ironically, Tony Jones fell victim to the democratic system and rules he helped put in place. He too became subject to re-election. He chose to resign but it was doubtless a difficult moment for him. He stood down as chairman in March 1990 but remained involved, both regionally and nationally and was awarded the MBE in January 1995 for his services to mountain rescue.

Volunteers wanted

Team members come from all sorts of backgrounds and in all sorts of shapes and sizes. As in those early days, some are mountain professionals — although this can present difficulties with attending call-outs during their working days. Often those who sit at desks for their day jobs stand a far better chance of being available to go on the hill when the SMS pings, but the list is long and varied — teachers, solicitors, health professionals, tree surgeons, web designers, police officers, shop and office workers, farmers... male and female, young and not quite so young! And it all starts with the trainees.

Now there is a very specific programme of training which every team member must follow, irrespective of their mountain experience. The active stuff starts with an initial hill day but, before that, there are a few criteria to fulfil. Applicants are expected to be active, all-season mountaineers with at least three years experience of general mountaineering. They must be familiar with basic rope work and capable of climbing a 'Diff' in boots in a safe manner — as opposed to being' a super-hard leader' — and able to climb Grade I snow gullies and fix simple winter belays. A good level of physical fitness and stamina is a must and they also need a good level of local area knowledge of north and east Snowdonia. 'In a nutshell', says Andy Harbach, they have to 'be mountaineers, navigate and carry stuff'.

Team and trainees must be sure they can commit to each other and work together. The first step is to fill in the 'blue form'. Then, if the committee approves them, they are invited to an initial hill day, an 'informal day out with a member of the training group or nominated team member' so both parties can get to know each other — usually under the more familiar wet and cloud of Ogwen. Although described as informal, the day is nevertheless structured. There are skills we expect them to demonstrate,' says Dave Worrall. 'They need to be able to lead a simple climb, cope on mixed ground and navigate'. Once accepted onto the list of trainee members, the applicant becomes a 'non-specialist' for police insurance purposes, picks up the necessary paperwork (training logbook, member guide and calendar) and, from that point on, is allowed to attend call-outs, albeit under supervision.

Before making it to full team member, they must achieve the expected attendance levels, join in the Scottish winter training trip, at least ten general training events and a first aid course. They are then reviewed every three months and assigned to one of three classes — Class 1: Training complete and ready for the final hill test; Class 2: Further training and/or assimilation time required; or Class 3: Rejection of application and removal from the list.

One of the most recent to make it up to full team member is Brian Robbins, who holds the dubious honour of being dubbed the team's 'oldest trainee'. He is also generally agreed to be one of the fittest! Defying the stereotypes, he joined the team aged seventy following a conversation with team member Tim Radford. He'd just completed his fourth 'Oggie 8' event. 'I said to Tim, if I'd been younger, I'd have joined. His response was, why not? You're fitter than many on the team!'

Now retired (but busier than ever) Brian's background is typical of many team members — parents who were keen outdoors people, a youth spent cycling, climbing, walking then a job secured in Caernarfon so he could be close to the mountains. Once there he was 'out on the hills every spare minute'. He took up fell running — completing all the major races and mountain marathons around the UK — got into diving, then paragliding at fifty and cross-country horse jumping at sixty. We can only speculate what eighty holds!

His first rescue was on Monday, 28 October 2013. 'The call-out came at 3.00am. I was enjoying a good night's sleep after spending Saturday and Sunday doing the OMM two-day mountain marathon in the Brecon Beacons and at the overnight camp fighting off hypothermia due to the lousy weather.

'Two males were attempting the Welsh 3000s. They'd set off at 9.30pm, up Pen yr Ole Wen but got totally wet through and demoralised. Chris Lloyd and I went up after two other team members who were looking for them. They'd had to come back down. We went up and found the men, got them down to lower levels and warmed up. The helicopter came in and took us all down to base.'

He applauds the formulated training structure. 'It covers everything — cascare, ropes, swift water and so on. You really progress through one stage to the next, with indoor scenarios followed by outdoor mock rescues on the crag, so you build a familiarity with the kit. The Scottish trip is very good — this year involved training in snow and ice, with a day off for bonding. You travel up Friday, train Saturday, have a free day on Sunday to climb, then there's a search scenario on Monday.

'You have to have confidence in the team members, especially on horrible ground. There's a lot of camaraderie in the team, everyone gels together and it works. It's good to feel you are a member of a team and the word team is what it's all about.'

The Scottish trip has been a regular feature in the team diary since 1992, and they have a habit of being uncannily eventful. 'We weren't getting good snow conditions in North Wales, so we

FROM THE ARCHIVE

Just one of those days, 31 March 1999: One family certainly had a day to remember during in North Wales. The May newsletter reports on a tale of disasters which started at home when the father dislocated his thumb while preparing to come to Snowdonia. Undeterred, they duly arrived and set off for a walk into Cwm Tryfan. Leaving his wife and one of the children in the valley, he struck out with his other daughter, who then slipped and bruised her leg. Trying to catch his daughter's fall, the father broke his wrist. (The record doesn't say whether it was the same hand/arm as the dislocation). The first report the team received was that the leg — presumably the daughter's leg — was broken and thirteen team members were involved in the rescue. Not the best of trips.

OGGI SNIPS

Volunteers wanted. Must live locally, have winter and summer mountaineering experience and be willing to carry ridiculously heavy loads at any hour of the day or night.

decided to go up to the Cairngorms to train,' explains Dave Worrall. 'On the first morning out of our second Scottish trip, we went up to the car park then, within two hours walking along the path, we came across a streak of blood. A guy had fallen from one of the gullies and slid a very long way. He was part of a family of four. We got to him and reported it. The Cairngorm team became involved and Ogwen were asked to support in the search for the other three members of the family. We were involved in three days of searches on the Cairngorm and Northern Corries. Various teams were involved in that rescue and eventually all four family members were recovered, unfortunately they had all died.'

On the ropes

The ability to work with ropes, and as a team, features high on the 'essentials' list for team members for very good reason: a high percentage of Ogwen's incidents demand technical expertise on very steep, otherwise inaccessible terrain. But there was a period, during the 1990s, when there was scant agreement about how things should be done.

'We fell into a void for about ten years on rope rescues,' says John Hulse. 'We'd send people on different courses, all over the place, trying to glean best practice but we couldn't seem to get all the threads together in a consistent way. The technique used on any one rescue was determined very much by whoever walked through the door to run the incident. There were four or five different techniques. It was all well-intended but there was definitely a negative impact in terms of quality and consistency. Lots of enthusiastic people but some unintended consequences.'

It was about this time that the work of Canadian Kirk Mauthner came to the fore. An international mountain guide based in British Columbia, Mauthner first got involved in mountain rescue in 1979, in the heart of the Purcell Mountains, and believes he was 'in the right place at the right time to witness change'. He took up the mantle of 'rigging for rescue', after serving as apprentice to the 'indomitable Arnor Larson', a pioneer of technical rope work who Ade Scott of 'Technical Rescue Magazine' described as 'being able to argue the hind legs off a donkey'. Larson's work laid the foundations for many of the principles still in play today. Mauthner continued to develop his work, building a reputation on questioning accepted practice. He consults and teaches technical rope rescue throughout North America and overseas, regularly visiting these shores to work with teams across the UK. He has also designed and tested equipment specifically for rescue purposes, such as the 540 Rescue Belay and the MPD (Multi-Purpose Device).

Mauthner first came to the UK thanks to Bill Batson, then chief instructor with the RAF Mountain Rescue Service. Batson, says Mauthner, 'was on a tour of rope rescue providers to see if they should outsource' and had travelled to Invermere, in British Columbia to do one of his seven-day courses, in September 1999. 'It was a revelation,' says Batson. 'I couldn't ignore it. I felt I had a duty to bring this thinking back'. Summing it up at the time, he wrote that 'the Old School has much to learn from the New World'. On his return, he went about changing the way the RAF did things.

'In May 2000, I arranged for Kirk to come over to the UK to deliver a 'Rigging for Rescue' course — as it was then called — at RAF Valley, followed a year later by a further course at Glenmore

troll
troll
troll

Lodge. This was attended by eleven RAF MRS personnel plus two civvy team members. We began to implement the techniques across the five RAF teams and I was invited to give a presentation at the mountain rescue conference and then a session at an MRC training weekend at Plas y Brenin. I delivered a total of five courses to the RAF MRS from 2000 to 2005 — the last one as a guest civvy and, where possible, I'd open up a couple of places on each course to civilian team members.'

Mike Margeson, then equipment officer for the Mountain Rescue Council (whose title had now segued, almost imperceptibly, from 'committee' to 'council') was also interested in Kirk's techniques. He organised a one-day seminar in Keswick in May 2000, which was 'absolutely transformational. It turned everything on its head. Kirk was saying, Okay, you've got a system but have you tested it?' Over the next two years, Margeson set up first a two-day workshop, then a six-day course at the High Borrans Centre, near Windermere, under the auspices of the MRC. Interest was growing across England and Wales but large pockets of scepticism persisted.

In Ogwen, Chris Onions was one of those who were keen to explore how this fresh way of looking at things might help the team. He and another team member approached the committee about attending one of Mauthner's courses in British Columbia but met with some resistance. 'They thought we were going on a holiday,' says Onions. 'And anyway, there weren't the financial resources available at the time. Our next step was to approach the region who were similarly sceptical.

'The attitude was that we were the experts, but we questioned that. We finally applied to Awards for All Wales and they offered the team the £4900 funding to go on the course and produce some resources. It was a useful amount of money for the time.'

Onions and his team colleague travelled to Wilmer, British Columbia for the seven-day course in September 2002. 'It was a great introduction to these techniques,' says Onions. The key thing with Kirk's work is that it's evidence-based, there's an underlying knowledge base behind it which then informs how you do things'.

John Hulse had been amongst the many sceptics who went along to the High Borrans course in 2002. His report in the team newsletter was as Damascene as Margeson and Batson had been before him.

'I was still only partly convinced the course would be beneficial but two other team members had attended the weekend session run by the MRC and were so impressed that they booked places on the full-week course in British Columbia. Here was an opportunity for me to attend the same course in the UK. This was too good an offer to refuse.

'The first day focused on theory, exploring the critical analysis of rescue systems and examining the worst-case events and loads that can impact a system. A new concept for me was the whistle test, which ensure the system retains its safety if everyone needs to suddenly abandon the lowering site for whatever reason — avalanche or rock fall and so on. The final element is destructive testing that identifies the point at which the system starts to fail, so allowing safety margins to be determined. We saw some amazing video footage of tests carried out by Kirk that showed the performance of different belay devices when subjected to a worst-case dynamic load. The following

Chris Lloyd as stretcher jockey: Stretcher training on The East Face of Tryfan © OVMRO.

days had progressively higher levels of practical work including stretcher work, pick-offs, steep slopes, high lines, compound pulley systems and moving over difficult edges.'

No longer the sceptic, Hulse returned home a firm advocate.

'There was a change management issue,' says Onions. 'We were keen to do things differently but the biggest hurdle was convincing others. John assisted with that — he wasn't frightened of change. It took some time before the committee said okay, we've had an insight, and suggested we got Kirk over from Canada to teach here in Wales'.

In fact, it was 2004 before Al Read, then training officer, reported that he hoped the team's 'technical rope rescue skills will now bring a period of consolidation'. In June that year the team paid for Mauthner to teach two courses at HMS Indefatigable, on Anglesey. The aim, said Read, was 'to teach a critical number of team members who had the right skill set so we could confidently deal with any technical rope rescue incident'.

'Kirk was great at sitting down over coffee and biscuits and looking at the sorts of rescues we did,' says Onions. He was genius at being able to absorb all that information, then run a five-day course aligned perfectly to our needs. He also ran a two-day weekend course for those who couldn't come during the week. It was a valuable part of the change process'.

Mauthner's philosophy is to have a standardised methodology, with everyone working to the same thing. He remains impressed with the way Ogwen dealt with the change. 'They'd picked up that something was amiss. They wanted to go light so I encouraged them to stay light. I also encouraged a huge amount of critical assessment — make sure you can answer the question: Why are you doing what you're doing? They invited me over to audit the way they do things. That revealed information I didn't have data on so they went to Lyon Equipment and did some tests.'

'We came away with our own emerging evidence base,' says Onions, 'which means we can spread the word with members and explain why we're doing things.

The ethos of allowing outside experts to audit their systems is long established in Ogwen. The first was in 1998, using assessors from the Langdale Ambleside and Aberdyfi teams. 'The objective was to see what we could learn from other teams and then use that as a vehicle to plan ahead,' says Hulse. 'We learned a huge amount from that and within a few years, much to our surprise, all the actions had been implemented!' A later audit focused on the team's water rescue capability.

'The audits have always been catalysts to change,' says Al Read. 'In the UK, we may be volunteers, but we've got some of the strongest mountain rescue teams you'll ever see. There's an immense sense of purpose and teamwork and with that you get great passion and a huge amount of professionalism'.

This formal audit process was taken up by the Irish teams, with Tony Jones as a regular independent assessor, assisted once by John Hulse and once by John Evans. 'A great learning experience,' he says.

Mauthner's technical rope rescue courses continue to influence mountain rescue teams across the UK. Some have remained true to the purist form of his teachings, others have continued to develop different aspects to their own needs. The early courses questioned the single rope procedures still common with many teams at the time and either no belay at all or the sort of dynamic belay used by climbers, such as a figure of eight or Sticht plate. Self-equalising anchors

The names of summits usually refer to local features: Y Garn, which resembles a large cairn, translates literally as 'the cairn'.

Team help save walkers in Cairngorms. Daily Post 12 February 2013: There's never a dull moment for team members, least of all when on their winter training jaunt to the Cairngorms. Sometimes it's as simple as one team member finding himself about to descend an icy path, only to discover his crampons were not in the rucksack as he imagined, but back in the comparative warmth and safety of his Land Rover, at the bottom of the hill (fortunately, he made it down to tell the tale). Other times, it's team members getting drafted in to assist with local searches. On this occasion, it was an overnight search for a group of students.

'The weather conditions up there were atrocious,' said Chris Lloyd, 'with strong winds, driving snow and a high risk of avalanche. Seven young men had been walking along a steep plateau in poor visibility when the leader fell about 150 metres down the Jacob's Ladder snow gully. He survived the fall and successfully walked uninjured but the second leader went to have a look and see what happened when there was an avalanche and he fell to his death. That left five inexperienced walkers at the top.'

The first leader raised the alarm and was rescued soon afterwards. The five still at the top also raised the alarm but had no idea where they were. They were told to walk along a bearing until they could link with other search and rescue teams. Finally, they heard a helicopter through the clouds, raised the alarm and were airlifted to safety during the early hours of the morning.

too were up for scrutiny. The thinking now is towards mirrored or dual capability systems where each rope in a two-rope system is fully capable and competent at being a mainline and a back up.

The Ogwen team went on to produce a definitive manual for team members, illustrated by George Manley. A professional illustrator and a mountaineering instructor, Manley had the drawing skills and an understanding of mountaineering. In 2015, the manual is heading towards its third version, as new developments gain ground. [Manley is also responsible for the illustrative maps on pages 12 to xx of this book]. Mauthner continues to work with the team and he too is constantly reviewing his systems in the light of new data.

Faking it

Clearly, whether it's casualty care, technical rope rescue, navigation, jumping in and out of helicopters, or swift water rescue — a huge amount of team training involves hands-on practice. Often, it involves a certain amount of play-acting — when team members, or their long-suffering friends and family, find themselves strapped to a stretcher as the 'casualty', in sometimes quite extreme circumstances.

When it comes to search dogs, pretending to be lost or injured can be something of an obsession for the 'dog bodies' who weekly volunteer to 'hide' in ever more inventive locations, in the name of dog training. Be it buried in snow holes, hidden by bracken or stranded on a ledge, there they will sit for hours on end, wrapped in their thermals, good book in hand, squeaky toy at the ready.

Sally Armond and her nine-year-old dog, Spin are currently the only 'search dog team' on the Ogwen call-out list, in contrast to earlier days. 'An enormous amount of time and effort goes into training a search dog,' says Armond, 'I've always been humbled by the experience of dog training and assessment because so many people volunteer to help out during our monthly training weekends — assessors, bodies, caterers and accommodation are all needed to help the training run smoothly.

'Within Ogwen, I owe much to Jed Stone, a very experienced, but now retired search dog handler. He was pivotal in helping me train Spin when she was a pup. He helped develop her tenacity and stamina during complex and difficult searches.'

Armond recounts a more recent training event when 'young' Brian Robbins, whilst still a fledgling trainee, volunteered to act as a body during a multiple body search exercise. The area was a large and very intricate mountainside, which needed to be covered within two hours. Brian was the first body Spin found, so she suggested he accompany her for the rest of the search, to get a better picture of how search dogs work.

'I though it prudent to warn him that I moved quickly on the hill when working Spin, but I said I'd keep an eye on him. A few minutes of hard, steep slog later, I turned round concerned I'd left Brian

behind only to find him practically on my shoulder, hands in pockets, skipping along nonchalantly!' Demonstration, were it needed, that one should never make assumptions about age and fitness!

'It's great that new team member Alex King has started training his dog Ben through the early stages,' adds Armond. 'And I'd love to see others come forward to train, despite the heavy commitment required.'

Sometimes, the role-playing involves getting very wet. In March 2011, team members joined a three hundred-strong group of rescuers from all over Wales for a 'flooding exercise' in Bala, to test their skills in real-life scenarios. Exercise Gwyniad — based on the prehistoric fish of the same name, indigenous to Llyn Tegid — formed part of Exercise Watermark, set up to test responses to severe flooding, following recommendations made by Sir Michael Pitt in 2007.

The set-up was dramatic, with RNLI volunteers being winched from the roof of a partially submerged caravan in the freezing-cold lake and team members from Ogwen and the neighbouring North East Wales team wading into the lake before having to swim to three stricken 'casualties'. They were aided by RNLI colleagues in their inshore lifeboat. One onlooker, safe on the lake shore, observed that it was 'good weather to test them. Really rough conditions.'

'There are three people stuck inside the caravan,' Chris Lloyd told the press, adding, a little dramatically, 'and we don't know whether they're dead or alive!'

Elsewhere, other dramas were unfolding, each one based on a real-life incident — one with the casualty trapped by his leg in a gate and fencing under water, another in which trapped canoeists were rescued from a weir on Afon Tryweryn. Meanwhile, rescuers using rope equipment traversed the Tryweryn higher up stream, to reach stranded casualties who had been winched and rescued to higher ground by an RAF Sea King.

'There was national level scrutiny of the capability of the exercise participants,' says Chris Onions. 'And it was without doubt that the voluntary sector, including mountain rescue team members, had performed exceptionally well. The adaptable and flexible approach taken by the mountain rescue community would serve the country well, given the likelihood of future significant flooding events.'

It was a significant exercise for the Ogwen team, because the floods of 2005 and 2006 had gone right to the heart of their community. Indeed, over the years, a number of individuals have made a significant contribution to the team's ability to excel at getting wet.

Preparing to winch: Sally Armond and her dog Spin prepare for transportation in the Sea King © Sally Armond.

CHAPTER SIX

Water, water everywhere

The Conwy valley is no stranger to flooding. Throughout its history, heavy rains have accumulated and spilled over the river's rim into the surrounding fields and farmsteads, drowning livestock and spoiling crops. But legend had it that these occasional floods were more than freaks of nature, they were the work of an enraged monster, the Afanc, who was said to break river banks when enraged. Variously depicted as a crocodile, beaver or dwarf-like creature or demon, the Afanc lived in Llyn yr Afanc (which translates as the 'Beaver Pool'). Many attempts had been made to kill him but his hide was so tough that no spear, arrow or weapon could pierce it.

The wise men of the valley held a meeting. The Afanc must somehow be enticed from his pool and removed far beyond the mountains, where he could cause no further trouble. They called for the finest blacksmith in the land to forge the strong iron chains to bind and secure the beast, and for Hu Gadarn and his two long-horned oxen, to haul him. But how to lure him from his lair?

The Afanc, it was said, had a liking for beautiful maidens. The villagers asked many beautiful maidens to volunteer, but none would do so — until one especially beautiful maiden, the daughter of a local farmer, volunteered. The wise men and all the men who lived along the River Conwy hid in the trees and bushes with the chains and the oxen ready as the maiden approached the water.

Softly, she called to him. The waters began to heave and churn and soon the monster's head appeared. Bravely, the maiden stood her ground, gazing fearlessly

Taking a leap: Swift water rescue training © Dave Worrall.

into the monster's green-black eyes, as her gentle lullaby floated through the air. Slowly, the great body of the Afanc crawled out of the lake towards the girl, his head gradually sinking to the ground in slumber, so sweet was her song.

The men rushed forward to bind the beast with their chains. But, just as they'd done so, the Afanc awoke. Roaring and snorting with rage, it tried to escape, sliding back into the water, but it was too late. The chains were long and very strong. The oxen braced their muscles and began to pull, dragging the captured creature from the lake. It took every ounce of their strength and every available man to pull him onto the bank. On and on they hauled him, to Llyn Ffynnon Las [commonly known as Glasllyn, above Llyn Llydaw], close to the summit of Snowdon. There the chains were loosed and, with a roar, the monster leapt into the deep blue water where he remains trapped forever, imprisoned by the sturdy rock banks of the lake.

Such was one of the many version of this myth. Yet, sadly, despite the Afanc's removal to that place far away, the waters have continued to be a threat. The successive devastation of 2004 and 2005 left homeowners fearful of when the next flood might strike. These were, they said, 'one in thirty year' events.

After succeeding John Hulse as training officer, Al Read had continued to maintain water training for the team, concerned about the high risk to team members of water operations combined with the lack of suitable equipment available to them. In January 2005, that training paid off. Ogwen was able to commit team members with local knowledge and suitable vehicles to support the emergency services. As floodwater devastated the entire length of the Conwy valley, four rescues were recorded: a Manweb engineer plucked to safety from the top of his van outside Trefriw, two council workers trapped in their vehicle by flood waters on the B5106 and an off-duty policewoman stuck on her way home from work.

'We were told that Trefriw had been cut off by the water, but we were able to access the village through the night without too much of a problem because we had suitable vehicles, local knowledge and dry suits — and we could walk along the sides of the valley. The mountain rescue bit was very much about access and egress. We also manned crossroads to discourage drivers from the A470.

'This was the start of our involvement with flood work. And, afterwards, the committee decided to support local flood operations in the future. We wanted to support the community and our capability was well-suited to that.'

This initial work led to Ogwen becoming a DEFRA Type C team on the national Water Rescue Asset Register — the first mountain rescue team to be so.

Now involved, both professionally and as a team member, with the development and teaching of water rescue, Read has helped deliver courses geared to mountain rescue which are disseminated across England and Wales. A key contact in this is Paul Amos, himself a water incident management instructor and also chairman of trustees for Mountain Rescue England and Wales.

The association with Amos began in 2007, when government funding required a key document to be written, leading to the Flood Rescue Concept of Operations (FRCO). Certain areas — search, rescue, communications, helicopters — demanded the unique knowledge and experience of mountain rescue. Read was invited to support the FRCO review meetings, keen as they were to

OGGI SNIPS

The Glyderau, with their boulder-strewn summits, means 'heap of stones, and Tryfan, with its three small peaks translates as 'the three headed mountain'.

develop a multi-agency approach to work in the flood environment.

With the Flood Rescue National Enhancement Project came two million pounds of DEFRA money, to develop the capability to respond on a national basis. Read suggested to the committee that there was a funding opportunity for Ogwen, if the team could generate a Type C response. The team leaders and committee said 'Yes!' to developing the opportunity but a firm 'No!' to taking the money — which would have amounted to just £56!

The result is that Ogwen team members are now available for national call-outs, wherever they may be required in England and Wales — although they have yet to be deployed nationally for flooding, because every time it has flooded nationally there have also been floods in North Wales.

Read joined Outreach Rescue in 2007, in an attempt to stop having to travel the 40,000-odd miles a year he was then doing. In his work there, he is regularly involved with training fire and rescue service personnel and has helped develop the National Resilience Assurance Team Tactical Adviser course for flood and water rescue. He became heavily involved in the fire and rescue New Dimension Project, concerned with urban search and rescue, post-911.

He believes standards within Ogwen have been maintained since the start, despite there not being many professionally-qualified team members involved.

When it all goes wrong

Without doubt, Read holds an impressive CV. Since that first 'long, cold and memorable night' on Tryfan, events in his professional and personal lives have seemingly conspired to deepen his mountain rescue experience. In 1988, when the town of Lockerbie was devastated by a terrorist bomb, he was working at Prestwick as the duty weather forecaster for the Royal Navy, his job to provide support for units in the theatre of operations. At the time there was a search and rescue flight based there, set up the year before. Read boarded an aircraft to go to the scene — being one of the few sober in that pre-Christmas period, due to being on duty. But at the last minute, they found a crewman, so he got out again. Despite a busy career in the Royal Navy, including living three years in the Netherlands, he regularly returned to North Wales and undertook call-outs, becoming a team leader in 1999, and team training officer soon afterwards.

In 2000, he left the Royal Navy and travelled straight to Greenland with fellow team member John Hulse, to cross the eastern ice cap. He returned to find his wife had secured him a job at BAE Systems in his absence. Alongside all his achievements on behalf of the team, he is now a fully qualified water instructor, rope rescue instructor, instructor in just about anything the team undertakes apart from confined space. Despite all of this, nothing could protect him from a 'life-changing' accident on 27 November 2009.

A group of kayakers were descending the River Conwy, late in the afternoon, on a recce for their canoe club but, due to the poor light they missed the all-important get-out point and ended up stranded on various rocks and ledges just past the road bridge. One of the group managed to scramble up the bank and raise the alarm. Before too long, fire service, police, ambulance, mountain rescue team members and 22 Squadron had assembled on the Penmachno bridge.

RX04 AFK

'The call came in at 5.30pm that two paddlers were trapped on the River Conwy below the Penmachno bridge. I was in the Cotswold shop in Betws at the time, buying a head torch (they were trying to close!) so I was only ten minutes from the incident site. I finished buying the torch, popped in the batteries and made my way down towards the blue lights on the bridge with both my water and mountain rescue kit. Sally Armond was already there. North Wales Fire and Rescue Service were already setting up lighting and starting to consider rescue plans.

'It was raining heavily but I could see two people in the eddy on the left-hand side of the river, fifty metres downstream from the bridge and twenty metres from the edge of the gorge. Just beyond that point, the river goes through a vertical drop and round a corner. Then, 150 metres further on, it meets the Conwy Falls — a life-threatening place.

'The fire service incident commander was with the retained crew from Llanwrst and Betws, so he knew I was an instructor. We devised a plan. As I was the only one there with both mountain and water kit, we'd set up a system to access the two in the river and pull them out of the water onto a ledge, then wait for a rescue system to be set up. Given the urgency, it was a single line process to get down to them.

'I was lowered into place, putting a throw line round a tree en route down, so I could tie them off once I got them out of the water. I got down to the water. The girl was hanging on to a handhold under water. And her friend was hanging onto her!

'There was a ripple on the rock, a one-inch wide ledge just enough to stand on. I got my feet onto it and from there I could lean down and stretch the rope to grab the shoulder straps of her personal flotation device (PFD). I pulled her in closer then grabbed her friend. Through a combination of lifting and pulling, climbing and kicking, I managed to manhandle them onto the ledge then the three of us shuffled about four feet upstream to a rock crevice, where I tied them off with the throw line. Then I got out of the water and waited.

'At that point, mentally, the high risk bit was done. The rope rescue system was set up above me, one of the fire service personnel was lowered down and the girl was hauled up. It's not that you relax, but the initial tension of figuring the logistics, then getting the casualties out of the water gives way to knowing the system is in place and there's a team up there supporting you.

'Then Bang!!

'My next recollection is looking down at my foot and thinking, Where's my boot? and then a jumbled rush of thoughts. I've broken my arm! Can't breathe! Why am I wet?...

'It didn't register then but I'd been hit by a boulder, hitting my shoulder, arm and chest on the right side. Bright lights glared in front of me. Comprehension slowly dawned… fingers moving but still can't breathe… the ultimate winding… sheer shock…

'Eventually, I managed to take a breathe, ribs crunching, body harness crushing into my chest with each attempt. Can't use right arm…

'You okay? The leading fire fighter shouts down but I can't reply, still struggling to breathe.

'Somehow, turning on the rope, I managed to get myself back onto the ripple ledge and shuffle into the crevice where one of the casualties was still waiting to be hauled. He hadn't seen a thing.

The changing face of water rescue: Top: Stewart Dethick, centre, in red during the recovery of a fatality. Bottom: The Flood Rescue response team, ready for action. Photos © OVMRO.

I was still struggling to breathe but, strangely, still having a conversation with the lad, making him aware of the next part of the rescue, oblivious to my own now more serious condition!

'Two minutes later the fire service had lowered someone down and, now the priority, I was swiftly attached to the system and hauled up. Time now more pressing than the need for finesse, the edge transition was enthusiastic — and exquisitely painful!

'Jed Stone, one of the Ogwen team leaders, who was managing the incident from the mountain rescue point of view, helped me out at the top. We scrabbled back to the road, climbing the ladder with one hand, onto an ambulance trolley and over the bridge to the ambulance, where I was cut out of my dry suit, given 5mg morphine and oxygen, and transported to Betws for a Sea King transfer to Bangor Hospital.

'I couldn't lie down and breathe, and my pulse and sats were low. As a triathlete, prior to the accident my resting pulse rate had been in the thirties, which caused a lot of problems for the nursing staff who had to keep resetting the pulse oximeter! Diane, my wife, summed it up: I didn't look well! But, X-rays done, four hours later they discharged me into Diane's care. As she is a trauma nursing sister, getting me home to her care seemed preferable to a Friday night in A&E! Once home, I was dispatched to bed — climbing the stairs a feat in itself — where I spent the next thirty hours, propped upright. I didn't feel like eating, struggled to drink, felt battered.

'By Sunday, Diane said it was time to get up and go downstairs. It took me an hour to get there, but get there I did, to spend the rest of the day on the sofa, a range of visitors helpfully reaffirming how poorly I looked. That said, I might not have been 100% better, but I was certainly a bit brighter.

'Then came Monday and a call from Dr Linda Dykes at Bangor Hospital. She needed to see me back there. Now! There were concerns about the mechanism of injury. Where originally they'd assumed I'd fallen onto the rock, now it seemed probable that the boulder had fallen from fifty feet above, onto me.

FROM THE ARCHIVE

From the online Guestbook, April 2014: I cannot believe it will be soon be fifteen years since our rescue from Heather Terrace. It was pitch black with gale force winds and horizontal rain. But your men traversed a waterfall all the same to reach us, as it was too windy for the chopper. Thank goodness someone saw us in the valley when I SOS'd my torch.

My girlfriend at the time was deaf, and so when we were finally guided down to the valley below only to be met by the bright lights of BBC cameras who were making a documentary on your team, we were sure we would be in it. However, we didn't make it in, which is probably a good thing, but the memories of the evening are alive and well, in my mind at least.

I'd like to extend my thanks and gratitude to the gentlemen on that evening who came and saved our bacon and to all those souls who continue to save the bacon of similarly silly persons such as ourselves. I have been back and scrambled Tryfan and Snowdon a few times since then, but tended to stick to the main routes as much as possible on those days. Keep up the good work — donation on its way!

OGGI SNIPS

From the 'pink' forms: November 2005: Having failed on an easy route, they continued to a longer, more difficult one with only limited hours of daylight. Bizarre.

'Ultrasound and CT scan were waiting for me. I'd walked into both but to my surprise there was a wheelchair waiting for me at the other end with instructions to get in and not move! A bed in ICU, IV catheters and gas lines, were ready and waiting for me. My liver was lacerated, with two haematomas — if they burst, I would die. I'd gone from healthy to intensive care in moments.

'That said, underlying the trauma-induced problem, I was probably the fittest, healthiest person there. What might have gone wrong in a less-fit individual, hadn't. Relative to my immediate neighbours, I was in good shape! Three days later, I was transferred to Fazakerley in Liverpool where further CT scans confirmed I was still bleeding. To make matters worse, my shoulder dislocated in the X-ray machine. On Thursday, I was in surgery, to put clotting stents in my liver.'

A week later, Read began the long road to recovery. It was four months before he was back at work but mountain rescue remained a draw. Set up with an airwave radio during the extended cold weather, he was able to manage mountain rescue responses from the comfort of home — including an avalanche at Aber Falls. Team members ferried him to and from incident locations where possible. On one occasion, this previously keen and accomplished ski mountaineer, even went out in skis and managed a 300 metre shuffle. 'A point of principle!' By early May, he was back in the swimming pool, barely able to manage a length of 'doggie paddle'. Still, six years on, his swimming hasn't returned to pre-accident level.

Nerve examinations on his shoulder showed that the brachial plexus was damaged. The following year he was referred to Oswestry, an orthopaedic centre of excellence, for a nerve graft to aid shoulder mobility but it failed to take. The accident has left him with what he describes as 'a level of disability'. Although he is far more active than most people, muscle wastage in his right shoulder means carrying a rucksack can be difficult.

Some weeks later, Read nervously went back to the incident site with team mate John Hulse. They scrambled down, trying to work out precisely where the accident had happened and whether they could see the boulder.

'The two years after April 2010 were about getting fit and better and coming to terms with this life-changing injury and disability. After the nerve graft there was the whole physio process to go through again and, prior to that, I'd been off work for a further ten weeks and not allowed to move my arm. But, since then, I'm now back skiing, walking, scrambling, running, even nervous riding of bicycles, and still doing swift water stuff, trying to live with the limitations of it.

'That time in hospital gives you plenty of time to think about what's important and find out what you want to do. I try to do what I enjoy doing but I do get tired more easily. It's surprised me the level of impact the accident has had on me in terms of physicality — from ultra-fit to struggling to climb stairs and swim. Then there's the psychological impact, the frustration, managing expectations. You have to find alternatives. For example, now I do more ski touring. I'm more conscious of living. Early on, I struggled with simple mental tasks, memory — as if the lack of mental stimulation switched off a previously active mind.

'But, in terms of that incident, I'd do the same again. You hear people shouting Help us, we're going to die! and you do something. We did the right thing. It could've happened to anyone.'

COBWEB CORNER

Sheep rescued from island, 14 November 2009: When two members of Global Rescue Services and three Ogwen team members heard that a sheep was stranded on an island, they quickly scrambled into action, out of the pub, up to the lake and into a dinghy. They reached the grassy thirty foot square island, some fifty yards into Llyn Elsi at 12.30pm, but the creature panicked and leapt into the water. Using the outboard motor, the nautical shepherds gave chase and dragged the heavy, waterlogged ewe alongside the dinghy to the shore.

Thunderous water

Dave Worrall had just joined the team during the team's first rescue at Conwy Falls, scene of Tony Jones's ingenious rope system in 1988. 'I was a bit fresh-faced but it was the most exciting thing I've ever been involved with! It's fair to say we were pretty dreadful at that sort of rescue. We made a lot of mistakes. I wasn't involved in the technical side. Doug Jones had gone down to pick up the canoeist. We were all lined up on the parapet and Tony got a really good rope system going. Doug went down with an aircraft strop to haul the casualties back up. Trouble was, when we were bringing them up, both of them instinctively reached out to grab the bridge, which loosened the hold of the strop around their chest. I still remember the look of sheer panic on everyone's face as they tried to get them back over the parapet before they slipped out of the strop!'

The incident certainly demonstrated that mountain rescue techniques were readily transferable to the water environment but it took Stuart Dethick to highlight the risks to team members, that using mountaineering kit in water wasn't necessarily best practice. He organised a 'river rescue day' on the River Trent, in Nottingham, in 1993.

'It was a very cold day,' recalls Al Read. 'Winter in a wetsuit is never ideal! But it moved the team on hugely in terms of technical knowledge. His input provided the reasoning to go back and keep training and this tied in well later, with the rigging techniques being developed by Kirk Mauthner. The whole process was bringing together mountain rescue and water skills, meeting most of the criteria for most of the rescues being undertaken at the time'.

Dethick was a canoe instructor at the time. 'It was a fascinating time,' he says. 'Canoes were getting smaller and stronger. At the same time, we were getting tourists falling into waterfalls. I was comfy in the water environment. My working week was spent in it. That first course at Nottingham was a good course. We looked at how you get hold of people, swim through fast water, throw lines and rescue systems.

Water incidents come in several guises. Canoeists missing their get-out at Conwy Falls is a regular feature. There's an urgency to those rescues, the fragile line between life and death ever-present. But there are technical systems in place now, developed through experience over the years, designed to minimise the risks as far as humanly possible.

OGGI SNIPS

Online Guestbook, 2008: Living on Anglesey I never had much time for going out in the mountains but after reading about your exploits I feel I want to go and explore.

When two kayakers got stuck in October 2013, their head cams recorded their frantic calls for help. They only realised they'd missed the exit when they'd passed under Penmachno bridge. Fortunately, they were able to paddle to an eddy and a passer-by heard their yells. Some other canoeists lowered a rope which one of the men was able to use to escape the river. His canoe became stuck in the eddy. The other paddler lost his canoe and was left next to the rock in the river. The team was able to set up a rope recovery system and haul the man back to the road. And, unlike those three early paddlers, whose request to recover their canoe was so summarily denied by Tony Jones, this time it was different. Another rope system was rigged and the second canoe successfully recovered.

In another incident in November 2000, a twenty-year-old Bangor student broke his leg when his canoe overturned in treacherous weather at Betws y Coed. The lad had ventured out in the rain and rough water with a group of friends but soon got into trouble at Fairy Glen. Ambulance teams were unable to reach him because of the depth of the gorge.

It was a challenging task lifting him to safety. 'We had to lift him out of the water on a stretcher attached to ropes,' said Chris Lloyd. 'He had to be lifted from a thirty-foot vertical gap.' It took fifteen team members to complete task but his ordeal wasn't yet over. 'Once he'd been lifted to safety, we had to carry him through the trees in appalling weather to get him to the ambulance.'

Then there are the accidental drownings in lakes and waterfalls, tragedies in which team members may be unable to save a life but work with equal care and efficiency to recover bodies and comfort relatives.

In August 2006, a group of teenagers watched in horror as their friend gave them the thumbs-up before sliding to his death down a waterfall at Cyfyng Falls, Capel Curig. Christopher Turnbull and his pals had arranged online, days before, to meet for a day out on the river. Describing that fateful day, at the inquest in December, one of the teenagers said he and three others had played in the water until it got too cold and then got out, dressed and changed. They found a café but it was closed and made their way to a bus stop at about 12.30pm.

'There was a waterfall with fast-flowing water. We saw Christopher [nicknamed 'Debs'] and another friend starting to make their way towards the top of a waterfall. By the time we got closer, Debs was sat on top of the waterfall. We realised he was going to slide down it.'

It was a manoeuvre Turnbull had apparently done before, without problem, but this time he jumped ten feet down the waterfall into the rock pool and simply disappeared.

'Debs had no fear,' said another. 'We couldn't see him. We thought he was hiding and having a laugh. We tried to save him but the current was too strong'.

Realising he wasn't going to resurface — and without a mobile signal — they began frantically knocking on the doors of nearby houses. Turnbull's body was later found by a police diver at the bottom of a rock pool. 'This is a desperately sad event, which has arisen from youthful high spirits,' said the coroner, adding that risks attract people and he couldn't 'fence off rivers for the whole of their courses'.

A month after his death, Turnbull's five friends joined his mother at the Falls to throw roses into the river. They were joined by the teenagers' family liaison officer, Mark Howell-Walmsley, and Ogwen's Al Read. Debbie Turnbull wore the gold, three Welsh feathers necklace her son had worn when she faced the heart-breaking task of identifying his body. Determined to save lives and educate youngsters to the dangers of rivers and sea, she set about raising funds to buy equipment for the team and other rescue organisations. The result was a raft bearing the words 'Christopher Turnbull's Barmy Army'. River And Sea Sense, a water safety campaign in memory of her son, was launched in 2008 to educate children and young adults about the dangers of water.

Even the relative tranquillity of a lake can be lethal. In July 1999, a twenty-two-year-old volunteer on a Prince's Trust course from Merseyside died when he and a friend apparently tried to take a shortcut across a freezing Cwm Idwal, fully dressed in mountaineering kit, including boots. Divers searched for five hours before finding a body. The other swimmer was found safe and well.

Roger Jones told the press, 'These lakes are deep and have all sorts of undulations. Even on the hottest of summer days they are cold. They never really warm up. You have got to take extreme care and people shouldn't take these places light heartedly.'

Machynlleth

On the evening of Monday 1 October 2012, in the quiet mid-Wales market town of Machynlleth, five-year-old April Jones was abducted from near her home. The search for this 'happy-go-lucky' little girl had a profound effect far beyond the small community that was her home. That fateful evening marked the start of one of the largest search and rescue operations in the UK for over twenty years. What began as a local search involving neighbouring teams from Aberdyfi and Brecon, quickly evolved into a multi-agency operation involving many services, agencies and members of twenty-three mountain and cave rescue teams, as well as four hundred willing members of the local community.

Ogwen team members were among the first to become involved because of their water ability. Dave Worrall couldn't get there at the start due to work commitments but wanted to get down there

COBWEB CORNER

Hoax calls: The 2007 Annual report describes an unusual incident which originated as a 999 call to the police, claiming the casualty was injured and also suffering life-threatening allergic reactions up in the hills. Obviously, this demanded a very rapid response, which the team duly made. Only the casualty wasn't where he claimed to be (not, in itself, that unusual), but he also wasn't making himself easy to find. After much searching by the police and RAF helicopters, plus Ogwen ground teams, getting very concerned for his safety as time elapsed, he was located. It turned out to be a hoax call, one more to add to many this individual had made in the past. 'Looking back at our response,' concluded Paul Smith, 'it is good to know we had people with the level of training and suitable equipment and medication to deal with the incident had it been real.

OGGI SNIPS

The famous, and well climbed, Idwal slabs are composed of Rhyolitic Tuff which is volcanic ash erupted from ancient volcanos.

and help as quickly as he could, like so many other people. 'I remember going to Dolgellau, conscious of the number of teams down there. There were a lot of groups doing bank searches and through the forest, but we were there specifically to search the rivers. Our involvement was very much water-based.

'I went to the leisure centre first for a briefing. It was pretty much night by then, so we were going out in the dark. The place given to search was pretty much where [suspect] Mark Bridger's home was, towards Dolgellau. People pointed out his house as we neared. We were taken to a bit of river closest to it. There was a lot of water in the river so it was a difficult search. Lots of parts we couldn't get into, it was too rough. There was a sense of wanting to not miss any clues. We searched in very difficult conditions for three or four hours then came back next day, further down the river. The water was dropping all the time. The longer it went on, we knew the less chance we had of finding anything.

'Even on the first night, TV news crews were following people around asking questions. The team was down there for pretty much all of the time we were required. Sometimes, in those conditions, you're as much concerned for your own safety, with the state of the water, but we were talking about a young child's life so you do take risks. Tim Bird was trying to access one bit and I could see him starting to get swept away so I threw him a line. After that we started to be a bit more circumspect. I'd heard him shout and, because of the training we'd done, it was automatic. I knew to get a throw line out to him — knew, because of all the training, that was the thing to do.'

'The sheer scale of the operation, the large rural area to be searched, and the incessant press attention produced many challenges for the search management team,' says John Hulse. With Tim Radford and Andy Harbach, he had been drafted in to take over the search management and relieve those who'd been working on it for four long days.

Radford had initially gone down on the Wednesday night, as part of the water search team, but after going home from the water search returned to help as a search manager the next day. 'It quickly became apparent that the in-place search management team were exhausted and needed to be relieved. So we took over. Andy was the planner, with John helping.'

Sally Armond was deployed with her dog, Spin. 'I was working in Swansea at the time, so other team members arranged for Spin to be delivered from North Wales to the search area three days in a row, so I could meet up and work her. There were dog handlers there from all over the UK. We were micro-searching with our hearts in our mouths. There was so little information.'

As the week progressed, the logistics grew ever more complex as more and more team members from across England and Wales arrived in Machynlleth to support the search. Search management resources expanded to meet the high demand for planning, identifying areas, documentation, briefing and debriefing — and the close collaboration between all the agencies involved was critical. Beyond mid-Wales, other teams were providing back-up for their neighbouring teams, absent from their patches. Rows of satellite trucks stacked up around the centre. Journalists and camera crews were everywhere. Hungry for news, they were 'filming us, filming the town and filming each other,' says Hulse. 'One recurring image was the sea of red mountain rescue jackets that provided that vital level of identification for our members in the field and at the leisure centre.'

Despite their grief, the generosity and support of the people of Machynlleth was unprecedented.

MOUNTAIN RESCUE

'It will never be forgotten by those who attended,' says Hulse. 'We were offered food, help, accommodation. It was a truly humbling experience to be there.'

On 6 October, local man Mark Bridger was charged with child abduction, murder and attempting to pervert the course of justice. He appeared before magistrates at Aberystwyth two days later, where he was additionally charged with the unlawful concealment and disposal of a body. He was remanded into custody and held at HMP Manchester pending an appearance at Caernarfon Crown Court, via video link, on 10 October.

In the absence of a body, the circumstances of April's death may never be known. Bridger's trial began on 29 April 2013. A month later, he was found guilty of abduction, murder and perverting the course of justice. Later that day, he was sentenced to life imprisonment with a whole-life tariff, dubbed a 'pathological liar' and 'a paedophile' by the judge.

After the verdict, it was revealed that Bridger had confessed to the prison chaplain that he had disposed of April's body in the fast-flowing Dulas, the river which flows past Bridger's house before terminating in the River Dyfi near Machynlleth. Dyfed-Powys Police, however, said they doubt the claims, believing he scattered April's remains across the countryside near his house.

The community of Machynlleth changed forever that day but their dignity was there for all to see, as pink ribbons fluttered across coats and collars in memory of their lost child. Her loss also changed forever the way mountain rescue teams approach multi-agency operations.

'There were clearly many learning points,' says John Hulse. 'Soon afterwards, we capture the views of all those attending with an online survey. We also surveyed members of the overhead team to look at the issues faced in managing and leading the operation for mountain rescue.

'From a purely personal perspective, the key challenges included our ability to rapidly scale up beyond the team-centric model, scalability of the search planning software, interoperability of IT between teams and regions, lack of structured communications between the mountain rescue regions, the challenges of working with entities that didn't know our capabilities, pressure from the media to perform and, finally, managing large numbers of resources in a timely manner. I learned a huge amount from this operation. It completely changed my perspective of search and rescue.'

The April Jones case was another step change in the team's perception of where it sits in the world. 'Originally,' says Hulse, 'it was mountaineers helping mountaineers but now it's about community. It's transformed over the last five years and April Jones was the most obvious aspect of that change. When the floods came, or when the snow comes down, many communities are cut off. Morally, we should help. It's our community and there's an increasing engagement there.'

It was also one of many tales which will hold in the memory forever, some tragic, some harrowing, some to which hindsight lends an ever-developing humour. And memory can be a fickle thing, so stories often differ and change according to viewpoint, individual involvement and the passing of the years!

Searching for April Jones: Top: Team members search the river margins. Bottom: Team vehicles set up at Incident Control. Photos © OVMRO.

2012

WHITE WATER AND VAUXHALL CORSAS

October 2012 by Dave Worrall

Stockton on Tees may not seem like the most obvious place to hold a course titled 'Rescue from Vehicles in Water' but the Tees Barrage International White Water Centre turned out to be a superb facility, purpose-built for swift water training and rescue.

The first morning found us in the classroom, with Chris Onions providing important reminders of the hierarchy of safety: Me, the team and then the casualty. Sounds harsh, but fast-flowing water is no place to compromise on safety. We'd all had experience of the swift water environment and attended similar courses in the past and this made for a very dynamic learning environment. Everyone had a clear understanding what was expected of them and what to do in given circumstances.

Next up was PPE: 'woolly bears', dry suits, footwear, buoyancy aids, helmets and, because of the environment, gloves. I'd forgotten quite how restrictive the various layers were and, combined with the need to swim, I felt distinctly clumsy. However, swimming was next on the schedule and, without hesitation, Chris led us to the side of the long course where we buddied up. Whilst one swam, the other person gave direction and encouragement to swim hard into the eddies and break-outs. It was at this point I wished I'd spent some time practising swimming harder than I would normally do.

This was followed by more swimming (this time defensive) with throw line rescues and careful thought about where to pull the swimmers in to, so they didn't disappear over the next rapid. Then, having gone through some basics of water rescue, we went to look at the Corsa.

Sitting on the floor of the short course, the Corsa — minus engine, so as not to contaminate the water — was firmly secured to the concrete floor with wires and bolts. We familiarised ourselves with the layout — doors, boot, sunroof — and checked to see if the radio worked. Again the emphasis was on a hierarchy of techniques depending on our assessment of the conditions and strength of flow of the water. However, the unbreakable rule was DO NOT STAND IN FRONT OF THE CAR. First up was going to be wading out to the vehicle. Chris asked for the water to be turned on to three cumecs (cubic metres per second) and within a very short space of time there was a substantial flow of water streaming past the Corsa. A casualty was placed inside the vehicle and, for this level of rescue, we were to wade out in formation supporting each other and, subsequently, the casualty.

OGGI SNIPS

From the 'pink' forms, August 2013: Their only navigation aid was Google maps on their phones, all of which had gone flat (after twenty hours on the hill).

The first step was to immobilise the vehicle with securing ropes, tensioning the line as best as we could. It was clear that two rescuers placed near the front tyre could do a substantial amount to divert the flow of water and reduce the effort needed to open the doors. It also provided the casualty with a safe haven to come into. Once out of the vehicle, we did a formation shuffle back to the side and safe ground. This technique was fine given the moderate flow but, once the rate went up to four or five cumecs, you had to question whether this was safe for all concerned. And so concluded the end of day one, a debrief back in the classroom and then something to eat and some beers. Or that's what we were all hoping for. Chris had other ideas.

Food was part of the plan and we had an impromptu barbecue on our patch of land. The sting in the tail was that Chris was planning an exercise in the dark. Thoughts of beer were banished as we kitted up in our PPE for a final round of swimming. At night-time, lighting and identification is vital so we added cyalumes and head torches to our PPE. Lit up like Blackpool illuminations, we must have been a very strange sight. The water in the main course was in full flow and the rescue technique this time was 'live bait', where the rescuer enters the water to catch the casualty as they are swept past. A line then brings them back into a convenient eddy. This can be achieved by leaping into the water from a convenient spot but, on this occasion we were expected to use our knowledge of water conditions to move out as near to the eddy line as possible. Then, swimming hard, we'd catch the casualty as they are swept past. A very valuable technique, with the added variation of using the water to help achieve the rescue.

Now we could have some beers!

Day two was much more about the Corsa and a variety of techniques to rescue people from it. So it was back into the PPE to carry all the necessary kit, including rescue sled, ropes and ladders, to the side of the short course. The Tees Barrage is a popular venue for all sorts of reasons. Plenty of canoeists and people taking part in rafting sessions. What was somewhat bizarre were the spectators who would stop for long periods and watch us carry out the rescues. We did feel a little bit as though we were part of some free show.

Back to the Corsa and, before we let any water into the channel, we had an exercise of immobilising a casualty with a KED board and then trying to remove them from the passenger seat of the vehicle. [The Kendrick Extrication Device (KED) is used in vehicle extrication to remove victims of traffic collisions from motor vehicles]. Even getting it into place was a nightmare and fitting any form of neck or spine immobilisation was a difficult operation. We did eventually get the KED onto our willing volunteer and the feedback was that overall it felt very smooth, although I

OGGI SNIPS

Newsletter 1990: Having got all excited at the late-November snow, I waxed the skis. I'd have been better off adapting the bindings to take a pair of wellies, then fitted them to the canoe.

have to say it didn't look it. It did highlight how difficult the process was and it was useful to practise.

Then it was 'Cumecs please', and the rush of water on the bonnet of the Corsa. The next stage was setting up a tension diagonal line. This was done relatively quickly and the rescuer was sent across to help the casualty in the Corsa put on a buoyancy aid and clip in to the line, to slide down the line to the far side. Simple but effective and we were able to practise this with a number of the delegates.

Next, we moved on to the rescue sled with a four-line tether allowing us to position — in theory — the sled alongside the car. The sled with rescuer on board provides a useful platform to rescue people but thought needs to be given how to get the person out of the car. Opening car doors with a rescue sled alongside may not be an option. In this case the boot was used but a sunroof could offer an option. Whichever way, careful positioning of the sled needs to be considered before you commit to the rescue. Similarly, we practised with a two-line tether as it's not always possible to reach both banks of the river.

Finally, we strapped a ladder to the raft. With rescuers standing in the water, we used the ladder to position the rescue sled in place. Again the positioning of the ladder and how it was strapped to the sled make a difference to what you can do. You need to get the sled in as close as possible to the person you want to rescue.

Rescuing from swift water isn't a one-size-fits-all. You need a variety of different techniques at your disposal for all eventualities. There isn't necessarily a right or wrong and each case will have to be judged on its own circumstances. Adaptability is the name of the game. It was a very intense two days, both physically and mentally. Next time I shall practise my swimming before I go…

Against the flow: Casualty care and victim recovery whilst working with the weight of water © Dave Worrall.

CHAPTER SEVEN

Ah yes, we remember it well

In its fifty years in operation as Ogwen Valley Mountain Rescue Organisation, the team has dealt with over 2500 incidents. Despite frequently expressed concerns about the 'rapid rise' in incident numbers, it wasn't until 2009 that the numbers suddenly jumped over the hundred mark. The early years may not have been as busy in today's terms, but some names always stir the memories — John Glews, Jimmy Haynes, Peter Dimond — founding threads in the weft of team history.

On Wednesday 2 June 1971, fourteen-year-old Jimmy Haynes travelled to North Wales, one of party of fifteen boys and three leaders from St Michael and All Saints Church Youth Club in Wythenshawe, on the outskirts of Manchester. It was meant to be a week of fun and exploration in the mountains, but somewhere during a four-mile hike from Nant Peris to Idwal Youth hostel, Jimmy Haynes disappeared.

Neil and Maggie Adam still have the black and white photo of Jimmy, handed to team members to inform their search. A smooth-cheeked young man, in a jaunty straw hat and aviator sunglasses, knapsack over his shoulders, squints into the sunlight and smiles. It's a group shot, one of his pals judiciously half-cropped out of shot. Police had already released the photograph with an appeal for anyone who may have seen him to contact any police station, but nobody came forward.

More than a hundred people rallied to the search — Ogwen team members, a twenty-strong RAF mountain rescue team from Leuchars, in Scotland, four SARDA

Wet weather stretcher slide: Rescue from the summit of Y Garn of a casualty with a severely gashed knee © OVMRO.

dogs and handlers and two army units. But, despite a thorough search of every tent, barn and hut in the area, he had simply disappeared in broad daylight. It was a complete mystery.

The party was led by the church curate, Rev Colin Tallworthy. Those who knew Jimmy described a strong lad, who'd travelled to North Wales before, albeit not to this particular area. His father, a lorry driver, spoke of 'a handy lad' who loved adventure. The piece of paper issued to the Adams read: 'Missing, since 2.00pm, Wednesday 2 June 1971, when he was last seen near the Devil's Kitchen and walking in the direction of Ogwen Cottage. Jimmy Haynes, fourteen years, height 5ft, blue eyes. Native Manchester. Wearing khaki shorts, ink shirt, brown boots, a trilby-type straw hat and carrying a light brown-coloured haversack.'

The hope was that he'd walked off the mountain safely but missed the youth hostel and would simply return later. One of the boys in the party told rescue leaders that 'Jimmy went off a long way ahead and said he wanted a good bed for the night,' adding that they knew it was him in the distance 'because he was wearing his straw hat, white shorts and dark glasses'.

The now brown-edged foolscap paper used to record the incident reveals that the team had another call-out that same day, for a missing mother and child, fortunately located by the RAF. Then the call came in that a boy was missing. Search parties were sent out, including dogs, until 11.00pm — with further searches planned up to 1.00am. The following morning at 6.00am, 'about 100 searchers were on the hill till about 9.00pm, when the search was suspended'. By 10.00am on the Friday, small parties were still out, but 'as nothing had been found by police, plans for a major search for Saturday were made, 1.30am'. Early on Saturday, a 'small party set off to cover the boys' route from Llanberis', numbers 'now amounting to about 250'.

FROM THE ARCHIVE

The adventures of Heidi, October 2009: Eight-month-old month old Border collie Heidi disappeared on the Carneddau range while walking up towards the summit of Pen yr Ole Wen with her owner Darren. Heidi ran ahead of him, disappearing into low cloud and that was the last he saw of her. But while Darren and his partner Melina worried about the whereabouts of their pet, she was tucked up nice and warm in a house in Bethesda, having found her way from Pen yr Ole Wen to the summit of Carnedd Llewelyn, the second highest mountain in Wales, where she was found by another walker and brought to safety.

Darren returned to the area on the Sunday, and team members scoured the crags with binoculars in case Heidi was stuck on a ledge. Notes were placed in the car parks asking other walkers to be on the look out for a lone dog but there was no sign of her.

Heidi was micro-chipped with her owner's details but, as the vet's surgery was closed and there was no dog warden service at the weekend, her temporary guardians had to wait until Monday to report having found her. There was no way the walker could have known they were out looking for Heidi on Sunday. As soon as the vet opened up, Heidi was examined, Melina got a call and the family was reunited.

OGGI SNIPS

From the 'pink' forms, May 2011: Team members found the lost couple sitting no more than three metres from the path.

It was hoped that three boys, who had been sunbathing near Llyn Ogwen at the time Jimmy was found to be missing, might have spotted the lad. But sadly, all hopes were dashed. At 2.30pm on the Saturday, three days after he had vanished from sight, Jimmy's brown-coloured haversack was found, out of sight of the path. Soon after, Jimmy Haynes was found at the bottom of a 300-foot deep gully in the left wall of Devil's Kitchen in Cwm Idwal. He was lying on top of his straw hat.

Dr Ieuan Jones was on duty at the hospital when Jimmy was admitted. He told the coroner that death had been the result of 'shock from multiple injuries'. It seemed that 'James had failed to follow a turn in a mountain pathway. It was necessary to get within feet of the body to see it. The area had been searched several times but the gully itself had not been closely inspected because it wasn't thought to be one of the highest probability areas. Tony Jones explained to the press that Jimmy 'was found in a difficult and dangerous place which involved a bit of scrambling to reach him.'

Rev Tallworthy said he'd impressed on the boys — mainly between eleven and fourteen, with two aged seventeen — that they should always travel as a group. He had stopped 'to bandage a finger for a member of the party and the group became rather straggled, although the distance between them was not great'. James had gone on ahead with a small group, and then probably went on again when the others stopped. He wasn't even missed until the party reached the hostel and even then 'it was not supposed he was still on the mountain as there had been a report that he had been seen down by a lake'.

Jimmy had apparently run on ahead, says Maggie Adam. He wanted to 'get the best bed because he hadn't the night before!'

After the event, the police needed to go up 'to do their bit', says Neil Adam, 'but it was impossible to reach the site with their wellies on. KC and Maggie were escorting the photographer up there — got halfway up and told the lads on scene to put a blue smoke flare up the gully. It went straight up like a chimney! The police took one look and decided it might not be a good idea! It would have been criminal negligence to take them up there. It sowed the seeds of the team doing this sort of scene of crime stuff'.

Jimmy's fate highlighted one prevailing rule of the mountains: walkers should stick together with their group, not be tempted to wander off alone. It was also recommended they shun the browns, greens and blacks common at the time, in favour of brighter clothing, so they might be more easily spotted by rescuers — a piece of advice which hasn't always been in tune with fashion!

Two years later, four young men — similar in age to Jimmy — prompted a similarly protracted search, but they were lucky. Setting off to complete their Duke of Edinburgh Gold Award expedition, their spirits were high, the weather fine. But by nightfall, the weather had closed in, leaving them huddled in a tent for four days and nights, singing hymns and sharing dwindling rations, as one of the biggest search operations the team had seen unfolded below them. Their story captured the public imagination, prompting a BBC film the following year. With the help of the boys, 'The Day Seemed so Good' recreated the events of that weekend and looked at some of the lessons to be learned. So significant was it for Tony Jones — who led the search — it even featured in his 'This is Your Life', with three of the boys, by then grown men, popping up to join in the fun. [Their story features in full on page 104.]

The search for Peter Dimond

The search for the four boys had involved 438 people on the fourth day. It was hugely demanding for team members, struggling to juggle their voluntary commitment to mountain rescue with the needs of family and employers. But, seven months later came a search which proved even more demanding.

Peter Edris Dimond left his home in Timperley, Cheshire on Thursday 15 November 1973, telling friends he was going for a day's hill walking, either in the Lake District or North Wales. When he failed to return by the Friday evening, they informed the police before driving to the Lakes on the Saturday to spend the weekend looking for his car. Why they chose to go north isn't documented. It was a fifty-fifty choice.

The first suggestion that there might be a person missing on the mountains was a telephone call from Bethesda Police Station, on Sunday 18 November, at around 3.30pm. Team members were asked to keep an eye out for Dimond's car, a gold Singer Vogue. Shortly before midnight, KC Gordon and Tony Jones received a further call. The car had been found in the National Park car park, between Ogwen Cottage and Tryfan. Now it was a missing person search.

Thirty-nine-year-old Dimond was head pharmacist at Pankridge Hospital in Timperley. Six feet tall, of slim build, with balding, greying brown hair and bespectacled grey-blue eyes, his friends described him as 'a loner', with 'ten to fifteen years mountaineering experience in various areas'. It was likely he would have more than adequate equipment for a day's walk in the mountains. A number of suggestions were made as to the likely routes Dimond may have taken but, according the incident report, 'even at the end of the major phase of the search, there were still only two concrete facts: Dimond was missing from home and his car was found in the Ogwen Valley'.

There had been no clear indication of his likely route. The two main possibilities were either 'the Idwal skyline, that is Tryfan, the Glyderau and Y Garn' or 'on the Carneddau, Gerlan, past Llech Du, up the ridge to Carnedd Dafydd and down to Ogwen'. The report noted that, despite Dimond's car being found in the car park, his friends had favoured the latter route.

Dimond had been missing for four days and nights. The main concern was that he might be lying injured somewhere, suffering from shock. The freezing temperatures would reduce any chance of his survival. Even had he found shelter, and experienced as his friends believed him to be, he might not survive another twenty-four hours.

During the early hours of Monday morning, KC Gordon, Tony Jones and Has Oldham planned an extended party search for the daylight hours. The RAF Valley MRT and 22 Squadron would join the Ogwen team for a 7.00am start, focusing on the two possible routes. Within an hour, eight parties were operational and the helicopter was in the air, where it would remain until dusk, flying numerous sorties with various rescue personnel as observers. During the morning, the facilities of the Gwynedd Constabulary were assembled at Ogwen Cottage. Both the police incident caravan and their mobile canteen were operational by mid-afternoon.

In the afternoon, Llanberis team members, staff and students at the Ogwen Cottage Mountain

Top: Helicopter winch from Braich Ty Du face. **Left:** Jimmy Haynes. **Right:** Guiding in the helicopter Photos © OVMRO.

School and Llanrug Outdoor Activities Centre joined the search. At this stage, the newly formed North Wales Accident Panel took over the running of the search, requesting further assistance from South Wales, the Peak District and other areas. With so little information, and keen to use the available resources to their best advantage, those coordinating the search faced tough decisions. They chose to focus their search on Tryfan and the Glyderau, and adjacent areas, 'the area of mountains between the A5 and the A4086 trunk roads, terminating in the north west at a line joining the Penrhyn and Dinorwic quarries' — approximately fifty square miles of rough and rocky terrain.

By the end of the first day, wrote Bob Maslen-Jones, in his account of the incident, more volunteers had arrived at Ogwen Cottage 'as news spread that a man was missing', and 'the original fifty searchers had grown to over a hundred, including several policemen'. Yet there was still no sign of the missing man and no further clue as to his movements.

According to the official report, this vast search area was now divided into forty-two sectors, with 'one or two specialist areas such as the east face of Tryfan'. By the time the search recommenced at 7.00am, 417 experienced walkers and climbers had been organised into teams, each with a designated area to search. The helicopter also joined the morning's search. All but two areas had been covered by dusk. All parties were safely off the mountain by 6.30pm. A number of items had been found, yet there was nothing that could be positively identified with Dimond. Despite ideal weather conditions and clear visibility 'the day's search had proved fruitless'.

On the third day, the search managers decided to 'concentrate on the Carneddau, the area to the north and east of the A5'. More searchers were needed, so a request went out to the Peak District and Mid Pennine teams for their assistance. From 7.30am until dusk, the search continued. 'The main area was sub-divided into thirty-one sectors. The two sectors on the south of the Glyderau that hadn't been completely searched, were re-searched. Meanwhile, small parties scoured the main cliff areas of the Carneddau and four peripheral sectors were checked by other small parties.' Various miscellaneous reports from Tuesday's activities were also followed up.

Since the search began, records Maslen-Jones, 'the police had signed in 560 people, making it the largest recorded operation of its kind in Britain since 1846'. The total number of volunteers during those three days had exceeded 1000, searching an estimated 200 square miles of ground.

Nobody, of course, could have dreamed that almost forty years later, a search for a missing child would far surpass those figures. By the week following the disappearance of April Jones, volunteer team members from across Wales and England were estimated to have contributed 9250 man hours to the search — a tally that would have taken one person well over five working years to achieve. By the end of the search, Mark Jones, deputy team leader of Brecon MRT, identified that the search area had covered an area 72.26km square with 208 search areas of median size 0.26km square. There were 1,075 'searcher days' given, with approximately 13,400 hours of time. And, in a reflection of how much the world has changed since 1973, more than 6,000 SARCALL SMS messages were sent supporting the operation — 2,670 on the Saturday alone.

The numbers may not have been as high in the search for Peter Dimond, but it was an intensive effort for its time. Many, said Maslen-Jones, were now 'inclined to the view that Dimond had deliberately disappeared, possibly to escape some personal problem'. As the third day's search proved fruitless, a meeting was called on the Wednesday afternoon. Dr Ieuan Jones, as the medical

OGGI SNIPS

'Rescue me, I've lost my glasses'. When a gentleman called to say he couldn't see after losing his specs, a team member walked him down and even found the lost specs .

adviser on the case, presented his assessment of the situation. The possibilities were that Dimond had either fallen a long way, such as down a gully, and been killed or drowned, or had sustained a minor, but incapacitating, injury to his legs. Alternatively, he may have suffered a heart attack or fallen victim to hypothermia. Only in the case of a leg injury did he think there was any chance of Dimond still being alive — and if he was, indeed, alive there was only a 50% chance of survival. Had this been the case, however, Dr Jones believed 'Dimond would have been likely to have been in sufficiently good condition to have attracted the attention of someone passing within thirty yards or so of him'.

As a result of the meeting, the official search and rescue teams were withdrawn. Tony Jones and the Ogwen team continued to look for Dimond, mainly at weekends, for several weeks longer, but in the end even this was dropped. Members of the public were asked to keep a watchful eye when in the hills and reminded to always leave a note of their own route, especially if walking alone.

On 10 April 1974, almost five months after his disappearance, Dimond's body was discovered by George Bridge — coincidentally also from Sale in Cheshire, not too far from Dimond's home. Bridge, records Maslen-Jones, had been 'looking for a cave at Quartz Pinnacle, east-south-east of the summit of Y Garn. He reported that a body was in a sitting position under a large boulder in a recess in the rocks'. Members of the team, with a police officer, went to the spot to recover the body.

Twiggy Price was one of those who searched over successive weekends, while staying in North Wales. She remembers being in Nant Gwynant and keen to get home early from her weekend in the valley when the police said a body had been found. They needed help with the carry.

Dimond was found sitting in a bivvy bag, well sheltered from the wind and weather and perfectly camouflaged to the distant eye. The 'cave' was later described by Bridge as 'more like a series of crevasses than a cave' with the opening going down about twenty feet. The pathologist later discovered a massive quantity of barbiturates in the body and this was undoubtedly the cause of death. 'One can only come to the conclusion,' he said, 'that it was taken with one object in view' and accordingly recorded a verdict of suicide. Those early suspicions, that Dimond had chosen to escape his own life, were proved to be true. The tragedy is that nobody knew why.

Remembering the first time

Everyone, it seems, remembers their first call-out, for a variety of reasons — not always just for being the newest face on the team. For Tim Radford, it was September 1998, as he related in a 'Daily Post' profile of the team's 'danger men'.

'A scrambler had fallen on Tryfan. He had arm and leg injuries and was in a lot of pain but the helicopter couldn't get in to winch him off the mountain because of poor visibility. We had to get him down the hill on a stretcher, with the rest of the party abseiling off too, until we were low enough below the clouds for the helicopter to pick him up.'

Radford stood at the bottom to meet the stretcher, which was being jockeyed by John Evans. 'The gully was unpleasant and the descent was obviously hard work with a lot of strain being put on the stretcher. Once we'd prepared it for lifting by helicopter, we noticed that one of the tensioning straps had come loose and the stretcher was starting to come apart.' It was an interesting job, he says, philosophically. 'I wasn't frightened or nervous, there were just too many things to think about. You have to go in and see what needs doing and then get the job done.'

He recalls another occasion, when two climbers set off unfeasibly late one afternoon in winter to climb on the East Face of Tryfan. 'We got the call late at night, by which time the wind was driving and there was heavy snow. Two guys had set off late. When they got to the top they realised they'd left their winter walking boots at the bottom and were in smooth-soled climbing shoes. It was blizzarding by this time and unpleasant up there. They only had one head torch between them.'

Summing up the mindset of the average mountain rescuer he adds that 'it honestly doesn't occur to me to be critical. It can happen to anyone. People genuinely need our help and don't usually set out to get themselves lost.' Although Roger Jones adds that he remains amazed just 'how many people are so blasé about losing people on the mountains, but what can you do?'

John Hulse recalls his first call-out, to a big fall down Glydr Fawr, in the early-1970s. He was just sixteen. There'd been a series of fatal accidents on Snowdon so team members were all out dealing with incidents. Hulse made the call to police summarising what the informant had told him. 'The operator said, Oh my God, not another one!' The team returned only to go straight out again to Idwal Slabs. 'I'd gone up ahead with Cliff Randalls, the hostel warden, and my brand new duvet, paid for out of my pocket money. The casualty leaked all over it! Tony Jones arrived, put the guy on the Thomas and hauled him away. It was a formative moment, a magnetic attraction!'

When Andy Harbach arrived at base for his first rescue, he was greeted by Roger Jones booming, 'Hey you! You've come from Bangor! Have you been speeding?' The answer was firmly in the negative, of course.

Other rescues might not be the first but somehow they stick in the memory. They're different in some way. And, frequently, they don't have a happy ending. In June 2007, Chris and Jennifer Parratt believed they were doing the right thing when they used a new guidebook titled 'Walks in the Snowdonia Mountains', to plot their way up Tryfan. Of particular interest was a chapter headed 'Tryfan the easy way'.

The couple had travelled to North Wales from Oxford, on a 'sporting break' and decided to go

COBWEB CORNER

'I'd take them to a slippery rock face at night to see how they like it', Daily Post October 2005: So said Chris Lloyd when thieves stole a dozen of the team's collection boxes from hotels, cafés and shops along the A5, in what was clearly a well-orchestrated operation. 'If I found the person who did this, I'd happily take them out to Tryfan in the middle of the night on a slippery rock face to see how they like it. People put money in the box to support us so we can carry out the work and provide a free service'. The boxes were practically full — an anticipated income of about £300 — when they were snatched from various collection points in Bethesda and Betws y Coed. Following the news, the team received an anonymous donation of £500.

OGGI SNIPS

Neolithic settlers began clearing areas for agriculture and creating homesteads in Snowdonia around 5,000 years ago. Evidence of their hut circles can still be seen.

up Tryfan with their Labrador Oscar, after buying the book, a map and compass in Betws y Coed. Both were keen sportspeople and experienced mountain walkers. They followed the recommended route towards the Heather Terrace and, despite becoming a little confused, managed to find their way to the summit, which was covered in low cloud. With conditions getting wetter, and not wanting to linger, they used the map to begin their descent down the north ridge.

'We'd lost confidence in the book on the way up,' said Jennifer Parratt later.

As they made their way down on the slippery surface they couldn't see the path and it became increasingly steep. They stopped for a while on a ledge and then Parratt turned to face the rocks and went further down. 'I stayed on the ledge and held onto the dog as he went down first.' Then, to her horror, she saw her husband lose his grip and fall backwards, tumbling about twenty-five metres down the slope.

By some miracle, she was able to scramble down to crouch beside her badly injured husband. For two hours, she administered first aid and CPR, until the team managed to find them in the cloud. Parratt was certified dead on arrival at hospital. His skull had been fractured.

The incident pops immediately to mind for Chris Onions. 'I was with Dave Jones and John Hulse, the advanced party. She was doing all she could whilst screaming for help. The clag was down so initially there was no hope of a helicopter arriving. Dave Jones and I were tasked with getting her away from the scene. Not easy. You have to be really forthright — you're taking someone away from the person they love. It's a really hard thing to do. I wanted to be compassionate but we had to get her off and to a place of safety.

'I got her down to base and she went straight into her family's arms. Then we went back up the hill to recover her partner's body, in darkness.'

John Hulse recalls that this was 'quite a technical evacuation' which went on all night. He later told the 'Daily Post' that he believed the text of the book was misleading. 'There is no easy way up Tryfan. It's a contradiction in terms.' It was amazing, he said, that they managed to reach the point where Parratt fell because it was such dangerous terrain, with steep, slippery grass and large rocks.

In fact, the same publication made news again later that year, when the 'cheap guidebook' [sic] was said to have led another walker to get stuck waist-deep in a bog. .Experienced walker Steve Savory claimed it had led him, his wife and sister-in-law into trouble on Moel Siabod, the previous summer. Ironically, Jennifer Parratt said that they had considered walking up Moel Siabod before deciding instead to climb Tryfan.

Savory too had bought the book in Betws but found the directions on the walk from Capel Curig unclear. 'It described one patch as wettish but in fact I went up to my waist in a bog and struggled and Chris went in over her knees. It was in June and we hadn't had a lot of rain in the days leading up to it.' Undeterred, the three considered carrying on but the path described took them up steep scree. 'With the weather closing in, and having less confidence in the book because it was so difficult to follow, I decided we'd better go back the way we came because it was safer. I was pretty sure I'd followed the directions properly but decided I might have misinterpreted them, until I read the report of the inquest and realised I'd been using the same book.'

Dave Worrall recalls another memory, in November 1989, when team members battled through heavy rain and 65 mph gales, to help a walker paralysed by lightning near the summit of Tryfan.

Two venture scouts had raised the alarm after leaving two of their colleagues at the scene to give first aid. An RAF Wessex tried six times to get close enough to lower rescuers to the scene but had to give up. Navigator Flight Lieutenant John Mullam told the Daily Post that gales were blowing down from the top of Snowdon. Even with full power they were unable to maintain a hover. Every time they tried, they were 'hurtled downwards by the fierce winds and downdraughts'.

It was almost nine hours before the victim was finally returned to terra firma on a stretcher. 'We had to carry him all the way off,' says Worrall, 'because it paralyses the nervous system and he couldn't stand up. It was a very difficult carry — we started in the afternoon and didn't finish until midnight. It did have its moments of humour though — someone asked, 'If we put a light bulb in your mouth, would it glow?!

'As part of Ieuan's course, he would show slides of people hit by lightning and it wasn't long after seeing those slides that it actually happened!'

That paralysed walker became the second person to survive a lightning strike in the same region in a matter of months. Less than six months before, a twenty-six-year old man had survived with severe bruising on Moel Tryfan. The powerful thunder flash ripped his clothes to shreds, singed his hair, burned one side of his body and caused a deep scorch mark around his neck where he had been wearing a gold cross and chain.

It's often claimed that lightning doesn't strike twice in the same place, but nothing could be further from the truth. Lightning does, can and will strike the same exact place or object more than once. The chances of a person being fatality struck, however, are quite low. According to the Tornado & Storm Research Organisation (TORRO) about 30-60 people are struck by lightning each year in Britain of whom, on average, three may be killed.

Derek Elsom, Professor Emeritus at Oxford Brookes University, documented twenty-five years of deaths and injuries from lightning in the UK, between 1988-2012. 'In terms of numbers, a lot more people who are struck don't register anything more than a tingle,' says Professor Elsom. 'The amount you experience can be quite variable.' Even when hit with a forceful bolt, there can be a 'flashover effect' where the electricity passes over wet clothing and skin, rather than through them — though this may still cause injuries. However, he adds that 'being on a mountainside is probably one of the worst places to be in a storm'. Indeed, lightning strikes are a common sight in Snowdonia, and far better appreciated from a safe distance.

There are recommended ways and means for avoiding being struck by lightning — not least being weather aware — but there's one aspect of mountaineering 'you can't mitigate by skill', reckons Worrall, and that's dealing with strong winds in the mountains. Walker John Knoxley was reported to be stuck on Glyder Fawr. A group of six went up to investigate but it wasn't long before the going got tough. 'We got up the Kitchen and Llyn y Cwn and we could feel the strength of the wind building up. On the plateaus, we were being hit by huge gusts. Because of my involvement with the marine trade, I had a little gizmo with me that measured wind speed. We found Knoxley, pinned him down into a shelter, then I stood up to test the wind speed. It was 90 mph!' The minutes also record one team member's narrow escape when he was swiftly grabbed by another before being blown clean off the mountain.

Newsletter February 1991. Grid search: An intense method of ground search which requires a great deal of people power and makes one think better of mowing the lawn.

The longest day

The Welsh One Thousand Metre Peaks Race takes place every year, usually on the first Saturday in June. Starting at Abergwyngregyn, on the North Wales coast, those who enter check in at Carnedd Llewelyn and Carnedd Dafydd, before cutting back and down to Ffynnon Llugwy and the Ogwen Valley. Next comes a climb over the lower slopes of the Glyderau towards Snowdon, dropping down to Pen y Pass, then up the Pyg Track, right for Carnedd Ugain and doubling back to Snowdon summit. It's a gruelling test of fitness, endurance and navigation skills, covering a distance of around 32 km, with 2500 metres of ascent — even in fine weather it is considered to be one of the most arduous events in the UK fell running calendar. The fastest do it in four hours. Even the 'short' course, designed for those who prefer a lesser challenge is still significant. Both military and civilians may enter.

In June 2009, 245 competitors set off into low cloud, rain and lashing wind. It was the start of quite a day for Ogwen team members, affectionately referred to as 'the longest day'.

The first call came in at 10.35am. A civilian runner was cold, wet, lost and exhausted. The team leader reported the incident to North Wales Police, only to be told of a second missing runner. This time he was from the army. He too was 'cold, wet and lost' somewhere by a fence line running east west. After a brief interview with him, his phone went dead and contact was lost. The police dispatched their helicopter to search the northern Carneddau but with low cloud and strong winds, there was little to be achieved.

'Just as we were deploying to search for these two, news came in of a third casualty on the ridge between Carnedd Dafydd and Pen yr Ole Wen,' says Chris Lloyd. 'This fifty-five-year-old man was exhausted. After several hours of unsuccessful search by our troops, RAF Valley MRT were also deployed. They eventually located him and bought him down below cloud base where 22 Squadron was able to lift him down to Oggi base.

'Meanwhile, a female army cadet was suffering from cold, wet and exhaustion and gone to ground near 3185 [a landmark spot height used by the team], on the dog-leg of the ridge between Llewelyn and Dafydd. Two passing walkers had found her and reported this to police. While we were preparing to send people up to her, she was joined by four other young cadets, who were inadequately equipped and poorly prepared for the conditions. Four army officers arrived on the scene and put the cadets into good quality bivvy bags and cas shelters and stayed with them.

'Just to keep the pressure on, the race organisers reported two more people needing assistance from the summit of Carnedd Llewelyn. As the party was being despatched from Ffynnon Llugwy to go to Llewelyn, the organisers then reported a further group in Foel Grach refuge shelter needing help. Fortunately, team members who had been deployed earlier were already in that area so they were diverted to check out these latest reports. The race marshals were moving the Llewelyn casualties to 3185 and the shelter turned out to be empty.

'Back to 3185, towards which two team members were now making their way. They came across two local mountaineers who had passed the large casualty party of cadets and officers and volunteered to return up the mountain to show where they were.'

At this stage the race had been abandoned. But yet another incident reported a fifty-five-year-

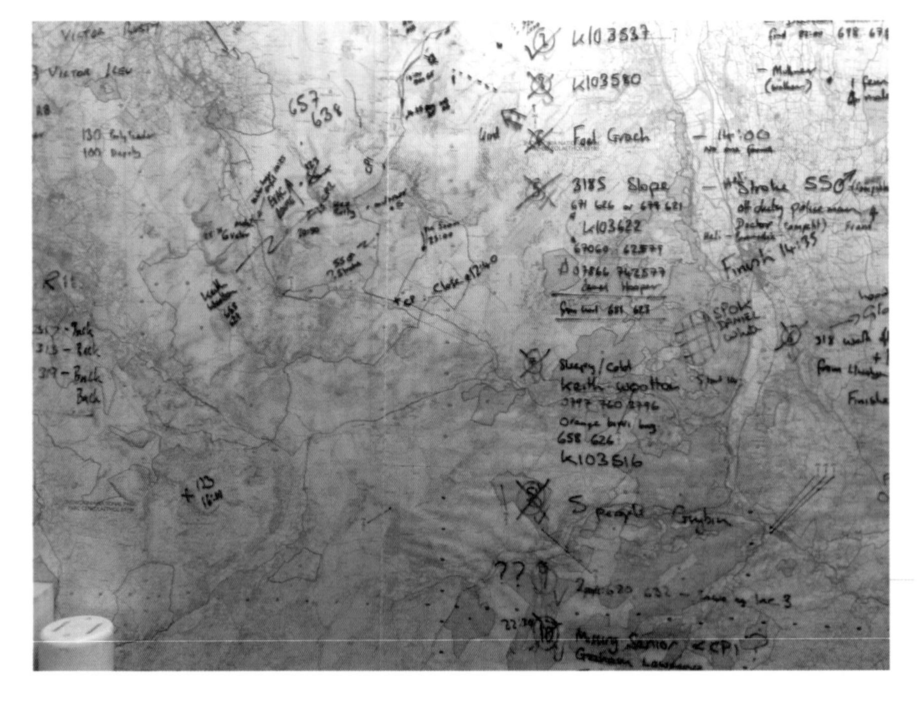
K103537
K103580
Foel Grach
318S Slope
K103622
Finish 14:35
Keith Wootton
K103516
5 people
Missing Senior

old man on the slopes near Fynnon Llugwy, who had allegedly suffered a stroke. He was with a doctor and a policeman. The air ambulance attempted to reach him, without success. Two team members were despatched, along with a request for assistance from 22 Squadron. After a short carry to get below cloud level, the casualty was winched and flown down to Ysbyty Gwynedd where it became evident he hadn't suffered a stroke but was hypothermic.

'Around this time, the Sea King developed a mechanical problem and limped back to RAF Valley. So, when we received a call that a group of five — nothing to do with the race — were cold, tired and wet, with their fifty-two-year-old female leader suffering from hypothermia, it was a Sea King from RAF Chivenor in Devon which joined the fray, picking up two team members and flying them to cloud base on the Football Field on the Gribin Ridge. These two — with the winchman — scrambled up to the summit and escorted the party down to the aircraft. They were then flown down to base.

'Back once more at 3185, the two team members, with the two informants, two local mountaineers, one female casualty, four poorly-prepared army cadets, three army officers and the two marshals who'd come over from Dafydd, all walked down to Oggi base... which was full of wet team members, cold, wet and exhausted racers and a National Trust group of footpath builders who had just arrived!

'The two who were first reported missing, were still missing. As a result a further party of three team members, who had just come off the Carneddau, were despatched to Aber Falls to help search that area. On arriving at the Falls, an original search party of two team members made a find above Rhaeadr Bach. It was now 5.00pm.

'The party of three were deployed to Llyn Anafon, just north of Foel Fras. They climbed onto the ridge to just south of Drum. The only information was that the casualty was by an east west fence. So the party split into two, one party heading over Drum to check a couple of east west fences before returning to just south of Drum and checking an east west fence going down into the valley leading to Cwm Dulyn. Meanwhile, the other party climbed to the summit of Foel Fras to see if there were any more east west fences that might not be on the map. There were none, so they returned to the second fence between Drum and Foel Fras and searched that, going into the valley leading up to Cwm Dulyn. The SARDA dogs had been deployed to search the main ridge again but the dogs picked up the Ogwen troops so didn't continue over Foel Fras but returned to base!'

By now, neighbouring North East Wales Search and Rescue team (NEWSAR) had also arrived to help. They were dispatched from Llyn Dulyn where, thanks to Google Earth, a new east west fence had been spotted. Around 10.00pm, the second casualty, a well-equipped member of the Territorial Army, was located by NEWSAR and evacuated by 22 Squadron to Ysbyty Gwynedd.

Memories of the day differ, largely depending on where a team member was at any given time. Tim Radford has his own take on things. 'It was just the chaos of the whole event — people scattered everywhere on the Carneddau. There were multiple things going on, not everyone knew what was happening. It had been a torrential, sleety cold morning. The initial call-out said a runner/walker was lost on a north-facing slope in the Carneddau, but there wasn't much to go on.

Top: Rescue on the West Face of Tryfan, June 2011 © OVMRO.
Bottom: The very heavily populated white board map at base during the 'Longest Day' incident © Dave Worrall.

Alex, Geraint, Kim and I were deployed to the hill. We drove in the Land Rover to the top of Aber then set off on foot. Geraint and I were on the mountain for most of the day looking for this guy and we didn't have a clue what was happening elsewhere. We kept making radio calls, trying to get information but we just weren't getting any.

'Eventually, we got that he was by a river so that narrowed the search down a bit, but I remember being on the radio and speaking to Paul Smith. We were a bit short with each other — we'd been asking for information and couldn't understand why we weren't getting any. Why were they ignoring us? We weren't aware there were nine other incidents going on.

'Around three or four o'clock, someone asked had we seen the pylons yet? What pylons?! The ones he can see, came the response. But that piece of information hadn't got to us. As soon as we knew that the casualty had described how the pylons lined up with a river he was near, we walked straight to the spot! In fact, we'd walked past it twice! He was in a bad way, completely poorly-equipped for the conditions, drenched, and he'd got lost almost immediately.'

'At one stage, we thought we had fourteen incidents on the go,' says Dave Worrall, who was back at base with Paul Smith, plotting the calls on a map. The pair were on duty the whole way through the incident, until the early hours of the Sunday morning. 'These days, you'd change the people on duty but we just kept going!'

The incident may have been dubbed 'the longest day', but one or two have since come close. On Saturday 4 November 2012, another 'epic thirteen-hour mission' saw fourteen people rescued in four separate incidents, which went on late into the night. The first call came in around midday when a thirty-six-year-old woman from London, who was attempting the ascent of Tryfan with work colleagues, was unable to carry on because of sciatica. The group had been going up from Llyn Bochlwyd. At about Bwlch Tryfan, she complained about her sciatica, so — breaking every rule about looking after the weakest in your group — they gave her the car keys and told her to go back down alone. A complete novice, she had no idea where she was but, somehow, managed to get to the lip of Cwm Bochlwyd before losing confidence.

Seeing her distress, a passer-by called 999. As luck would have it, a team member happened to be passing and, after a quick chat with the incident controller, she walked down slowly with the woman. Two hours and a number of 'camera stops' later, she was back at her car but, rather than leaving her to get cold there, they left a note with the car and retreated to the warmth and hot tea of Oggi base. It was several hours later before she was collected by her companions.

Shortly before 5.00pm, two men made a 999 call close to the Devil's Kitchen. The pair, aged sixty and forty, had climbed the North Ridge of Tryfan and Bristly Ridge, then come over Glyder Fach and Glyder Fawr. En route, there had been some squally snow showers, so by the time they came to descend to Llyn y Cwn above the Devil's Kitchen, there was no sign of the descent path. They followed a runnel which took them to the cliff face, about fifty metres east of the main chasm. While trying to scramble down, one of them took a short slide on the soft snow and steep ground. They re-evaluated their predicament and rightly called for help.

Five minutes later, a further call came in. A group of students from Merseyside had walked up Y Garn and then along the ridge to its north west limit. Descending from Carnedd y Ffiliast, and within 200 metres of the road, one of them, a nineteen-year-old girl, slipped and broke her ankle. And,

OGGI SNIPS

Newsletter, February 1991: Please don't lend kit to outsiders. Someone lent out a long chisel to help retrieve a dog from a rabbit hole. The dog seems to have taken the chisel with him.

while she was doing that, her four male colleagues were deciding what to do after having an 'epic' on First Pinnacle Rib on the East Face of Tryfan. They'd started up the climb late morning, the four twenty-year-olds climbing as two pairs but then they lost the prescribed route. Much of the rock and holds had a sprinkling of fresh snow cover. After a couple of short slips, they were only halfway up the crag. Dusk was falling and the weather deteriorating. With only two torches between them, they called at 5.00pm to ask for advice. They'd tried to abseil, but found this difficult. The advice, as you might expect, was to stay put 'before someone has an accident. We will come to get you'. Good advice but it proved easier said than done.

A hasty party of two headed out to get above them and give them a top rope. Meanwhile, back at the Devil's Kitchen, a second hasty party of three located the two men and were preparing to lower one troop with a view to bringing the men up. A further three team members followed, with a couple of 100-metre ropes, ironmongery and pulleys.

Responding to the girl with the broken ankle, two team members sought support from ten members of RAF Valley MRT who had just completed a long day on the hill. They made their way up the slope and proceeded to stretcher her down, ready to meet the ambulance. Job done, the troops were free to head for Tryfan. It was 7.43pm.

Meanwhile, the two cold men on the Devil's Kitchen were hauled up and taken down the correct path — something of an eye-opener, as realisation dawned just how vulnerable their position had been. Back at Oggi base by 9.00pm, they too took advantage of the warmth, happy to devour hot tea, hot soup, pasties and pizza.

Back on Tryfan, team members fought their way up the North Ridge, followed by a further party of RAF and Ogwen with all the heavy gear. Snow continued to build on the ground and the intermittent squally showers were punctuated by a starry, moonlit night and some spectacular lightning.

The crew of an RAF Sea King from 22 Squadron was flying back from Stoke after a patient transfer. Had they arrived ten minutes before, they might well have been able to snatch the four but this was no longer possible. Hopes of a rapid denouement to this particular incident, so swiftly raised, were now firmly dashed. It was 9.30pm.

'We continued on,' says Chris Lloyd, 'with the hasty party arriving thirty metres above the four. Then, at about 10.15pm, the helicopter returned. They crept up the East Face, showered by clouds of fresh snow. Their spotlights lit up the rock face until they could identify the four. Holding a hover close to this 800ft cliff and with the downdraught and clouds of snow obscuring any clear vision of the rock face, they managed a very quick snatch of the two pairs of climbers, then flew down to base for 10.30pm, where the four were treated to the log fire, hot tea, hot soup, pasties and — you guessed it — pizza.

'Meanwhile pizza was also being delivered to the crew on the aircraft which was parked, rotors running on the landing zone while the pilots reviewed the previous ten minutes or so.'

It was just too risky to attempt the lift back to the two team members still about thirty metres above the incident site. Left to find their own way down, they climbed up to complete the route then followed the mixed party of Ogwen and RAF troops down the mountain, arriving at Oggi base about 1.00am. 'The good news,' said Lloyd, 'was that there was still a log fire burning, hot tea, hot soup, pasties and pizza!'

Poorly equipped and ill-prepared

The majority of Ogwen's rescues involve experienced, well-prepared and suitably equipped people. They've planned their route (leaving a route description in some appropriate place), acquainted themselves with the weather forecast and togged themselves up with whatever kit they need for their day's activities, with a bit to spare. They might well be carrying a mobile phone or GPS device, but they'll also have a map and compass at the ready. The picnic will be sorted, the flask filled, water bottle charged. And they'll make sure there's a torch to hand, in case the day turns nasty or darkness closes in sooner than anticipated.

And then there are those whose naivety threatens their very lives. In March 2015, one terrified young woman clung petrified to the Adam and Eve pillars, as high winds conspired to loosen her grip. She was with a group of two men and four women from London, who had travelled to Snowdonia for the weekend. Despite the forecast of strong winds, they seemed determined to tackle Tryfan — lightly clad and without any suitable equipment. They had inched their way slowly as far as the North Tower before they realised the challenge was too great — apart from the one girl, who made it to the summit. She was the first to be found and returned to the sanctuary of tea, cakes and burning logs at base. Meanwhile, it was dusk before a second hill party found her five companions two-thirds of the way up the hill. Not a single one of the party had a torch, map or compass. 'As they refuelled with hot tea,' says Chris Lloyd, 'they were advised of their inadequacies for the scramble up the notorious North Ridge of Tryfan in these conditions!'

In August 2012, two fourteen-year-old girls were lucky to be alive after collapsing in drunken stupors after a drinking binge on Conwy Mountain. One of the girls had drunk so much she was unconscious. The alarm was raised just after midnight when they were seen in a drunken state on the mountain. When paramedics arrived, the girls' ten-strong group of friends scattered, leaving them alone on the ridge. A Sea King lifted them off the steep ground, then returned to search the mountain with a thermal imaging camera in case there were other teenagers still on the mountain. 'Intoxication and mountains do not mix,' says Chris Lloyd. 'If you fall on a mountain, you could fall a long way.'

Sadly, as in the case of Peter Dimond, there are some who retreat to the harsh beauty of the hills to end their lives. In March 2008, one death caused a media frenzy which threatened to obscure the tragedy itself.

Fifty-year-old Michael Todd was chief constable of Greater Manchester Police. A charismatic man with an impressive CV, and widely regarded as one of the country's most talented senior police officers, he had graduated from the University of Essex with a first class honours degree in government in 1989 and a master's degree in politics in 1994. The university named him their alumnus of the year in 2003 for his contributions to policing and the community. He joined Essex Police in 1976, and the Metropolitan Police on a management exchange programme. His progress through the police was swift, through assistant chief constable with Nottingham Police, to deputy and then assistant commissioner with the Metropolitan Police, to his post in Manchester in 2002. He was also vice president of ACPO. His death shocked all who had come into contact with him.

North Wales Police mounted an extensive search for Todd when he was reported missing by his

OGGI SNIPS

'Trail' magazine, January 2014: 'Tryfan has a unique aesthetic and has always been a mountain close to the heart of hill walkers who love a challenging afternoon out'.

official driver on the Monday evening. It appeared Todd had taken the Monday off work to go walking in Snowdonia. The search began in the early hours of the following morning. A mobile phone message traced Todd to the Felinheli area so coastguard teams and the Beaumaris inshore lifeboat spent two hours searching the Menai Strait between Britannia Bridge and Caernarfon. But, when two walkers reported finding possessions belonging to Todd, the search switched to the mountains. It later transpired that the signal from his phone may have pinpointed the incorrect position as his phone was found on him.

On the Tuesday afternoon, Todd was found on Bwlch Glas, about 300 feet beneath the summit of Snowdon. His body was covered in snow, his winter jacket discarded just a few yards away. News of the grim discovery spread quickly through the small community.

Members of both Ogwen and Llanberis teams were asked to assist in the recovery but efforts were hampered by atrocious weather. High winds hampered the helicopter and there was snow underfoot. It took thirty-six team members four hours of punishing effort to carry their heavy load over difficult, rocky ground with teams of six at a time operating in a relay system.

Speculation about suicide was rife but a subsequent report by Sir Paul Scott-Lee, stated that the circumstances of Michael Todd's death were 'subject to thorough investigation by North Wales Police' at the direction of coroner Dewi Pritchard. The 'narrative verdict' returned was that Todd 'had died of exposure when the state of his mind was affected by alcohol and drugs and confusion, namely his personal situation'.

One of Britain's top police officers, once tipped for the top job at Scotland Yard, Michael Todd was publicly honoured by Greater Manchester Police and civic leaders at a memorial service at Manchester Cathedral on Friday 11 April.

Challenging the elements

Sometimes, tragedies occur when people go into the mountains clad in little more than running vest and shorts to push their own personal boundaries of endurance and fitness. In June 2007, two years before the 'longest day', a serving soldier with the Parachute Regiment fell to his death during the same gruelling event. Rescuers rushed to save the thirty-seven-year old, who fell on Carnedd Llewelyn above Ffynnon Llugwy reservoir, but their efforts were in vain.

It was an interesting day for a group of trainees and their two, more experienced, mentors from the Rossendale and Pendle team in Lancashire. The group were visiting RAF Valley for the day to undertake their basic helicopter training when matters took a surreal turn in the form of a call-out for the crew.

'Safety briefing done, fear about the imminent death awaiting us should we grab the wrong this, clutch the wrong that suitably instilled, we prepared to wander back from the aircraft for a welcome brew in the mess,' says Judy Whiteside, one of the trainees in question. 'No sooner had our bums left those seats than Bing Bong! went the station tannoy. Job on, said Chas, the winchman paramedic. A female casualty had apparently fallen above the Ffynnon Llugwy Reservoir in Snowdonia. As it was a mountain job — and at this stage it was unclear whether the Oggi team had been called — Chas requested that Andy and Barry (our Rossendale and Pendle team leader

and deputy) assist him. Whisked off to the operations room, via the boots of their respective cars for appropriate kit, they emerged moments later complete with flying helmets to enable access to radio traffic. We watched them board the aircraft and disappear into the gathering Welsh cloud.

'Abandoned by our leaders and locked inside a military base, there was nothing more to be done than loaf about on the leather sofas, fight for the remote control, catch up on the tabloids, and avail ourselves of the Valley tea caddy. All the while believing they'd be back in a mo and our training would resume.

'Two hours later, the aircraft landed. Out went the fuel tanker, back came the fuel tanker and back up went the Sea King. Word came that they'd left the winchie at the site. Rumour had it there were now two casualties, the second a heart attack and incredibly from the same party. But where were our two?

'Later still, back came the aircraft again, and once again our hopes fluttered higher that this training we'd looked forward to for so many weeks would continue. But back out went the fuel tanker, in came the winchman, back came the fuel tanker and back went the winchman. Still no sign of our lads. They're off to Leeds now, someone said. Hospital transfer. What? Are our two walking back? And yet, still, we wondered about the possibility of a resumption in proceedings but an afternoon of tea and music channels had taken its toll. We'd grown decidedly listless. People had anniversary parties to get home to, beer to drink. Then in came a member of the ground crew. Sorry but the training's off. You can go home. Just as well really, we'd run out of tea bags.

'And then, almost simultaneously, a call from Andy. They were en route to Oggi base. Could we drive up there to meet them? So off we set up the A5.

'Back at Oggi base, I was fortunate enough to sit in on the debrief. I heard of the tragedy that had unfolded, and the sheer professionalism of this small group of volunteers in dealing with its consequences, as we'd bantered our way restlessly through an idle afternoon.

'Who knows what passed through his head that morning, as Sgt Paul Upton prepared to join

Map? Compass? Torch? Who needs 'em? March 2003: A fifty-year-old man set off with no map, compass or torch on a day with low cloud. He went up via Bochlwyd and the side of the Bristly Ridge and across the Glyderau by asking other groups which way to go. He also reckoned he'd been this way once before in clear weather. In the area of the summit of Glyder Fawr, he lost his way and at 4.45pm made a 999 call to say he was lost. A search party with a SARDA dog set out to look for him using his information, in the area above the Devil's Kitchen. Later, he said he could hear cars and occasionally see lights. He was eventually found by a party on a night exercise above the Pen y Pass Youth Hostel. After contact had been made with him from the road, he promised to buy a map, compass and torch. And the less said about his steel-toe capped boots and motorcycle jacket, the better...

Winter stretcher lower: Photo © OVMRO.

his companions in the gruelling race? Doubtless he was fit, doubtless he had been training for many months for this very day. But, somewhere above the Ffynnon Llugwy Reservoir, as he crossed Carnedd Llewelyn, he lost his footing and fell 150 metres to his death.

'The disjointed information which filtered through to us trainees whiling away our time at RAF Valley was no less confusing to those at Oggi base. The initial call from North Wales Police, at 10.55am, had indeed suggested that a woman had fallen and been unconscious with injuries. Both land and air ambulances were en route and the ARCC contacted regarding 22 Squadron. The map reference, plus the information regarding ambulance resources, gave the impression the incident was at, or very near to, the road head at the dam.

'Ten minutes later, a call from the police stated that the air ambulance would not be not attending — just as it flew overhead the casualty site! Another five minutes and another call suggested there was also a thirty-five-year-old male with a heart attack, at a similar grid reference.

'Chris Lloyd called the informant who confirmed there was only one incident, the road ambulance was at the road head but the casualty was, in fact, 200 metres away. The air ambulance radioed in saying it was unable to assist on the steep ground and that 22 were already on site. 22 Squadron radioed in stating this was a fatality and, in line with fatal incident protocol, Oggi troops would now be required at the scene.

'Meanwhile, our lads on the aircraft listened to the radio traffic as the Sea King flew across Anglesey, following the A5 as it meanders through the Ogwen Valley towards Capel Curig, before turning left just after Ogwen Cottage and up the hill to circle the reservoir. It would be a snatch and run, Chas explained, his intention to treat the casualty as an MI. He would go down with either Andy or Barry, then the other, their task to perform CPR and bag and mask. The basket stretcher would be lowered, casualty loaded and winched and off would fly Chas, leaving Andy and Barry to fend for themselves on the hill.

'As they approached the lake, they saw several vehicles, including the land ambulance, and Helimed was just leaving. The casualty lay on very rocky ground and it didn't look good, so down went Chas alone. As the aircraft came out of the hover and flew a couple of orbits round the reservoir, he quickly diagnosed life extinct — a heart attack brought on by massive trauma. No longer a snatch and run, this was now a job for the coroner.

'Leaving the winchie with the body, the Sea King transported our two back to Oggi base, in exchange for Oggi team leader Jed Stone and Chris Lloyd, who still believed this to be a simple fatal heart attack incident. Only as they approached the cas site did they realise this was going to be more unpleasant.

'In line with the fatal incident protocol, the area had to be thoroughly photographed and recorded. Aware that 22 might not be available for too long, given the shift in urgency, Jed requested the collection of further troops and kit. Back to the site went our two with a couple of Oggi boys, then the aircraft returned to refuel.'

'This gave us valuable time to gather and record evidence before we bagged the body and readied it for the winch up,' explains Lloyd. 'The aircraft returned with another two troops and some technical kit. The body was then moved from the mountainside and we set about trying to find the cause of the accident.' As they ascended the steep grass and scree slope they identified evidence

OGGI SNIPS

January 2010: A torch found floating in water after an avalanche at Aber Falls sparked a major search involving thirty members and three dogs but, fortunately, it was a false alarm.

of the fall. Clods of earth and impact marks, and the everyday detritus of an outdoor life — Mars bar, Nutrigrain bar, a shoe and a sock, map — each marked with an orange flag. Soon a fall line became obvious — a diagonal straight line from the body to a point two-thirds of the way up the hill, and the foot of a fifty-metre vertical crag.

As team members made their way round to the top of the crag, they identified a departure point. Anchors were set up and John Hulse abseiled down the line. He found scuff marks and part of a water container. All of these were photographed and he was lowered to the bottom of the crag.

All the evidence was photographed, bagged and sealed, GPS reference noted, and then signed for. By 3.00pm they had left the scene for the Oggi Land Rover parked at the road head, some ten minutes away.

Back at Oggi base, having pottered up the valley under late afternoon sunshine, Judy Whiteside watched the Land Rover meander down the hill and along the road to Bryn Poeth, still little appreciating the tragedy her fellow team mates had become embroiled in. 'Jed's firm reiteration that, if anyone had been emotionally affected they could access the critical incident experts at North Wales police for guidance, underlined that this was no ordinary call-out. I recalled Barry, in similar circumstances on our own patch, reminding team members that despite his thirty years as a serving police officer — dealing with more than enough death and trauma — he still never knew when an incident might come back and bite him. Frame of mind, time of month, family conflicts, emotional stress, personal bereavement, whatever. So many other factors in the mix at any one time. Experience does not inure you to horror.

'And, as we set off back to Lancashire, Jed, John and Chris remained at Bryn Poeth, collating the information. Later, a police officer came to collect the evidence and rolls of film and the following day, Jed collated a more thorough report.'

As press officer, Chris Lloyd spent the Monday fielding calls from the press, many picking up on a comment to the BBC about the weather. 'There was a very big change. They started out under beautiful sunny, clear, blue skies but would rapidly have climbed up into heavy cloud and would have relied on good navigation to find their way.'

Despite speculation that the change was unpredicted, a Met Office spokesman suggested their forecast for Snowdonia had said cloud would thicken and lower into the afternoon and that the cloud base would be around 500 metres.

Wherever the truth lies, should organisers still have gone ahead? Lloyd saw no reason why not. 'It's a navigational exercise and that's part of the challenge. There was no wind or rain and though cloud is an adverse condition, it's not an extreme condition. You frequently get it on the summits so I see nothing wrong with running the race with a bit of cloud cover. There were no strong winds and the weather was mild. You just have to take your time and be careful with your navigation. Whilst the low cloud probably contributed to this tragic accident, the differing weather forecasts did not.'

An inquest in August heard that Upton had been warned by doctors not to do 'any strenuous exercise'. A member of his family said he had been going back and forth to America and had come back with a deep vein thrombosis. He still had a month to go on his tablets yet he was apparently seen as medically fit enough to take part in the race. Major David O'Brien, who was running in front of him, said they were running as quickly as they could through cloudy conditions but because of the descent he'd started dropping back. Upton was almost directly behind him and he shouted 'Steady on'. Then he heard the noise of him slumping. 'I saw him fall until he came to rest at the bottom.' O'Brien followed him down. 'As I approached, I shouted but there was no response. I was aware he had a bad injury to his head.'

Pathologist Mark Lord said death had been caused by a fractured skull due to a fall from height. Before the race started, it was revealed that Upton had received a medical examination when the DVT and Warfarin had been discussed but he was declared fit. He knew the risk he was taking. He knew the exertion he would be required to put in to this race. Deputy Coroner Nicola Jones described it as 'amazing bad luck', saying he had lost his footing descending the mountain.

With any incident, once the job is complete, normal life resumes — whatever that may be. For team members, it's back to the long-suffering family or accommodating workplace. For the family and friends of Paul Upton, and for those running the race with him, it would never be quite the same again. A thirty-seven-year-old divorced father of two, he was still young, still serving in the 1st Battalion the Parachute Regiment, based at Brize Norton, still looking forward to the active life ahead of him. He was due to remarry later that year.

For team members, the image of his death may fade into the background, emerging again when least expected, a haunting moment of sadness. One of the party of trainees had spent the day worrying whether the female casualty was one of his mates, out on the hill in that same area whilst he was 'playing with helicopters'. Even as he drove away from RAF Valley he'd had little reassurance that this was not the case. Doubtless he was somewhat relieved to meet with those friends again, safe and sound.

COBWEB CORNER

Finding Shergar: A group of walkers were descending off the hill, late one afternoon, their progress slowed by one of their number. Eventually, the slower member of the party sat down to rest, assuring the others he'd meet them at the car. In the rapidly failing light, he gently cast his eyes around him, drinking in the view. Suddenly, to his horror, he saw a skeleton close by. All thought of tired limbs were gone and so was he!

Following his call to the police, the team was called, an early start planned for the following day. With thoughts of murder in mind, the police sent a more senior officer to Bryn Poeth — not just the Bethesda bobby for this one. The 'informant' made several attempts to remember where he'd made his discovery. Then, at last! 'This is where I sat —and there are the ribs!'

Team members quickly moved to the site and reported to base that they'd made a find. Bryn Poeth buzzed with excitement as the police officer asked for further details. But the mood quickly changed for the ribs belonged to a pony — news which was greeted with disappointed silence down at base. The hill party was just about to return home, when a message came from base. 'You'd better bring that skeleton down! Shergar's worth a million pounds!'

OGGI SNIPS

January 1996: A lucky paraglider survived the night on the mountain in heavy rain, and with an injured ankle, by wrapping himself in his parachute in the manner of sleeping bag.

Chris Lloyd spent the evening at a fiftieth birthday party thinking about a widow and fatherless children. Andy Simpson travelled home the 120 miles to Bury, near Manchester and a family outing to the local pub garden. Pint in hand, he gazed at the sky. What should fly overhead but the very Sea King from which he had been winched to an unforgiving Welsh mountainside not six hours earlier — en route back from Leeds. What are the chances of that?

'And as for me,' concludes Whiteside, 'hearing the debrief and Barry's lucid account of the day en route back home, the image of another similar death and subsequent body recovery, in a local quarry, sprang to mind and stayed with me for the evening, superimposed on the events of the day. I was also reminded that the spirit of voluntarism, the care and concern for a fellow mountaineer which drove our predecessors to form a more organised mountain rescue service, is still alive and well in our mountain rescuers today. Long may that continue.'

Air and car crashes

The mountains of Snowdonia can be far from hospitable to humans, much less to aircraft. In 'No Landing Place', his study of aircraft crashes in the region, Edward Doylerush describes the peaks of the Carneddau, the Glyderau and the Snowdon range as an 'impenetrable barrier to aircraft flying a straight east to west course in cloud below 2000 feet, an altitude that might be comfortable over East Anglia'. September 1937 saw one of the first crashes 'because the mountains are there', when an Avro Anson Mk1, of 220 Squadron, Coastal Command, returning from 'bombing practice at Penhros, flew into mist as they approached Penmaenmawr'. Finding his way 'blocked by a mountain', the pilot 'pulled the Anson steeply upwards only to lose flying speed', nose-diving 'into the sea with the loss of the crew of three'.

Many of the crashes since have been military, a consequence of war and the need for trained personnel to fight it but, as Doylerush concludes, 'one cannot fight a mountain in an aircraft and win'. However, history changed on 10 January 1952, when an Aer Lingus Dakota, en route from London to Dublin, crashed in flames in a gale of hail, rain and sleet near Moel Siabod. A simple stone still commemorates those who died in what was Ireland's first air disaster.

The St Kevin almost buried itself in bog on Y Cribau at 1200 feet, east of Llyn Gwynant on the slopes between the peaks of Moel Siabod and Moel Meirch. Twenty-three people were killed, many of their bodies forced deep into the bog by the impact. There were no survivors.

The plane had departed London Northolt at 5.25pm and was due to land in Dublin at 8.10pm. The last message received was a report to the Nevin Radio Station, south of Anglesey which reported that the St Kevin was flying normally. The cause of the crash was never established, although it was believed that the atrocious weather conditions may have led to mechanical failure.

The alarm was raised when a farmer heard the crash and ran half a mile to the power station at Nant Gwynant to alert the police. By midnight, more than a hundred rescuers had battled by torchlight through blizzard conditions to the blackened wreckage, broken bodies and personal possessions scattered all around. It took three days to complete the clearing up, wading knee-deep through the bog, but only twelve bodies were recovered. The remainder had to be left inside the aircraft as it slowly sank deeper into the water-logged ground.

Dr E Gerald Evans, the pathologist to the Welsh Regional Hospital Board and Home Office, said at the inquest that death had been instantaneous for the three crew members and twenty passengers, adding that the bodies were mutilated by the impact of the crash. Four were never accounted for, while others could not be clearly identified. The twelve recovered victims were buried in a mass grave in Llanbeblig Cemetery in Caernarfon and later in the year, the ground was consecrated in memory of those who died.

The Dakota crash stood apart from earlier air crashes in the area because of the size of the aircraft involved and the sheer number of casualties but it has proved one in a continuing line of civilian and military air crashes. Since 1968, the team has noted nine small aircraft crashes amongst their incident reports, although there have been others. Most of these have been fatal. Fifty-one-year-old Stephen Lovatt, however, had a lucky escape. When he crash-landed his two-seater plane into the side of 3028ft Elidir Fawr, team leader Roger Jones told the 'Daily Post' that it was 'absolutely remarkable that someone can land an aircraft in Snowdonia and survive!'

Lovatt was a classic car restorer from Nottingham. He was flying to Caernarfon to inspect two vintage Rolls Royces when his engine failed and he was forced off course. He remained trapped in the single engine Piper Tomahawk for about five hours until rescuers found him at 2800 feet, cut him from the wreckage and airlifted him to Bangor by Sea King. He'd suffered head injuries and was in critical condition but stable.

Speaking after the accident, Al Read said Lovatt was 'lucky to be alive. He was in the cockpit and still alive. Initially, I thought he was trapped by the rudder pedals but these fears were

unfounded. We were more concerned about his injuries and decided to call for more help to lift him out of the aircraft and onto a stretcher. He was very close to steep slopes on three sides. The aircraft was badly damaged but still intact and there was no fire.

More than twenty members from both Llanberis and Ogwen teams had responded to the call, after walkers reported hearing an aircraft and a bang. Four rescuers were dropped off by Sea King at Llyn Marchlyn, 600 feet below the crash site. It appeared that Lovatt was able to belly-land without the aircraft catching fire and softly enough to avoid even a fuel leak.

Yet, despite a glowing testimonial from the chief flying instructor at Nottingham airport and Lovatt's own avowal that adequate safety checks had been made — and that he was simply the victim of bad weather — the accident caused some controversy. Air accident investigators said Lovatt was lucky to be alive. An inquiry by the Civil Aviation Authority Air Accident Investigation branch found he had called Caernarfon airport to check flying conditions. Although weather forecasts predicted bad weather for west Wales and the mountains, there was no other evidence of weather checks by Lovatt. The report said, 'Whilst it is possible that the pilot obtained weather info from another source, the only evidence of his checking the weather is the phone call to Caernarfon airport before he left his place of work. Given the pilot chose to fly his fair-weather, direct route, it seems likely that he was aware of the poor weather over the mountains and that he had based his decision regarding the suitability of the destination weather only on his phone call'. The report also revealed that Lovatt had not filed a flight plan.

Needless to say, Lovatt was disappointed at the findings. 'It was just severe weather which got me stranded. I was asked for my opinion but my opinion wasn't there on the report. There was nobody about to witness what happened so it's just personal opinion.'

In September 2006, sixty-year-old Brian Vaux owed his life not just to the quick work of mountain rescue teams, but the quick thinking of a young woman who ran down the mountain to raise the alarm. Unfortunately, his passenger, seventy-three-year-old Stuart Kingsbury, was not so lucky. The Cessna 152 had just taken off. One rescuer said if the pilot had been able to fly the stricken craft just a few feet higher, he may have cleared the mountain top. Weather conditions along the coast had been bright but the aircraft hit low cloud on the Carneddau, clipping the mountain top and flipping onto its side on a grassy boggy slope of about 15-20 degrees.

A year later, Vaux still had no recollection of the crash, he told the inquest. The last thing he remembered of that day was flying over Caernarfon bay at 2300 feet. He said the passenger had remarked that Snowdon was to the left of the plane. He couldn't remember landing, refuelling or taking off afterwards, nor the incident itself. The pair had taken off from Caernarfon and just a few minutes later the aircraft came down in cloud. Experts said it had crashed while flying 'straight and level'. The force of impact pushed the wings forward causing the fuselage to bend over the cockpit. 'It looked like a ball,' said the report.

Vaux had planned to fly directly from Caernarfon to their home base but poor weather forced them to return to Caernarfon to refuel and he decided to take a more northerly route, along the North Wales coast where the weather was reported to be better. Still recuperating from the accident,

Air crash wreckage: The remains of the crash at Drosgl © OVMRO.

he appeared at the inquest in a wheelchair. He would, he said, forever be haunted by the death of his passenger.

Keith Conradi of the Air Accident Investigation Bureau at Farnborough said he had visited the crash site the following day. Inquiries revealed that Vaux had marked the chart with his intended route and crashed within a mile of that track. Asked by the coroner what Vaux should have done, Conradi said, 'He should have navigated around the low cloud. If you are in any doubt, especially in bad weather, it is best to keep away from high ground'. As Edward Doylerush had noted.

Pathologist Dr Susan Andrew said Kingsbury suffered a deep gash to the forehead in the crash which probably knocked him unconscious. He also suffered fractures to sternum, right leg and ankle. 'The cause of death was the inhalation of vomit due to the traumatic injury of the chest.'

The AAIB report concluded that his unfamiliarity with the area and the deteriorating weather conditions may well have disguised the danger that the rising terrain presented and led to this controlled flight into terrain. 'An early climb to the minimum safe altitude, which was accurately marked on the pilot's flight log, or an accurately flown track over the Menai Strait would almost certainly have prevented this tragic accident.'

In 1998, a light aircraft crash into the East Face of Tryfan led to a British Red Cross award for team member Peter Gadd, after he risked his own life to recover two bodies from the wreckage. Gadd's daughter Mel, a youth worker with the British Red Cross, nominated her father for the award. He had been first on the scene of the accident with fellow team member Dave Williams, a police officer from Conwy.

The two-seater Cessna 152 had been en route from Leicester to Blackpool, in dense cloud and drizzle when it smashed into rocks, 500 feet below the summit. Pilot Shaun Booker, and passenger Paul Pountney both died in the crash but Gadd went to extraordinary lengths for the sake of the men's families, effectively amputating Poutney's foot to enable his body to be extricated.

'It was a catastrophic impact,' says Dave Worrall. 'The two guys in it wouldn't have known anything about it. The team was called out swiftly because the crash was heard. We sent a lot of people up. The biggest thing was having to secure it to stop it tumbling down the hillside. We used every bit of rope we could lay our hands on, tying it to rocks. There was aviation fuel everywhere as the tanks had ruptured — and, at that time, a lot of the team were smokers so we had to warn them not to light up!

'Once it was secure we were faced with the problem of having to remove the two bodies from the aircraft. Pete and Dave crawled inside and tried to get them out. One came out relatively easily but the other was trapped with his foot under the pedals. For the families' sakes we had to get them out and down to the road. The RAF were also involved guarding the site.'

The team lost a lot of equipment that day, including five or six ropes, because it was all contaminated by the aviation fuel. 'We were recompensed by the crash investigation people,' adds Worrall. 'Of all the air crashes, that was definitely the most memorable.'

Karen Pountney, the passenger's widow, was obviously distraught by the accident. Needing to make sense of her loss, she asked the team whether anyone could take her to visit the crash site. Gadd volunteered for the difficult task, safe in the knowledge that Karen didn't know exactly what had gone on in the plane during the rescue. Or so he thought. However, during the scramble up

OGGI SNIPS

July 2003: Given the explosion in the indigenous rabbit population at base, a new idea was floated, that the Rabbit Reaction Force now would be first to respond to an incident.

to the crash site, with her daughter and sister, Karen revealed that she was fully aware of the details — something of a shock to Gadd — but that the only emotion she felt towards the team was 'deep thanks for rescuing Paul's body and not leaving it on the mountain'.

Later still, Gadd carried a marble plaque to mark the spot, high on the south side of Tryfan. He also took another relative to the scene on the anniversary of the accident.

'Pete was very surprised to find he'd been chosen as a Wales region winner,' wrote Mel, in the December newsletter. 'He thought that was that, but the Red Cross didn't think so and he was invited down to London as a national winner. There were about fifteen national winners in all and they'd all done such brave and caring acts that I know he was proud to be counted among them.' Gadd accepted his award on behalf of the team. 'I just happened to be one of the first up there at the time'. He still felt he'd done nothing special, added Mel.

Car crashes also seem to be a regular occurrence, with team members frequently on hand to deal with the aftermath. One such collision, right outside Roger Jones's house left three people seriously injured. The first car to pull up was Roger Pyves, Pete Evans, John Lindsey and Lyn Roberts, a casualty nurse at the hospital, on their way to Bangor for a curry and a few beers.

'You couldn't have wished for a better team of bystanders,' says Jones. 'The car was starting to burn, one passenger had gone through the windscreen'. It seemed an age before the fire crew arrived, but they'd come all the way from Caernarfon. The local GP turned up, realised there was someone else in the car, in the footwell. He got an IV line into her, saved her life.

'We do seem to attend an inordinate number of road traffic collisions along the A5 and outside base. Bill Dean had his car written off by a motorcyclist on the evening of a committee meeting.

'In another incident, team members were returning to base following a day of training when this car just stopped at the end of the drive. Karl glanced out the window and commented it was a strange place to park! We went up to investigate and there was a very blue looking man in the driving seat, with a very old lady sat next to him. We later found out she was 107! He'd had a serious heart attack. We pulled him out and started CPR. We had to close the road to vehicles. Someone called the air ambulance so they landed in the field. We brought the old lady up to base — didn't want her sat in the car whilst we were giving CPR to the man we thought was her husband. She was very confused, didn't understand what was going on. Turned out she was the casualty's mother and they were on a trip round Snowdonia after lunch at a local hotel.

'A big part of the confusion', explains Dave Worrall, 'was that the lady was a native Welsh speaker. It was only when Tim Radford and Jo Worrall started to talk to her in Welsh that things became clear'.

2011

TABLE D'HÔTE: A TALE OF SANDWICHES, SAUSAGES AND SAUCE, WITH LASHINGS OF HEATHER

by Matt Sutton

The call came in the afternoon, a warm, sunny Saturday in July: an accident on Craig yr Ysfa involving three climbers, injuries sustained but not thought to be life-threatening. This magnificent, remote cliff demands respect in any conditions and a rescue always presents a major challenge. I was disappointed I couldn't attend. I knew it would be a great experience.

Dave Worrall was the designated team leader. He sent an immediate request to 22 Squadron for assistance. First indications were that the fall had taken place on Amphitheatre Buttress. A hasty party had been taken by Land Rover to the end of 'Mac's Highway'. From here, a short but steep climb leads to the summit of Craig yr Ysfa. As they arrived, the Sea King flew overhead, in the direction of base. Kim wondered if they'd already plucked the party from the crag but then the Sea King reappeared. Flying low past them it went into a hover a little way ahead. It was an open invitation and they made a dash for it.

Back at base, Dave formed a team to discuss how best to extricate the three from the cliff as the facts became clearer. Rather than Amphitheatre Buttress, as first thought, the party had attempted to climb Great Gully. Below the Great Cave Pitch, with their abilities tested to the limit, they'd tried to bypass the difficulties by following a rock chimney on the right only to find themselves on steep, difficult and vegetated ground. The leader of the party was reasonably experienced but his two seconds had almost no rock climbing experience. During the traverse the leader took a fall, dislocating his shoulder and leaving his inexperienced second to hold him. With their leader immobile and without the technical experience to rescue themselves, this expedition was neither going up nor down.

The team had two choices: either go in from below and climb up to them or descend by abseil from above. As they were already high on the cliff, the latter was the logical option. Also, in most cases, it is much easier to set up and operate a rescue system from above than below. If conditions and terrain allow, this gives the additional benefit of continuing down once the party is retrieved. The law of gravity stays on the side of the rescuer.

While this was clearly the best option, the summit of Craig yr Ysfa is almost 1,000 metres, so the first challenge would be getting the equipment and team up there. A lot of equipment and a fair number of 50 and 100-metre ropes would be needed. The cliff is over 300 metres

OGGI SNIPS

In the early-1970s, a honeymoon couple on a wild camp were somewhat shocked when a search dog, working the area during a night search, shot through their tent flap to join them.

high. While climbing to the summit of the mountain would not present a challenge, the weight of the equipment draws valuable energy best preserved for the rescue. 22 Squadron willingly obliged to get people and equipment to the right spot, a ridge overlooking the cliff from which the abseils could be set up for the team to descend to the incident site.

Communication is a crucial aspect of any rescue in Cwm Eigiau. The four kilometre-long ridge that divides the Ogwen Valley and Oggi base from Cwm Eigiau means that, once you drop below the ridgeline on the opposite side, radio comms fail. The only solution is to set up a mobile communication point lower down the cwm and relay messages from base to the troops on the hill. Al Read lives not far from the spot and he was on hand to take his own Land Rover up to fulfil the task.

Dave now had enough team members to get his plan into action. The hasty party had arrived on the ridge and begun setting up an abseil. A second team, including Glynne Andrew, would join them on the cliff. As an orthopaedic surgeon, Glynne would play an essential role dealing with the particular injuries sustained by the casualty. Chris Onions and Chris Lloyd would serve the backbreaking role of taking additional ropes and equipment by foot while Jed Stone and Roger Jones took on the logistics and transportation as well as supporting Dave at base. With the Sea King's noisy arrival there was no time to waste.

It was now past four o'clock. As the second group arrived on the summit, Geraint — in a moment of precognition — declared his thought that they wouldn't be off the hill until dawn. Those around him immediately scotched the idea, declaring midnight would be the most likely time. Yet, without doubt, the cliff would present unforeseen challenges. Its size and terrain would be the first but the lack of familiarity would be another. Tryfan takes the lion's share of technical rescues and this cliff, no less demanding, sees a lot less climbing and therefore fewer rescues.

It took three abseils to reach a suitable ledge, approximately level with the casualties. Frustratingly, the party were still below the level of the belay and horizontally 15-20 metres away. If only they'd remained in Great Gully itself, it would have been more straightforward but now there was no easy solution. Dusk was approaching and, at the point you want things to start fitting into place, it was getting ever more complicated. Day or night makes little difference to how the team operates but night always takes longer. As more team members descended to the ledge, the task of setting up a rescue system to reach the casualties began. In poor light and with precious few reliable anchor points for the rope systems this proved time consuming. The problem was mitigated to some extent because Geraint had secretly stashed a bag of pegs, recalling his dad's advice that finding good anchor points was always difficult on Craig yr Ysfa.

It was at this point everyone realised this was going to be a very long job. Food and drink would be an issue. Many team members would not have eaten since lunch and those on the hill had been on the go for over five hours. There was no chance of resupply from the top as the ropes used for the initial abseil were now needed for the rescue. The only option was to send food and drink in from below as people came down.

It was eight o'clock and I was now at home. I'd noticed there'd been no 'stop message' for the job but thought maybe it had been forgotten. Then a text came: 'More troops required.' Considering the time, more than five hours on, this was unusual. Clearly this wasn't a straightforward job. I rang in to confirm my availability. 'Hey mate!' said Jed. 'Tim's coming up too and we need you guys to take supplies up. We think this job is going to go on all night.'

I set off immediately. It was a beautiful evening, warm in the setting sun. As I arrived at base, Tim was just getting out of his car. The front door was open and the smell of cooking filled the air. Something was being prepared but this wasn't just biscuits and Mars bars. I walked into the crew room and the table was laid out as if for a well attended party or function. Platters of sausages in Pyrex dishes, bacon, a wide variety of sauces, Snickers bars, tubs of margarine, roll of tin foil, loaves of bread, flasks of hot tea, cutlery, paper plates — all ready to go. Ken Dwyer appeared at the kitchen door with a broad smile, tea towel in hand. 'Wow Ken, looks fantastic!' I was inspired. The boys and girls would love it and we were going to deliver it.

For some reason none of us had considered the practical problems of transporting this feast onto the hill. Even with the seats down in my Peugeot 406 Estate, there was barely room for both the food and our sacks. I spent some time neatly laying it all out before we set off. As we drove to Betws to take the long way round to Cwm Eigiau, we started up an interesting conversation on the subject of crop circles. This phenomenon, particular to the chalk uplands of Wiltshire and Hampshire and close to my parents' home, had interested me for many years. Any thought about what was in the back of the car or the task in hand was relegated to background consciousness. This was unwise as we negotiated the steep narrow lane that leads up into Cwm Eigiau.

By this time it was getting quite dark and I had to stop quite suddenly for the first of the sheep gates. Tim jumped out to open and close it before we continued, keeping up our quick pace. A few humps and bumps in the road led around a sharp bend. 'Gate!' cried Tim, as the next metal five-bar gate appeared through the gloom. I slammed on the brakes. The contents of the boot shot forward, spurred on by the weight of our sacks. 'Sausages!' Tim cried out again, a split second after his first warning. The problem wasn't lost on me. Given the momentum, the now upended platter of sausages would, without a doubt, end up in the footwell. I released the brake. Next came a jarring, clanging impact. The gate sprung open. By some miracle, we sailed through to a gentle

OGGI SNIPS

When a 52-seater coach broke down outside base, team members rushed to help, pushing and pulling the vehicle to unblock the road, as all 52 passengers looked on. From the coach.

halt, just ahead of the gate's return. 'Shall I shut the gate?' chuckled Tim.

We continued on to the car park where Roger, Jed and Al were waiting. At this point, Al confessed that he'd already been supplied with supper, courtesy of his wife who had ridden up the hill and across the moor on her horse to deliver it. I doubt there is a more chivalrously supplied dinner in the history of mountain rescue! Anyway, it did mean we had one less mouth to feed. It was only when I opened the boot, the reality sank in: how do we transfer the contents of the boot, more appropriate to a Sunday lunch party, into two rucksacks already loaded with climbing kit? And failure wasn't an option.

Platters of sausages in Pyrex dishes, bacon, a wide variety of sauces, Snickers bars, tubs of margarine, roll of tin foil, loaves of bread, flasks of hot tea, cutlery, paper plates... but, for some reason none of us had considered the practical problems of transporting this feast onto the hill.

We devised a plan: Wrap food in tin foil, pop in margarine, bread and cutlery, and a single bottle of tomato ketchup, and make the sandwiches on the hill. Snickers for pudding, all washed down with tea. Hey presto! Though this wouldn't include the full range of sauces, I was looking forward to offering 'á la carte'. Then it was into the Land Rover for the final part of the journey to the end of the track. There, we unloaded, said our goodbyes and turned to begin our walk in. Until that point we'd had some sort of light whether from head torches, the fading daylight or even the headlights of the Land Rover, but now it was dark. Pitch dark. And no reference point on the hill where we'd expected to see the head torches of rescuers. We made our lonely way across the boggy moor.

Back on the mountain, painstaking progress was being made. There were now 800 metres of rope in use on the hill and a rescue team of nine to manage. It was the type of challenge that Kim, as leader on the hill for the night, relished. From his central position, he could keep tabs on the comings and goings. To reach the casualties a dual main and safety line was set up and Alex was lowered down to the injured casualty. Once Alex was attached the casualty, it had to be converted into a raise using a pulley system. On very difficult ground, with no stances or belays, it was a challenge. Also Alex could only bring the one injured climber and had to leave the other two. There was no way of speeding up the process without compromising the safety of the operation.

In the meantime, a second system was set up for the eventual evacuation from the cliff, so the injured climber could be lowered to the foot of the cliff while the rescue of his two other colleagues took place at the same time. Geraint was sent down to find a way down off the crag. He found a stance just above the final steep section of Great Gully and the eventual easing of this mighty cliff. At last, an end game was in sight. Yet this wasn't the end of the challenges. Glynne Andrew was now able to assess the condition of the injured climber. He attempted to put his shoulder back into place. This would have made the descent a little easier and less painful, but he was unable to do it because the injury, thought to be simply a dislocation, included a fracture.

It was at this point that we arrived at the foot of the crag. After half an hour of walking we'd spotted lights and were able to orientate ourselves and reach the correct location more quickly. We climbed up the hillside, which grew ever steeper and more heathery. At last we reached the foot of the crag. We could communicate by radio with Geraint who was only around sixty or seventy metres above us waiting for the arrival of the injured climber. After a brief recce into a very wet and boggy lower section of Great Gully, Tim and I decided to return to the foot to the climb. We unpacked the food and I began the task of preparing the sandwiches.

This was not easy. There was a lot of food and a lot of extras. I hadn't been able to fit in the plates so, once I'd made a number of sandwiches, there was nowhere to put them. There was no solid ground as we were surrounded by heather. Balanced on these, any movement could send the sandwiches and sausages into the thicket. To make matters worse, the bread was of the thick white and dry variety and I couldn't close it or put it into a bag without the whole thing falling to pieces. Above me, my colleagues were engaged in a heroic effort to rescue three climbers in big trouble and here was I juggling with bread. Finally, by arranging my rucksack with two Tesco bags I'd discovered, I found I could accommodate a large number of sandwiches in neat piles.

I kept Tim at a reasonable distance, lest the tottering arrangement collapse, then turned to sit down and admire the view. By now, our eyes had fully adjusted to the darkness. What had been a hazy dark sky had cleared. In the far distance, the lights of civilisation cast an orangey glow above the rugged mountain horizon, while the stars sharpened above us. Suddenly, I caught sight of a tongue of deep orange flame rising above the hills opposite us. 'Look Tim!' But Tim was a little way off looking for a suitable spot for the helicopter to collect the injured climber. I assumed it to be a heather fire. It grew quickly, getting higher and broader at the base. Flushed with confusion, I struggled to figure out what I was looking at. It wasn't a fire. What the hell was it? Then, suddenly, it was obvious: it was a slow rising crescent moon! Tim had finished his task and came over. 'Look Tim, it's the moon!' I said, quite excited. But Tim was clearly a bit puzzled. The radio crackled into life. 'Rescue 22 inbound.' Glynne and the climber were now only a short way above us.

OGGI SNIPS

February 2006: Team members rescued a novice group from John Moores mountaineering club, one wearing wellies, another trainers. They had been walking in low cloud and rain.

Long before I heard the helicopter, I spotted the regular flashing of its strobe and the red and green of the sidelights. Then that familiar low drone, distant at first but rising on the breeze. The sound woke me up. I let out a four-letter swear word, then again and again in quick succession. Less than a minute before the Sea King would be here. I was screwed. Completely screwed! Soon the entire area was going to be subject to a violent downdraught, a gale force wind directly onto my delicate work. There was no way out! Fifteen seconds to go. I couldn't just capitulate. I stood at the foot of the rucksack facing outwards, then leaned back to lie as if crucified, my back and extended arms shielding the sandwiches from the wind. A series of violent gusts filled the air with fumes and a twister of heather whipped into a frenzy. It lasted as long as it took to get the casualty winched safely on board and on his way to hospital, which must have been a full ten minutes. I knew the result would be bad and once the helicopter had gone I struggled up, not wanting to look down. It was a mess. Sausages and Snickers strewn about wantonly, bread and margarine in various states of deterioration, devoid of filling but still adorned with ketchup, garnished with sprigs of heather.

I'd no option but to stuff the remnants into the two Tesco bags. Tim formed part one of the reception committee offering the tea and then they were passed on to me. The anticipation and expectation must have been intense. 'It's a lucky dip,' I said apologetically, as each one came for his or her rations. I thought of poor Ken and his culinary pride, now been reduced to a quick fumble in a Tesco bag. But, such was the level of hunger, I even got a few compliments.

Once fed, people began to sit down in the heather. The two or three team members left on the cliff were now stripping gear and retreating down from the route. The sky had remained clear and the moon was high in the sky. It must have been around 2.30am. Two team members chatted a little distance away but I couldn't tell who they were in the darkness. It was almost hypnotic, the gentle movement of the breeze and the slow discernable passage of the moon and stars above. We sat peering out into distance, lost in our own worlds, exhausted.

As we finally made our way down, there was an almost imperceptible increase in light. Bit by bit, the shadows reduced. We were quite a large group and there wasn't enough room in the vehicle for everyone. As Tim and I had been on the hill for the least amount of time, we stayed behind and waited for the others. I stared down the valley to the rolling mist and cloud welling up lower down the mountainside. It moved across from left to right, billowing and dispersing as it went. After what seemed like an eternity the others finally returned. Everyone and everything was loaded aboard and we set off for a big breakfast at base. It was now fully light and a new day was with us.

CHAPTER EIGHT

Inspiration, perspiration and innovation: equipping the future

Change has inevitably brought resistance from time to time, as each 'old school' gave way to successive 'new school' thinking, but the trend has always been towards more efficient ways of doing things, optimum care for the casualty. The team has tested and developed new equipment, had themselves audited, taken on board the best of practice from around the world — and they've also led the way, particularly in the field of technology.

Russ Hore first came into contact with the team in 1977, as a schoolboy, when Bill Dean was his biology teacher and ran the school climbing club. By 1993, he'd been to college, fancied joining the team, did his hill day and a year later he was a full team member. He did twenty years — living in the Midlands, commuting to Ogwen at the weekends to climb and go out on rescues — and remains an honorary member.

In 2005, Hore was IT officer for the team. He began to look at how they might get information such as ECGs, video and photographs from the hill to base via the radio. During his research, he discovered GPS mic handsets and it occurred to him that it would be good to track team members' radios while they were on the hill. Coincidentally, Dave Binks and Rob Brookes had already been doing similar

Radio comms 1968-style: Photo © OVMRO.

FROM THE ARCHIVE

Life-saving Psion has more byte than a St Bernard, January 1998: 'It's an emergency. A lone walker is lost on a vast inhospitable range of hills. A day passes before the alarm is raised with the rescue services, so he could be anywhere. What happens? The man at the mountain rescue station asks a few pertinent questions, presses a computer key —and pinpoints to within yards the exact area where this particular walker should be found.' So ran the opening lines to the Guardian's tale as teams 'merged futuristic vision with an old-fashioned British talent for making do'.

Ogwen team member Martin Hayes wanted to improve search efforts through computerisation and reached for something in his own back pocket: a standard Series 3a Psion. 'It's easily portable,' said Hayes. 'You wouldn't want to lump around something as heavy as a laptop in your rucksack'.

What he did was simple. The key search equation involves putting numbers on the likelihood that a missing person will be in a certain area, and the chances of him being spotted during a search. These two figures are then extended to cover all sectors of a search area, enabling resources to be focused where most appropriate. Forswearing traditional paper and pencil, Hayes programmed his palmtop to do the work for him, with encouraging results. His hope was to put palmtops to greater use in the field in mountain rescue in general.

'You can fax from a palmtop,' he said, 'so exact details of the injury could be sent over with no possibility of error. Some palmtops also have a stylus drawing facility which would be useful for assessing search clues such as an item of clothing. To describe it over the radio and identify if it belonged to the person you were looking for, could be very difficult. But to sketch it would be easy. The same would apply to a footprint'.

He believed other possibilities would emerge as teams got used to handling technology. Hard to believe, in this digital age, but many were sceptical about hauling any kind of electrical apparatus on to the hill, but Hayes was convinced such progress was just around the corner. His Psion never took off as a mountain rescue accessory but the principle was sound. And, only very few years later, walkers and rescuers alike willingly embraced the carriage of any amount of communication equipment in their pockets and rucksacks. How times change.

research in the Lake District. Rob Brookes, a Kendal team member at the time, had been looking at ways to transmit GPS position reports over a mountain rescue radio for some years. 'The original system was fairly easily assembled using amateur radio technology,' explains Brookes, on the MRMap website. 'This worked but it was designed to operate either as a fixed location system or from a moving vehicle. No hardware existed that would allow operation via a hand portable radio such as the ones used by mountain rescue teams.'

After many years of developing, trialling and securing the necessary permissions, the system

OGGI SNIPS

February 2000: Team members sent out to investigate 'calls for help' in the area of Y Gribin eventually found the culprits — a herd of mountain goats.

took shape with the software required to run it written by Dave Binks, of Duddon and Furness MRT. That software, MRMap, is currently used operationally by over fifty rescue teams across the UK and Ireland. With Rob and Dave's help, Hore introduced North Wales to MRMap around 2007. Now, whenever there is a call-out, or team members are on the hill with their radios, their movements can be tracked on a map back at base.

'Dave had solved the problem,' says Hore. 'But this spurred me on to something else. MRMap works for team members, could we do the same for the people who call in needing our help?'

He started looking how he could get a GPS location from a phone. Within two or three hours he'd written a 'very simple bit of code'. That evening, he tested it with Brookes. It blossomed from there — SARLOC was born.

There are many apps for smartphone which show the phone's location, but these rely on the lost person having the app installed before they get lost. SARLOC uses the web browser installed on the smartphone to interrogate the GPS and locate the person, normally to within a few metres.

The team simply sends a text message with a link to a webpage. Clicking on this link opens a page in the phone's browser which queries the phone to identify its location. This data is then displayed to the user and automatically added over the internet to the MR Map database. Whoever is handling the call-out can then see the caller's location displayed on a digital OS map display.

Can it go further? 'When it doesn't work, it's generally the phone that's the problem. It needs to be a smartphone, with a connection to the internet and the location services switched on,' says Hore.

Use of SARLOC has grown exponentially over the last few years, far beyond these shores. It works anywhere in the world. Now used by most teams in the UK, it's been taken up by mountain rescue organisations in Ireland and Scotland, the Joint Rescue Coordination Centre of Norway, quite a few teams in the USA — one in particular is the Rocky Mountain Rescue Group — then there's Hong Kong, Sweden, the German Red Cross. The list grows ever longer and it's all free. 'My legacy to search and rescue,' says Hore. 'Hopefully, it will get better as phones get better.'

Sally Armond is a great fan of the system. 'It's changed the face of search and rescue! Through SARLOC, Russ alone must have saved countless lives.'

One particular incident sticks in the memory. In November 2011, two male walkers set off from Capel Curig to walk up Moel Siabod in very poor weather conditions. They had limited equipment and eventually became totally lost and disorientated in the cloud. As the light faded, they called for help but only had a vague idea of where they were. One of the gentlemen was a diabetic and feeling very unwell, so search parties were sent out immediately. 'The initial route information we had suggested they could be anywhere on the western side of the mountain from the summit to Pen y Gwryd, a potentially vast search area in such poor conditions. But thankfully, one of them had a smartphone, so we managed to fix their location using SARLOC.

'We quickly discovered they were on the eastern flanks, a long way away from where we were originally due to commence our search. I'd taken Spin, but didn't need to use her at all! When we finally arrived, having used the pinpoint precision of SARLOC, we found them soaking wet through and cold, while the diabetic gentleman was hypoglycaemic and on the edge of losing consciousness, unable to keep his eyes open.

'We were able to quickly get some oral glucose into him, which he devoured. He rallied sufficiently to carefully stand and eventually walk off the hill with assistance. By the time we got back to the road he felt fully recovered and warm, had full capacity and didn't wish to go to hospital so we left him in his friend's care, with advice to consume complex carbs as soon as possible and seek urgent medical attention if he began to feel unwell again.

'Without SARLOC, we'd have spent the night searching the wrong side of the mountain, and the outcome for this gentleman could have been very poor indeed.'

Andy Harbach recalls another incident when a couple phoned in to say they were lost on Y Garn. 'They didn't know exactly where on the mountain they were so we sent a SARLOC text. This gave a result with a ten metre accuracy and we were able to tell them to use their compass and walk west until they hit a path which they could follow down to Nant Peris. We asked them to click the link again on their descent so we could follow their progress down the mountain. When they reached the bottom they were advised to get a taxi back round to Ogwen to collect their car. Without SARLOC we'd have had to go up in to the cloud to find them because we wouldn't have known which direction to send them in. It probably saved eight or more members several hours on the hill.'

Lost en route

Mobile phones are a mixed blessing for mountaineers and mountain rescuers alike. In August 2001, a 'Weekly News' article damned their use as 'a menace' due to climbers and walkers 'ignoring the basic safety precautions and becoming over-reliant' on their phones. Hill goers were 'shunning traditional map and compass as a guide' in favour of calling for mountain rescue at the first sign of dilemma.

Increasingly, teams are called to deal with the uninjured, 'lost' on recognisable footpaths and oblivious to the significant number of people setting aside whatever they were doing to go help, without any sort of remuneration. The danger is that resources might become severely stretched, life-threatening emergencies hampered. Readily available mapping software on GPS-enabled phones means more and more hill goers are navigating without map or compass. The consequences can be serious.

In September 2010, one walker got into difficulties when he used his iPhone to guide him up the 3000ft Y Garn. Ill-equipped and inexperienced, dressed for the high street in black leather jacket, denims and gym shoes, he'd set off in poor conditions to look for a mountain waterfall. Having checked out 'waterfalls' on the internet and noted that the Devil's Appendix is the highest single falls in Wales, he'd set off early from his home in Leicester, arriving in Ogwen mid-morning. Using his phone as a satnav he set off up Y Garn.

Not knowing anything about mountain rescue he emailed his father back in Leicester to say he was in trouble. His father called the local police who then contacted North Wales Police and eventually the team were called out. Soon after he had contacted his father, his battery failed.

Team members went to the area to search for him before darkness fell. 'The weather was poor with low cloud and heavy showers,' says Chris Lloyd. 'Three small search teams went up into Cwm Idwal to try to find this moving target before dusk. Fortunately, the cloud lifted and the guy was

OGGI SNIPS

From the 'pink' forms, April 1990: Blissful ignorance on the part of all four. Cannot blame the dog!

able to walk down to above the Devil's Kitchen — but then missed the main descent path, nearly walking over the cliffs between the Twll Du and the Idwal stream!

'We could see a lone, lost figure waving, very cold and very wet. He was given a fleece jacket and walked off the mountain. He had no rucksack, no food and no way of keeping warm — and he was blissfully ignorant of the position he'd put himself in.'

The internet search simply showed the waterfall as a red tag on the map. It wasn't even a proper map. Whilst the Devil's Appendix is indeed the tallest single-drop waterfall in Wales at around 300 feet, it isn't easy to pinpoint, located where a small stream falls off the Clogwyn y Geifr cliffs into Cwm Idwal. Most of the time it's really only a trickle, requiring a real downpour to become visible.

In 2011, one ingenious walker facilitated a speedier rescue when he sent a photo of where he and his party were 'lost'. Team members recognised it as the north gully of Tryfan and were able to make their way to the spot without further ado.

'Sending us a picture seems to be a very sensible and useful idea to give us an indication of their position,' said Chris Lloyd, soon after their recovery. The couple, from the Chester area, had taken the North Ridge route to the summit and decided to descend by the mountain's east face. They were aiming to find the Heather Terrace. But they strayed into the north gully, which has a couple of vertical drops, and realised the ground was too steep for them'.

On this occasion, the walkers were experienced and well-equipped for the conditions and rightly called for help.

'There was some confusion as to where exactly they were on the mountain but when they sent us the photo we were able to recognise the spot straight away. We were able to get above them, drop down a rope and help them find the right path. They were unhurt, but we took them down to base for a short debrief.'

Control, we have a problem

SARLOC revolutionised the way teams can pinpoint the location of those asking for help. Another system, also devised by an Ogwen team member, has revolutionised the way teams and the emergency services talk to each other during an incident and become the only multi-agency land SAR system in the UK and Republic of Ireland.

Prior to 2006, the 250,000-odd 999 calls handled by North Wales Police each year were split across three control rooms — Central, West and East — staffed by people with strong local knowledge. Relationships with mountain rescue teams were good. Then things changed. With the creation of a single communications centre at St Asaph, the quality of 999 calls needing a mountain rescue response deteriorated. 'We went from an environment in which we knew the person at the other end of the phone, to delayed calls to teams, the wrong teams being called for the area in question — which meant delays for the casualties — and poor information gathering,' says John Hulse.

'Operationally, it was causing issues. So I found out who the communications centre supervisor was and contacted him. As luck would have it, Dave Simcock was equally concerned. He also had an interest in the outdoors, so a very good relationship developed.'

Hulse suggested a root cause analysis. 'It turned out that different teams went through different call-out routes — we thought the police were the problem but the eight teams had eight different call-out methodologies and that caused problems for the new staff at the centre. Some teams were called by phone, some by pager, some by SMS some by a bureau. It was pretty shambolic — to the point of embarrassment!'

Hulse's day job was engineer manager for a telecoms company, so he had some understanding of the technology. 'Having some experience in web-based technologies and the Worldtext SMS platform successfully used by several very busy teams, I innocently volunteered to deliver the application! We needed a simple web page with links to the teams and an SMS page in the background. I put the prototype together and showed Dave. He became the system's internal champion within the North Wales Police.'

The next step was to negotiate with all eight teams, while Simcock dealt with the police aspect, encouraging everyone to engage with the new system. It took a couple of months but once everyone had accepted it, suddenly 'calls were going to the right teams, information was suitably supplied'. And somewhere along the way, the system acquired a name: SARCALL.

Following initial trials with the Ogwen team, the North Wales region went live with the system in August 2009. Almost immediately, the overall quality of the initial stages of call-outs has improved dramatically. The police reported that they were getting far faster responses from team leaders to the call-out — in some cases, the time between the police operator logging into SARCALL, selecting and contacting the team, and the team leader's response, was less than three minutes — which can only benefit the casualty.

With the system accepted in North Wales, Hulse did a number of presentations to teams nationally. Simon Harris, from Bowland Pennine MRT, was very interested in persuading the Mid Pennine teams to take it on. Paul Horder took it to the Lakes, John Beavan to North Yorkshire, Jon Whiteley to Devon and Cornwall.

Since then, the roll-out has continued apace, with all teams in England and just two in Wales now looking at the system. North of the border, almost half the Scottish teams use SARCALL and a programme is well underway to have all those teams called out direct from the new Police Scotland Control Centres. By autumn 2015, there were ninety teams and fourteen police forces and ambulance services using the system which has directly supported more than 4,000 call-outs.

There has also been a steady stream of minor but important improvements, mostly focusing on major incident messaging between teams and improving the security and resilience. By summer 2015, Hulse anticipated a new release to add team-level asset declaration for major incidents, the ability for team members to manage their own availability in the system by SMS and also new work on an online, integrated incident form for trial in specific areas.

A major exercise in the Lake District in January 2015 provided the largest ever single test for the system — six regions, thirty-four teams and four police forces joined the exercise at varying levels during the event. Even at this level, there was a lot of capacity available for further concurrent major operations. A remarkable outcome from one man 'innocently volunteering' to find a solution to a local problem which, in the event, proved to be a problem for every other team and police authority.

So how does it work? In the first instance, the system makes it easy for the calling authority to

OGGI SNIPS

The Snowdon lily is found around the northern hemisphere from the Alps to the Rocky mountains and from Greenland to Mongolia.

select the right team by means of a medium scale regional map marked with the team boundaries. With a hover-click, the operator can call the team and access geographic descriptions and a comprehensive list of climbs and local features in the area, as well as the more common names or keywords. Once the team has been selected, the operator uses just one simple screen to create and send an SMS message to the team.

Once the team leader has established the need for a team response, the entire call-out is played out on screen with team members, the emergency services and other relevant parties able to access, follow and update details. In North Wales, the hospital can also log on and make decisions about treatment and alerting the trauma team. The ambulance service can decide when to send people to the helipad to meet the incoming aircraft. The Bristow helicopter bases at Caernarfon and Humberside actively use the system in conjunction with the ARCC at Kinloss and two of the RAF MRTs.

And what of the future? 'I would love SARCALL to become the default platform for land search and rescue call-out and incident management in the UK and Ireland, with everyone on it. That would bring significant operational gain — although politically, I'm not sure it will ever happen.' We should watch this space.

Keeping an eye on things

The team has been fortunate in having a number of savvy IT people as members. At a time when not many teams had their own websites — certainly there were none in Wales — Russ Hore and Tim Radford wanted to create a website which would better inform the public about their activities. 'The big thing was all the work behind the scenes,' says Radford. 'We wanted to put some real data up there to show the public so we had to write the back end database to record incidents. This was before the advent of SARCALL.' By 1996, the team was noted to have 'established a presence on the World Wide Web'.

Next came the need to manage training events but the existing 'off-the-peg' systems 'weren't dynamic enough'. The resulting 'Team Manager' enables team members to log in, update their profile information, indicate whether they would be available for talks and tours of base, claim mileage expenses and look at a whole diary of events — from training and leadership duties, through to base visits, fundraising events and opportunities for fun. The latter invariably includes liquid refreshment at some stage.

Andy Harbach was responsible for much of the programming behind the system. 'Team Manager keeps a record of what team members have done and their attendance at call-outs is logged, which means we can generate stats about what they're doing, what they've attended, training activities and skills covered. Every member has access. The incident officer logs the attendees at each call-out, training is logged by the training officer or the event organiser. At the click of the button the system generates a spreadsheet. Members are able to see whether they need to refresh core skills and whether their attendance is above the minimum level required.'

Innovative though the initial website was in its day, in 2015 a replacement website was launched,

SM

DIAMOND

PETZL

which fulfils all the original requirements but also interfaces with social media. 'We had one of the best websites out there in terms of functionality,' says Harbach. 'We had the Oggie cams and live weather information for the valley but it was looking dated.' The 'Oggie cams' were installed over the winter of 2009. 'The main problem with the installation was the weather. It was rarely good enough for the engineer to go climbing on the roof, so he spent quite a lot of time weather watching — if only he'd had a web cam to allow him to see the conditions at base!

'The main benefit of the webcams is to the public. We don't really use them operationally a great deal, unless it's curiosity, when we might zoom in to watch the helicopter winching. The public find them extremely useful to get up-to-date conditions, and this is especially true in winter. If the cameras are down for a day we invariably get emails telling us — it does sometimes seem that people don't realise we are volunteers and that base is a remote location where the broadband can be temperamental. Fortunately, since we gave up with phoneline-based broadband and moved to satellite we've had fewer issues, bar the odd lightning strike.'

The growth of social media has brought another pressure, with the need to maintain a presence online, continually informing, educating and entertaining the public. It's also a great medium for reuniting people with their lost kit. In March 2014, the team's Facebook page alerted followers to the discovery of a 'camouflage rucksack', found on Bristly Ridge and recovered for safekeeping at Bryn Poeth. A flurry of shares later, camouflage rucksack and owner were reunited.

Social media has also been known to reunite heartbroken dog-lovers with their lost animals. In June 2013, a fourteen-year-old cross-bred King Charles spaniel was hailed a hero when he alerted climbers to his critically injured owner's plight after a 600-foot fall near the Atlantic Slabs on Carnedd y Filiast. No sooner had his sixty-year-old owner been airlifted to hospital, however, than Sutty disappeared from sight. A social media campaign asked hill goers to be on the look-out for the dog but it was ten days before he was found.

Rob Shepherd and Sian Williams, both members of the Llanberis team, were heading off for a climb, when they heard whimpering. Coincidentally, they'd spotted a 'wanted' poster of the missing pooch en route. Shepherd made a difficult ascent on steep and broken ground to find Sutty sheltering on a very small ledge. Concerned about the location, he called the team for help with additional ropes. Ogwen member Paul Smith made his way to the spot, but without any additional equipment, so the pair created a ropeway and Sutty was lowered down in Sian's rucksack and in remarkable condition, given his ordeal.

Calling Oggi base... over...

Efficient communication has always been an important feature of the team's work and key to this are the radios. For many years, Tony Jones was responsible for the upkeep and care of these valuable items of kit. In the team's Silver Jubilee newsletter, he looked back on those first twenty-five years. According to the minutes of a meeting held in March 1965, 'Pye having supplied a base

Top: The portable Genny. **Bottom:** Sutty the spaniel, wiith Sian Williams after his adventure © OVMRO.

Robert J. Chapman 04

set and two small portables, money was required to pay for them'. The base set was a Pye Handy Cambridge, the two small portables were Pye Bantams. Not long afterwards, these initial radios were 'donated' to mountain rescue. In 1967, the organisation bought three additional Bantams, the team was operating on 86.325 MHz, AM and the call sign OGGI with numerals 20-29 was in regular use.

During those early years, there were 'all sorts of problems with the use and abuse' of the radios, generally solved by the finding of more 'reliable batteries, reliable aerials and reliable users'. There were times, he said, 'after particularly soggy operations when troops were dried out on top of the Aga and the Bantams in the oven'. It was a constant source of amazement that they continued to work, but they were robust sets. They had to be, because in the minutes of a meeting in 1968 it was decided that a maintenance contract with Pye, at a cost of £80, was beyond the organisation's means.

Another issue — although not seen at the time to be a problem as such — was the 'blissful ignorance or wilful neglect' with which the radios were operated without licence. By 1971, 'questions were being asked and the answers tended to be evasive'.

There was 'slow and erratic increase in the radio holdings, both in numbers and type'. In June 1974, the ownership of all the team's radios was transferred to North Wales Police. The equipment listed in the transfer document was: Pye Bantam base set, Pye Vanguard (mobile), Pye Bantams, GEC Couriers and Pye Pocketfone 70s. The transfer meant that, from then on, the police would be responsible for the licensing, maintenance and eventual replacement of the radios. The radios were effectively on permanent loan to the team.

By the mid-1970s, details were in progress to develop effective ground to air communications with the search and rescue helicopters from RAF Valley on the frequency used by mountain rescue. A link scheme was also put in place, which enabled the team to speak directly to police headquarters. By 1979, the government had introduced a dedicated search and rescue channel (SRC) and within three years, all the team's equipment had been converted to accommodate this. 'No longer,' writes Jones, 'was the channel shared with a multitude of other users such as construction companies and crane drivers!'

Soon afterwards, the Dymar 980 became the standard hill set, but 'they did not react at all well to being dried in the AGA oven'. Rather, 'much loving care' was necessary to keep them working.

Towards the end of the 1980s, change was in the air again, this time prompted by the Association of Chief Police Officers (ACPO) who had begun looking at the whole issue of communications for land search and rescue. They recommended a switch to FM, and that the radio equipment holdings for the larger teams in busier areas should be one base set, six mobile sets and twelve hand-held sets for taking on the hill. Their recommendations were accepted by North Wales Police and the changes implemented in 1989. Two types of radio were brought into service: Pye Whitehalls for base and mobile sets, and Pye PF85s for the hill sets.

Meanwhile, just as the hardware was developing, alterations were being made in the way team members communicated with each other over the radio. In 1983 the radio call signs of OGGI 200 and upwards were brought into use. Team leaders were allocated numbers 201 to 209, with team

'I find all I need is one of these': Cartoon illustration © Rob Chapman.

FROM THE ARCHIVE

Lost and found thanks to her mobile phone, 21 March 2009 : Diminutive Beverley Burkitt dropped her mobile phone while enjoying a wander through the woods with her similarly diminutive pet, Pebbles, then became completely disorientated trying to find it. Unable to call for help, she spent the night cuddled up with the tiny Chihuahua lying across her legs to keep warm, until help arrived. Fortunately for them both, it was a mild night. Back at the Ty Coch trekking centre in Penmachno, where they had been staying, her fifteen-year-old daughter, Jasmine, grew increasingly worried that her mother had not returned from her 'short' morning walk.

Rescuers searched for over twelve hours before they found Burkitt. 'Every time I heard the helicopter go by, it broke my heart,' she said. Then, on the Sunday morning, a search party found her mobile phone and the police helicopter located Burkitt with its heat-seeking equipment. 'It took our team ten minutes to reach to her. We had to cut our way through the forest,' said Chris Lloyd, 'and across a river.'

Three feet eight inch-tall Burkitt had clearly taken note of her daughter's keen interest in survival methods. She set about using moss to filter water and made a giant cross from Pebbles's bright orange poop-a-scoop bags to make their location more visible.'I just tried to stay warm and keep my spirits up, talking to myself and to Pebbles. When I got cold, I danced and sang and shouted. Pebbles just stayed by my side, he was brilliant. He kept me warm and I kept him warm.'

The search had involved five mountain rescue teams, two helicopters and search dogs. There were concerns about her wellbeing as she is asthmatic but she was given a check-up by a paramedic at the scene and given a clean bill of health.

members using OGGI 210 and upwards, depending on the order they went out on a call-out.

There is a wealth of anecdote about radio transmissions — some arguably unpublishable — but Jones recalled his favourite from those first twenty-five years, concerning 'a long period of inactivity during a call-out'. Those sitting in base were surprised when the radio cackled into life. 'I'm bored!' exclaimed a voice. One eminent person (who we suspect may have been Jones himself) got to the microphone before anyone else. 'Station calling Oggi base. Identify yourself!' The reply was inevitable. 'I'm not that bored!' In the way of all good anecdotes, as Jones then concluded, 'the ensuing hilarity still brings tears to many eyes'.

Of course, technology has continued to develop at an ever-increasing pace, often necessitating the team as a whole to adopt a brisk walking pace just to keep up. Technology didn't always feature in everyday life for every team member. The arrival of a computer at base — now so central to every operation and take for granted as a piece of vital kit — was announced with some flourish. In 2004, Matt Sutton noted 'a communication problem akin to deafness' which was being

OGGI SNIPS

October 2001: A climber who fell 300 feet was saved from certain death when his arm became caught in a crack, preventing him from falling any further.

'addressed' by team members 'brushing up on their technical skills'. A working group began to look closely at communication abilities and seek solutions — noting that this would inevitably result in 'further expenditure'.

Four years post-millennium, the team was 'dragged kicking and screaming into the twenty-first century', says John Hulse thanks to the arrival of 'high band' VHF. 'For many years, we operated using low band VHF and managed reasonably well by using our local area knowledge and careful operating practice. But, as part of national spectrum reallocation, mountain rescue as a whole needed to move up to high band which, due to the laws of physics, immediately resulted in far worse operational communications. I estimate we had radio coverage of less than 25% of our area from Oggi base. At times, we couldn't even reliably talk from Idwal to base, a distance of only two miles!

'Tempers quickly frayed and teddy bears were flung far and wide from team vehicles. This level of coverage was totally unacceptable. It was degrading our operational effectiveness and safety.'

'At one point it looked like we'd have to resort to smoke signals and flags,' said Jed Stone.

The best way to explore new options was to see how other teams were coping with the change. Langdale Ambleside and Keswick teams in the Lake District are two of the busiest teams in England and Wales, covering relatively small areas compared to many but their geography is such that they too were struggling but had successfully implemented networks of repeaters and sophisticated aerials to achieve acceptable performance.

A number of ideas had been put forward, but it was a meeting with the Chief Constable, Richard Brunstrom which brought about real solutions. 'He was more than surprised to hear about the dire state of our operational communications,' says Hulse. 'We were directed to talk with Keith Williams of the North Wales Police Information Management Group and the NWP communication technical support provider, Arqiva. The result was a near-miraculous improvement. Mr Brunstrom recommended and agreed to supply advanced Airwave Terrestrial Trunked Radio (Tetra) to all mountain rescue teams in North Wales.

'We were the first teams in the UK to have this tremendous facility to link into the police networks. The new radios had already seen good operational benefit and enable the team leader at the scene to talk direct with the police control room and other officers over a secure network.

'On top of this, North Wales Police funded the provision of two new repeater sites which would provide radio coverage over more than 95% of our area resulting in far higher operational efficiency and improved safety. A further four repeaters became operational over the following three or four months, providing good radio coverage over most of North Wales — a major asset for all North Wales teams. Again, we were the only region in the UK to have this type of network mostly funded by the police.'

Work continued in the background to improve the reliability and effectiveness of the radio network, with the team investing in external aerials as well as experimenting with cases, different headsets and microphones.

In June 2009, the team agreed to provide each full and trainee member with a waterproof GPS radio compatible with the MRMap system. It quickly became apparent, however, that 'waterproof' wasn't always a reliable descriptor. By 2013, 183 'defective, leaky radios' had been returned in the North Wales region, replaced by sets from a different manufacturer. The new radios were warranted as 'fully waterproof', a characteristic which Hulse deemed 'absolutely essential for the safety and success of operations in extremely challenging circumstances'.

Dealing with this problem alone placed a huge burden on team members — or one in particular. Paul Smith took on the task of working with the new supplier to get the radio firmware working which would enable the radios to report their position using a GPS facility — a task which took longer than anticipated as Smith had to test each candidate release of code and then work with the supplier to resolve any issues he found.

I-Spy and Welsh lessons

In March 2004, the changeover from low band to high band radio sets caused considerable confusion in the rescue of two young men in wintry conditions, two young men who owed their lives to a Snowdonia national park warden and an impromptu Welsh lesson.

Just after three o'clock in the afternoon, Nikki Wallis, a SARDA dog handler and Llanberis team member, was making her way down the familiar zig-zags of the Pyg Track beneath Yr Wyddfa, when she heard distant faint cries for help. What had begun as a routine patrol with her dog Jacob, was to become a long and challenging ordeal — not just for Wallis, but for all concerned — fraught with communication problems and severely hampered by treacherous conditions.

Before making her way to investigate, Wallis glanced round. Had anyone else heard the cries? Some way off with his group, an instructor and fellow team member had also heard something but continued in his work, too far away for Wallis to call out to. Unable to raise a radio response from the Warden Centre at Pen y Pass, she eventually managed to make contact with fellow warden Bob Ellis Jones and Meirion Thomas, who were also out on the hill, underneath Lliwedd. She told them what she was doing and asked Ellis Jones to remain where he was. Thomas, meanwhile, returned to Pen y Pass to liaise with the rescue team and use Ellis Jones as a radio link to the warden centre. A position, incidentally, which he subsequently held for many hours.

Climbing up the steep, ice-rimed grass, impossible to negotiate without crampons and ice axe, she discovered two young men. Despite one of them wearing only trainers, they had somehow managed to make their way across Crib Goch and Crib y Ddysgl when they lost their rucksack, which contained only a few biscuits. No torch, no map, no first aid equipment. When one of them slipped and disappeared over the edge, his friend believed he must surely have died. Somehow, he managed to climb down to where his friend lay, his leg broken, before crying out for help. The injured boy lay precariously across the scree gully line, gradually sliding towards it and, from the position of his leg, he appeared to have suffered a fractured femur.

From the start of the incident there were difficulties with communications. At 3.21pm, a call was registered with the police from a mobile phone. The report was of a French couple, one with a broken leg, on a ridge. At 3.30pm, there was another report of a male, stuck and possibly hurt. The description was vague, but appeared to indicate Crib Goch. It later transpired that one of the boys, unsure what to do in case of emergency, had dialled up a friend in Nottingham who had, in turn, called 999. The 'French couple' was a bit of a red herring — accident reporting by Chinese

OGGI SNIPS

July 2007: A missing walker turned up safe and well — in north Germany — after a major search operation in the hills above Conwy and Penmaenmawr, which spanned a weekend.

whisper — but it would be several hours before that became clear. So, for the rescuers involved, there initially appeared to be two separate incidents. Through the boys' mobile, Wallis was eventually able to establish a direct contact with both the police and Pen y Pass, but there was further confusion with the radios.

North Wales teams were still in the changeover period to high band radio sets. Wallis had made her call to Pen y Pass, and her colleague, using her National Park high band radio. John Grisdale, leader of the first party to be deployed low down by the RAF Sea King, was one of the few with the National Park high band frequency on his set. The Llanberis team members who responded to the call were working in low band. Not only did they not have radio contact with Bob Ellis Jones, they were unaware he was even in position for some hours. Phil Benbow described the situation as a 'nightmare in terms of knowing who was where and doing what'.

As a handful of Llanberis team members were airlifted up to the Miners' Track daylight was beginning to fade. The first party deployed had contact with Wallis via John Grisdale, but communications began to really deteriorate when Wallis's battery started to go flat due to the length of time she had been scanning and transmitting messages. Whilst still able to transmit, she took a bearing from their location straight up to her position so that when communications were finally lost, they could accurately locate them. With only a vague idea where she might be, it was agreed that Benbow and another team member would go on ahead to establish where she was before darkness fell. Leaving the stretcher behind, but equipped with sufficient kit to deal with a fractured femur, they set off to Glaslyn and climbed up to the Pyg Track, on to Bwlch Coch, then on to the Rock Step before beginning their traverse underneath Crib y Ddysgl on the notorious sheep track. With hindsight, they started their traverse too low. Less than 200 metres from Wallis and the boys, their whistles clearly audible now, they reached a series of buttresses. It wasn't easy mountaineering terrain, and with the wind gusting and the difficulties of finding a solid placement for an axe, there was a real possibility of a slip becoming a fatality. Reluctantly, they were forced to turn back.

Back on the Pyg Track they met up with another group who had attempted a different route, climbing up from below, with similar success. The lead climber, finding himself strung out, with no secure placements, stuff falling off around him, had no alternative but to reverse down. 'He thought he was going to die', said one team member. In fact, there were several occasions throughout this rescue when the possibility of losing one of the rescuers seemed all too real. Back at Pen y Pass, there were difficult discussions. Decisions to be made. Should they leave Wallis up there until conditions improved and risk losing the casualty? As time went on, it became clear that this was not a fractured femur, but a knee injury. Thus far he had supported himself with his broken leg, but he was very cold and still in danger of slipping.

'It was literally a case of cutting bucket seats in the snow, using the wet snow to form a splint as far as possible for his leg injury, and supporting him on the lower side so he didn't slide down the mountain,' said Wallis. However, there were also concerns for her wellbeing. As a keen mountaineer, actively involved in encouraging fellow diabetics to enjoy the mountains despite their medical condition, she is well-rehearsed in looking after her own sugar levels. Her team mates knew she would have spare clothing and a ready supply of food in her sack. Yet, despite her reassurances via the mobile that she was fine, there were still concerns that she may be hypoglycaemic. Tough call.

Meanwhile, the Ogwen team had been called to assist, with Aberglaslyn as back up. Under the impression that Llanberis team members were at the incident site and had all the kit they needed, Ogwen set off, expecting a 'nice simple carry off'. But things proved anything but simple. They were a strong group made up of members from Llanberis and Ogwen team members, every single one a competent mountaineer. They included Mal Creasey, experienced mountain guide and instructor and Tim Bird, also a mountaineering instructor. All well versed in the mountains and the conditions they found themselves in. Yet, at a point on the traverse where it became difficult to distinguish the path of the goat track, as they negotiated frozen turf and ice and a series of bluffs and buttresses, the thought occurred to Bird, 'One slip here and we're gone'.

Communications confusion continued. A message came through at Pen y Pass that all the kit was in one place and all the troops in another. The weather was deteriorating rapidly, visibility down to zero. All in all, not quite so simple as expected. As members of the two Ogwen parties met up, a message came over the radio of another job — a walker at Llyn y Cwn between Nant Peris and the Devil's Kitchen had twisted his ankle — stretching manpower capabilities even further. And not forgetting that, at this point, they still believed this to be a third job, the mystery of the 'French couple' and the 'stuck male' yet to be resolved. Aberglaslyn team members were diverted to the task.

Bird and Creasey worked together to take bearings and navigate a route up. Just past the avalanche fences on the way up to Bwlch Coch they spotted footprints in the snow and névé. At Bwlch Coch, they began their traverse line, pushed on at some pace by their group, who were unhampered by heavy kit and keen to keep moving. It was at this point they got the message that Benbow and the other Llanberis team members had been forced to retreat.

So, while the Ogwen group were going across the top, Benbow and company were back down on the Pyg Track. By this time, Wallis's radio had gone down completely. Benbow had intermittent comms via mobile with Pen y Pass. Two of his party of four had decided to either go home or return to base — too cold, wet and exhausted to safely continue. The two remaining were aware of the bigger group coming in from above but didn't think they'd have an easy time of it, so decided to approach again from below then walk to the zig-zags, coming back along the goat track in the other direction.

COBWEB CORNER

Newsletter, summer 2011: The chairman noted an 'interesting observation' from an incident on Carnedd Llewelyn. 'Two walkers were attempting the Welsh 3000s using what they thought was a GPS mobile phone as a navigational aid. It turns out it was just a normal phone, but they thought it had a GPS as it always knew their location when in an urban area. Mobile phones use a combination of techniques to derive position information. Along with GPS (where fitted), they use triangulation based on mast positions and known WiFi hotspots. WiFi transmitters are not yet available in the middle of the Carneddau so it's not surprising that the app they were using stopped being useful!'

OGGI SNIPS

Rotary Wing: An aircraft whose wing spins about and makes a terrible noise. A helicopter.
Fixed Wing: An aircraft whose wing doesn't spin about and make a terrible noise. An airplane.

Back with the casualties, her radio batteries spent and, by now resolved to being on the hill for the night, or at least until weather conditions improved, Wallis worked hard to keep the pair awake, and hypothermia at bay, with 'I-Spy', word games and Welsh lessons, oblivious to the drama unfolding around her for her fellow rescuers. This, whilst continuing to blow SOS signals on her whistle. Each time the boys asked, 'How long will the rescue team be?' all she could answer was, 'Very soon'. Battered by wind and snowstorms, the situation could have been very different without the group shelter she carries, alongside everything else, in her rucksack. Jacob, who seemed keen to stay outside the shelter listening for the sounds of the approaching people, was frequently completely covered in snow.

Finally, just before midnight, a very relieved Wallis heard shouts as Bird and his group approached from above. The separate groups — above and below the incident site — made contact, radio comms were established and the relevant kit taken to the appropriate locations. No mean task. The Ogwen group now realised that there was insufficient equipment at the incident location as members of the Llanberis team had not actually made it to the site earlier on. So now the teams were faced with bringing up ropes and stretchers and more equipment from all the members who were below the incident site just above the Pyg Track. The uninjured lad was taken out first, and Wallis moved to a safe position up the hill, anxious not to be involved in any further decision making apart from her own safety, as by now she was also cold.

Benefiting from extra group shelters and extra basic mountain kit, two of the Ogwen troops were able to improve the casualty's insulation from the freezing ground. The casualty examination indicated lack of long-bone injury but a possible incomplete left patella (kneecap) fracture, which was appropriately strapped. Oral analgesia and glucose were provided to the casualty, followed by a further wait while the stretcher was assembled and secured in challenging ground and weather conditions. Then rescuers set about stretchering the casualty directly down the hill to the Pyg Track — first down a thirty metre bluff, then a series of ten to fifteen metre bluffs across steep scree — and on to the Miners' Track. It was a hazardous descent, with the continuous danger of stretcher inversion and prolonged, difficult stretcher jockeying. Once on the track, there was a carry of about thirty minutes before the party met with the rescue Land Rover. Here, the Ogwen team doctor was able to further examine the casualty, in slightly more favourable surroundings, before arriving at the Pen y Pass Warden Centre in the early hours of the morning. Once the lines were in place, what had been an epic became a routine rescue.

It was 6.00am the following morning before everyone involved was down from the hill and the incident closed. Fifteen and a half hours. Involving forty-two team members working 611 man hours. Had Wallis not heard the boys' cries and found the pair, she is in no doubt that they would eventually have lost their footing on the frozen ground and slipped, with tragic consequences. Press reports said they were lucky to be alive. Lucky indeed. For her part, Wallis remains adamant her actions were only one small factor in the rescue operation, that all she had to do was sit there and wait. It was her friends and colleagues, working together under extreme pressure, in extreme circumstances, who did the hard bit.

To have and to hold

When Ron James formed his rescue team in the early 1960s, apart from items such as stretchers, team members mainly operated using their own kit, be that vehicles, first aid kit, boots or clothing. The result was a multi-coloured hodgepodge of clothing, of varying standard and suitability. And there was no perceptible difference in appearance between team members and any other walker or climber.

In 1995, certain key items were issued for the first time, with an allowance made for a helmet, harness and first aid kit. Team members were allowed to choose the harness and helmet they felt most comfortable with. Others used the money to replace equipment damaged on rescues or stuff that was past its sell-by date. But it was during Dave Worrall's time as chairman that the idea of investing in the team overall really took hold, beginning with the issue of radios to individual team members.

'Previously, the radios had been strictly controlled by Tony,' says Worrall. 'They were given to members when they turned up at base for a call-out and returned at the end. But we thought every team member should have a hill set radio.' It put the onus on team members to look after their radio, keep it charged up and ready for action with their hill kit.

Worrall also oversaw the first issue of team jackets from Vango, a deal negotiated by Paul Henshall. 'We were trying to go for a corporate look. It didn't necessarily go down well at the time but it was a conscious switch from a group of amateurs, mountaineers who knock around together and turn out when there's a job, to a very professional, serious organisation, trained, equipped and ready.'

Tim Radford believes that 'the casualty is greatly reassured to see a team turn up that can be identified as such'. It also helps to be easily identifiable when talking to passers-by during incidents. He recalls an incident several years earlier, when he was the first responder to an incident on the North Ridge of Tryfan but unable to find the exact location of the casualty. It turned out he was less than 100 yards away, but in the meantime, he asked some passing walkers if they had come across anything. Their response was quite indignant. Who are you and why should we tell you? I could see their point, but it was frustrating!'

It was some years before a fully corporate look was achieved, however. In 1990, Flight Sergeant Peter Kirkpatrick, formerly NCO in charge of RAF Valley MRT, described his earliest recollections of clothing worn by team members as resembling that 'worn by mercenaries who hadn't been paid for three months and were about to change sides'. The 2006 annual report describes the vision which may have greeted a casualty barely twenty years earlier: moleskin breeches, woolly jumpers, slack-rumped tracksuit bottoms and chunky fibre pile jackets. A far cry from the hi-tech activity trousers and windstopper soft shells of today. Thankfully, the average casualty was more interested in being recovered to terra firma than calling the 'fashion police'. This was the year which saw the introduction of the orange and blue colour scheme, since superseded by red and black.

Resistance continued to what many then considered to be 'uniform by the back door'. By

Colour coordinated: Team members wearing jackets provided by Páramo for the Princes' Charities Activity Day in June 2015 © Páramo.

comparison with today's waterproof, the Vango jacket was heavy and 'not as versatile or waterproof as we had perhaps hoped,' noted Chris Lloyd, in something of a recurring theme where the ingress of water is concerned.

From such tentative beginnings, every team member can now boast a complete, layered rescue 'wardrobe' to make any mountain fashionista proud, all the way down to their breathable undies. But, better still, they no longer need to dip into their own pockets to buy it. In 2014, being a member of the team became cost-neutral. 'We pay travel expenses for call-outs and training, and other mountain rescue-related events. We say to the members, you tell us what kit you want and we'll get it. There are limits in place, but if there's any bit of kit they need that's rescue-related, we'll supply it. No piece of kit is excluded, so thermals, soft shells, boots, crampons, ice axes, torch, rucksack, the lot — and that includes everyone, even if they only go out once or twice a year.

'It took the team a lot of soul-searching but we're being realistic. People do ask what the public might think about this use of funds but we believe our supporters like the fact they're funding a definite piece of equipment. We're an emergency response organisation. It's not a hobby any more.'

Footwear, of course, is a highly personal choice. A casual inspection of any team member's car or home might reveal a number of pairs of boots and trainers — some lightweight, some more sturdy, some more suitable to the rockface, some to winter conditions, and in varying degrees of dampness. Then there's the first aid kit, personal rope tech kit, map, compass and whistle, emergency bivvy shelter, spare clothing, head torch, spare batteries — all the stuff that goes in the rucksack, which before 2014, represented a costly commitment for team members.

Suffering for their art

Equipment officers, perhaps more than most, suffer the slings and arrows so lightly thrown in their direction by their fellow members when things don't go according to plan. As Dave Salter observed, when he was the team's equipment officer, looking back over the first twenty-five years, 'In the middle of the night, when it's the wrong size, the wrong shape, doesn't work or is too heavy, who do you call ?' He himself was the brunt of much, mainly due to his 'supposedly lightweight designs' but he laid the foundation of tidy, well-serviced kit, arranged in easy-to-find order. Salter helped with many of the equipment developments, gathering a reputation for acquiring bits and pieces of scrap and aluminium in the creative pursuit of solutions to whatever problem presented.

Illumination on night-time rescues has always been a problem. Team members in the early days often returned home 'with their clothing in smouldering tatters after carrying 12-volt lead-acid car batteries around the hills all night'. In an attempt to improve matters, two 2-stroke generators were acquired. The so-called 'Amp Champs' were, 'a pain to start and keep running'. They were succeeded in the early 1980s by two Japanese-manufactured machines, which were up-rated to take one gallon fuel tanks and 150 watt, 150,000 candle power spotlights. Quite apart from still being 'as noisy and smelly as their predecessors', they would doubtless horrify health and safety sensibilities today.

This period also saw members coming forward, says Salter, with 'revolutionary ideas that went

OGGI SNIPS

From the 'pink 'forms, November 1976: Ambulance man: 'Where is the casualty?' Ogwen team member: 'Heather Terrace'. Ambulance man: 'Which number?'

against established practice — the pirate era of rescue. With no new idea safe from prying eyes'. Methods of testing new equipment were pretty unorthodox too with, for example, 'Land Rovers being sent down the old A5 at a rate of knots to be brought to a sudden stop as the system under test came into operation'. Equally, it wasn't unusual 'to find the chairman hanging upside down under a helicopter simulator to test the strength of stretcher bed stitching'.

The 'ledge sack' was the first to receive analytic treatment, being so heavy only 'body building fanatics' might lift it. As ever this involved a public house, the offending sack being carried there and emptied on the floor. All the unnecessary items were rejected and a new sack devised 'based on a mechanic' tool roll system, with no space to accommodate extras. This could be carried in the cragsman's sack along with his own equipment. The first aid sack followed suit. So now, both first aider and cragsman could move fast and light to the incident site. The rest of the equipment was converted into a modular system, allowing the back-up party to bring only what was necessary.

Subsequent equipment officers have continued to develop and research new pieces of kit, and ensure that all kit is inspected, repaired and replaced to the required standards. In 2015, equipment officer Dave Jones reported that the team had been 'evaluating carabiners', one of the critical factors being 'the maximum load we might apply in a worst-case event'. Stretchers were also a focus for concern, as helicopter provision transferred to Bristow. But he reckons the best bit of kit has been the industrial dehumidifier. 'It turns a room full of soaking wet ropes and kit from a soggy weekend of rescues into dry kit that can be repacked by the following Wednesday.' For its provision, he thanks Al Cook, who organised the 'Get Wet to Get Dry Ogwen Swim' in January 2013, to raise the £1500 to buy it. It was a novel way of celebrating the new year and effectively banishing any lingering effects of the previous evening's celebrations. The plan was that a number of hardy souls would swim across Llyn Ogwen on New Year's Day. At 300 metres up in the Ogwen valley, the lake is close to the team's base, overlooked by Tryfan, the Glyderau and Pen yr Ole Wen.

By New Year's Eve, there was already £800 raised in sponsorship money. The weather was set to be okay, with the winds dying down and swinging to north-west, the temperature about eight degrees. As their Facebook page said, 'Just a matter of getting wet and biting the bullet now!' And we already know how good they all are at that! By the end of the day, eight swimmers, five support paddlers and many supporters knew they were many soggy steps closer to their dehumidifier.

Daily Post, 13 November 2004: Two climbers tried to scale Tryfan during the late afternoon, with nothing more than a toy phone, a dead mobile phone and no survival equipment. The men, in their mid-twenties, who claimed to be experienced climbers, were finally plucked from the summit by a Sea King. Stuck in the dark, unable to move either up or down, they had tried to abseil down but their rope rapidly got jammed and they found themselves dangling down the face of the mountain. They had only enough power left in their phone to call police. All their survival equipment, helpfully, had been left in the car.

HM COASTGUARD
COASTGUARD
RESCUE
G-MCGJ

CHAPTER NINE

Friends in high places

In October 2009, when interviewed about his a fifty-year career in mountaineering, Ron James spoke about how 'he once helped world renowned climber Sir Chris Bonington off the face of Tryfan when the pair were both teenagers'. Bonington too recalls the incident. It was 1952. Still at school in Hampstead, he had just completed his A-levels when he persuaded his mother to write a sick note to say he was in bed with flu, so he could squeeze a few days climbing in North Wales.

'Off I went, climbing with a Scottish pal, Mick Noon. We went up to Terrace Wall to do Scars Climb. It was a straight VS then but it's now classified as a hard VS. We'd plimsolls on our feet and a few slings round our necks. Our protection was a few runners over minuscule rocky spikes.

'We just kept going. My leading standard then was about hard VS so I thought I'll cream this one. I was having to do a bit of layback but there was nothing for my feet and I fell off. Came hurtling down. All the runners fell out. At the bottom is a grassy angled slope. I tumbled down that too.

'I think I was slightly concussed, I'd damaged my arm and sprained my wrist. But I was able to walk down helped by various people — Ron being one of them. It's amazing since then how many people reckon they saw me fall!

'I was taken to the docs in Bethesda — it may have been Ron who took me. My memory is that the doc patched me up and the next day I hitched back to London. Then of course, I had to explain how I had a patched-up head and a patched-up arm when I was supposed to be at home in bed with flu!'

First call to Idwal Slabs: The newly operational, Caernarfon-based S92 helicopter, called to Ogwen for its first mountain rescue incident © John Carrie.

His mother, he says, was 'amazingly calm and cool' about all his various adventures. He began his National service with the RAF because he had aspirations to joining the RAF MRS. 'Because I'd been to a public school, they suggested I apply for a commission and I decided to make a career of it and got into Cranwell, the Royal Air Force College to train as a pilot. I was no good at that, didn't want a ground job, so applied to enter Sandhurst.'

He spent the summer of 1963 in Snowdonia doing his 'board' — thankfully without mishap — ultimately becoming secretary of the Sandhurst Climbing Club, so it holds a special place in his heart. At the team's special anniversary dinner in March 2015, Sir Chris was principal guest, sealing an association which began so many years before on the Tryfan rock.

Right Royal connections

The organisation has long attracted the attentions of those in high office. Prince Charles visited the original Bryn Poeth in 1977 and the Secretary of State for Wales, William Hague paid an official visit in 1997. A keen mountaineer, Hague was given an outline of the team's work, before taking off into the mountains in a Wessex helicopter from 22 Squadron, RAF Valley. He then walked back to base before going on to Bangor by air to officially open the new helipad at Ysbyty Gwynedd.

But the Royal connection developed in a way few might have expected when the Duke of Cambridge graduated as a search and rescue pilot in September 2010, having begun his training at RAF Valley the previous January. Not since Henry VII had a member of the Royal Family lived in Wales. His first rescue mission, as co-pilot of a Sea King helicopter, was in October 2010, during his first full operational shift. With the other three crew members, he flew from Valley to an offshore gas rig in Morecambe Bay to attend a man who had suffered an apparent heart attack on the rig.

Ogwen team members became accustomed to hearing the voice of Flight Lieutenant Wales over the radio as the Sea King joined their rescue operations. His three-year posting ended in September 2013, by which time he had graduated to captain or 'pilot in charge' of a Sea King.

Search dog handler Sally Armond recalls an incident above the Devil's Kitchen, which was widely reported in the media. Two people had been reported missing for seven hours in severe winter conditions. 'I'd been on a traverse of the Glyders with Spin that day, and witnessed walkers struggling with the snow and hard ice, so I already knew conditions were poor. We got the call late that night that they were overdue. We knew they had mobile phones but we couldn't make any contact with them so we were beginning to seriously fear for their safety. Parts of Snowdonia were beautifully starlit that night, but the Glyders were enveloped in a thick blanket of cloud, which severely reduced visibility and hampered any helicopter search of the mountain.'

Sally, her dog Spin and navigator, Anne Margerison, were dispatched to search the Glyderau via the Devil's Kitchen. 'It was treacherous underfoot. Making progress was extremely hazardous without crampons due to the sheet ice. We climbed up to Llyn y Cwn en route to Glyder Fawr when Spin took us into two people huddled in a bivvy shelter. They were very happy to see us and gave

Top: A young Chris Bonington on Dinas Cromlech in 1954 © Chris Bonington Picture Library.
Bottom: Left to right: Elfyn Jones (National Trust warden), Paul Henshall, Bill Dean and William Hague © OVMRO.

Spin a welcome cuddle! Fortunately, they were both uninjured, but very cold. They seemed well equipped for most conditions, but as they didn't appear to have crampons, ice axes or torches they were unable to descend in such serious conditions.

'We could hear the helicopter was airborne in the Ogwen Valley but due to freezing cloud it couldn't access our location, meaning Anne and I may have had to perform a long and potentially risky extraction. Luckily, while we were assessing the situation, Anne spotted a narrow break in the cloud overhead, through which we were able to see stars. I contacted the helicopter to ask if they could come and assess the risk of attempting to reach our location and they replied that they'd take a look. Sheer skill enabled them to manoeuvre the aircraft down towards us, to hover just shy of the ground about 150 metres away from the bivvy site.

'As freezing cloud began to be sucked downwards by the aircraft, Anne and I grabbed the pair, stashing their kit, and manhandled them over the ice towards the aircraft. There was just enough time for the winchie to snatch the couple before having to make a hasty exit into the cloud. Relieved that the casualties were being taken to safety, we three made our way down the mountain, finally arriving back at base at 4.00am. Upon our arrival, we were passed a message from the pilot, Prince William, relaying his apologies that he couldn't pick us up as conditions were too hazardous.'

It's a constant source of amazement that the pilots manage to get their aircraft into the places they do, often in weather conditions most people cannot stand up in, but history is littered with tales of their bravery and skill in doing just that. Number 22 Squadron, C Flight began operations out of RAF Valley in March 1955, having reformed as a search and rescue short range unit, equipped with Whirlwind helicopters. The Whirlwind had a crew of three, a single turbine engine and a sixty-foot winch. Initially formed at Gosport in 1915, 22 Squadron had already enjoyed a varied history of disbanding and reforming through the two world wars and the intervening peacetime, in various roles, using various aircraft types. Flight Lieutenant Tony Dewhurst, a navigator with the squadron in 1990, took a brief look through 'the Squadron scrap book' for Ogwen's Silver Jubilee.

The squadron's primary duty was to rescue downed airmen but their encounters with 'the Oggis' probably began on 20 September 1965 when 'Flight Sergeant Mitchell, Master Navigator Mabbs and Master Signaller Williams were scrambled by Caernarfon Police to search for a young girl in the mountains south of Conwy. The area was searched in cooperation with the police and mountain rescue teams. The girl was found by the aircraft and taken to Llandudno Hospital. She had been missing for nineteen hours.'

The first time Ogwen received a specific mention in the Flight's dusty archives was on 12 July 1967 when Flight Lieutenants Ridge and Daniels and Master Signaller Vernon were called to an injured climber at Ffynnon Caseg. He was rescued by Ogwen team members and flown to hospital in Bangor.

On 29 September 1968, C Flight was requested to search for a crashed aircraft near Llyn Ogwen. Bad weather meant nothing was found that day but the crew returned the following day, along with a second aircraft. Team members and police personnel were ferried up to the crash area by 'Pedro 22' and 'Pedro 23'. The crashed aircraft was located by the ground parties and the pilot's body airlifted to Bangor.

OGGI SNIPS

From the 'pink' forms, November 2003: Their embarrassment was intense, especially as he was chairman of the mountaineering club.

'A number of learning points gained during the conduct of the job resulted in the first tentative — and in those days illegal — mutual training between C Flight and Ogwen. There's a saying somewhere about mighty oaks and acorns,' says Dewhurst adding that, 'incidentally, a certain Tony Jones had just started work at Menai Bridge that same day'.

In May 1969, a 'Mr Gordon of Ogwen Valley MRO requested a heli-lift for a fallen climber on the east face of Tryfan. The senior medical officer was lifted to Ogwen Cottage for briefing. Two Ogwen Cottage guides and the medical officer were then lifted to the scene. The body was found at the end of his rope in a small gully.' He had died of severe head injuries.

The first mention of Tony Jones by name was on 6 August 1970. 'Two crews and Jones were involved in the recovery of a heart attack victim from Snowdon. On a very hot day, six Valley MRT troops, Dr Ieuan Jones and Tony Jones were deployed low on the hill (the single-engined Whirlwind, altitude and heat were not a happy mixture) and, after travelling by road, foot and rail, the body was eventually airlifted to Bangor.'

Roger Jones gets a mention for the first time on 27 September 1976, at which point, says Dewhurst, 'our radios became redundant overnight' — a reference to Jones's reputation as the high-volume 'Voice of Ogwen'. Later that day, they attended the handover from Whirlwind to Wessex. The Wessex also had a crew of three but had more power to hand from its twin turbine engine and had a 100-foot winch (later 300 feet).

Continuing the long-running theme, he concludes that 'the number of mutual incidents can only be exceeded by the number of mutual beers quaffed' and lists his highlight of the first twenty-five years as an incident in March 1989, when the Oggi White Stick was awarded jointly to Flight Sergeants Chris Jones and Chris Kirkup. 'Just why this should have been, is so highly classified that it doesn't appear on our records, but the honour is obviously a high one!' But more of 'the white stick' later!

During the first forty-two years of Whirlwind and Wessex operations, they were involved in 5,232 missions. On 8 June 1997, the Wessex was finally replaced by the Westland Sea King helicopter, described as 'much more capable', an all-weather rescue aircraft. Sixty years on from the formation of C Flight, this sturdy old workhorse too had reached the end of its career. Between April and July 2015, the familiar yellow helicopters gradually disappeared from the skies, as Bristow Helicopters, on behalf of HM Coastguard, took over the provision of helicopter search and rescue.

It may have been dirty, noisy and smelly but the long-planned demise of the Sea King, and the end of RAF involvement in mountain rescue, evoked strong feelings. Since its establishment in 1955, C Flight, 22 Squadron had carried out thousands of rescue missions — its 10,000th working alongside Ogwen team members in the rescue of an injured walker. The incident was just one of four rescues on a busy Saturday over Easter 2015, including one for a cragfast dog.

In July 2015, the colour and shape of helicopter rescue changed forever. Bigger, squarer and displacing a considerably stronger downwash, the distinctive red and white Sikorsky S-92 is set to become as familiar a sight in the Ogwen Valley as its predecessor, operating from a brand new base at Caernarfon Airport. The transfer of service, from the RAF to private operator presented challenges for mountain rescue teams across the UK, particularly in terms of training and operating procedures. Ogwen's John Hulse and Pauline Hallett were instrumental in helping smooth that

RAF
RESCUE

process, along with Phil Benbow, of Llanberis MRT, and Mike Park, of Cockermouth. Thanks to their efforts, a staged training process is in place for team members. At its centre is iSAR, an online package which allows teams and their members to record and monitor their training progress. 'Thanks to the strong, professional and trusted relationships we're now forging, between the teams and Bristow crews, our teams and casualties will continue to get the world class search and rescue service they've come to expect,' says Hulse.

Barely hours after 'going live', the S-92 was in action. The day had started out warm and sunny. Two young couples from Somerset, who were staying in North Wales for a couple of days, decided to climb Y Garn. By the afternoon, the skies had turned grey and rain was falling. The four had descended Y Garn and the path by the side of the Devil's Kitchen, continuing along towards the base of Idwal Slabs. En route, the path crosses the Idwal stream at a little gorge. This 'difficult' step is renowned for incidents. The eighteen-year-old girl slipped on the wet rock, sustaining a painful ankle injury. She tried to continue but the pain was too severe.

'We were called at about 6.00pm,' says Chris Lloyd. 'We felt a helicopter evacuation would be preferable so the request was made. As team members arrived at Ogwen Cottage, the S-92 was inbound to the casualty. The hasty party, complete with Titan stretcher, quickly joined the Bristow's winchman on the path in the shadow of the Kitchen. The S-92 circled in Cwm Idwal, while other team members made their way to the casualty site.

'Working as a team, the winchman and Ogwen members had soon treated the casualty, giving analgesics and splinting her injured ankle. The aircraft came into a hover below the towering black cliffs and, using the 300 feet per minute winch, she was quickly winched aboard and whisked down to hospital. We then walked off the mountain with the remaining three of her party.

It was an unfortunate incident. Both casualty and team members were grateful for the prompt response by Bristow as well as their expertise in winching from this area'. A new era had begun.

John Hulse's involvement in the helicopter migration holds a certain irony, given that he himself will not fly on an aircraft if at all possible, having found himself in a life-threatening situation on three occasions. The first was in the early 1990s and involved a German pilot on secondment and a Wessex helicopter. 'The casualty had a severely fractured ankle. We got it back into alignment and on the stretcher, then hooked the cable to the stretcher and gave the thumbs up. Unfortunately, the stretcher stayed where it was. One of the aircraft rotors had hit rocks, showering us with debris. One of the rocks came down, narrowly missing me but landing on my rucksack. I still have it!

'The second occasion was a casualty and group on the west face of Tryfan. This time I was in the aircraft when it hit an air pocket and lost several hundred feet before the pilot found air. It was heading straight for Oggi base. I heard 'Brace! Brace! Brace! And saw the winchman hurl himself across and grab stuff. We were spinning round and round. The door was still open — all I could see was Tryfan, lake, Tryfan, lake...

'The third occasion involved a flight up to Craig yr Ysfa, when the severe icing of the airframe meant the pilot had great difficulty keeping full control of the aircraft.'

Helicopter at work: Sea King in front of Gribin Facet, Cwm Idwal, with Idwal Slabs in the background © Judy Whiteside. **Inset:** Three RAF Wessex helicopters and a Luftwaffe Huey at rest behind Bryn Poeth, circa 1981 © Chris Lloyd.

Mayday! Mayday! Mayday!

Team members know the risks of working with helicopters. It's drummed into them at every opportunity. But an episode on New Year's Day 2009 really gave cause for reflection.

'Winter had arrived with a vengeance after what had seemed an indefinite break,' recalls team member Matt Sutton. That particular day had been a little milder, damp and overcast but higher up the mountain, above freezing level, the wind, cloud and snow made navigation difficult. Sutton had been climbing that day, with his pal Pete, when the text came in: 'Ogwen Valley Mountain Rescue call-out. Job starting in Devil's Kitchen. Possible femur injury. Rendezvous Oggi base'. It was already dusk. Having only had two honey sandwiches and a rushed cup of tea on the summit, he'd gladly accepted an offer of dinner that evening. Hoping the helicopter would get in and winch the casualty to safety, he hoped to be back down by eight.

'The track to base was snowbound to all but four-wheel drive vehicles so I parked on the A5. Ahead of me I could make out someone's shadowy figure unloading gear from their boot. It turned out to be Alex Bath who like me had just returned home after a day on the hills. As we walked, Paul and Pauline arrived with the Land Rover and had base open by the time we made it up the track.

'A climber had taken a huge fall from the top pitch of the Devil's Cellar ice climb in Cwm Idwal — maybe forty metres. Suspected broken femur. The guy's climbing partner had managed to hold the fall and she was now trying to descend to him. Two other climbers had managed to reach them and secure the man.

'Straight away I knew this was going to be a serious job. The approach to the climb is steep and exposed, on shattered rock and poor ice. Furthermore, a helicopter rescue below the route would be highly unlikely due to the size and proximity of the cliff. I grabbed my flask and stuffed my pockets with Mars bars. This was going to be my dinner after all.

'Alex, Pauline and I loaded first aid requirements into our rucksacks, including oxygen, morphine, traction splints and a casualty shelter. As first to base, we were to form the hasty party. The seriousness of the accident wasn't lost on us: in the case of a broken femur, if there was a severed artery or protruding bone, internal bleeding could mean death within two hours. The task of meeting the medical challenges was going to fall to Pauline as the advanced first aider. For Alex and I, the task was simple: get there as quickly as possible and ensure everyone's safety. Other team members began to arrive. They would form a second, larger rescue group bringing the big ropes, technical equipment and stretcher. These were heavy loads but the hope would be for their arrival to coincide with our stabilisation of the injured casualty, so we could evacuate him without delay.

'Cloud hung low over the hills. Beyond the car park lay darkness. I led the way with powerful torches over each shoulder, locating a path to avoid snow that was knee deep in places. Once we reached Llyn Idwal we could make out head torches high on the hill above and, as we approached via the snow slopes below the climb, I could clearly make out pools of light with figures silhouetted against the rocks. But perspectives were distorted and this created a strange impression. The torchlight wasn't enough to show their position in relation to the surrounding terrain. They were just little round cameos, surrounded by intense blackness.

'Our final approach took a steep line up to the base of the cliffs and onto a ledge around two

From the 'pink' forms, August 1993: More like jungle rescue than mountain rescue.

metres by a metre. An impressive spike of rock provided a belay as we fixed our crampons. The party were now just twenty metres above us and at last we could communicate with them. Alex went up to make the primary survey of the casualty while I traversed into the gully to make an operational assessment of what we faced.

'The casualty, a chap called Rob in his early twenties, was secured by a rope system that Mark, one of the climbers who had come to assist, had set up and was now overseeing. The other assisting climber, a lad called Jonah, and the casualty's partner Alys (who to her considerable credit had managed to abseil from her belay forty metres above), were beside Rob comforting him and trying to keep him conscious. Heavy blood loss due to a bad break would lead eventually to medical shock and loss of consciousness and they had been at this point for nearly two hours, in temperatures well below freezing. I climbed up to check Mark's ropes but he'd done very well to secure them all. Due to the steepness of the gully and the precarious position of the casualty's party, I untangled the remaining rope and set up a security line to the lower ledge for other rescuers later in the operation.

'As we were bringing Pauline up, the drone of the Sea King could be heard making its way up the valley. The plan was for the helicopter to make a rescue attempt from the position we found ourselves in. If this failed, we'd attempt to lower the casualty using the stretcher, to a point low enough down the mountain and clear of the cliffs, for the chopper to make the pick-up. As team members, we knew what to expect from the approach of the helicopter, this close to the cliffs in winter conditions but there was no time to give the others more than the most basic instructions: don't look at the helicopter with head torches, which might blind the crew using night vision glasses, and make secure any loose items.

'The beating of the rotors grew steadily louder until the all-pervasive noise forced all activity to cease. Suddenly the hillside lit up as bright as day. The helicopter's landing lights found us pinned motionless to the cliff, the thudding of the blades vibrating through our entire bodies. Then came the downdraught, throwing up furious gusts of spindrift laced with ice crystals and the stench of aviation fuel. Where a minute before had been darkness, there right beside us was the massive yellow frame and, up through the maelstrom, the clear outline of the rotor blade tips spinning within a few metres of the cliff. As the crew searched for somewhere to put the winchman down, I withdrew into the hood of my jacket to breathe free from the choking cocktail of ice and fumes. The intensity was unbearable, the emotion overpowering and then, as if unable to bear it itself, the helicopter banked away and the pounding slowly receded into the distance leaving us surrounded by silence. A direct rescue was going to be impossible.

'While I remained at the belay with Mark, the others descended down to Rob and Alys to set up a shelter and assess his condition. Soon Alex emerged to discuss the situation with me. 'We've got to get him out of here now,' he said, under his breath so as not to alarm the others. 'Pauline is very concerned about Rob's condition. We think he also has a broken ankle, as well as head and chest injuries.' Any movement was causing him terrible pain and he was getting ever colder. Alys picked up on the concern in our voices and at one point I heard her reminding everyone in a cheerful voice that everything was going to be okay. This attitude required great courage in the circumstances and I sorely hoped we could repay her faith.

'After some ten minutes we had word on the radio that the helicopter had returned to RAF Valley to refuel. Worryingly, it had also sent news that bad weather was expected within the next half hour. If we didn't get him down for a pick up quick we'd have to carry him out. We were concerned he wouldn't survive, as it would take three brutally punishing hours to get him to the road. The tension mounted considerably. The lights of the stretcher party now flooded the valley and slopes below, though their help was still more than half an hour away. I descended to survey whether we could lower him out of the gully on the rope to save time. The first thirty metres looked good, not too steep, but then came a vertical drop of around fifteen metres. The risks involved in sending his broken body over the edge without support from a stretcher would be unjustifiable. We had no choice but to wait for the others to arrive.

'Alex and I discussed how best to undertake the evacuation. It presented a major challenge. The cliff above us rose vertically into the night. The gully we hoped to lower him down lay directly below and it was steep, laced with bare ice and broken rock — dangerous and insecure. While our training and experience meant we wanted to set up a rescue system above the casualty, it was just too risky. So we decided to use the original belay ledge, some five metres below us, as the anchor point for the technical team. As this was below the casualty we'd have to lower Rob on the rope some of the way before we could get him into the stretcher for the vertical drop. We also planned to get him down the gully by the time the stretcher was ready. It was a tough ask. Simply to find enough anchor points on the ledge would be a challenge, let alone building a stretcher in such a confined space.

'The medical challenges were no less daunting. Pauline wanted to splint the leg with the traction device but it was difficult to apply on the steep ground. Lowering him over rough snow risked catching the device so she had to abandon this idea and improvise tying his legs together, using his good leg as a splint. This meant we could sled him down part of the way and, as we prepared to lower, she delivered a shot of morphine.

'After half an hour the stretcher party arrived on scene, along with Glynne Andrew, our team

COBWEB CORNER

Shakespearean actor Abercrombie Lewker — 'Filthy' to his friends — takes off for a climbing holiday in Wales after a season on tour. On the way, he picks up pretty Hilary Bourne, a novice climber who's seeking a break from her dreary job in the city and they discover they're headed in the same direction — in fact, staying at the same guesthouse near Tryfan. They meet an interesting mix of characters: a glowering minister, his long-suffering wife, his repressed daughter and some equally complex friends, including a nuclear scientist and his assistants. Tension abounds and when one of the climbers dies in a fall, Lewker suspects it wasn't an accident and teams up with his new friend to investigate before alerting local police to his suspicions. So goes the tale. 'Death on Milestone Buttress' by Glyn Carr was initially published in 1951.

OGGI SNIPS

From the 'pink' forms, August 1979: A man of total inexperience.... eighteen hours from Capel Curig to Llyn y Cwn.

doctor. While the stretcher and anchor system were being constructed, he supervised how best to move Rob. He asked Alex and I to descend and cut out a ledge just above the vertical drop for Rob's transfer onto the stretcher which, having been put together on the narrow ledge, now overhung the void like a cantilever. Chris Lloyd, realising only three of the four joining pins had been fitted, could no longer reach the fourth pin and asked me to help. It was a crazy position. I climbed up from below and leant out to fit the pin as if on an overhang of a rock climb.

'The task of jockey fell to Al Cook. He was to go down with the stretcher and keep the lowering process going by making sure the stretcher didn't get snagged on rocks or tip over. On steep ground, in deep unconsolidated snow, this was the toughest of jobs. The worst moment came when Glynne, Alex, Al and I had to lift Rob onto the stretcher. His cries of pain were heart-rending despite the morphine. We wrapped him up in the casualty bag. He shivered uncontrollably, but this was a good sign as, in advanced hypothermia, the body can no longer try to warm itself by shivering. Safely strapped in, the stretcher team took over the lower and we could start to relax.

'I climbed back up to where Mark had remained without shelter, on belay duty for over three hours now, a passing climber selflessly helping out two people in big trouble. He remained very cheerful and great credit is due to him. He was getting an experience he would never forget! By the time we'd cleared the casualty site, the stretcher — following the training of our winter trips to Scotland — had been lowered 180 metres off the mountain, through a belay station at 100 metres, in around twenty minutes. An impressive achievement.

'I descended to where Chris Onions and Chris Lloyd were dismantling the belay at the ledge. Soon the red and green lights of the helicopter came into view and we stopped to watch. This is the true moment of rescue for us. As we passed our responsibilities into the hands of the RAF, Rob's life would be safe. Looking down from our perch, the bowl of Cwm Idwal was thick with snow and the mountainside below peppered with the torch lights of our colleagues. As we anticipated the moment, the cloud suddenly thickened, swirling around us and sending icy blasts of wind across the face of the hillside. Was this the promised bad weather? The torchlight below dimmed as the mist descended threatening to fall below the helicopters altitude. If this happened the pick up would have to be aborted and we'd lose our opportunity.

'Slowly the helicopter made its way towards us, then on came its searchlights, an orangey-white halo of light passing over Llyn Idwal. The soft light lit the hillside, eerily revealing features previously hidden. The noise returned, the thudding amplified by the close proximity of the mountains. As a spectator I felt increasingly detached from this extraordinary scene, yet oddly aware of my own presence, as if watching a scene from a movie — the helicopter, the lights of the rescuers, all players in an epic staged drama. The closer the chopper came, the greater the sense of drama. I'd never seen a scene like it. Not even Steven Spielberg could capture this.

'As the helicopter descended to its target, huge columns of spindrift went spiralling upwards, enveloping the aircraft before dispersing in great arcs. It was terrifying to watch. The snow, like sweeping curtains of cloud, must surely have blinded the pilots at times. I could only imagine what it would be like for Rob and the team members caught up in the fury of the downdraught directly below. Yet down came the winchman, who appeared to land, secure the winch wire and begin the lift, all in one movement. One could only stand in admiration of the crew's skill and teamwork. The winch seemed to take forever, such was the anticipation of success. Great hunks of accumulated snow, illuminated by the landing lights, fell from the stretcher as it rose, but finally it was gone from view and, in an extra burst of power, the helicopter began a vertical ascent that went on until it disappeared into the cloud above. Silence returned and the emotion of the moment passed into one of deep satisfaction. We stood around for a few minutes exchanging exclamations of awe over what we had just witnessed before I turned to begin my descent.

'I'd gone maybe ten metres when Chris Onions called me back. His voice came across with an unusual authority. Chris Lloyd was stuffing his sack in a distracted sort of way. The helicopter had just sent out a radio transmission of Mayday, Mayday, Uncontrolled Descent. I stood speechless, turning to look out over the valley, an awful physical sensation of horror passing down through my body as Chris Lloyd added, 'We think the chopper's gone down'.

'Utter disbelief. No one spoke. Just stood there staring out into the night. We could hear the radio communication from Oggi base with the ground party back at Ogwen car park. It was Paul calmly going through a list of questions. When was it last seen? Did you have a sighting of it? Did it appear to go down in the Nant Ffrancon. Can you confirm it was last seen heading over the Gribin? I looked out towards the Gribin Ridge. There was nothing to see but cloud.

'I was aware of standing there wondering at my body's capacity to continue working and then thinking, I've been out on the hill now for fourteen hours but really I don't feel too bad. Then, slowly, the sheer scale of dealing with a helicopter crash started to sink in. It would overwhelm the capacities of our team. It was too big. I had a definite sense of our collective fragility in the face of a tragedy on this scale. I couldn't begin to address what we would find at the crash site, or the full implications of having gone through all that we had, just to lose everyone in a stroke. We continued to stand there, lost in our own little worlds until Chris suddenly said, 'There's nothing we can do here. We might as well go down.'

'I'd descended about ten metres ahead of the others and was no longer able to hear the radio communication, when Chris Onions called down to me again in an excited voice. The helicopter had recovered!

'At first, I couldn't take in the news but then, almost as one, we broke into guffaws as if we had been subject to some appalling practical joke or 'Candid Camera' sketch. We continued down the mountainside, occasionally breaking into pained giggles, the contrast between a moment of absolute horror and one of total elation psychologically too great to bear. From then on it was like any other successful job: banter, laughter and a huge jolly meeting of rescuers and their helpers at the Ogwen car park, as news came through that Rob was safely in hospital and his condition stable. We decamped to base for a midnight curry, more laughter and endless tea before heading home. I woke around eight to let Pete and Angela, my would-be dinner hosts, know all was okay and then promptly fell back asleep till eleven.

'That night, I went up to their house for the dinner we'd planned for the night before. Pete had a friend staying, and they'd climbed the Devil's Cellar that day. I asked whether they'd found evidence of our handiwork, thinking of all the people that were there and the snow ledges we'd constructed. 'Not a thing,' said Pete registering his own surprise. 'The whole hillside was virgin, not a footprint, no tracks or ledges.'

OGGI SNIPS

The pleistocene epoch commonly referred to as the last Ice Age began about two million years ago. During this period there have been repeated glaciations...

'I was dumbfounded. All that work and no physical imprint remained just twelve hours later. The snow and wind must have taken it away in the night. A moment in time that Nature had covered over. All that remained was a memory.'

It was only later that team members understood what had happened. 'Due to the onset of bad weather and low cloud, the helicopter was climbing to a point above the surrounding mountains. However, in the ensuing snowstorm, the rotors had become so heavily iced, the pilots no longer had the power to remain airborne. This led to a rapid, uncontrolled descent. Battling to keep the chopper in the air, they broke cloud cover on the descent, thankfully avoiding striking the mountains, and managed to regain enough control to land safely at the hospital in Bangor. It was a close call.'

As for the casualty, Rob Dyer made a full recovery, despite his many injuries. He recounted his story in the Winter 2014 issue of 'Summit' magazine. Climbing his final pitch of the day, battling cruddy ice, he describes going for his last steep step up. 'The whole section fell to bits and I took the whole ride: stripping the whole pitch (apart from one ice screw protecting the belay) and falling forty metres. I bounced off the gully's side walls, to land unconscious at the bottom of the first pitch with a broken femur, fibula, tibia and a few snapped ribs.'

He describes the 'long and protracted' rescue, the four-hour lowering in rope length and eventually the helicopter winch. 'On the way to the hospital, iced-up rotor blades meant that it pretty much fell out of the sky. The pilot sent out a full-on Mayday crash-landing call, but managed to regain control seconds before hitting the deck.'

Dyer spent nine days in hospital 'followed by very possibly the worst car journey of my life, back home in a Renault Clio — not ideal for tall people with a leg in a cast — through mid-Wales in a blizzard, as I was coming down off the various hospital drugs'. Six months later, he entered the Oggi 8 challenge to raise funds for the team, slipped on wet grass on the Carneddau and re-broke his fibula, had another helicopter rescue from the same team and ended up back in hospital!

A different kind of torch

In July 2012, the relationship with the Duke of Cambridge brought a unique opportunity for John Hulse. Since becoming patron of Mountain Rescue England and Wales, the Duke has been keen to support mountain rescue nationally by association with the Royal name. So when plans were being laid for the Olympic torch to process around England and Wales, prior to the 2012 Olympic Games, he asked that a mountain rescue team member be invited to take on the torch in London. The Duke and Duchess of Cambridge and Prince Harry each selected one of their charities to carry the Olympic Torch in the vicinity of Buckingham Palace. With 1,000 rescue operations under his belt in over thirty years, Hulse was an ideal choice.

His section of the route ran from Buckingham Palace up Constitution Hill, to a changeover at Hyde Park Corner. From there, he would be escorted by the Household Cavalry Mounted Regiment. At this point, he says, fear and uncertainty took over from the elation. This was getting a bit serious!

'The day before the run was one of the hottest of the year with perfect blue skies, rather than the normal drizzly, drab grey pallor of that year's Snowdonia summer. London felt vibrant and ready to party. Union flags mixed with the London 2012 Olympic symbols wherever you looked. Big BMWs emblazoned with London 2012 logos sped past traffic queues, whisking their cargo through the busy roads. Taking the opportunity to recce the route, we made our way to the Palace amidst all the preparations for the Olympics. Security was tight, military and police highly evident around all the usual landmarks. Police helicopters droned overhead doing figure-eight circuits above the Palace and Mall. The usual throng of tourists snapped at the beautiful building through the railings. It seemed surreal that the following day, I'd be inside those railings looking out!

'Constitution Hill rose, with a gentle gradient by Welsh standards, flanked by trees, heavy with full leaf, for several hundred metres to the magnificent Wellington Memorial at the top. The traffic at the top looked so far away. My immediate concern was could I cope with the crowds? Give me Tryfan at night in snow and ice any time. There was only one sane option and that was to run the route to learn the pace, gradient and timing for the section. Practice, practice and more practice has always served me well, on and off the hill. After six repetitions of the route, together with pacing a contingent of the Household Cavalry up the Hill, I became far more relaxed about the run. Initially I was too focused on completion and found myself racing and looking just ahead at the arch of the Monument. To help combat this excessive focus, I devised the mantra Slow, Steady, Smile and Wave!! repeated over and over again. This was intended to switch my focus from the destination towards enjoying sharing the time with the people who were coming to watch the event.

'On one repetition, I met one of the London 2012 Games Makers who was helping tourists at the top of the Hill. He told me thousands of people were expected to be at the Palace for the relay. I quietly told him I was running that stage for mountain rescue. He started laughing. Many years ago, he had been posted to RAF Valley and flown with 22 Squadron to near the top of Snowdon — what a very small world! He was delighted to meet the mountain rescue runner and shook my hand, promising to be in the crowd the following day. This left me feeling more humble than ever.

'The big day arrived. Official preparations were gathering pace with newly-erected barriers keeping the tourists a little further back from the Palace, the Household Cavalry rehearsing the route and more helicopters and police clearly visible. Tension was growing. Messages of support from many people involved in different aspects of mountain rescue all over the UK and Ireland were hitting my phone — this was so welcome and encouraging. The MapAction runner, Ming Lee, and I met the organising committee at a hotel near the Palace and joined a group of forty young aspiring Olympians who are very strong prospects for the 2016 Rio Games. I got changed into my pure white tracksuit, a polar difference to the usual black and red hill gear. No rucksack, no phone, no radio: I began to feel a bit vulnerable. A security and protocol briefing, then we were herded onto a coach, bound for the Palace. The chatter and excitement from those young aspiring Olympians was a good distraction. Once in the inner courtyard, we were soon joined by the Duke and Duchess of Cambridge and Prince Harry, tall and stunningly fit in their Team GB kit. Within seconds, they made us all feel at ease.

Top: Left to right: Wai Ming, the Duke and Duchess of Cambridge, Prince Harry and John Hulse outside Buckingham Palace © Press Association. **Bottom:** A health and safety challenge for the Queen's Golden Jubilee © OVMRO.

'Prince William and I briefly chatted about rescues on Tryfan. Before this day, my only contact with him had been on the VHF as 'Rescue 122' to his Sea King, in the security of the more familiar surroundings of the Ogwen Valley. I always thought that if I should meet him, it would be in the mountains and not on his home territory. We were all on our very best behaviour as I heard there was a very special grandmother in the Palace keeping a careful eye on us.

Then, at the allotted time, we made our way through to the Palace forecourt to a phenomenal roar from the crowds. Helicopters and an airship circled overhead, crowds were clinging to the Victoria Monument and a phalanx of press cameramen were enclosed thirty metres away.

'Within minutes, Ming of MapAction appeared through the south gate and steadily walked to the assembled group. The torches were 'kissed' and the flame was now alight on my torch. The weird combination of elation and extreme nervousness rose again, together with the fear of messing up for mountain rescue with the eyes of the world on me. There was one moment when my newly-lit torch came uncomfortably close to Prince Harry's hair, but his Apache pilot reactions took rapid evasive action. I was gently ushered forward by the police torch relay escort team leader and started the big walk holding the torch aloft, trying to share the moment with all the crowds and the many people supporting me. 'Slow, Steady, Smile and Wave!!' kicked in and my grin increased to painful proportions. The crowd noise rose to new levels as I approached the Palace gates.

'There were cameras everywhere. Ushered on, I was joined by the thirty-two members of the Household Cavalry Mounted Regiment. The crowd noise, helicopters, cacophony of the hooves and regalia added to the celebrations of the crowds, at least ten to fifteen people deep, all the way up the hill. To keep up the roughty-toughty mountain rescue image, I started a gentle jog up the hill, waving and grinning widely to the crowds alongside the barriers. The Cavalry formed up and we all moved steadily on.

'A few hundred metres on, I was brought to a halt to pass the flame to the next runner. It was over far too soon. I was ushered into a waiting BMWs and we followed the cortège up the hill and into Hyde Park, the adrenalin rush subsiding. Tomorrow I'd be back amongst the mountains.

'As is often the case, rescues and mountain rescue activities displace planned events. The Ogwen team was called out the evening of this torch relay to deal with a broken leg, high on the Gribin ridge, which meant most team members were unable to see the live coverage of the relay! However, a contingent of Ogwen members, returning from a white water course in the north east, stopped at Tebay services and cheered — much to the bemusement of the other diners — when the torch being carried for MREW appeared on the live BBC broadcast. Amazingly, some footage of that Royal Torch Kiss briefly featured in the Olympic Opening Ceremony, so mountain rescue managed to be global for a little while.

'Back home, after the sheer exhilaration of the previous few days and so many kind messages of support, I found myself on a call-out carrying a big sack of four large hand-lamps, to help on the evacuation of a severely injured casualty from Glyder Fach cliff — a totally different sort of torch carrying! Back down to earth with a bump and business-as-usual in the team! I am exceptionally grateful and honoured to have been selected to carry the torch for Mountain Rescue England and Wales. The day will stay with me forever. It was such a special privilege to be part of that iconic event and I am so proud to be a member of our unique search and rescue community.'

... and the current warmer Flandrian inter-glaciation began around 11,000 years ago.

Working together

Royal patronage of the national body comes with the expectation that the various charities which comprise the Princes' Charities Forum will find ways of working together for their mutual benefit. The Charities Forum is the collection of charities, of which the Duke and Duchess of Cambridge and Prince Harry are patrons. William and Harry founded the forum in 2006 as a way to bring their individual charitable interests together and explore how they could best support them all. In the case of mountain rescue, this has manifested as a day of activities for disadvantaged and poorly children and young people, hosted by a different mountain rescue region each year. The Ogwen team has undertaken this now on two occasions, in collaboration with their neighbouring teams.

On a sunny afternoon in July 2015, four young people and two staff from Centrepoint in Sunderland, six children from Child Bereavement and two families from WellChild descended on the Towers, near Capel Curig. A quick chat on the workings of mountain rescue gave them a brief insight into the following day's activities then it was off to bed for an early night.

The following morning, six children and four adults from Place2Be in Burnley joined the party. The skies looked grey but team members were too busy setting things up for the day's fun to notice. At the London Crags at Gwern Gof — otherwise known as 'Big Willie's campsite' — members of Llanberis and Ogwen teams were rigging the crags, and at the Towers, a fleet of gleaming Land Rovers arrived to taxi Centrepoint and Child Bereavement to the crags. As they arrived at Big Willie's, it looked like the weather might turn wet but this was not to be. While this group was kitting up to begin the rock climbing and abseiling experiences, the Land Rovers returned to collect the children and adults from Place2Be. Before long, these six children were on the crags too, impressing their supervisors and parents with their new-found skills.

Back at the Towers, the remaining three WellChild families had arrived. The set-up was ideal for these quite poorly children, confined as they are to wheelchairs. Far from being restrictive, every single one experienced both abseiling and a zip across the pond on a wire.

Meanwhile, members of neighbouring NEWSAR were busy setting up a small search exercise high up in a cwm in the shadow of Carnedd Llewelyn. Here, a reservoir is serviced by a steep tarmac road. The views of the Ogwen Valley from the reservoir car park are impressive — and all from the comfort of a car seat.

After the abseiling and rock climbing, the larger group was taken to Bryn Poeth for lunch. There they were briefed by a police officer that two men had been descending Tryfan when one had slipped and injured his leg. The other man continued on to get help, but he too had an accident. The rescue team would have to go out to search for the two men, then treat them for their injuries, carry them on stretchers off the mountain. Quite a task.

A NEWSAR Land Rover escorted the five WellChild families high up into the mountains at Ffynnon Llugwy where they also learned about searching. A SARDA dog gave a demonstration of his impressive search and sniff skills and the police helicopter landed on for all to see.

Back again at Oggi base, tension was mounting as the search and rescue parties clambered into the vehicles for the short drive to the foot of Tryfan, where the exercise began. Shortly, both of the men were located. Hand-held flares — used under very close supervision — went up to indicate the finds. Young voices transmitted details of injuries and treatments over the radio to base. The casualties were loaded onto stretchers and sledged and carried to Gwern Gof Uchaf.

The police officer supervised the crossing of the A5 by the stretcher parties as they carried the casualties all the way up the drive to Bryn Poeth. All that then remained was the magnificent spread of food, laid out for all to enjoy — and a goody bag for every child. But the highlight of the day was the hat trick of helicopter sightings. Not content with just the police helicopter, events conspired to bring the familiar Sea King through the valley, not once but twice, tipping its chassis at base in a final hello. Then, late in the day and without warning, once again the valley filled with the sound of rotor blades — the new S-92 on a training flight to check the LZ at the back of base. It touched down only briefly but it was a thrilling sight nevertheless.

With all the guests gone, washing-up complete, kit packed away, and stacks of sandwiches wrapped in cling film, the remaining team members trickled down to Siabod Café for a well earned bowl of goulash and a hefty chunk of gateau.

'The sun shone on Ogwen that day in so many ways,' says Chris Lloyd. 'None of the guests had visited the area before and they were all impressed by their surroundings. The young people enjoyed new experiences and skills. And team members could be satisfied that, through hard work, they had put smiles on the faces of so many disadvantaged young people. Worth every moment'.

COBWEB CORNER

Pedant's corner: Sometimes it's the words that trip us up, January 2011: Email to the Ogwen press officer: 'You mention 'hill troops' being sent to one incident. Surely the terminology is incorrect as this would imply a military involvement? The OVMRO is made up of volunteers and the reference to troops seems misguided.'

'Fair comment', replied Chris Lloyd, politely. 'We're civilian volunteers giving our free time, work time, home time and sleep time to assist people in distress in rough terrain in northern Snowdonia. The term 'troops probably comes from working closely with RAF MRTs and having a number of ex-military within our team. Troops is used as a collective noun for trained personnel but as you correctly point out, it does imply the military'.

The correspondent remained unconvinced, however, replying. 'Regardless of the close cooperation with military and ex-military personnel, the mountain rescue teams are not military organisations and the use of hill troops as described in the report is parallel with mountain troops, something that mountain rescue teams will never emulate either in organisation or ability.' Ouch...

...although, in defence of the esteemed press officer, the Oxford English Dictionary definition of 'troop(s)' allows for a wider definition than the purely military, citing 'a unit of 18 or 24 Girl Scouts or Boy Scouts organised under a leader' and — more generic still —'a group of people or animals of a particular kind: a troop of musicians'. That'll do for us.

OGGI SNIPS

1984: Reports of a flashing light on Conwy Mountain. Team members found the source: a workman's flashing Traffilamp. They failed to find the hole in the road to which it belonged.

As seen on TV

Judging by the number of TV appearances clocked up over the years, Ogwen team members are clearly a photogenic bunch. Quite apart from featuring on 'This is Your Life', they have taken part in and advised on reconstructions of significant rescues and training events, appeared on CBBC and even represented mountain rescue on 'Songs of Praise'.

It was in February 2000, in preparation for St David's Day on 1 March, that the BBC approached the team to appear on their Sunday evening celebration of hymns. They wanted a link between the hospital and the team but, somewhere along the way, this seemed to be forgotten and Chris Lloyd found himself 'volunteered' for the job.

'The BBC also wanted the Sea King to fly the presenter, Aled Jones, around Snowdonia,' says Lloyd. 'So, having politely offered the services of OVMRO, I found myself taking time off work to act as radio link between aircraft and ground-based film crew. Foolishly, I'd supposed they would film my interview straight afterwards. After all, everybody was there. The weather was good. But no. My interview was scheduled for some other time, to suit the BBC and not my employers!'

When his turn came, it was a very wet afternoon. When the 'Songs of Praise' film crew arrived — complete with 'red lipstick and mink hat' — they were surprised to be met by another BBC film crew, who were making a documentary about the team over the course of a year. 'Initially, there was some reluctance from the 'Songs of Praise' crew to go out in the 'Ogwen' rain but, after I'd dropped into the conversation that our resident — more intrepid — crew had spent the previous night with the team, buried in a snow hole at 3000 feet in the Cairngorms, we all ventured out onto Little Tryfan.

'Duly assisted by my off-camera roadie, Rob Grant, I abseiled down greasy rock. Time and time again. Each time the camera was at a different angle but the questions were the same. The problem was, each time the answers were different as I grew more and more frustrated with the whole affair! Finally, it was back to Oggi base for a cup of tea and a dry out.

'So what about the cathedral service? I asked, yet again. Oh yes. I've got you tickets, said the red lipstick from underneath a drowned mink. I couldn't get to the rehearsal but managed to make it to the cathedral for the recording. Still wearing my Vango jacket, I'd hoped I might appear on camera again but, having missed the rehearsal, I was seated at the back. I'm glad I asked where I should sit for there were a few choice words said when people found their seats from the rehearsal taken by others who wished for a better view! Three hours and a packet of cough sweets later, I was relieved of my duties representing the religious side of the team. Quite an experience!'

The programme put together by that other, more intrepid, BBC Wales film crew, which aired on Tuesday 12 September, was a far more considered and representative piece. 'Mountain Rescue' showed the life of the team through a year of filming. They even followed team members up to Scotland for their annual winter training and, only marginally less exciting, filmed committee meetings. Sadly (from a TV point of view), there were never any 'good rescues,' says Tim Radford, who had the dubious privilege of being a squeaky new trainee at the time. His final hill day assessment was filmed in its entirety — 'so no pressure!' Another potential trainee also featured but, early in the process, he was advised he wasn't up to standard.

Jim Langley and Chris Lloyd have both appeared in CBBC's 'Hero Squad'. 'It was about showing the kids about life in a mountain rescue team,' says Langley. 'They get to experience something of what we get up to — driving round in the vehicles, making a belay, stretcher lowering. When it came to that we put an egg in a Perspex tube with a GoPro attached to see if they could do the lower without cracking the egg. No one did. We gave them the opportunity to abseil and then the stretcher lower. It was very windy when we did it so they did well.'

Langley made a truly dramatic entrance at the start of the show. 'The kids were stood at the bottom of the cliff in Tin Can Gully. Rav Wilding asked whether they were ready to meet their mentor and I whipped down on an abseil'.

Pressing matters

Cultivating good relationships with the press and media has always played a major part in team life, on so many levels. It facilitates fundraising, raises awareness of the team's work (which, in turn, also facilitates fundraising) and helps publicise events (facilitates fundraising...). After every incident, press officer Chris Lloyd will spend time putting together a press release. In the case of a major incident, finding the right words then fielding the avalanche of calls and emails might take several more hours besides. Sometimes, it prompts controversy — like the torrent of opinion which poured forth online following a simple observation, in November 2014, that an increasing number of incidents occur in the same spot and maybe this should be investigated. And, frequently, it can be used to educate those heading out to the hills for fun that there are risks involved, because

even the most experienced of hill goers can forget to pack a vital piece of equipment, or get their bearings wrong.

In January 2014, the reporting of a rescue from Tryfan in the grip of winter reminded readers that navigating on the mountain could be a challenge, even in good conditions. 'Maps cannot really represent the topography. GPS readings are sometimes incorrect, possibly due to the shape of the mountain, and the geology seems to lure people to the West Face,' wrote Lloyd.

That same month he stressed the importance of groups staying together on the hill after three men were rescued from Tryfan when one of their party slipped and injured himself. Their three companions, all more experienced scramblers, had gone ahead and reached safety, leaving them behind to pick their way down the mountain. It was an incident which could have had much graver consequences.

In September that year, Lloyd had warned that loose rocks were becoming more common, after another scrambling incident left a man with head and leg injuries. The rock had simply come away in his hand.

With North Wales Police, Snowdonia National Park and the North Wales Mountain Rescue Association, the team is also involved with the 'Mountain Safe' campaign, which aims to keep people safe on the region's mountains. 'We want people to continue to come and enjoy the beautiful mountains of North Wales,' says Tim Bird. 'But before they set out they need to ask themselves are they properly clothed and equipped, do they know the weather forecast, have they got the mountain skills needed for the terrain they're about to tackle?'

So, there's little doubt that a good relationship with the media is invaluable, but there are other people too, without whose support team members and the team as a whole would find life a lot more difficult: the families and friends who regularly find themselves abandoned while their 'mountain rescue' companion heads off up the hill, and the 333 supporters who work hard to raise funds and support the team in a variety of ways.

COBWEB CORNER

March 2001: Team members are renowned for their practical jokes on each other. 'Repetitive sabotage of vehicles comes to mind,' says Chris Lloyd. 'On one occasion, a team member ran off the hill and jumped into his Land Rover, only to find there was no forward motion. Ah hah, he thought, they've jacked up the rear wheels. No problem, just slip it into four-wheel drive. Wrong! All four wheels were spinning in fresh air.

The same driver, on another occasion, was assisting his team mates when he returned off the hill to find a distinct lack of seats in his Mark 1 Ford Escort. After locating the missing seats, he was stuck for a spanner. Purely coincidentally (of course), one team member not only knew which spanner would fit but just happened to have the correct one to hand. Amazing!

Hero Squad 2013: Team members and kids © OVMRO.

2002

FALL FROM BRISTLY RIDGE

The Royal Humane Society Award received for the rescue of Andrew McCluskey

The team received its first bravery award, in July 2002, thirty-seven years after its formation. The Royal Humane Society Award, presented by Deputy Chief Constable Bill Brereton, was in recognition of a rescue the previous October, to recover a man who had plunged 200 feet off Bristly Ridge.

University student Andrew McCluskey had just started his first year of a sports science degree at Bangor University. Like so many before him and since, he'd been attracted to the coastal campus because of its easy access to Snowdonia. He was an accomplished hill walker and a regular visitor to the mountains since the age of eight, with his father, a mountain leadership trainer. He and a friend were hiking on the exposed side of a col on Glyder Fach at the same time as a school party made its way up the other side. The twelve-strong group of fifteen year olds were on the first leg of a six peaks challenge with Wellington School's Combined Cadet Force, led by teacher David Armitage.

Twenty-seven-year-old Armitage, an experienced mountain walker, had already spotted a climber with a large backpack above a dangerous sheer face just across the col. Then, as he was telling his party to put on waterproofs, a cry went up from one of the boys. The climber's had slipped on a clump of grass. He hit his head and started free-falling.

'I heard Stephanie Toase, another teacher, saying he'd fallen,' said Armitage. 'I felt this jolt of adrenaline and said 'I'm going'. I'm respectful of the terrain and I'm very safety conscious but somehow I buried that. I charged down the horrendous cliff, just jumping from rocks to boulders. All that was in my head was, Don't be dead!'

He couldn't see McCluskey and had no way of knowing whether he was alive but as he raced down the cliff, he kept shouting out to him. Within five minutes he'd reached him, fifteen metres from the cliff edge. His head was crumpled onto his legs. 'I wanted to see if he'd broken his back so I ran my fingers down his spine. I checked his pulse which was strong but when I put my hand around his mouth he wasn't breathing.'

As he tried to turn him over, the scree shifted beneath them. He managed to pull him on to his back but the injuries to McCluskey's face were so severe that mouth-to-mouth resuscitation was impossible. He tried chest compressions. After three minutes, McCluskey began to breathe but they were still slipping closer and closer to the edge.

OGGI SNIPS

Volcanic eruptions around 440 million years ago form the foundation of the rocks found in Snowdonia.

'It was nerve-wracking,' said Armitage. Six metres from the edge, he pulled the boy, who was going into convulsions, onto his lap as they continued to slide. Just as McCluskey's feet began to slide off the edge to another steep drop, another climber emerged from below. He'd heard their shouts and scaled the near vertical wall to help. Armitage made a sling with a rope and used that to hold the student, while the other man kept up the pressure on his feet, holding him off from the edge. Meanwhile, Stephanie Toase shouted to the second climber's friend to call 999, spelling out their grid reference.

Team member Chris Cooksey had popped into base to pick up a radio when the call came in. He and Tim Radford were lowered from the Sea King, with Rich Taylor, the winchman, in itself a hairy situation. 'I could see the rotors whizzing past the rocks,' said Cooksey. 'It was a long winch of a couple of hundred feet and I was spinning wildly.

'Andrew was a mess when we reached him. A couple of times we thought we were going to lose him. There was an awful lot of blood and we gave him oxygen because of his erratic breathing. We got a rope attached but it was a very dangerous situation.'

'We were desperately trying to find belays to hold the stretcher,' says Radford, 'and stop it sliding off towards the edge of the drop.' But, finally, McCluskey was winched up on the stretcher and flown to Bangor. Team members proceeded to help the school group safely off the mountain and lower Armitage from his still precarious position.

McCluskey himself remembered little of the accident. In fact, he had no recollections of North Wales at all. 'My memories start again with four weeks of physio at Stevenage hospital,' he told the 'Daily Express', prior to the launch of their Life Savers awards scheme. The paper had taken him back to the scene with Armitage, to build up a picture of what had happened and thank his saviour in person. Doctors said it was because he was unconscious and his body limp as he fell, that he was saved from death, but the two climbers were key to his survival.

For David Armitage, the experience was something of a personal revelation. 'When I look back at my decisiveness on that day, I am surprised. I have a tendency to procrastinate but I knew I was the only person who had a hope of saving him.' He received a Royal Humane Society Bronze Award. That he was still around to receive it was down to the actions of the Ogwen team and the helicopter crew, who saved both men before they slid off the mountain.

'We've never had an award before,' said Chris Lloyd, after receiving the award. 'People just let us get on with our jobs. But it's nice to be recognised for our efforts as volunteers, that all the time and effort we put in doesn't go unnoticed'.

The incident featured in a TV programme, some time later but, disappointingly, there was no mention made at all of the team's involvement!

CHAPTER TEN

Life is but a weaving: The people who made Ogwen

As Tony Jones observed, the team would be nothing but for its members, past and present — a rich and motley mix of personalities and professions, drawn from far and wide. With one common purpose: mountain rescue. The innovation and drive which key individuals have brought to the team is well documented, but there are many, many more who have contributed simply by being part of the team, doing the job they signed up for.

As long as mountain rescue teams have been in existence, people have been volunteering to join them — and grumbling about what their particular team should get involved in, team member commitment, even the need to actually turn up. And in this respect, Ogwen is no different to any other.

In August 1974, Neil Adam debated the case for the team undertaking 'standby' duties, weighing the merits of team members languishing at base on the off-chance of a call-out, against the need to maintain hill-fitness by getting out there. He also expressed concerns about some people still considered to be members of the organisation who hadn't been seen around for a very long time. 'It would be nice,' he said, 'to see their faces more often than once or twice a year'. He called all members — of a team he considered 'one of the best in the country' — to show their faces. They were needed!

Nowadays, the problem of a member dropping out of contact is addressed by keeping an eye on the attendance log. There may be many reasons why an

Jubilee sunset: Photo © OVMRO.

individual's commitment to operational duty wavers — the dynamics of family life, the demands of work, personal fitness and health all wax and wane over time. But what to do with those members who no longer wish to be involved at the sharp end but still feel a commitment to the team? The Treble Three support group is the perfect solution, allowing members to remain involved, assist with base duties and fundraising — and be on hand should the voice of experience be required.

Conceived in 1996, to address escalating running costs, Treble Three is an integral part of team life, boasting around 750 members in 2015. Back then, those escalating costs amounted to just £25,000 a year. Fundraising has always been a necessity but attitudes towards it have varied. Clive Swombow, chairman of the group from the beginning, recalls a time, years before, when it was suggested that mountain rescue might learn some lessons from the RNLI, and generate funds by sponsorship and a policy of active fundraising. 'Eyebrows were raised,' he says, 'to put it mildly, and the matter was tactfully ignored'. But, as time passed and the diversity of tasks widened far beyond simply 'mountain' rescue, drastic action was required.

A working party was set up and a first meeting held in April 1997. The Marquess of Anglesey and the chief constable of North Wales Police, Michael Argent, kindly agreed to be patrons and the terms of reference were set: to raise funds for the organisation by forming a support group. Treble Three was formed, taking its iconic name from the telephone number at base: 'Capel Curig 333'. At its inaugural meeting on 13 September 1997, Swombow was appointed chair, Bill Dean treasurer and Barry Pinion secretary. Other members took on responsibility for developing membership, distributing collecting boxes and general fundraising. Treble Three already had 115 members, raising the received income from membership to £1800 plus additional donations. 'By 2004,' says Swombow, 'the cost of running the team had reached well over £30,000 but this was offset by income from 333 of over £11,000 — virtually a third.' By then, it had been accepted that without the efforts off 333 the team would have difficulty in meeting its financial needs.

Since its formation, many other teams throughout the UK have tried to emulate Treble Three, with varying degrees of success. Swombow firmly believes they 'set the standard in what is given to members in return for their support'.

While fundraising may be the group's key purpose, there is a huge social aspect to it too and this was evident with the organisation of that first inaugural meeting. More than just a meeting, the day comprised a walk out on the hill with team members, a tour of base and the inevitable slide show. Paul Henshall was amongst those who trawled through the records of the previous thirty years, extracting some 1400 names and addresses of people the team had assisted in some way. Every one of these was invited to come along on the day.

From the start, there was a vital synergy between supporters and team members, that spark which makes people feel involved. Ian Logan was one of the early membership secretaries. Following the inaugural day, he wrote how impressed he was by the welcome from team members. 'Best of all was the fact that I arrived in the morning as a stranger but left in the afternoon feeling I had spent the day with old friends.'

Treble three members are encouraged to visit base at any time. In fact, they often take on minor roles which don't require mountain rescue experience. Many are expert mountaineers and people who live out of the area. Each year, a list of activities they might engage with includes courses such

OGGI SNIPS

From the 'pink' forms, February 2003: He had left his walking boots at home and decided to risk going out in his street shoes. This may have caused the resultant broken ankle.

as tracking, navigation, first aid and GPS training, fundraising events such as the Oggie 8, climbing and camping weekends and social evenings at the Siabod Café. Membership continues to grow. Casualties are handed a leaflet, encouraging them to join and support the team.

In 2015, the cost of running the team is an estimated £70,000 a year. Treble Three brings in approximately £15,000 in membership and £7000 in other income, with the Oggie 8 bringing in another £6000 plus. And since setting up the group, the team has attracted a lot of legacies.

Sad losses

Treble Three is undoubtedly a success story for Ogwen, and a handy segue for team members no longer wishing to be operational. But, sadly, there have been many who never reached that opportunity. For any mountain rescuer, arguably, tragedy goes with the territory but it becomes immeasurably more hard to bear when it's one of your own. John Evans, Bill Galston and Izzy Lindsay in particular hold a special place in memory for their loss, so young.

Isobel Lindsay was just twenty-six when she tumbled to her death down a frozen hillside in November 1977. She had been climbing the snow-covered back wall of Cwm Lloer with her dog Sheba on a lead when she slipped and fell. Her abdomen was penetrated by her ice axe, severing her vena cava. Eyewitness Peter Butler, a student, later told the coroner that 'Mrs Lindsay fell past the dog until she pulled it down on top of her. They collided and went down in a tumble'. Sheba escaped with just a broken leg.

Neil and Maggie Adam recall the horror of that day. 'Izzy was going up a snow gully with a group of team members when her crampon came loose. She told the rest to go on to the top and she would catch up, but she never did. When they looked back, she was at the bottom of the gully. We never knew whether she'd slipped first or the dog. There was the added difficulty of having radio comms because we knew her husband John — also a team member — was out climbing on the hill and he would hear it.

'The helicopter took Izzy away and the crew planned to come back for the dog but got diverted elsewhere, so we brought Sheba down on a half Thomas stretcher and put her in the back of an

COBWEB CORNER

October 2003: A large group of RAF personnel were carrying out an exercise in the forestry around Llyn Elsi, Betws y Coed, when they heard shouts for help accompanied by banging. They carried out an immediate search, calling out to see whether there was any response, but found nothing so they called for help from the team. An initial search of the area was carried out with physical and telephone checks to houses in the area. At the very last house, the owner admitted he had a dog called Hal which he had been calling in by shouting and clapping — at about the same time the RAF heard the shouts! He was all but deaf and had not heard any of their calls. It was a false alarm but, at least the intention was good.

Allegro Estate car. The vet said, tell John not to worry, the dog is safe, she's survived. He really looked after her.'

The inquest heard that Lindsay had been trying to pull the dog up a steep slope. 'Unfortunately,' said Tony Jones, 'the dog was the direct cause of the accident'. Izzy often took the dog with her on a climb. 'The dog went quite well,' he added, 'though whether it enjoyed the experience was a matter for debate'.

Coroner Dewi Pritchard Jones considered it 'quite obvious that if she had been walking without the dog she probably would not have fallen in the way she did'.

Lindsay's accident was one of four recorded in Snowdonia in the same period, described as being 'alpine weather up on the peaks with hard packed ice underfoot'. Arthur Clarke, chief instructor at Plas y Brenin said there was new snow up to a foot deep in the higher gullies, with the snow line on the mountains down to about 200 feet'. Conditions were treacherous.

Recovering the body of a team colleague is particularly harrowing but, says Tony Jones, you just have to get on and do the job. Post-trauma therapy then largely consisted of chatting to your team mates over a pint or a cuppa. Nowadays, team members have access to more structured counselling, if required.

Three years earlier, in July 1975, Bill Galston fell to his death while practising for the Army's Welsh 3000s. Galston had been a keen team member for many years. A plumber by profession, he spent most of his spare time as a mountaineer and Territorial Army member.

The team's newsletter reported that there was no better way to pay respect to a missed colleague than to echo the sentiments of his obituary, published in his battalion's Part 1 Orders of

6 June 1975. Bill Galston was 'an enthusiastic and competent mountaineer. A tough, fit infantryman and a good companion both on and off the hill. He was a competitor in the first Welsh 3000s competition in 1963 and had taken part in every competition since. His leadership, drive, energy, patience and good humour have been a source of inspiration to countless Royal Welchmen as well as his many civilian friends. His untimely death leaves a big gap in our ranks but one which we would wish to see rapidly filled by volunteers determined to follow the high example which he set us all.'

Of course, not all those who leave this life do so under such traumatic circumstances. Ken Dwyer, had been a member of Ogwen team since 1966. When he died after a short illness, in September 2011, it was peacefully at home, surrounded by his family. Remembering their friend, team members described 'a stalwart of the team, always there when needed. More often than not, he would be the first one to base and he could be relied upon to make sure that everything was up and running before the rest of the team arrived'.

Coming from a family with strong mountaineering links, Ken had followed in the footsteps of his father George, also known as Scotty, a renowned mountain guide in the 1940s, 50s and 60s. He had lived in Capel Curig all his life and was well-known by many people in the area. He met Ann, his wife, while they were in their teens and they had been together ever since — childhood sweethearts who raised their two lads Gareth and Carwyn in the village. A true Capel family. It was fitting then, that on his last night in hospital he had a glorious view of the Carneddau bathed in the setting sun. As if in a final tribute, an RAF Sea King took off from the hospital landing pad and flew past the window.

Jed Stone recalled one occasion when the team had deployed and he and Ken thought they were going to 'get away with it staying at base providing support from the warmth of the ops room. Then the call came in that the troops on the ground requested a support party, as they kept losing sight of the climbers stuck high on the cliff and needed some spotters to direct them in.

'So we duly headed off to an area called the beach on Llyn Idwal, loaded up with flares and lighting that would make even today's Army proud. Just as we arrived, we noticed a young couple setting up camp, tent up, sleeping bags out. We introduced ourselves and apologised for the noise and firework display we were about to produce in the cwm. Not much further on, we set up our stance, sheltering behind the stone wall to get out of the wind and heavy drizzle that had started. A few flares later and with the search lamp lighting up the location of the stuck climbers, we started to direct the troops in towards them.

'Some time after this we started to hear noises on the wind. Comprehension dawning, we realised that the camping couple were getting up to what young people get up to when on their own in a tent. We looked at each other and popped our heads up over the wall. Sure enough, carried on the wind, the noises were amplified further. Both of us slid back down the wall. I have never heard Ken giggling as much as we did then.

'Eventually, the peace of the night returned but every now and then we would look at each other and start giggling again. But it didn't end there. All of a sudden, shouts and squeals could be heard

Paying respect: Team members unite as a 'family' to pay their respects to long-standing team member and friend, Ken Dwyer © George Petry.

and, once again, like naughty schoolboys we slid up the wall. This time to see, through the drizzle and haze, two ghostly figures jumping about and splashing each other at the edge of the lake.

'No, I thought, I don't believe this. As I turned to say something to Ken, I suddenly notice the search lamp beam start to wander off the stuck climbers, over the cliff and down towards the lake.

'Initially, I thought it was falling over, but no, there was Ken, about to shine it on the couple, lighting them up as if it were daylight. Now normally, I'm the naughty one of the team, but there he was outdoing me. There was that mischievous side. Fortunately, discretion took over and he didn't actually go through with it and we resumed our position sheltering behind the wall. But, for the rest of the night, all that could be heard from our side of the wall was giggling as every now and again, one of us would start the other off.'

In April 2009, Mick Parsons, another stalwart from the 1970s, also died after a period of illness. Described by his friend Raj as a 'joker, piss-taker extraordinaire — and sometimes a royal pain in the ass, which didn't endear him to some — a self-contained comic and straight man in one', Parsons took part in many rescues over the years, 'happy in the contribution he was able to make and comfortable and open about the limit of his capabilities. He had a good head on him, capable of analysing situations and responding correctly, a safe pair of hands'.

Mick became a full team member in September 1977 after moving to North Wales to set up business as a plumber and electrical contractor. He was highly committed to the team, 'frequently attending call-outs and greatly assisting in the maintenance and development of Bryn Poeth, where he was often to be seen as part of the Wednesday evening gang. On top of this he serviced numerous collecting boxes and tirelessly recovered a great deal of money for the team through the Gift Aid scheme'.

The family factor

It's a mark of the 'family' that is mountain rescue, that those who die are remembered with such warmth. Ask the average rescuer what mountain rescue means to them and that characteristic, the supportive nature of the wider mountain rescue 'family', will invariably form part of the answer. But what about the real families, the wives, partners and children left to continue the threads of life while their loved ones disappear up a hill for hours at a time? Childcare forces practical considerations, but sometimes both husband and wife are involved operationally. Other wives continue patiently at home, keeping the house running, the children fed, the lawn mowed, the shopping done, while also offering support with fundraising activities. And some get stuck into the administrative side of things. (If you can't beat 'em...)

Twiggy and Willuck, otherwise known as Sue and Pete Price, met through the team in the late 1960s, while camping out with the crowd beneath the trees at Ogwen. 'He was just one of the lads,' says Twiggy. 'but one day he parked next to my van and asked me where I was from. Turned out we lived twenty-nine miles from each other and we'd been travelling up separately for so long!'

The relationship blossomed but, in typical mountain rescue fashion, when the pair celebrated

OGGI SNIPS

Online Guestbook: I bought your calendar today. What fantastic photos. I got home tonight to watch 'Calendar Girls'. Great film. How about it boys? I'd buy it.

their engagement in October 1972, it was by climbing different mountains, thanks to the demands of two separate rescues. While Twiggy was leading a stretcher party down the 3000-foot peak of Pen yr Ole Wen in the dark, Price was climbing down another with a different group of rescuers. Guests at their planned engagement party may have been without their hosts, but for them it was business as usual: another Saturday evening taken up with twelve hours-worth of rescue operations. It was 3.00am before they were both done and, as Sunday was still a 'dry' day in Wales, there was nothing else to do but postpone their celebrations.

Roz Hulse has been contributing to the team for almost as long as husband John, so she's well versed in the nature of mountain rescue life. 'You don't marry a mountain rescuer, you marry a mountain rescue team!' She has a series of sage one-liners for those embarking on married life with a team member. 'Never assume a birthday or anniversary will have a higher priority than a call-out. Never invite more than two mountain rescue people to a dinner party — they have a habit of being called away during the second course. The family tent will not be used by the family — unless, of course, it is somebody else's family, lost on a mountain. Accidents at home are merely photo opportunities for casualty care courses. And that late night de-brief is never quite the thrill you were expecting!'

Mountaineering socks, apparently, will always be carefully put away in pairs, whereas work socks are 'always odd'. In fact, socks feature heavily in any anecdote involving the Hulses. Legend has it that, many years ago, before his wife 'brought him under control', the young John Hulse was renowned for the aroma of his socks. 'Team members, being the tolerant types they are,' says Chris Lloyd, 'finally decided enough was enough and the socks were forcibly removed, feet washed in bleach and the cold Idwal stream, and the socks set alight'. Wool will usually burn with relish. However, sweat-compacted sock soles do not. 'A gallon of petrol was produced to complete the job. There were no witnesses to the pyre, though a photograph does exist somewhere of a team member carrying the can! And strangely enough,' adds Lloyd, 'three years later, when some roadworks were being carried out in the Idwal car park, the ghostly sock soles reappeared!'

Roz Hulse can divide her husband's mountain rescue career, and its impact on her, into handy decades, her tongue firmly in cheek. 'In the 1970s, he said he wanted to buy flares. I thought trendy clothes, he meant bright lights. In the 1980s, he said he wanted to listen to my heartbeat. I didn't realise that meant I'd be connected to his latest invention, a heart beat amplifier — and I had to run around Cwm Idwal to test it out! In the 1990s, John started to use his comms expertise in mountain rescue and began exploring ways of recording voice activated radio messages received and transmitted at Oggi base. But recalling what I'd said to him not thirty minutes before had nil result.

'In the 2000s, there was a choice to be made — expedition to Greenland with his mountain rescue pals or silver wedding anniversary with me. Yep, the Ice Cap won. Finally, in the 2010s. John said he needed a new torch — I didn't appreciate at the time he'd be giving it a test run out of Buckingham Palace! He said he should get a medal running behind those horses — and guess what happened in 2015!'

Summing up, she reckons the 'best piece of kit for helping the friends and family of a casualty is a hug' and this aspect best demonstrates her direct contribution to rescue. 'For ten years, I was a 'specialist team member' as an 'informer carer' (looking after friends and family of those being rescued). The role came with voting team member status — the first of its kind within the team — and this had both its challenges and rewards. Used with care and sensitivity, I found the most useful and underrated tool to help friends and family, sometimes at quite distressing times, was a hug. I guess I was helped by being designed for hugging rather than climbing mountains. Also in the tool kit were good ears for listening. Sound knowledge of how a rescue is undertaken and its timings was essential to answer an array of questions — why was the helicopter not being used? What's a coroner's inquest? Will the body be damaged being carried down the mountain? Do you organise the funeral too? Can we join the team? An up-to-date contact list of bereavement and disability support workers was always useful, as was a soft, fluffy, lilac-coloured fleece and a bottle of Miss Dior! The fleece was to help identify me from the red-clad rescuers and Miss Dior ensured folk weren't cuddled in the aroma of damp mountaineer.'

In the summer of 2015, John did indeed get a medal and a return trip to the Palace to collect his MBE. He is, incidentally, one of several team members, past and present, acknowledged for their contribution to mountain rescue with a Queen's honour. Tony Jones and Roger Jones preceded him. And Ron James, founder of the team, received an honour for services to mountaineering.

Jill Jones has been married to Roger for 'forty-odd years'. Her memories of married life with a mountain rescuer hinge around the impact of a husband fleeing to call-outs on bringing up three children and running a small bed and breakfast. She feels strongly that 'everyone needs an identity, something to do in life' and she was happy for Roger to carry on. It could just as easily have been golf or fly fishing!' That said, once she had the kids, she was 'a stay-at-home mum', through the 1970s and 80s, and also trying to run a modest business. 'It was very hard. It could have been awkward — I had a house full of young blokes and it was just me and the baby. I'd sometimes say to Roger, I think you should come back now and he would.

'The kids took it in their stride and we even bred another mountain rescuer with Geraint! Over the years, there have been wives who are, shall we say, more high maintenance. Those that were, made it difficult for their husbands to carry on. And some of the men would actively exclude their families from team life.

'When the family grew up, we went more into holiday accommodation and self-catering, so that was a big pull on Roger's time. I always felt it was important for Roger to have something outside family life. His first commitment was always to the family but there were others who were committed to the team above and beyond for a part-time interest. You have to keep a balance. The team has to be secondary if you want a good life, a good family life. Some marriages haven't stood the test.'

She quickly adds that there are several who have, and for several decades. But it's an acknowledged fact that mountain rescue — or rather all the extra voluntary activity which surrounds it, fundraising, admin, dealing with the press, training, equipment maintenance — can quickly eat up every available moment in an individual's life. Maintaining a balance isn't always easy.

Prior to the introduction of 'cost neutral', and certainly when the family were young, 'it was very difficult, because we were financing it — you know, using our own cars and kit. We had very little money. Roger would use all his old kit. On one occasion, his very first Ventile anorak was so rotten, one of the sleeves fell off. They called him the 'Antiques Roadshow'! If he'd had the kit he gets

OGGI SNIPS

'The reason for accidents is still a lack of awareness of danger. You don't run across a motorway but if you'd never seen one, you might be tempted to try!' Ron James, 2005

now, it would have been fantastic. To be fair to Roger, he never had to have the newest and best of everything, we could never afford to do that, but I could see how that might be a bone of contention with some'.

Roger and Jill Jones have always lived in the Ogwen Valley, handy for call-outs. He agrees it 'all stands and falls on the families' and he's been 'well-supported in that'. There have been moments of clear choice, team versus family. He recalls the air crash on Moel Siabod when, aware that Jill was close to her due date for Geraint, he literally took a step back as the team leader organised team members for the airlift up to the site. 'I'd have been a real Mr Popular!'

In 2008, when Jones stepped down as a team leader there was some relief at 'no longer having to miss my Sunday evening dinner! Makes you realise how many family things you should've been there for but the family have put up with it, this grumpy old git coming back at 3.00am wanting food!'

Geraint Jones remembers little of the 'grumpy old git' coming home, which his mother attributes to him invariably being tucked up in bed asleep. 'It was interesting, growing up. I always had an interest in what was going on. I guess Dad was my idol and Mum always reckoned that at least she knew what he was up to'. He does recall that call-outs often seemed to happen at tea-time. 'He was only usually away for a couple of hours or you'd get up in the morning and find he was missing. He'd been out all night. I do remember the big yellow helicopters going over the schoolyard and wondering if Dad was in it.'

Like father, like son, he grew up with an interest in the outdoors but went away to university to study engineering with no real idea where he might end up. 'It took going away for me to come back and appreciate it here. I'd climbed through university so when I got back, I did the initial hill day, about ten years ago. I was a trainee for a while. It was a bit more easy-going then, as long as you turned up on call-outs and were a good pair of hands, it was okay.

'When you first join, you want to go on every call-out, get there first but I'm a bit more circumspect these days. I try to strike a balance with my personal life. From being around the team for a long time, I'm amazed how people often don't strike the balance. They want to be there for everything and it can impact on family and social life'.

It's arguable, of course, whether there is ever a 'good' time for the SMS to ping. If it's between the hours of 9.00am and 5.00pm, the chances are the pocket it goes off in will be at its owner's place of work. Up to midnight, it's going to intrude on family responsibilities, hobbies or social life — and it's quite a test for any blossoming relationship. And after midnight, well, there's sleep to be had. But whatever time it beeps, those who can get away will do everything in their power to do so. It's what they signed up for.

In December 2000, Dave Worrall wrote about a funny thing which happened to him 'on the way to the theatre. The team had been asked to attend a sports award for Conwy Borough Council at the North Wales Conference Centre. We were to provide a small demonstration and, for our efforts, receive a cheque for £250 from Cotswold. Within ten minutes of reaching the conference centre, the pager went off.

'Now any team member will tell you the pager never goes off at a convenient time. Or should I say, any team member's partner will tell you the pager never goes off at a convenient time! You might be on the way to pick up the kids, going out for a meal, having people round for dinner,

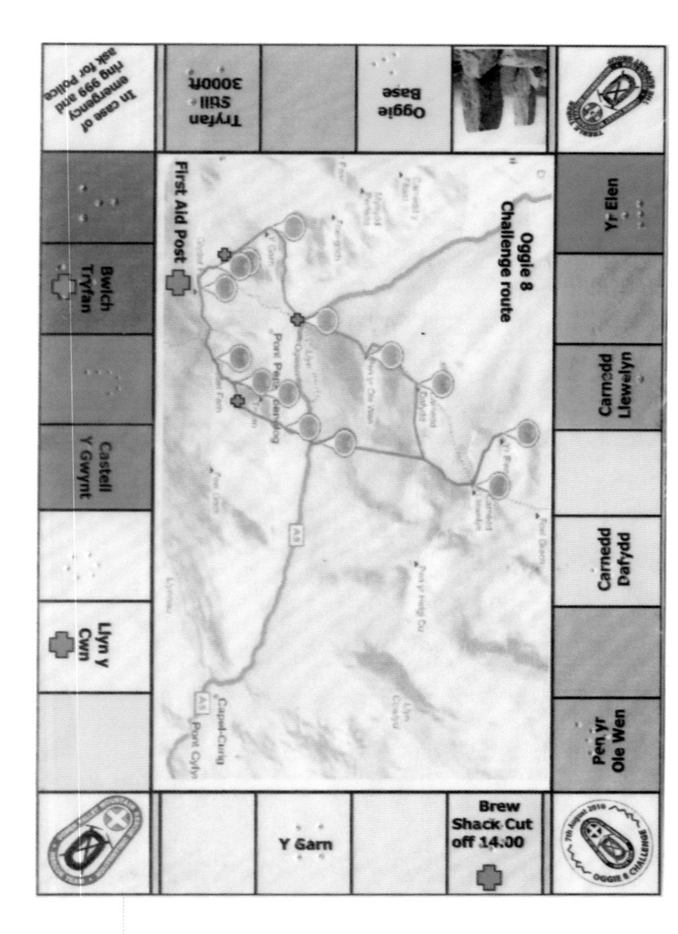

Oggie 8
Challenge route
First Aid Post
Pont Pen-y-benglog
Capel-Curig
A5
Pont Cyfyn
Yr Elen
Carnedd Llewelyn
Carnedd Dafydd
Pen yr Ole Wen
Brew Shack Cut off 14.00
Y Garn
Llyn y Cwn
Castell Y Gwynt
Bwlch Tryfan
In case of emergency ring 999 and ask for Police
Tryfan Still 3000ft
Oggie Base
7th August 2010
OGGIE 8 CHALLENGE

whatever... the list is endless. The one constant is the dilemma: what do you do? The urge is strong to attend the call-out but there's a balancing act. We all have lives outside mountain rescue. I imagine we all think we make a reasonable compromise but in truth, we probably don't. Invariably we head off leaving loved ones to sort out the chaos we've left behind with the token apology: I'll phone when we're off the hill. For my part, I'd like to apologise. We really are hopeless cases.

'However, on this occasion the dilemma was two-fold. The event we were to attend was team business and we were to receive a donation. I now also knew there was a job on. I was torn but, after a call to the police, I decided to stay at the centre and receive the donation. I guess it shows that commitment to the team comes in all shapes and sizes and that the actual rescue is the top of the pyramid.

'We all joined to help those in trouble on the hill but these days it takes a lot more than taking part in call-outs to make the team function. I'd like to thank all those who work in the background for the job they do and the help they bring. It's not all glamour is it?'

As the 'loved one' left behind in this instance, Jo Worrall is very much of the 'can't beat 'em, join 'em' brigade. Already married to Dave Worrall when he joined up, she has always been a firm support, but became more involved during his time as chairman. It escalated a little from modest beginnings when the pair agreed to take on producing the team newsletter. That led to the annual report, then involvement with Treble Three and finally, in 2011, putting herself forward as treasurer. It's a time-consuming role which is well-suited to a non-operational team member. She was also heavily involved with the plans for the anniversary celebrations.

Being involved does bring experiences for team members and their partners which, were it not for mountain rescue, might never have come along — invitations to the Palace, garden parties, involvement with the Royal Family and other charities, meeting people and making friends far outside the Ogwen Valley. During the last days of RAF involvement in search and rescue in North Wales, team members were invited to a last reception at RAF Valley. 'A few of the wives were there too. We were shown round the base and heard a couple of talks from crew members,' says Jo, 'then it was out to the airfield where two Sea Kings were parked up nose to nose. The pilots were there, explaining how things worked but when they invited us to have a look on board, we all hesitated. Eventually, one of the wives said, well I'm going, so I did too and ended up sitting in the driving seat! I'd never have had that experience but for mountain rescue'.

It's clear the 'other halves' must be pretty resilient because, as one team member said, 'it's almost as if people make lifestyle choices to stay with the team'. But what drives the average rescuer to make such a commitment, one that can risk the balance of every other aspect of his or her life? To put something back... because it might be me one day... accident of circumstance... the satisfaction of a job well done... it's incredibly rewarding... more fun than golf or fly fishing... there's no one definitive answer but, as Roger Jones says, fifty-odd years in, 'if I hadn't enjoyed doing it, I'd have stopped doing it'

Top: The very first Raft Race **Bottom:** The 'Oggie 8' route map © OVMRO.

Fun and games

The social aspect of the team has been a key factor in forging bonds. Frequently these events threaten, if not life and limb, then a momentary loss of dignity of those who dare to join in. Maggie Adam set the benchmark in 1974, during her stint as treasurer.

'I thought it would be fun to have a raft race on Llyn Ogwen. We negotiated with the national park, fishing clubs, police and local authorities and one of the conditions of being allowed to do it was that we picked up all our debris and there were no engines used.

'We started with thirteen entries but only seven survived the ordeal. The teams came from all over the place. One team turned up with what looked like aluminium tubes, with pointed ends, on top of their Land Rover. They set off but it quickly became apparent that these were cardboard tubes. About halfway down the course, they began to unravel!

'One raft had a bike on top. The wheels created a sort of turbine in the water. Or that was the theory. In practice, it didn't work. With the four team members on top as well, it was too heavy, got about a yard offshore and sank. Another entry was a couple using a tyre inner tube. He fell off but his wife gamely carried on, towing the inner tube with her. KC had another raft — he put up a sheet as a sail.

'We'd persuaded a couple of people to donate bottles of whisky for the finishers and the most outstanding boat. There were a couple of races in the early days, then a break, then a couple more. We tried it ourselves one year with a bed frame, with plastic bottles underneath. I paddled up front and Neil pushed from the rear'.

That October's newsletter recorded that the first race was a 'great success'. After an ominous start to the day, the weather had perked up and so 'with a mild, following breeze, grey skies and quaking hearts', the brave mariners set sail at 4.30pm from the weir towards Tal-y-Llyn Ogwen. Of the seven entries, one 'failed to make the starting line and the remainder either fell apart, sank or the crew gave up the ghost'.

The winners were Nigel Shepherd and Paul Johnson on 'The Idwal' and the retiring entries included a 'half drowned' Peanuts, John Hulse and 'rather wet girlfriend, who is now not speaking to him', Doug and Kev, 'morally deflated when a drifting barrel passed them', and John Evans and John Norris, whose craft broke up at the start but the former made a 'commendable effort to swim the distance pushing the barrel'. Entries from the Calder Valley and Rossendale teams, who had travelled all the way from Mid Pennine for the dubious pleasure of entering the race, had also retired, defeated.

Needless to say, these events were hugely entertaining to unsuspecting onlookers who were generally happy to throw a few bob in a passing collecting tin.

Also in 1974, the creative juices flowed with another event, the first RAF Valley MRT Bike Race round the Snowdon Horseshoe. 'A team of three had to carry a bike round the Horseshoe,' explains Neil Adam. 'It had to be rideable on the summit of Snowdon and then had to be ridden out on return to Pen y Pass. The circuit route went across Crib Goch, Crib y Ddysgl, Snowdon, Y Lliwedd and down again. One year, we had a kiddie's trike — we only got away with it because Maggie

OGGI SNIPS

'I've seen all sorts of footwear on the mountains, from stilettoes to flip flops'. KC Gordon, Wales Online, 2005.

could just about ride it on the car park. Another time, the RAF guys kept their bike in one piece, attached to a pack frame on their back'.

The Murder Ball was another RAF-related bit of fun. 'Once upon a time,' says Chris Lloyd, 'the pubs were dry on a Sunday in Gwynedd. Over the Whit weekend, RAF Stafford or similar would camp on Bryn Engan fields, just opposite the Bryn Tyrch Hotel. On the Sunday, the pubs being closed, there would be sports and a barrel of beer at the camp. The inter-team sports included Murder Ball in which anything went except in the case of serious injury. And there was a tug of war across the river with a real incentive to win. One year, a climbing rope was used and snapped. The recoil whipped across one of the girls, spraining her wrist. She didn't dare tell all those eager first aiders that it bruised her chest as well. And then, with all the water about, everyone seemed to get dragged in for a swim as well. Or was that someone lurking in the depths in a wet suit dragging the opposition in? And there was the bonfire and singing. We should do it more often!'

The dreaded stick

The annual team dinner is an important fixture in the team diary, not least because it provides an opportunity for one team member to take to the floor and entertain the crowd with tales of wrongdoings and mishaps amongst team members and those associated with the team. Roger Jones initially undertook the role of Master of Ceremonies. He was succeeded by Jed Stone, and Karl Lester took on the role four years ago.

The awards consist of the White Stick, given in recognition of some gross error in the navigation department, the Four Wheel Drive Award, for misdemeanours involving a mode of transport, the Joe Hero Award, an honour bestowed upon those who have given service above and beyond the normal expectation and the Golden Spanner, awarded for general incompetence. Those in receipt of the awards take them with a mixture of embarrassment and pride.

John Banks was the first to be honoured in this way, at the annual dinner of 17 March 1984. Earlier that winter, he had radioed base that he was on Bristly Ridge, though his backpack generator headlights could be distinctly seen heading up the North Ridge. Along with the White Stick, he was presented with a giant demo model Silva compass, later returned to its rightful owners.

Bill Dean was a later recipient. 'Over Whit Bank Holiday,' reports a subsequent newsletter, 'Phil, Claire, Dave and I went up to Glencoe — two excellent days on the hill doing the Ring of Steall on the first day. A very fine walk covering four Munros. The next day was a circle above the bridge at Ballachulash with a further two Munros. A great pity both days were in thick mist and on the second day we actually had to take the dreaded compass out. But not until we were lost, of course. We took bearings and walked for about an hour when we met two people coming towards us. Guess what? We were both supposed to be walking down the same way!

'Oops, we'd walked in a circle! I think Claire was a little concerned when she saw my face. However, after a short period we found the way off but must confess there was a time of concern and confusion. I don't know where the other party came down — we never saw them again!'

Chris Lloyd received the award for sending three members to the new Western Ops Room which he 'thought was housed in the new wing of HQ in Colwyn Bay. Alas, the police had been busy building in Caernarfon too!' Many others have had the pleasure of holding this award, including 22 Squadron, as Flight Lieutenant Tony Dewhurst reported earlier. The Hulses held it for two years — once for John and once for Roz. Sadly, the newsletters don't record all instances.

The Joe Hero tends to be awarded for acts of gallantry because, says Roger Jones, 'sometimes people do daft things', like the team member who saw a lone hand, peering out of the bushes. On investigation, he found a little old lady had fallen into her septic tank. Without further ado, he jumped in and hauled her out.

Since these early beginnings, there have been a host of events where challenge meets social fun — stretcher races, Great Oggi Bike Rides — which have also drawn modest funds into the coffers. But one of the most successful events in terms of fundraising has been the 'Oggie 8'.

'I had a notion,' says Dave Worrall. 'I'd read somewhere, something about the Lairig Ghru walk which the Cairngorm team organised and thought why not do something similar here. I was in the ops room at the time. It came together quite quickly, almost a series of coincidences. It was initially conceived in 2008 and we'd wanted to run it on the eighth of the eighth of 2008 but the first event was on 7 August 2008. We drew a route on the map and a few of us thrashed out a few ideas about where it should go and ultimately finish. We had about a hundred people the first year.'

The fiftieth anniversary year saw the eighth Oggie 8, with the event now recognised as the team's main source of fundraising. For the first time, there was also a shorter route option for those who wanted to take part but lacked the confidence to tackle all eight peaks. The Oggie 4 began at the Brew Shack next to Llyn Ogwen and followed the second half of the route over Y Garn, Glyder Fawr, Glyder Fach and Tryfan, finishing at base for a goodie bag and after-event party.

The event has become a 'national institution', attracting teams from all over the country to pit their strength, stamina and endurance against the Ogwen Valley's 3000-foot peaks. The target is always for a hundred entrants, with sponsorship of £100 each and the 2014 event raised a tremendous £6596, with winners Siabod Shifters completing the route in just seven hours and fifty-five minutes. In 2015, Siabod Shifters beat this record with a time of five hours fifty-four minutes.

'Treble Three has taken over the running of it now,' says Worrall. 'The route is the same. And we

FROM THE ARCHIVE

Where not to take a car: The annual report 2007 reported a' bizarre incident' in which the team was called to assist a group of 'motorists' who had decided it would be a good idea to drive from Rowen to Aber via the old Roman Road — at night, in January — rather than the more conventional A55 route. During this adventurous journey, their navigational abilities continued to fail them and their three cars ended up so far from the rough track, wedged up against a mountain wall, having slid down steep grassy slopes. Team members managed to recover the sheepish motorists and local farmers had the opportunity to claim salvage on a handful of cars.

OGGI SNIPS

From the 'pink' forms, August 2000: Equipped with map, Mickey Mouse compass and rudimentary knowledge. Allegedly, 'a very experienced and competent hill walker'.

finish near base so it's easier for people to drop out early if they need to. We always have food and a decent goody bag. We want people to feel part of the team, not that they're just raising money for us. Often people hang around till quite late, eating, drinking, chatting. It's a great profile-raiser.'

Of course, fundraising isn't just about the 'big events'. Since the 1970s, Bill Dean has been urging people to think 'Stamps, stamps, stamps' in the name of the team. Back in 1979, he reported that one pound in weight would yield 70p to the team. Once a year, Dean would advertise his 'Mountain Rescue mixture' in 'Stamp Magazine', the cost of £12.50 to do so, a contribution to team effort. 'That ad alone usually brought a response of half a hundredweight of stamps. Many collectors don't respond to the ad for several months, so after the initial deluge there are small requests through the year'. Orders regularly came in from South Africa and New Zealand. 'The word gets round that we're good value for money, 'says Dean.

A good mix of stamps might be mostly ordinary small stamps with a scattering of regional stamps and larger commemorative stamps, together with the occasional foreign and older items. The stamps are sold with their bit of envelope attached. These days, the availability of used stamps is dwindling, but he continues with the task nevertheless. In 2014, it raised £643.

A number of significant donations have come from the bereaved families and friends of casualties fatally injured in the mountains here and abroad. In April 2002, the team received its first major donation. Mrs Marion Brewer's brother had died in Snowdonia in 1972 and when she died, she left almost £55,000 to the team in his memory.

In February 2005, a group of friends donated £2,162, in memory of a colleague killed in an alpine climbing accident. Liverpool estate agent Richard Elliott, of Connah's Quay, died after he was stranded alone in a blizzard in Italy's Argentera Valley in November 2004. He was found after his climbing partner raised the alarm. The men had been separated in the snow storm and forced to spend the night in the open. Despite being hypothermic, Paul Field managed to reach a mountain hut where he used an emergency phone to contact relatives in the UK. They called the Foreign Office and alerted the police.

Staff at City Residential, where Elliott was a branch manager, collected the cash for the team after his family asked for donations to the charity. They donned costumes for a 3.5 mile Santa Dash around Liverpool city centre and organised other fundraising activities. Elliott had helped set up and run the company for three years and he was 'deeply missed'. The company's managing director, Alan Bevan, said he would have been proud his colleagues had raised so much money for a charity so close to his heart.

There are benefits to being allied to the national body, in terms of certain items of equipment and the availability of training courses, funded centrally. The Welsh teams also benefit from a small grant from the Welsh Assembly. But overall, over half a century of rescue, it has been the efforts of the team members themselves which has brought the greatest rewards.

CHAPTER ELEVEN

And here's to another fifty...

In fifty years, the voluntary ethos of mountain rescue hasn't changed, but the demands on those volunteers has and those demands gather ever quicker pace. It is no longer simply mountaineers rescuing mountaineers.

'Up until my retirement as an operational team leader four years ago,' says Roger Jones, 'I was getting involved in rescues in sports not invented when I joined — extreme canoeing, parapenting, mountain biking, canyoning. There are as many people in the Ogwen Valley on a Wednesday as there would once have been on a bank holiday forty years ago. With the A55, you can finish work in Manchester at five on a summer evening, and be climbing in the valley two hours later.

'Like most MR teams, we're becoming more and more community-focused but we're a versatile bunch of people prepared to give up our time to help where we can.'

Asked where he sees mountain rescue in ten years time, he's adamant it's a question the 'younger guys' have got to seriously start addressing. 'Are we going to stay as we are? Will people have to start paying for rescue? Unfortunately, we've lost the search and rescue service of the military, who used to chalk everything up as training, now it's a commercial operation running things — we don't know yet how that might impact on things. Of course, if people did have to pay for rescue, that would bring more paperwork for us.'

There's a recurring theme in conversations with older members, and those who've moved away, that there comes a point when you no longer wish to hare up a hill with 'the young blood'. Some step aside, others continue in non-operational

Looking down the hill from the Tryfan Skylight: Photo © Andy Harbach.

jobs, their expertise and experience still called on when required. But there's no doubt that the future of the team is in the hands of the younger members. Fortunately for the Ogwen team, there's a ready supply of youngsters, who continue to come to North Wales to study and be close to the mountains.

'We're attracting young people who are far fitter than we were — and we thought we were fit!' says Jones. 'One lad recently came from the top of Tryfan to the road in eight minutes!'

Al Read believes mountain rescue is 'on the cusp of change. In North Wales, we welcome it. It's a recognition of what we've done already. We may struggle to evolve but I think we will. The 'volunteer professional' is a phrase I think we'll use more often, because that's what we are now'.

He too believes the younger people joining the team now are different to when he joined. 'Ogwen still has the ethos of mountaineering but it's perhaps less important than it was. We need people with the capability to develop as well. The challenges are different, we're a much bigger team — there were thirty calls a year in the 1980s, now its 130+. We're where the RNLI was a hundred years ago.

'The total independence of teams has softened over the last five years and this is down to us being more busy. Where once there were territorial issues, the strength of feeling between teams has gone towards helping each other'.

FROM THE ARCHIVE

Climbers rescued after man spends five hours on summit of Tryfan waiting for his friends, July 2015: The group of three, in their late-20s were attempting a rock-climbing route on the mountain when they got into difficulties. A miserable start to the day had deterred them from climbing in the Llanberis Pass, so they opted for the easier but longer classic route of Grooved Arête, on the East Face of Tryfan.

'After the first pitch, one member decided to abseil off and scramble to the summit via the South Ridge,' said Chris Lloyd. 'The other two continued the climb but lost the route just below the Knight's Move. Their colleague reached the summit and patiently awaited their arrival — for five hours. Without mobile phone contact and no response to his shouts, he made a 999 call at about 8.45pm.

Team members managed to make visual and telephone contact with the two on the East Face, but mobile phone battery life was short-lived. They were instructed to make their way to the Eastern Traverse at the top of the rock climbs. Meanwhile, two hill parties of two were dispatched. One went to collect the lone man on the summit and the other to locate the two rock climbers. After some searching, they were located down Green Gully. They were invited to climb back up to the Eastern Traverse, from where they were shown the descent via the North Ridge.

'A late start, damp rock, a route-finding error, low battery life on their phone and the lack of torches resulted in this call-out,' concluded Lloyd.

OGGI SNIPS

Online Guestbook: Love the website, visit it daily. Always check the web cams.... any chance you can clear the snow off?

Currently serving as training officer for Mountain Rescue England and Wales, Read would also like 'to see our own national body having a national function, fully supported, so they can do a good job for the teams'.

'We've a great future,' says John Hulse. 'The people coming through are open-minded, collaborative, they want to innovate but recognise our limitations and that we need other people to help us sometimes'.

The biggest change of recent years has been changing the team's status to a charitable incorporated organisation (CIO), which went live in June 2015. People have been working on it for a number of years, in order to mitigate the financial risk to the trustees. It's an option which the government only made available in 2013. As chairman, Andy Harbach has been instrumental in driving that forward, through a new constitution, changes to the lease, banking arrangements and all the minutiae of running what is now, in many respects, a business operation. 'There's a lot to it,' he says, in something of an understatement. 'We've more call-outs now, so need to find a more efficient way of managing things'.

Mountain rescue is clearly a rewarding way of life, capable of drawing in and holding people in its thrall for many years, despite the occasional brush with tragedy. 'The chores, fruitless searches and the fatalities are far outweighed by the positive experiences,' says Roger Jones. 'You get the satisfaction of a job well done as a team, and the camaraderie of working with people'.

In fact, it's that sense of camaraderie that is the glue which binds the team together and it's been a constant from the start. There's a seam of black humour, always has been — possibly the only way to make sense of what can be very challenging circumstances. And the creativity which has consistently explored innovative ways of operating, raising funds and having fun — was evidenced almost monthly through the summer of 2015 as the team sought every opportunity to celebrate fifty years of mountain rescue work in the Ogwen Valley.

Anniversary antics

In time-honoured fashion, anniversary festivities began — and will likely end — with the enjoyment of good food and wine, beginning with an impressive (and very tasty) 'Tryfan rescue cake', baked and decorated by Anne Aspinall. This was swiftly followed, later the same day by a Grand Dinner at the Venue Cymru in Llandudno, a glittering occasion attended by invited guests and team members past and present. Founder member Ron James was there and Sir Chris Bonington too came along to say a few words and share his memories of climbing in the valley.

The anniversary antics continued apace in April and May, with two very different events. The first of these was the Tryfan Skylight, an idea conceived by Jim Langley. He'd seen something similar done on the Matterhorn, thanks to a YouTube clip — a line of lights in the night sky, all the way to the summit. Wouldn't it be amazing, he thought, if we could do the same thing on Tryfan and set about making it happen.

John Rowell took the spectacular images of the event, proud to be part of such a historic occasion. From behind the lens, he was in a unique position to see the evening unfold. 'The team

2015 Anniversary antics: Tryfan Skylight images © John Rowell. Raft Race victors , Anniversary cake, Extreme Dining and Beach party © Dave Worrall & OVMRO.

is well known to us in the Moel Siabod café, which hosts our photographic gallery 'Soul of Snowdonia'. We regularly raise funds for the team with talks, quiz nights and by donating prints. Earlier in the year, Jim told me he had a vision to place people with head torches on the ridge of Tryfan. Did I think it feasible and would I organise the photography? It was yes on both counts.

'We worked out some possible dates via an app called TPE (the photographers' ephemeris), based on the lengthening evenings following British Summer Time and where the sun was setting behind the mountain. We wanted some ambient light to the right in the night sky, not directly over the ridge. Now, anyone who knows the Welsh weather will know how fickle it can be. We decided on Friday 17 April, with a reserve date a week later.

'We wanted to keep it low key because so much could go wrong. Jim contacted all current and past members and the Treble Three group. He'd hoped to get fifty people on the mountain but the response was overwhelming and the figure quickly reached over a hundred, including a team from RAF Valley who were keen to be part of it.

COBWEB CORNER

Nearly a white stick, 1998: In the September newsletter, Dave Worrall recalls how close he came to the prestigious award. I'd decided it was time to further my education and enrolled on a business computer course at Bangor Tech. Jo and I were in our third week and beginning to get to grips with the complexities of Windows when the hushed silence was interrupted by a persistent beep, beep, beep. 'Missing person Pen Quarry Contact Base.' Do I abandon the class or drink from the fountain of knowledge. No contest! With apologies, we left college and, turning to another recently acquired modern appliance, phoned up base on the mobile. The instructions were clear: get to the entrance to Pen Quarry and rendezvous with the other team members. Did I know where the entrance to Pen Quarry was? Did they think I was stupid? Of course I knew where it was!

We set off down the A55 and turned off into Pen. The entrance was somewhere on the right, I informed Jo, who was clearly unimpressed by the whole episode. Finally, the signs indicated quarry workings and I turned onto the tarmac road to the quarry. The road climbed up the hillside to a series of zig-zags, passing a huge clock face. It became clear we were the only car travelling this road and that there were no signs of activity to indicate the presence of other team members.

'Where are they then?' asked Jo. 'They said Pen Quarry,' said I. Clearly something was wrong. Time to admit defeat. Sheepishly, I turned the car around. We returned to the main road and drove back home. When later asked why I hadn't made it to the call-out, I made some feeble excuse about finishing dealing with some megabytes and microchips. How was I to know there was a back entrance to Pen Quarry? I know now but at the time I didn't admit to the error to avoid the embarrassment. Which all goes to show you should always check where you are going rather than assume you know!

OGGI SNIPS

From the 'pink' forms: February 1987: Grossly overweight.. expected to be carried until she was told the facts.

'The next step was to break this number down into teams, each with a team leader. There were nine teams in all. Each was given a place on the ridge and would be equipped with a radio. A project sheet was plotted with key placements and times they would need to leave base to be in position. It would still be cold after dark and they needed to spend as little time as possible standing or sitting in one position.

'With two weeks to go, we went for a dummy run. Two people went onto the ridge while we went to one of the designated places we'd decided to shoot from. Our first problem was that, although they thought they were on the ridge, they weren't — they were at least five metres below. Another quite unforeseen problem was that Warner Brothers was making a movie in the valley and large areas were closed off! We went to see them in a mountain rescue vehicle and, thankfully, this seemed to exempt us from any closures. The dummy run had proved a worthwhile exercise. Jim worked out a strategy to ensure that people were actually on the ridge and the other point to come from it was the decision that each team would carry a powerful rescue torch, in addition to the many individual head torches, so that all light sources would not be the same size.

'As the event was nearly on us, a team was charged with cooking a stew for over a hundred hungry people. It was agreed that a final decision would be made on the Wednesday prior to the event, based on weather forecasts for the area. The original date was a goer. Texts went out to all participants to arrive at Oggi base at 5.30pm for a briefing at six, before the groups were despatched onto the mountain at their allotted time.

'When we arrived, it was overcast and cold with a promise of clearing skies around dusk. There was intense excitement as people began to arrive, all keen to make Jim's vision happen and be involved in something that would be very special. At the briefing, Jim was quite emotional — this had taken months of organising and now it was about to happen.

'Petzl provided torches for anyone who wanted a more powerful one. The first groups began to leave and the skies began to clear. We made our way to our selected shooting point, nervous but excited. The plan was to shoot in three phases at 8.30pm, 8.45pm and 9.00pm. All participants were asked to stand pointing their head torches to the Land Rover headlights after the first flare went off and to make sure they could see clear sky behind them. Reports began to filter in that they were experiencing a fantastic sunset to the west and all were in good spirits. Then, problems... Jim set off the flare, the lights lit up the mountain and the smoke engulfed us, ruining our shots!

'Radio contact was made asking people to continue to point their head torches at us and we were blown away by the sight in front of us. Then, a frenzy of activity as we captured what would be a once-in-a-lifetime opportunity. As promised, the Sea King came into view and sat just above Adam and Eve, the two upright plinths that mark the top of the mountain. The light show could be seen for miles around. People were stopping their cars on the A5 to take pictures. We knew from the banter that people were enjoying it.

'As we returned to base, teams started to filter in, huge smiles on their faces. It was dark now and streams of head torches were making their way down the mountain. Without doubt, it was a huge success. I was privileged to be part of it and an evening I will never forget.'

Langley remains stunned at the response to his idea. 'One woman asked could she be near Piccadilly Circus, from where she'd been rescued. Another group were with the son of a man who had died ten years before, to the day. It had been windy conditions and he slipped and fell from the summit. They wanted to commemorate it. His wife came and drank tea with us at base.

'It was a very emotional day for the whole team. People who'd never been on a mountain were walking up in the dark! We didn't know who were the mountaineers so we put team members in each group and divided up the ridge section — two team members in each section. We allocated 333 members into different parts along the ridge line and team members went to the summit. It was a real community event — and very poignant for the RAF guys too.'

Barely a month later, team members and off-duty crew members from C Flight, 22 Squadron RAF Valley were back up the hill again, this time dressed in their finery for an extreme dining experience. About thirty team members, along with wives and partners, carried everything to the summit for a black-tie event. And, lest anyone think they were off-duty, there was even a brief interlude to carry out a rescue when a call came in that a local man in his fifties, and part of a well-organised hill walking group, had pulled a leg muscle whilst descending the South Ridge. He had tried to continue but found the pain too great so OVMRO was called. A hasty party was preparing to deploy when a Sea King flew into the valley and winched the casualty and his partner from the mountainside to deposit them at Oggi base.

'Meanwhile,' explains Chris Lloyd, 'the rest of the casualty's party made their way down the mountain, passing heavily laden mountain rescue troops heading up Tryfan carrying tables, chairs, stoves and dinner! Staff from the Conwy Falls Café prepared a slap-up meal of Welsh lamb with

COBWEB CORNER

In their own words: Summing up the sentiments of so many of those who Ogwen team members have rescued and helped over the years, these are just a few of the comments left on the Ogwen website guestbook.

April 2009: Rescued from Moel Siabod by these fine people. Embarrassed but so glad to have got down safely. After 20 years of hill walking I hoped I would never have had to ask for mountain rescue help. I never felt so scared before as I did being stuck on that small ledge and as time passed that feeling just grew. I never felt so happy before as I did when I saw the Ogwen team coming up the hill. Thank you to each and every one of you. Heroes who put your lives on the line to help others for no material benefit to yours.

January 2012: I cannot thank you enough for your assistance. I have always been over cautious in the mountains, why I suddenly thought I knew better I'll never know. Your kindness and prompt help instantly calmed me down...

August 2010: I have been visiting Snowdonia to walk and climb for many years, and hoped the day would never come when I needed to call on mountain rescue. However, I am infinitely grateful that when I did, you heeded my call. The speed at which team members arrived from the valley floor was nothing short of astonishing, and the care I received before I was flown out by chopper was fantastic.

August 2008: Diolch yn fawr...

OGGI SNIPS

Bog asphodel, a plant with bright yellow flowers, can be seen flowering in upland bogs across Snowdonia. The fruits have been used as a colourant to replace saffron in food.

fresh vegetables, mint sauce and gravy followed by an 'Ogwen Mess' of fresh summer fruits, and a cheese course complete with fresh grapes and coffee with personalised after-dinner mints, made by a local confectioner with the outline of Tryfan on their face.

'Being a formal dinner, the Ogwen lot were in black tie and the RAF chaps were in mess dress, complete with medals. The ladies wore long dresses — though they did need a fleece or two in the cool breeze.

'A couple of hill walkers were surprised to top out on the evening summit, to find a formal dinner party in swing. They were welcomed to join in the feast and liquid refreshment.

'After prizes for the most imaginative table, complete with candelabra, the tables were cleared and packed up once more. It was the end of the day, the end of dinner and, with the ending of our long relationship with RAF helicopters, the end of an era.'

The celebrations continued, through a draughty summer, with a beach party on the shores of Cwm Idwal and a raft race on Llyn Ogwen which left a few team members a little damp behind the ears. In July, team members were joined 'on the beach' by members of Treble Three, friends of the team, past team members and also crew members from Bristow's new base in Caernarfon. What had begun as a picnic developed into a Hawaiian Beach Party and barbecue, hampered only by the winds which threatened to blow away the newly sprouted palm trees (carefully inflated earlier in the day), as white horses scudded across the lake.

The raft race made a return to the calendar, this time in somewhat more sophisticated fashion. Time was when participants set off down the lake with nothing more than a confection of cardboard tubes, an old bed sheet and hope in their heart, to keep them from a dunking. This year, at least they had the benefit of full swiftwater rescue kit to keep them from the elements.

This impressive string of anniversary events culminates with this very book, a celebration of the challenges, tragedies, joys and extraordinary people which have made today's team. The idea of a book has been brewing for many, many years. Chris Lloyd summed it up in 1999. 'The real history of the team is not laid down with pen and paper but by tales of heroics on the mountains and misbehaviour in the pubs. One day,' he said, 'someone must write 'The Book'. But before too much is lost by members retiring from the organisation, a précis of the antics and a list of punchlines must be recorded.'

It's said that to know where you are going, you must first understand where you came from and, now 'The Book' has been written, that foundation has been laid. No one can know what challenges the next fifty years might bring but one thing is certain, members of the Ogwen Valley Mountain Rescue Organisation will face them as they have every other, with enthusiasm, compassion and creativity — and, in the main, a contented smile on their faces.

Acknowledgements

This book is the culmination of eighteen months work, delving into the dusty files and distant memories of so many of those who have shaped the Ogwen team throughout its fifty years — and for some time before that. It would not have been possible without the collaboration of many individuals, and their willingness to share their personal recollections. There are many too whose words have been quoted from previous texts and publications. We have credited those whose thoughts and commentary we have used throughout the text, but for completeness we list everyone here also. If we have missed anyone out please forgive us!

Maggie Adam
Neil Adam
Dr Glynne Andrew
Sally Armond
Stephen Attwood
John Banks
Bill Batson
Tim Bird
Sir Chris Bonington
Rob Brookes
Dave Canning
Rob Chapman
Stuart Dethick
KC Gordon
Andy Harbach
Russ Hore
Peter Howells
Clive Hughes
John Hulse
Roz Hulse
Barbara James
Ron James
Dr Anthony Jones
Geraint Jones
Dr Ieuan Jones
Jill Jones
Roger Jones
Jim Langley
Chris Lloyd
Harvey Lloyd
Chris Onions
George Manley
Kirk Mauthner
Pete Price
Twiggy Price
Mike Margeson
Tim Radford
Al Read
Hazel Robbins
Brian Robbins
Elved Roberts
John Rowell
Paul Smith
Jed Stone
Matt Sutton
Clive Swombow
Marion Waters
Dave Worrall
Jo Worrall.

Bibliography & Sources

Online

- bbc.co.uk/wales
- en.wikipedia.org
- folkrealmstudies.weebly.com
- genesreunited.co.uk
- historic-uk.com
- J and J A Venn's Alumni Cantabrigienses, online edn
- kirkmauthner.ca/technical.html
- ogwen-rescue.org.uk
- mountain.rescue.org.uk
- murderuk.com
- mrmap.org.uk
- riverandseasense.com
- rmets.org
- snowdonwales.co.uk
- snowdonrailway.co.uk
- strangedayz.co.uk
- thefreelibrary.com
- venn.lib.cam.ac.uk
- walesonline.co.uk
- weatherimagery.com
- Who Was Who, online edn, Oxford University Press, 2014

Newspapers

- Burnley Gazette
- Caernarvon and Denbigh Herald
- Cambridge Independent Press
- Daily Graphic
- Daily Post
- Dundee Courier and Advertiser
- Grantham Journal
- Lancashire Evening Post
- Manchester Courier and Lancashire General Advertiser
- Manchester Guardian
- News Chronicle
- North Wales Chronicle
- Sunderland Daily Echo and Shipping Gazette
- The Times
- Western Daily Press
- Western Gazette

Books & other sources

- Archer Thomson, J.M., **Climbing in the Ogwen District** (London, 1910)
- Doylerush, E., **No landing place** (Midland Counties Publications 1985).
- Greenstreet, W.J., ed., **The Mathematical Gazette**, Vol. III., No., 47, (October 1904).
- Hankinson, A., **The mountain men** (Mara Books 2004).
- Hudson, R. W. H. T., **Kummer's Quartic Surface** (Cambridge, 1905)
- James, B., **Itching to Climb** 2nd Ed., (Baton Wicks 2014).
- Jones I. A., **Climbers' Club Guide to Wales. Ogwen and Carneddau** (Climbers' Club 1993).
- Maslen-Jones, B., **A Perilous Playground** (Wrexham, 1998).
- March, T., **Great Mountain Days in Snowdonia** (Cicerone 2013).
- Sharp, R., & Whiteside J., **Mountain rescue** (Hayloft Publishing 2008).
- Richardson, S., **The team** (Mill Field Publications and Cockermouth MRT 2002).
- Whiteside, J., **Call out mountain rescue? A pocket guide to safety on the hill** (MREW, 2010).

- **A history of stretchers** by Peter Bell (The Oracle, www.mountain.rescue.org.uk).
- **A short account of Caernarvon and Bedd-kill-hart, or Beddgelert &c** by Thomas Pennant. Printed by T Roberts.
- Court papers and letters relating to Wilson Hey's pursuit of morphia, MREW archive.
- **Dr Ieuan Jones** by David Allan. (The Oracle, www.mountain.rescue.org.uk).
- **Johnnie Lees** by Judy Whiteside. (The Oracle, www.mountain.rescue.org.uk).
- **Notes and recollections of an angler: Rambles among mountains, valleys and solitudes of Wales** by John Henry Cliffe.
- Ogwen scrapbooks, newsletters and annual reports.
- **Some thoughts on the organisation of mountain search and rescue operations** by Dr ASG Jones with **Notes on mountain rescue first aid** by Dr IW Jones.
- **The Census of England and Wales** 1871 & 1911.

Acronyms, initialisms & explanatory notes

A&E	Accident and Emergency
ACC	Assistant Chief Constable
ACPO	Association of Chief Police Officers
ARCC	Aeronautical Rescue Coordination Centre
ATLS	Advanced Trauma Life Support
BCRC	British Cave Rescue Council
CPR	Cardio-Pulmonary Resuscitation
ECG	Electro Cardiogram
ECMR	Emergency Care for Mountain Rescue
EMT	Emergency Medical Technician
GPS	Global Positioning System
MCA	Maritime and Coastguard Agency
MOD	Ministry of Defence
MPD	Multi-Purpose Device
MR	Mountain Rescue
MREW	Mountain Rescue England & Wales
MRC	Mountain Rescue Council Mountain Rescue Committee
MRT	Mountain Rescue Team
NEWSAR	North East Wales Search & Rescue
NWMRA	North Wales Mountain Rescue Association
OVMRO	Ogwen Valley Mountain Rescue Organisation
OS	Ordnance Survey
PFD	Personal Flotation Device
PPE	Personal Protective Equipment
PHTLS	Pre-Hospital Trauma Life Support
RAF	Royal Air Force
RN	Royal Navy
RV	Rendezvous
SARDA	Search & Rescue Dogs Association
SMC	Scottish Mountaineering Club
SOP	Standard Operating Procedure
SOS	Save our Souls
UKSAR	United Kingdom Search & Rescue
USAF	United States Air Force

Ampoule	Small sealed glass container
Arête	Sharply defined ridge
Barrowboy	Team member who holds onto and guides the casualty and stretcher over the edge and during a lower from a high crag. Also known as the 'stretcher jockey'
Gully	Narrow valley or split in rock face
iSAR	Online system adopted by teams in 2015 for the initial stages of training to work with search and rescue helicopters
Karabiner	Metal loop with a spring-loaded gate used to quickly and reversibly connect components, in safety-critical systems
Prussik knot	Attaches a thinner rope to a wider rope for the purpose of taking a load. When tightened the knot 'bites' to enable loading but, when the load is released, it can be moved easily
Misper	Missing person
MRMap	Software for tracking MR personnel during training and call-outs

Névé	Old snow turned to ice
Ridge	High crest between two valleys
Rime	Ice build-up on rocks, stakes and other objects
SARLOC	Enables teams to locate people on the hill through the browser on their smartphone
SARCALL	System for calling out and managing aspects of an incident online
Scree	Loose rocks/boulders
Sea King	Helicopter used by the RAF for search and rescue purposes 1978 to 2015
Tricouni	Hard steel nail embedded into the sole of a climbing boot
Tyrolean	The Tyrolean traverse or cableway is a method of crossing through free space between two high points by means of a rope system, used in casualty evacuation
Wessex	Helicopter used by RAF for search and rescue purposes 1976 to 1997
Whirlwind	Helicopter used by RAF for search and rescue purposes 1955 to 1979.

'OGGI' or 'OGGIE'? THAT IS THE QUESTION...

There's no doubting that 'Ogwen Valley Mountain Rescue Organisation' is a somewhat lengthy title and, sometimes you just need something more succinct. Consequently, news reports, annual reports and newsletters over the years have tended towards the use of 'OVMRO' for the more official or impersonal, and the more affectionate, 'Oggi', when speaking colloquially. And the call sign too has been 'OGGI' from the start.

Sounds simple. But somewhere along the way, an extra 'e' crept in so, for example, the team's major fundraising event became the 'Oggie 8'. The webcams at base are the 'Oggie cams'. The jury is still out on which is 'correct' — but we have chosen to use the longer established 'Oggi' throughout the book, given the historical precedent, except where specific usage demands otherwise.

The language of the mountains

Aber	Confluence of waters or river mouth
Afon	River
Afon Denau	Narrowing of the river
Bethesda	The area set up around the Non-Conformist Chapel
Braichmelyn	Sun shining on the spur of the hillside
Blaen y Nant	Head of the stream

Braich Tu Du	Dark side of the spur
Braich Ty Du	Spur of the black house
Bryn Poeth	Hot hill
Bwlch	Gap, pass or notch
Bwlch y Brecan	Pass of the coarse cloth
Bwlch y Ddwy Glyder	Pass between the two Glyder
Bwlch Eryl Farchog	Pass of Eryl the Knight
Bwlch Tri Marchog	Pass of the three knights
Capel Curig	The chapel of the holy man Curig
Carnedd Dafydd	Dafydd's cairn
Carnedd y Filiast	Cairn of the Greyhound bitch
Carnedd Llywelyn	Llywelyn's cairn
Carreg Mianog	Craggy rock
Castell y Geifr	Castle of the goats
Castell y Gwynt	Castle of the wind
Cefn yr Orsedd	Rear of the chair/throne
Clogwen Castell	Castle cliffs
Clogwyn Llys	Cliff with vegetation
Creigiau Gleison	Grey-green rocks
Cwm	Valley
Cwm Cneifon	Valley of the shearers
Cwm Clyd	Secluded valley
Cwm Cywion	Valley of the young animals
Drws Nodded	Sheltered pass
Ffynnon Lloer	Well of the moon
Ffynnon Llugwy	Well of the bright moon
Foel Goch	Red bare-topped mountain
Y Garn	The cairn
Gallt yr Ogof	The cliff of the cave
Glan Dena	Edge of the river Denau
Glyder Fach	Small pile of stones
Glyder Fawr	Large pile of stones
Y Gwyliwr	The watchman
Gribin	Comb
Gwern Gof Isaf	The marsh of the Smith Lower farm (Big Willie's)
Gwern Gof Uchaf	The marsh of the Smith Upper farm (Little Willie's)

Hafod	Upper farm
Helyg	Willows
Llymllwyd	Grey sharp ridge
Llyn Bochlwyd	Lake of the grey cheek
Llyn Caseg Ffraith	Lake of the piebald mare
Llyn Clyd	A secluded lake
Llyn Cowlyd	Beloved lake
Llyn y Cwn	Lake of the dogs
Llyn Idwal	Lake of Prince Idwal
Mynydd Perfedd	A central mountain
Nant	Stream, river or vale
Nant y Benglog	Vale of the skull
Nant Ffrancon	Vale of the beavers
Mynydd Du	Black mountain
Pen y Helgi Du	Head of the black hunting hound
Pen Llithrig y Wrach	Slippery summit of the witch
Pen yr Ole Wen	Head of the white light
Penywaen-wen	Head of the white marsh
Pont Pen y Benglog	The bridge at the head of the skull
Pont Rhyd y Goch	Bridge of the red ford
Rhaeadr Ogwen	River Ogwen's water falls
Tal y Braich	End of the arm/spur
Tal y Llyn Ogwen	End of Ogwen Lake
Tal y Waen	End of the marsh
Tai Newyddion	New houses
Tryfan	Three peaked
Tryfan Bach	Little Tryfan
Twll Du	Black hole (Devil's Kitchen)
Ty Gwyn	White house
Ty'n y Maes	House in the field
Yr Wyddfa	The tumulus.

Team members & officers, past & present

Many, many hours have gone into searching through the archives to create a definitive list of team members since 1965. It hasn't been easy, not least because, in the earlier years, there was little documented evidence of team membership! The following list is far from conclusive and any omission is unintentional. Further information will, almost inevitably, come to light once published. The list notes the date an individual first appeared in the team's official documents — latterly, this would be when they passed their final hill day. Space does not permit us to detail length of service, nor to acknowledge that several team members have joined, left and rejoined the team over the years.

JOINED	
1965	Neil Adam K C Gordon Ron James Emyr Jones Roger Jones Sgt R Jones John Lindsay Barbara Lunt (James)
1966	Dr A S G (Tony) Jones Dr Ieuan Jones Cedric Milner Dave Siviter
1967	J Hesketh D Llewelyn John Ellis Roberts Dai Rowlands
1969	Richard Alwyn (RAJ) Jones Maggie Boley (Adam) John Cooke Peter Davies Bill Dean John Dean John Dore Graham Dingle Ken Dwyer Carol Eaton (Rickard) Andrew P Frazer Mark Gladwyn Merion P (Butch) Jones Trevor Jones Duffy W Lee G J Little

JOINED	
1969	Peter Martin Frank McLaughlin G N Mollard Phillip J Morris Mike O'Nions Eddy Osbourne Robert (Wally) Owen J Martin Quale Ken Robbins Nick Rushby Geoff Shuttleworth Pete Smith Bernard Snowden Ruth Townson (Greenall)
1970	Lew Costello Ray Greenall J H Lewis Chris Wharmby
1971	Rhys Davies Gwen Moffatt E Wallis A Burgess Niall G (Noggin) Evans Sgt Ian Sanderson Selwyn Thomas Ron Williams
1972	Charles (Peanuts) Binyon L Burrows R (Bob) J Cooper I Mosey Davies Pete Douglas Dave Fildes

JOINED	
1972	GR Fildes
	John A Finlay
	Bill Galston
	Dave R Headley
	Mike Hold
	Sue (Twiggy) Hurst
	Pete Jardine
	P Doug Jones
	Merfyn O Jones
	Ken McCoy
	G Bill Pardoe
	Pete Price
	Cliff Randles
	John (Og) Roberts
	J Alun Roberts
	Vic Simpson
	Robin Trangmar
	Rob Walker
	Ron Weeks
1973	John D Evans
	Clive Hughes
	Jimmy Logan
	Maj Phil Williams-Jones
	John (Sunshine) Rogers
1974	John Banks
	Richard Brice
	Ron Cooper
	P Davies
	Dave Hardy
	John Hulse
	Brian Jones
	John Murray
	Dr Trefor Owen
	Jon Robinson
1975	Pete Gadd
1976	Richard Brindley
	Bill Fedrick
	Paul Johnson
	Bill Highton
	Isobel Rennie
1977	Dave Butler
	Chris Lloyd
	Mick Parsons
	Malcolm (Max) Williams
1978	Barry Pinion

JOINED	
1978	Anne Rook (Rogers)
	Dave Salter
1979	Jack Baines
	Robert (Bob) Chapman
	Gareth Dady
	Bob Eaton
	Bryan Roberts
	Mark Williams-Jones
1980	Ada/John Cobb
	Jerry Galliene
	Gareth George
	Cliff Jones
	Davey Jones (Pen)
	Dr John Mithan
	Roger Pyves
	Nathan (Naff) Sharpe
	Huw Thomas
	Russ Vaughan
1981	Martin Barnicott
	Jim Evans
1983	Arthur Bowman
1984	Stuart Dethick
	Pete Evans
	P Rickard
1985	Colin Dickenson
	Arwel Johnston
1986	Phil Davies
	R Bob Lewis
	Ian Pilling
1988	C Richard Bates
	John Burson
	J Arwel Thomas
1989	Dave Worrall
1990	Adam Charlton
	Kevin de Silva
	Dave Williams
1992	Alison Backhouse (Donnely)
	Justi Carey
	Pauline Hallett
	Mike Hendry
	Russ Hore
	John Swinburne

JOINED	
1993	Martin Hayes Chris Onions Alistair Read Huw Rogers Simon Owen Chaz Goddard Paul Stevens
1994	Paul Henshall Alan Jones
1995	Steve Howe Dave Norris Dr Ian Williams Jenny Wilson
1996	Ro Howe Dave Parry Owen Samuel Clive Swombow Mike Thomas
1997	Dale Howard
1998	Marianne Davies Colin Kimber Wayne Roberts Jed Stone Stuart Woodward Harry Wordsall
1999	Mel Gadd Pat Gadd Roz Hulse Tim Radford
2000	John Carrie Rob Grant David Jones (Conwy) Andy Nelson Jock Stewart Matt Tuck Pete Ward Marion Waters (Hughes)
2001	Ginge Farrar
2002	Chris Cooksey Dave Meeson Simon Melia Paul Smith

JOINED	
2003	Tim Bird
2004	Matt Sutton
2005	Biddy Baxter Gerwyn Lloyd
2006	Mark Handford Allen Ince
2007	Kim Burnham Mark Edwards Geraint Jones
2008	Alistair Cook Jim Langley Jo Worrall
2009	Glynne Andrew Sally Armond Alex Bath Andy Cornford Paul Edwards Andy Harbach Karl Lester Simon Worth Sally Wrigley
2010	Andy (Big Andy) Jones Tim Vollum Howard Winston
2011	Denise Conford Anne Margerison
2012	Tabitha Codd (Angle-Smith) Jen Young (Edwards)
2013	Stuart Kato Mike Pinches Jim Quinn
2014	Pete Frost Danny Hinson Brian Robbins
2015	Chris Campbell Craig Jowitt Alex King